ET   6295   2

P9-AON-592

Psychological theory and educational practice

H S N McFarland

Professor of Education
University of Durham

Psychological theory and educational practice

Human development learning and assessment

 London   Routledge & Kegan Paul

First published in Great Britain 1971
by Routledge & Kegan Paul Ltd
Broadway House
68–74 Carter Lane,
London EC4V 5EL
Printed in Great Britain by
Western Printing Services Ltd, Bristol
© H.S.N. McFarland 1971
ISBN   0 7100 7009 8 (*C*)
ISBN   0 7100 7010 1 (*P*)

Contents

List of tables and figures

Foreword and acknowledgments

Readers will see that Chapters 3 to 5 deal with the theme of child development, Chapters 6 to 8 with human learning, and Chapters 9 to 11 with human assessment. The first two chapters are both fundamental introductions. Chapter 1 analyses the problem of relating psychological explanation and educational practice. Chapter 2 concentrates on the position of teachers, faced with their own learning problems as well as their pupils', and with the problem of learning how to teach as well as how to master the knowledge and understanding on which that teaching must be based. There is a sense in which Chapter 2 encapsulates many of the problems discussed in other chapters.

The individual chapters have been planned to stand on their own feet to a considerable extent, even although they are also knit into the larger pattern just described. The 'perspective' section at the end of each chapter is not so much a summary of contents as a concluding reflection, aimed at putting the themes in their proper place. Five considerations have influenced the discussion of each theme—(1) to make it clear that one is dealing with problems, not closed issues; (2) to present a fair sample of the relevant empirical evidence; (3) to stimulate critical thinking about the concepts used; (4) to draw attention to some of the methodological problems that accompany psychological enquiry, and (5) to hazard a good deal of practical suggestion, in defiance of the rift that some psychologists and educators try to maintain between their respective territories.

A book which aims, like this, at a wide but critical perspective is necessarily indebted to the writings of many people. The bibliography should be read as part of this acknowledgment and not just as a list of the main references that have contributed directly to the text. Material used in tables is acknowledged by reference in each case, but particular acknowledgment should be made for the substantial Table 16, which has been reproduced from Appendix B of the Underwood Report on Maladjusted Children, 1955, by permission of the controller of Her Majesty's Stationery Office. To make special mention of authors who have been particularly stimulating is tempting, but the task would be invidious.

Working with young graduates preparing to be teachers and with experienced teachers improving their academic and professional qualifications has itself been a contribution to the writing of the book, whether the contribution came in sceptical or idealistic form. I should like to conclude with an expression of particular personal thanks for the friendly support of immediate colleagues, encouragement and criticism from my wife, and the cheerful typing of the manuscript scrawl by Mrs Maureen Chrystal and Miss Anne Shipley.

Psychology and education

There are two extreme views of the relationship between psychology and education. One views psychology optimistically as a kind of dispensary handing out specific psychological remedies for sundry educational ills, if not a universal panacea. The other view is the pessimistic one. Psychology has to do with artificial situations in laboratories, with rats and machines rather than human beings, and, therefore, is irrelevant to the practical world of education. A more accurate assessment of the relationship lies somewhere between these extremes and it will be the business of this chapter to try and make such an assessment. This is important both in itself as a step towards clarifying fundamental questions and for the better understanding of subsequent chapters dealing with particular areas of educational psychology.

Teachers, parents and administrators

Since teachers are the main users of educational psychology, it is justifiable to look first at the problems that confront them. In doing so one remembers that there are other groups of educators—parents, administrators, or counsellors, for example—who have their own interests in psychology. But we shall take teachers first and divide them into student teachers and experienced teachers. Student teachers are typically concerned with certain immediate practical problems, such as how to maintain or restore order in a class of pupils, how to organize a lesson or other section of school work so that it fits both the available time and the capacities of the learners, how to create and sustain interest and activity in learning, how to organize work so that there is cumulative learning over longer periods of time, how to deal with typically diverse rates of learning, and particularly with slow learners, how to reconcile their own ideas about tasks and methods with the human, organizational and physical constraints of particular schools, and, generally, how to sustain and develop their self-esteem in relation to a professional task that can be extremely demanding in personal terms.

Experienced teachers mostly lose the earlier anxieties of the student teacher. They do not expect to fall off the bicycle. Having fairly complete responsibility for a job helps one to make a job of it. Increasing practice in specific skills (class control, work organization, use of suitable and interesting material, etc.) helps to make these skills more fluent and effective. Relative or complete acceptance of the assumptions and supporting social apparatus of a particular school diminishes the areas of doubt about what one's assumptions ought to be and about the means there may be to uphold them. Student teachers may have greater doubts because of their relative inexperience and because their tutors properly encourage them to spend part of their time in critical doubt about some established practices. Experienced teachers can give and receive satisfaction by conforming to a clearly established norm within a particular school, whereas student teachers must to some extent confront detailed appraisal against ideal norms.

These models of the student teacher and experienced teacher are, of course, only first approximations. Pursuing the bicycle-riding analogy, one recognizes that some teachers keep on wobbling for a long time, just as some student teachers are immediate candidates for the Tour de France. But, generally, experience of the right kind does count, and the experienced teacher, if he looks to psychology for help, is not looking for solutions to elementary problems. Once he knows that he can work within a particular scholastic mould he may begin to consider how the mould itself could be improved. Once he can teach his children and his subject competently he may want to excel rather than just be adequate. He may want to relate his particular classwork more fully to the broader educational achievement of the school community, or to the social community outside the school. He may come against new practical problems for which he has had no special preparation—serious scholastic backwardness; alarming delinquency; radical innovations in curriculum, method, or examinations; reorganization of the school system itself. These professional challenges throw a teacher back to first principles, including his whole conception of the psychology of children and their learning.

Teachers typically have to deal with children in relatively small groups—thirty or forty at a time, or smaller groups still. Sometimes, as in primary schools, they spend most of the time with one group. Sometimes, as in secondary schools, they may spend rather limited periods with a greater number of groups. One can contrast these situations with that of parents on the one hand and educational administrators on the other. Parents naturally concentrate their educational and psychological attention on their own few darlings. Administrators must, in justice, try to act in the interests of very large numbers of individuals. These different and understandable circumstances may suggest why different people look for different kinds of educational help from psychology. Parents can reasonably be expected to take an interest in the idiosyncrasies of individual psychology, while the administrator may be more professionally interested in techniques of assessing, guiding and providing for whole categories of children, including some with very special needs, such as the physically, intellectually, emotionally or socially handicapped. Teachers occupy an intermediate position. They try to treat children as individuals, but they cannot be parents (except to their own offspring, of course). They share the administrator's concern with just categorization and guidance but probably repudiate the apparent impersonality of administrative justice. These varying orientations may be relevant to some of the conflicting emphases that can be detected in attitudes towards the psychology of education.

Educational administrators are largely responsible, within politically determined policies, for the material and major organizational equipment of the educational system, for its different kinds of schools, different special and ancillary institutions and services, and different development programmes. Psychological considerations are only one set among many—political, economic, social, religious, historical, etc.—that must enter into the administrator's calculations, but they sometimes have particular importance. Psychological evidence and techniques played a vital part in the pattern of English secondary schooling between (roughly speaking) 1930 and 1960, just as newer psychological evidence has been used to support different patterns in more recent times. Psychological evidence and techniques have been essential in defining various categories of intellectual and emotional handicap, in identifying individuals apparently coming within the categories, and in developing suitable educational treatments. The psychological measurement movement has made administrators, as well as teachers, more critically aware of how to use and interpret examination marks, test results, individual reports and personal information: none of this in the simplistic sense of 'Psychology tells us . . .', but in the sense that psychological evidence, techniques and criteria have been *part* of the basis for educational decision and action.

Enough has now been said to illustrate the situations of those, particularly teachers, who are professionally interested in educational applications of psychology. The next chapter will look at the psychological aspect of the teacher's role in more detail. What matters in this chapter is to establish the teacher's understandable concern with practicalities, that is, with techniques for solving specific current problems, preferably without delay, and in the context of things as they are, not as they might be if painful, laborious or expensive changes were made. There is some tendency to put a low estimation on what is called 'theory' (even if there is also reluctance to recognize the different uses of this word and their different implications). The 'theory' problem will be taken up again later. What can be seen now is the need to analyse this gap that is commonly felt between the educational problem and the psychologist's contribution to its solution.

The educator's viewpoint—some problems

The problem arises from the fact that there is only a partial overlap between the kind of interest taken in human behaviour by an educator and that taken by a psychologist. Some psychologists in virtue of their jobs are particularly interested in the applications of psychology, but these applications may be limited to special areas. Academic psychologists are not primarily or even at all concerned with applications but with developing scientific explanations of observed behaviour. What constitutes a scientific explanation will be discussed shortly, but the main criterion is not immediate practical utility. Educators, on the other hand, are primarily interested in initiating people, and particularly young people, into the values and skills which adult society wishes to perpetuate or foster. This poses two different kinds of problem. The first is to decide what values and skills ought to be instilled. This is a question of aims and purposes and cannot be answered by psychology, even if it would be folly to disregard psychological fact in the process of deciding what values to pursue. The second problem is to decide the best ways of instilling whatever values and skills ought to be instilled. Here psychology might have more legitimate advice to offer, although actual psychologists vary considerably in the caution or rashness with which they offer it.

The facts that psychology is only marginally relevant to the problem of deciding one's educational values and purposes, and that even legitimate applications of psychology are a secondary interest of the psychologist as scientist, are not the only obstacles to a facile marriage between education and psychology. A third difficulty can be expounded via an analogy with maps. Anyone who has tried to find his way on foot or by car with the aid of maps knows that there are many snags *en route*. Many of the detailed problems can be paralleled in attempts to educate children with the aid of psychological maps. From what point of view is one looking? Is the available map just a rough sketch or done accurately to scale? Is it a large-scale representation of a small area or the other way round, or something in between? How professionally competent was the map-maker and how old is the map? Was the map simplified for unsophisticated users or drawn with some particular bias—economic, political, or any other—which may not coincide with the bias of the user's interest? Then there are problems about the user. How intelligent, experienced or conscientious a map-reader is he? And problems about the changing face of the landscape—new roads and buildings since the map was made, old landmarks obliterated, periodical fogs that remove convenient clues, changing seasons that make the same scene radically different in appearance. Briefly, there is no reason to expect that psychology, any more than maps, should give sure and detailed guidance unless much effort goes into studying and interpreting it. The landscape of human behaviour is certainly no less complex than the landscape of geography.

A fourth difficulty arises from the way social and educational decisions are made. Even if psychology offers clear and sound guidance on some educational matter and the decision-makers understand the relevant psychology perfectly clearly, there are further factors that enter into the situation. Many decisions must be complex compromises, not mathematical solutions to clear problems; attempts to minimize worst consequences rather than bring about the unqualified best. Simon (1964) opposes the view that decisions are simply a matter of pursuing an obvious route to a specified goal with the suggestion that 'it is easier, and clearer, to view decisions as being concerned with discovering courses of action that satisfy a whole set of constraints'. Peston (1969) expresses a similar line of thought in terms which will strike a sympathetic chord in the minds of teachers:

> The straightforward formulation of a problem, its analysis, and the bringing to bear of relevant evidence, all as careful preparation for the application of criteria of value are not the commonplaces of decision makers at any level of administration.
> Plunging in the dark, reacting to crisis, and making the best of overcommitment, are much more favoured activities.

This applies to the teacher, not just the administrator. Or one can say that every teacher is partly an administrator, establishing rules and patterns of organization within his classes, promulgating a constant stream of minor, occasionally major, decisions on their interpretation and implementation. Psychology, even once understood, must take its educational place among a complexity of other considerations. Here again psychologist and educator must tread somewhat divergent paths.

A fifth difficulty about the relationship between psychology and education is the false assumption frequently made that, because there is a name, Psychology of Education, there is some quite distinct branch of study corresponding to it which ought to be able particularly to emit answers to educational problems. Of course, if one looks at the assumption in a sufficiently loose kind of way, it is not utterly false. There is undoubtedly such a study which has helped to solve some specific educational problems. The point is that it is not 'quite distinct' from psychology in general. It is those parts of general psychology—the study of children's development and behaviour, to give one example—which have relevance to educational problems. But those parts of psychology, as much as all other parts, depend on the chances of human purpose for their applications. They represent usable knowledge, but it is the users who must define what the uses will be and work out the practical details. Bridges must obey the laws of physics but it is engineers that design and build them. The maintenance and restoration of health must accord with the laws of physical science, but one consults a doctor, not a physicist. Even within the physical sciences themselves, the reported experiments and theories are mathematically neat and elegant for publication, but may surface from a sea of abortive experiments, untidy notes on envelopes, odd hunches in prepared minds, professional rivalries and so on. One has to work at translating the general into the particular, and vice versa.

A sixth difficulty, and the last that will be mentioned in the present context, is the problem of so-called intangibles. Perhaps this is really a by-product of the preceding difficulties. It is not surprising that many people should have difficulty in seeing their way through situations that are complex by their very nature. This being so, there is a strong temptation to retreat from the complexities and attribute significance to vague intangibles which are thought to influence what must happen in unanalysable ways. The danger of this is that present incapacity to understand something will be used to argue that the something cannot be understood, even should not be understood. This seems to be a pointless obscurantism. If it is believed that there is not even a chance of understanding, one had better remain silent. Of course, the tangible/intangible dichotomy has various possible meanings. Can the thing be observed or not? Identified or not? Specified in detail or not? Expressed in quantitative terms or not?

In this series, any one question might be answered positively and yet the ensuing questions negatively. Not to want to persist through the series as far as possible is to want not to think. This can be defended, for mysteries sometimes generate a pleasurable emotion, but only as a self-indulgence.

It is clear that the educator must struggle with the problem of conflicting values, that he can use psychological help only as part of a much more complex operation, that he must expect to work hard at psychology in order to understand its true contribution to understanding, that he must develop the intellectual and practical skill of applying his psychological understanding appropriately and subtly, and that he must not be driven into the comforting, mildly exciting world of intangibles as a *substitute* for thinking hard about the intricacies of human behaviour. But it must not be imagined that the educator alone faces the difficulties of the partnership, and it is now time to look at the psychologist's side of things.

The language of psychology

It is an almost irresistible convention of language to speak about *the* psychologist, *the* educator, *the* child, *the* anyone-else, although these species really contain a wide range of differing individuals. Many professional psychologists are as concerned as any teacher with working out practical solutions to immediate problems arising in the hurly-burly of everyday life. Like teachers these must strive with all the complexities already outlined, for they are called upon to recommend, decide, and act—not just explain in general terms. However, those psychologists whose job it is to teach psychology and to advance their subject by research tend to be less immediately concerned with detailed applications and more concerned with sustaining the image of psychology as a scientific discipline, sometimes in the teeth of scepticism among their colleagues in the physical sciences.

Given this strong and reasonable aspiration towards scientific status, it is understandable that psychologists should sometimes seem particularly eager to dissociate themselves from traditional associations that might impede their aim. This could be illustrated from many psychological texts. To select one arbitrarily as an example, Cattell (1965) puts literary and philosophical approaches to psychology firmly in their place:

> Undoubtedly there *are* gems of scientific truth about personality, lying available in this literary approach, but there is no way—except through the fresh start of scientific research—to separate the living truths from the pasteboard shams.

He goes on to point out the defects of early clinical approaches to personality, with their undue stress on abnormalities and lack of a proper quantitative foundation. The quantitative and experimental approach of real science alone can produce nuggets of psychological gold. Psychology, in Cattell's conception, becomes wedded to mathematics, the queen of the sciences. Psychology is psychometrics—conventionally and etymologically, mental measurement, or, to be more scientific, behavioural measurement.

Not all psychologists, of course, pin their faith so firmly on statistical analysis of collected psychological information. For some, science means physiology, not mathematics. Zangwill (1950) and Walter (1953) illustrate a physiological and anti-psychometric bias that can be found in other writers too. Particular points of view assert themselves sometimes by slashing away at apparent rivals, sometimes by pursuing their own bent as if there were no rivals. Piaget, who has contributed so much to psychological understanding of children's developing behaviour, is not particularly concerned with physiology and not at all with statistics. Skinner, who has concentrated so intensively on developing techniques of behavioural control and written extensively about their practical educational relevance, is concerned only very incidentally with physiology or statistics and purports not to be concerned with psychological theorizing. It is clear that, even among psychological researchers, the conception of what constitutes scientific analysis covers quite a range. There is nothing wrong about this, for, in the physical sciences too, the general principles of science are broadly consonant with a great diversity of kinds of enquiry—so much so that, as is often said, specialists within one broad discipline (let us say physics) may not understand one another precisely.

Something more should be said about the relationship of psychology to literature and philosophy. There is no doubt that the scientific study of behaviour, so far as it can be pursued, is something different in kind from literary or philosophical analysis. The psychologist as scientist was glad to see literature and philosophy pitchforked off the psychological field, and occasionally seems to feel a degree of alarm that these archaic disciplines might still slip back through a side-gate and give psychology a bad (that is, an unscientific) name. The threat appears more real by the fact that at least one whole modern movement in psychology, the psychoanalytical movement, has had a tremendous literary, philosophical and popular impact, and is still strongly and professionally sustained, despite the slightness of its scientific basis.

The case for attempting to pursue a science of psychology seems sufficiently strong to justify a policy of not tilting against adjacent windmills unnecessarily. A literary analysis of Cattell's sentence quoted above would draw attention to the psychologist's own rhetorical and linguistic (not purely scientific) techniques of discrediting opponents or imagined opponents. There can be a failure to grasp the kind of claim that would be made by an intelligent person for the psychological insights of literature. These are, and usually are meant to be, illuminating illustrations, sometimes models, of action and reaction in particular circumstances—not, on the whole, generalizing formulae about behaviour. In case this seems to put too much onus on a single sentence, readers can study how Hunt (1961) gives a fine polemical display while mocking his opponents' polemicism, or how Skinner and others achieve an intimate mix of persuasive rhetoric and substantial argument. And if psychology wants to disown its philosophical relations, one might ask whether Peters's *The Concept of Motivation* (1958), Komisar's *Psychological Concepts in Education* (1967), or Louch's *Explanation and Human Action* (1966), do not leave one with a strong sense that psychology can profit from philosophical analysis of its concepts, even if the substantive study of psychology is conducted scientifically.

A substantial thesis could be written on the linguistic style of psychologists as a reflection of differing modes of psychological analysis, but a few brief examples may serve to make the point clear. They leave a sense that psychological enquiry, however closely it approximates to a theoretical model of scientific enquiry, will be—at least as much as the other sciences, perhaps more so—strongly coloured by the differing values and styles of individual psychologists. There is a sense in which all human enquiry is a kind of enquiry into human nature, even the most impersonal sciences reflecting the pattern of human curiosity. This is not least true of psychology itself. The following examples are selected from writings that merit serious study; they are not from wayward, questionable sources. Also, while they must lose some clarity from being taken out of their context, they are not violently wrenched out of context.

One school of psychology tries to see how far aspects of behaviour can be understood by analogy with machines. It would be naïve to attack such an attempt as inhuman, for surely what is *distinctively* human must be pursued by distinguishing it from behaviour that may follow a mechanical model. One sample of language from this 'machine' psychology is given in the following fragment from Annett (1969):

In practical terms the simplest form of perceptual task is detection ... The detection problem arises when stimulus energy is not much greater than energy from non-stimulus sources, for example a sinusoidal tone may be embedded in a background of random white noise. ...

Annett's whole book is particularly clear, even if the uninitiated may have difficulty with 'stimulus energy', 'sinusoidal tone', or 'random white noise', but its language strikes a quite different note from, let us say, the following from Fish's *Outline of Psychiatry* (1968):

> All ideas have a charge of energy or cathexis which produces the emotion appropriate to the idea, when the idea becomes conscious. Some ideas give rise to anxiety when conscious because the associated instinctive drive is not approved by ego or superego. If this occurs, the unwanted idea is unconsciously pushed out of consciousness by the mechanism of repression. . . .

There is a reference to 'mechanism' here too, but the language of 'cathexis', 'instinctive drive', 'ego', 'superego', and 'unconscious' is a far cry from the world of servo-mechanisms.

Sometimes established fact and speculation may be deceptively mingled. Tanner (1961), discussing higher intellectual functioning in relation to the brain, writes:

> These structures must be units of organization widespread through areas of the cerebral cortex, rather than local areas like the motor area. Their maturation is probably signified both by increasing size and myelination of some cells and fibres remote from the primary centres and by an increase in connectivity.

This reads perfectly sensibly for anyone who knows a little physiology, but 'units of organization' and 'increase in connectivity' are phrases that incline towards speculative abstractness. Speculative physiology has been a long-standing and, of course, unavoidable temptation for psychologists.

The language of psychologists sometimes runs to a degree of abstruseness that does not seem justified by the substance of the ideas. For example, one may come across a sentence like the following in Piaget and Inhelder (1969):

> As we have already seen, affectivity constitutes the energetics of behaviour patterns, whose structures correspond to cognitive functions, and even though the energetics may not explain the structuration, or the structuration the energetics, neither one can function without the other.

Or a whole jargon may be generated that casts its own stylistic spell, perhaps particularly on those who most warmly embrace psychological science and repudiate stylistics. Wallach and Kogan (1965) provide the following example:

> We have found that diverse means of operationalising the physiognomic sensitivity concept lead to dimensions of individual

differences which possess little relationship with one another.

Sometimes a definition emits a sense of conciseness and trenchancy that conceals many problems. Allport (1966), repudiating the notion that attitudes can be labelled either 'mental' or 'motor', comments that 'such a practice smacks of body-mind dualism, and is therefore distasteful to contemporary psychologists'. The tone reminds one of Queen Victoria in one of her we-are-not-amused moments. Allport then defines attitude in the following sentence:

> Attitude connotes a neuro-psychic state of readiness for mental and physical activity.

What this reminds one of is the old logical rule that the *definiens* should be clearer than the *definiendum*, that is, that the definition should be clearer than what you are trying to define. Whether Allport's definition honours the rule or not is at least discussable.

Moving from verbal to numerical symbols does not abolish stylistic influences if one considers the matter in a wide perspective, for the very sight of tables of figures and reports of statistical findings can bring a gleam to the eye of the enthusiast or a sigh to the breast of the innumerate. Suppose one takes, again quite arbitrarily, a sentence like the following, referring to the relationship between certain students' intelligence test results and referees' reports:

> Relationships of AH5 and Referee's Report are negligible in 1964/6, but in 1966 were significant at $p < \cdot 01$ for Part I and for Total, and at $p < \cdot 05$ for Part II.

Although AH5 is simply the reference name of a well-known adult intelligence test, the particular symbolic form may carry an added irrelevant suggestion of scientific or mathematical formula. And, although $p < \cdot 01$ simply means that the probability is less than $\cdot 01$, or one per cent, or one in a hundred, that the discovered association is merely a matter of chance, the symbols and figures create a seemingly impenetrable mystery for a very large proportion of even sophisticated readers. They would pick up the message more readily if one wrote, 'If you repeated this enquiry a large number of times, you would get a similar result more than ninety-nine times out of a hundred.' Or, where it says $p < \cdot 05$, 'If you repeated this enquiry a large number of times, there is less than a five-per-cent chance that you would get a very different result. More than ninety-fives times in a hundred you would get a similar result.' But, once the symbolism is understood, it would be tedious indeed not to say simply $p < \cdot 01$ or $p < \cdot 05$.

The examples of psychological language just discussed are intended to make two main points. One is that psychologists cannot escape from the rhetorical or stylistic features of the language they have to use. *Le style, c'est l'homme* and *le style, c'est le psychologue*. In whatever way the psychologist may strive justifiably to objectify his study of behaviour, the process of enquiry, like a mirror, reflects the features of the viewer. The second point is that the student of psychology must be prepared to cope with the different kinds of language generated by different lines of psychological enquiry. It might be agreeable to have a common psychological language, but, as things are, there is as much conflict of tongues in this as in other realms of human discourse. Since science represents a principle of free and open enquiry, this must be counted a good thing.

In concluding this minor excursion into the language of psychologists, it must be stressed once more that the few examples used, while arbitrarily chosen, are meant to be fairly typical examples from important writings, not the more dramatic but unfair examples that could be picked up in the writings of extreme or inferior psychologists. They are meant to alert readers to the influence of emotional (or emotionless) tone and persuasive intent, to aspects of language that go beyond literal meanings, sometimes in quite subtle ways. However, the fact that these influences are almost inescapable does not mean that scientific enquiry is not possible. It is time now to discount language and style and ask what substantially constitutes a scientific explanation, for, unless one has some sense of what is to count as an explanation, of what the criteria of explanation are, one will never know whether or not any pattern of behaviour has or has not been explained.

What is an explanation?

If something unexpected happens, that is when the man in the street begins to wonder what the *explanation* might be. He may ask himself what could have *caused* the unexpected happening. He may even begin to formulate a *theory* about what must have happened. The italicized words are central in this realm of discussion. Of course, the unexpected is not the only thing that invites or receives explanation. There are many things that are expected and accepted but not really understood. One could not give a rational account of them, beyond straight description, nor control nor influence them in predetermined ways. The weather is a commonplace example. In this case, some rational account can be given of it, but not to the extent of being able to predict in much detail or for any long period ahead exactly what the weather will do. Similarly, men and women can be expected to be sexually attracted to one another and to behave in accordance with fairly predictable general patterns, but, despite the importance of this phenomenon, the details that matter to individuals are not so predictable, perhaps because chance factors play a large role alongside the systematic ones.

Psychology is quite often blamed for merely giving dazzling insights into the obvious, for providing expensive proof that rewarded behaviour tends to recur more often, or that children of well-to-do parents attending good schools go further than those whose parents are poor and whose schools are inferior. Some research workers in any science may grow blind to the pedestrian character of some of their work. There is certainly plenty of unilluminating hack work in the physical sciences. But this is inevitable, for one ideal of scientific endeavour is to give a systematic explanation of all the relevant phenomena, the pedestrian as well as the astounding. And, in any case, psychology, like other sciences, does sometimes show that the obvious expectation is false. Children with working mothers ('latch-key children', as the emotive phrase has it) do *not* show up badly in educational attainments. Intellectually bright children are *not*, as was once and perhaps still is popularly supposed, physically or socially retarded, but rather the opposite. Even where explanations are nearer to what may be considered obvious, the layman is apt to be wise after the event. He will tell you that something *was* obvious after he knows the scientific evidence, but less often make a firm prediction before the matter is put to scientific test. Furthermore, he is typically satisfied that his opinion was *more or less* the same as the scientific verdict, whereas the value of the evidence lies in its precision, its quantitative techniques and specifications and in its formulation of the conditions and exceptions attaching to any generalization. One knows not just that there is a relationship between several variables but what the size of the relationship is; not just that some phenomenon shows wide variation from person to person, but the exact details of the distribution.

It is a fact of language that the same word may have different meanings. Much futile dispute arises from an apparent refusal to recognize this. Each person wishes to assert that his meaning is the only true or correct one. It is more profitable in these situations to ask certain questions. Given any one meaning of a word, what is the context or what are the circumstances in which this meaning is a useful one, and, in that context, what kind of use does the meaning serve? And, given an actual problem or context which one is confronting here and now, which of several meanings of a word is most useful for present needs? Contestants sustain futile arguments not only because one or the other is intellectually obtuse (which, of course, he may be), but because each person sees a different problem.

Even common sense occasionally throws into such a dispute the observation that 'We're not talking about the same thing at all'. These considerations can now be applied to the word 'explanation'.

The explanations sought and given in most ordinary conversation do not have to satisfy particularly difficult requirements, nor are the requirements necessarily the same from one situation to another. (Why did you buy that hat? I just took a fancy to it. It's exactly what I've been looking for. Well, I am getting rather thin on top. It's to help with some tests the Consumers' Association are doing. You're not dressed without a hat. We've always worn hats in our family. The Party's tightening up on the wearing of hats. It was going for a pound. Don't you like it? It's for the wedding. Everybody's wearing them now. It's so different from all the other hats you see.) Sometimes a justification is sought, that is, evidence that the incident to be explained comes under some accepted or acceptable rule. This, of course, leaves aside the difficult question about what makes a rule accepted or acceptable. Sometimes it is not a question of justification, but simply of filling in a gap in the picture, of supplying the missing piece of information that will remove the questioner's puzzlement and restore him to a normal state of feeling that he understands. The question about the hat, depending on whether its tone was one of challenge or just curiosity, would evoke a corresponding justificatory or simply explanatory tone in the answers. And the answers illustrate how casual personal explanations foreshadow some of the major modes of systematic intellectual explanation—psychological, scientific, political, economic and sociological.

What distinguishes systematic explanation from the casual explanations of every day is, firstly, that the criteria or tests of what may count as a good explanation are much more demanding, and secondly, that different *kinds* of explanation, where they exist, are explicitly recognized and appropriate specialists allowed to develop and formulate their own criteria. Some of the main criteria, of course, will be common to all disciplines. Professional logicians may investigate the problems of what constitutes logic, but all disciplines of enquiry accept that arguments must be logical in some sense, whatever else they may have to be as well. Professional mathematicians may extend and modify their conceptions of mathematical reasoning, and give different personal evaluations of various parts of mathematics, but one does not expect psychologists or historians or economists to deny the validity of mathematics in general, whether they themselves use it or not. Professional physicists may and do dispute hotly (or coolly, which may here amount to the same thing) about fundamental theories of the physical world, but no one suggests that the whole physics enterprise is being done in the wrong way, or that a political scientist or sociologist can propound theories in which apples rise off the tree instead of falling to the ground.

Although logic, mathematics and physics have a general intellectual force and relevance that cannot be denied, they are not all in the same category of enquiry. Physics is clearly different in respect of its use of experimental method, whereas logic and mathematics are more purely intellectual studies. Logic and mathematics have a close affinity, to the extent that each may be tempted to claim the other as a subsidiary branch. Mathematicians are particularly proud of the fact that their enquiries are independent of any utility, apart from their own satisfaction in the particular intellectual exercise. However, while the mathematics itself is in some sense independent of empirical considerations, the mathematicians as paid professionals are not. In this sense, both mathematics and logic are sustained by the community for their ultimate applied utility.

The points that matter in the context of discussing psychological explanation are that psychology too must respect the whole set of criteria implicit in logic, mathematics and physics (here taken as the type of all physical science); and that logic, mathematics and physics, although so universally unchallenged as fundamental modes of rigorous intellectual enquiry, are not themselves all of the same nature— physics as an experimental science being clearly distinct, and even logic and mathematics not precisely the same thing despite their specially close affinity. Because experimental science *uses* mathematics so extensively, graduates in science particularly may fail to appreciate that mathematics itself is a pure intellectual system—perhaps more like theology than physics. Applied mathematics would then, presumably, be more like so-called pastoral theology. If all disciplines share the discipline of logic, and all experimental disciplines (at least in some sense) the discipline of physics, the questions arise how far a science like psychology can actually satisfy the empirical criteria of science, and whether human or social sciences must have criteria of their own.

If there is a central feature of scientific method, it is that phenomena are studied and measured in precisely controlled circumstances with a view to developing general explanations or theories that will account for, or subsume, as much of the evidence as possible. A theory may be anything from a tight mathematical system to a set of rather loosely associated general concepts. The power of this method arises from the detailed logical and experimental precautions that are taken to ensure that there are as few loopholes as possible in the final argument. One has to have a complete analysis of the logical possibilities of any situation being studied, that is, of the various causal patterns that might be operating. Then one has to devise experimental means of showing what difference each relevant factor does or does not make to what is observed. Science, ideally at any rate, differs from a good deal of common sense in the thoroughness with which it explores different possible explanations, and in the scepticism which it brings to bear on its own findings. The layman is more quickly satisfied with a plausible explanation and does not typically try to disprove one that pleases him. Science is as much an attempt to disprove theories as to prove them. Good theories prove themselves by their resistance to disproof. 'The exception proves the rule' should mean that the exception tests whether or not the rule can accommodate it, not, as is commonly imagined, that the exception proves the existing rule to be correct. (This is rather like the saying, 'a custom more honour'd in the breach than in the observance,' by which most people mean that something is more often not done than done, whereas they should really mean that something is *better* not done than done.)

A scientific *theory* is not a substance, like a sausage. It is a way of looking at phenomena and fitting them into an intellectual pattern of a certain kind, a pattern characterized by careful logical and mathematical reasoning on the one hand, and carefully controlled empirical measurement on the other. Similarly, a scientific *cause* is an element in the pattern that is made (a cause is not a sausage either). When something is called a cause, one is saying that it must come at a certain point in time and space and satisfy any other specified requirements on any occasion when a certain pattern of events is reliably observed. It is the human need to group things into patterns, partly in order to control them, that generates the notion of cause.

The fact that cause is a logical, categorizing concept can be illustrated by referring back to the example of the hat purchase. What caused the hat to be purchased? What was the necessary precondition? One is not now asking for moral justification. It is not a question of whether it ought or ought not to have been bought, but of what in fact caused it to be bought instead of not bought. And the answer would differ with the profession of the questioner. The psychologist might give his account of how men or women like that tended to buy hats like that; the economist of how at that time a pound was the critical dividing line at which a certain percentage of people were likely to buy hats like that; the sociologist or historian of how hats like that were a typical status symbol for persons in that class of society at that time, and so on. How far is the psychologist's theory or explanation likely to be really scientific? Can one trace a scientific pattern of causation in behavioural phenomena?

Problems of psychological explanation

Some of the problems are obvious. First, behaviour, and particularly human behaviour, is not so scientifically manipulable as the things that interest a physicist, or even a biologist. Mostly one cannot pop human beings into bell jars or dissect them (while alive and without surgical excuse) or even isolate them for very long. Secondly, it is diffi- cult to control the range of variation and the instability of behaviour patterns in human beings. This is so true that much psychological research has been done on white rats, although even they have given psychologists plenty to quarrel about. Humans, individually and still more so when viewed across different times and societies, are shaped by myriads of uncontrolled chance factors. A statistical analysis of this variability, if it were possible, might show that more variance was due to unassessed chance factors than to any that could be assessed. This speculation is made a shade less improbable by the fact that, even in statistical analyses of very limited aspects of human behaviour, the proportion of the variance that is not accounted for is sometimes quite large. The necessary attempt to set up more controllable situa- tions, as in psychological laboratories, limits the range of relevance of any results. At least some academic psychologists vie with mathe- maticians in repudiating any intention of immediate utility. But, in the psychological case, this represents a curtailment of explanatory responsibility.

Thirdly, psychological or behavioural measurement is not, and perhaps cannot be, so refined and stable as physical measurement. The physical ruler, or any extension of the same idea up to the most subtle measuring devices of the physicist, has such stable conventions that both empirical observations and mathematical calculations can be made with high reliability and sophistication. Psychological rulers —the intelligence test result, the scaled measure of attitude or emo- tionality, the table of responses in relatively standard experiments— lack these merits. Some psychological rulers are more stable and more acceptable than others. They mostly have points of superiority to the layman's crooked branch broken off the nearest psychological tree. They have helped psychologists to delimit the field of observa- tion and the requirements for valid conclusions. They are scientific in principle. But they are not as scientific in effect as the physicist's tools.

Fourthly, there are problems about what kinds of concept are dis- tinctively psychological. This problem was hinted at in the earlier discussion of psychological language. The concepts of the psycho- metrically inclined psychologists are founded on the complex statisti- cal analysis of various psychological data—multivariate analysis.

Psychological significance is sought where statistical significance has been demonstrated, although, of course, statistical analysis shows rather what patterns of numerical association are possible or probable rather than what these patterns mean psychologically. A psychometrist has suggested jocularly that if success in a certain job was highly correlated with the length of candidates' shoe laces he would would be prepared to select them on shoe-lace length, despite the absence of psychological plausibility in this imaginary association. To take a situation nearer life, one might be justified in using an intelligence test to select candidates if the test results had been shown to correlate highly with later success. It does not follow from this operational definition of intelligence, or of likely success, in terms of a particular test that no more can be said about what constitutes intelligence or success. These might have many aspects to them. Other tests might also give good predictions. But a successful prediction is not a complete explanation. Statistical concepts belong to the methodology of psychology, even if some writings may suggest that they constitute the central substantive concepts of the study.

If psychology is not simply statistics, neither is it simply physiology. Most psychologists today would make a clear distinction between these two, but there is a standing temptation to reduce psychological to physiological explanation. This is perhaps because physiology is more clearly rooted in the physical world, and, since psychological phenomena (leaving aside certain disputable areas) depend on physiological, it may seem that the gradual physiological unveiling of the mysteries of glandular secretions and nerve-cell connections will dispel problems that at present are considered psychological. This reductionist fallacy seems to be based on a misconception about the different kinds of explanation. Since explanations are intellectual constructions that people make, partly out of sheer curiosity or urge towards intellectual manipulation, and partly to facilitate the management of different kinds of problem, there is no reason why explanations should be reduced to a single kind.

After all, one could equally speak of reducing physiology to physics as being the subject concerned with nature's ultimate particles, or physics largely (perhaps not entirely) to mathematics as being the only subject that can provide physics with sufficiently sophisticated models of analysis. But by that time the psychologist might as well make a come-back and suggest a psychological analysis of what makes mathematicians bother their heads with such abstractions, or prevents physicists from accepting the world as it comes without probing into it, or motivates physiologists to become what they are instead of becoming physicists or psychologists. There is no escaping the great fascination of unravelling the physiological events on which all behaviour depends, but it is not really possible to conceive of a world in which nobody used any kind of psychological or behavioural explanation. Psychological explanation, whatever it amounts to precisely, represents a distinctive level of practical and theoretical human interest, just as physiology and physics represent different levels and kinds of conceptual analysis.

If psychology is not just statistics or physiology, is it just engineering—a study of behavioural servo-mechanisms, like the electric fire or iron that switches itself off or on at certain temperatures, the traffic lights that vary with the number of vehicles crossing pads in the roadway, or, to take a physiological example, the mechanisms that produce bodily sweating with excessive heat or shivering with excessive cold? So long as machines were simple, it was easier to comfort oneself with the complexity of the human 'machine', but now that computers can achieve some results much more quickly than their manufacturers, the machine analogy or model can perhaps claim a new lease of life (if one may turn the tables on the machinists and be anthropomorphic). Perhaps those who react against mechanical analysis are fearful of the 'smart' computer-could-do-that attitudes of some of the machine enthusiasts, but extremes of enthusiasm or hostility simply miss the point. Much human behaviour may be machine-like, but human beings are not machines; just as much adult behaviour is childish, but that does not lead us into confusing the meanings of child and adult. The value of the machine model is that it disciplines one to look for behavioural patterns that can be specified precisely and completely rather than vaguely and incompletely. It is not a question of humans being machines, but of units of behaviour being machine-like in specifiable respects.

The behaviour unit in such analysis has been called the TOTE—an acronym for Test Operate Test Exit. The idea can best be explained by an illustration. This is given in Figure 1. A plan of action set out in this way is called an algorithm. While an algorithm is just a systematic diagram of a plan of action, a TOTE is thought of as the unit of behaviour of a person who completes some distinguishable operation or set of operations in accordance with such a plan. An algorithm is an illustrative device with a specific directive purpose. A TOTE is also an illustrative mode of analysis, but it does not direct one to do anything. It is just a possible way of looking at behaviour, namely, as a series of servo-mechanical units, in each of which a set of operations is governed systematically by the operator's knowledge of what must be done to achieve a specified end. It is fairly obvious that many practical problems involving perceptual and motor skills might be usefully analysed via this model. As one moves towards more purely intellectual areas it becomes difficult to apply the model, for

Figure 1 Algorithm for making a local telephone call from a call box.
The words in capitals and brackets illustrate a TOTE analysis. An
algorithm is simply a plan of action set out in this particular way.
A TOTE is a unit of behaviour of a person following the plan.

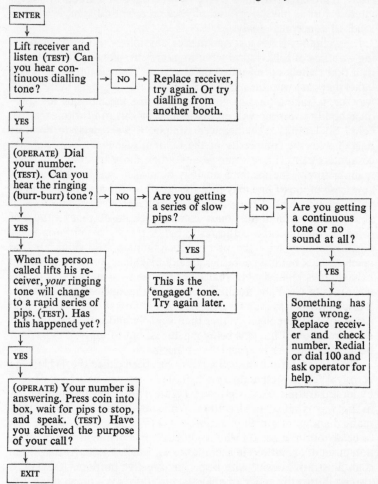

so many of the operations and tests are conducted symbolically inside
the human black box.

The term *feed-back* is used to denote the influence on a unit of
behaviour of one's knowledge of the effects of the last unit. The public
speaker is struck by a well-thrown tomato and decides to advance his
departure time, or gets a hearty response to his funny story and goes
on to tell another. The student is given a prompt assessment of his

work and knows what he must do to sustain or amend his performance; or, alternatively, he is not told how he has done and, consequently, does not know how he should proceed. The driver sees clearly
what is happening around him and acts decisively; or, with misted
windows, cannot see much very clearly and runs into trouble. This
is simply the servo-mechanical model again, but the jargon of feed-
back can be irritatingly misleading in its tendency to suggest that we
know as much about human 'black boxes' or brains as we do about
mechanical ones, or computers. There is the whole problem of what is
implied by 'knowledge' when we mention knowledge of results (KR
in jargon). Even viewed in servo-mechanical terms KR is a mechanism with a difference, notably its complexity and the fact that we
cannot manufacture the 'black box'.

Compared with psychometric, physiological and servo-mechanical
concepts, those of psychoanalytical psychology take one almost into
a world of myth. The dictionary definitions of *myth* illustrate the
problem. The more sympathetic one runs, 'a usually traditional story
of ostensible historical events that serves to unfold part of the world
view of a people or explain a practice, belief, or natural phenomenon'.
The less sympathetic is, 'an ill-founded belief held uncritically especially by an interested group'. A sentence from the psychometrist
Cattell (1965) is typical of critics of psychoanalysis:

> Even the father of psychoanalysis, Freud, based his generaliza-
> tions on so few cases that a statistician can only blush for him,
> while critics can assert that the conflicts he described were
> peculiar to middle-class Viennese in a *fin-de-siècle* culture.

A neat rhetorical stab—or is it two, one in the front and one in the
back? At any rate, some workers in the psychoanalytic tradition,
while they have had little success in providing statistical backing for
their traditional concepts, have attempted to curb their more extreme
mythopoeic tendencies, and to bring their ideas down to earth in the
recognizable world of social psychology.

Psychoanalysis may provide the kind of psychological illumination
that, it was suggested earlier, is given by literature. This is a vivid
sense of particular, rather than generalized, actualities and possibilities. One says to oneself, 'Yes, things are sometimes just like that,' or,
'Things could sometimes be like that.' What literature does not supply
is a statistical analysis of how often things are like that, or a prediction of how often or how closely they could be like that. But, since
people have so much practical use for such illuminations, which often
have both a strongly *felt* relevance and a real potentiality for personal
use, it is not surprising that literature and psychoanalysis should
continue to flourish. Scientific psychology, constricted by the rigorous

demands of its own criteria and less accessible to non-professional understanding because of them, holds grimly on to its place in the scientific sun at the cost of being less useful to individual lay persons. It may benefit individual laymen but mainly by the professional mediation of applied psychologists in institutional contexts. The psychoanalytical approach has something of the vividness of literature together with a greater degree of generality, albeit not the statistical or otherwise disciplined generality of science.

Earlier psychoanalytic writing, and still some of today's, maps out the psychological world as if it were a physical realm. Here is the most important country of the Unconscious. It is governed by Id (all the unrecognized selfish and sensual urges) and Superego (the distorted version of our parents' apparent moral values that took up residence in childhood and continues to be influential). The longings, urges and mythical notions that inhabit this territory are apt to try and get out and invade the adjacent land of Consciousness, but there are frontier guards who wage a persistent but not wholly successful battle to prevent migration. A powerful sexual urge makes a bid for freedom but is thrust back into the Unconscious, and can get near the frontier again only in the guise of a naughty dream or a day-dreaming fantasy. A thoroughly aggressive fellow is rebuffed for threatening to attack his own parents, but turns up instead as a militant pacifist, like those politicians who say Peace as they increase the nation's arms expenditure. A real mischief-maker tries to disguise himself with loud protests that 'It's these mischief-makers that are to blame'.

One could make more fun of the reifying tendencies of some psychoanalysts, their representation of patterns of behaviour as if they were substantial things (Ids, Superegos, etc.) instead of just conceptual patterns. But, while this reification is useless as scientific explanation, it should be remembered that more scientific psychologists are not immune. They may laboriously explain that certain speculative concepts are just intervening variables, terms of physiological or statistical convenience, or what not, but they often seem to take on a more substantial life than that once they are allowed over the threshold of psychological discussion. It could then be asked whether there is not a difference of degree rather than kind between the loosely controlled concepts of psychoanalysis and the less than one-hundred-per-cent-controlled concepts of behaviourism.

Psychoanalysis, even if it has been weak in experimental controls and mythopoeically self-indulgent, has nevertheless focused attention on widely significant features of behaviour that are of great interest. The most important in general terms may be the distinction between aspects of behaviour that are recognized by the person behaving and aspects whose significance he persistently fails to notice, although it may be clear to others. He argues aggressively for peace, pruriently for chastity; offers self-satisfied reasons for doing what benefits personal interests; blames others for misdemeanours typical of his own; puts on a childish tantrum if frustrated in adult desires; lets slip his hidden thoughts in slips of tongue and pen ('I've just seen Mary—sorry, I mean Margery'); forgets what he wants to forget; and dreams fantastic delights and horrors.

These mechanisms of reaction-formation, rationalization, projection, regression, repression and fantasy are certainly conspicuous once one is alerted to them. Their recognition is important as an aid to seeing oneself and others realistically and honestly, even if they may not represent a tight conceptual scheme, and may often fail to provide *decisive* interpretations. (Did the imaginary character in the last parenthesis wish he *had* seen Mary? Or was he frightened that he might have and glad he did not?) The critics complain that the psychoanalyst cannot lose. The mechanisms of the Unconscious are all-purpose. A little adjustment and they will do the trick—any trick. This kind of ironical attack may be possible only because psychoanalysts are professionally more concerned with clinical work than with perfecting statistically reliable techniques of categorization.

If psychoanalysis has not evolved a really scientific conceptual system, it has served to remind people of the extent of irrational factors in human life. This may seem obvious, but psychoanalysis has thrown up a great number of suggestive lines of approach which help one to see the detailed forms that irrationality takes and the possibilities of diminishing its influence. It helps one to make allowances that are not made by those who have not seen this particular light. It has been helpful too in thinking about conflict, particularly the conflicts that may rage within an individual and be so difficult to resolve. None of this apology is meant to suggest that irrationality can be finally dismissed (*Naturam expellas furca, tamen usque recurret*), but one has at least a more analytic way of looking it in the eye. This may not qualify for the cachet of science, but it is a practical convenience.

In looking at the conceptual modes that are associated with psychology we have tentatively placed psychometry, physiology, servo-mechanics and psychoanalysis. If psychology threatens to disintegrate on one side into smaller-unit study, whether physiological, servo-mechanical or clinical, it must, on the other side, distinguish itself from the larger-unit study constituted by sociology. Sociology too is concerned with behaviour, but in relation to the structure and influence of the social groups and institutions within which the individual grows up rather than to laboratory learning situations, psychometrical tests or psychoanalytic appraisals. Berger (1963) says:

As to the exact definition of the 'social', it is difficult to improve on Max Weber's definition of a 'social' situation as one in which people orient their actions towards one another. The web of meanings, expectations and conduct resulting from such mutual orientation is the stuff of sociological analysis.

This does not quite distinguish sociology from social psychology. The only means of differentiation seems to be in terms of the larger, more complex conceptual units that interest the sociologist—social class, status, power, conflict and institution. The concept of *role* is prominent in sociological analysis but is also used in social psychology. Perhaps the sociologist is more interested in the public aspect of role—the pattern of what a person does in a position which has public expectations attached to it, such as the role of teacher, politician, clergyman, etc. The psychologist is perhaps more interested in the individual's own expectations of himself, but the two notions are clearly associated.

Sociology has probably been even more criticized than psychology for its jargon and for conceptual woolliness. Certainly the generality of even a standard concept like *class* invites loose usage by people who have not gone into the problems of definition. Then the difficulty or impossibility of looking at social institutions and relationships without ideological bias makes it less likely that sociological enquiries will be scientific in a fundamental sense. Like the psychometricians, the sociometricians may perfect the techniques of collecting representative samples of accurately recorded information, but it is the fundamental assumptions of their enquiries that are challengeable. Why investigate that particular topic or those particular aspects of it? Questionnaires, however technically impeccable (and of course, not all of them are), are liable to be ideological broadsheets in disguise. Someone is out to prove something, even if it is only that he ought to get a degree for his little piece of research, or that Radiant Television Incorporated is something worthy of your humble opinions.

One can perhaps implicitly distinguish psychological from sociological analysis, and also reach a more positive general statement of what psychology is centrally concerned with, by reference to Lunzer's *The Regulation of Behaviour* (1968). Lunzer, allowing that an introspective and empathic approach to human behaviour and experience has its utility, goes on to question the sufficiency of concepts like knowing, striving and feeling 'as irreducible explanatory concepts'. He sees scientific psychology as a study of 'the interconnectedness of behaviour'. Pattern and direction in behaviour are the produce of the brain's hierarchical modes of operation. Sequences of physiological and corresponding behavioural activity develop, based on some elements facilitating, others inhibiting, one another. These sequences are called *strategies* or *schemata*. There are also assumed to be central, that is brain, mechanisms called *links*, which respond differentially to combinations of cues from the senses. They are minor strategies—transformations of sensory input in the brain. The whole set of these supposed links is given the name of the *comparator system*. Lunzer stresses that he is not giving a physiological but a structural and functional account of the regulation of behaviour. A physiological account 'would specify the anatomical locus and the physiological mode of action of all the elements envisaged', which, of course, is not possible—at least, not so far.

Any piece of behaviour will be a product of the environmental stimulation acting on a person at a particular time (the sensory input) and the operational state of the hierarchy of strategies (the 'black box', one might say). Any strategy already in operation will tend to run to completion unless the sensory input proves inadequate and the hierarchy is forced to rearrange itself. However, a predominant role in the regulation of human behaviour is attached to

> the capacity for the representational reconstruction of experi-
> ence by means of strategies which depend on a series of inputs
> that is largely within the control of the subject, and free of
> environmental constraints.

Language is one form of this general representational function.

An account developed by Lunzer in about four hundred pages can hardly receive more than summary justice in two paragraphs. But the point is not to give a full account of a particular theory of behaviour, but to draw attention to the mode of psychological conceptualizing. It is one with strong physiological and servo-mechanical affinities, but attempts to assert itself as distinctively psychological by claiming to be a functional explanation. The problem is that the explanation has most clarity and force at those points where one can envisage a physiological or a computer model, but then we have only partially penetrated the literal technology of the brain. Where the talk is of strategies—a term that is very much at home in the world of intro-spective, empathic psychology—one can see that this is a way of cate-gorizing behaviour but not so clearly that it has much stronger explanatory force. Words like 'strategy' and 'function' derive mean-ing from some assumed standard of achievement—strategic or func-tional for some assumed goal. And when Lunzer speaks of 'a series of inputs within the control of the subject', the word 'subject' seems to readmit the little man in the machine, the introspected 'I', for *all* inputs seem to be largely within the control of the hierarchy of strategies, if that is what the psychological organism is.

Psychology was once thought of as the study of mind but is now characteristically defined as the scientific study of behaviour. We have seen that the pursuit of such a science poses the four special problems of manipulation, control, measurement and conceptualization. Psychology stands, in a sense, between physiology and sociology, dependent on the possibility of developing explanations of behaviour at a particular level of generality—more general than physiology but less general than sociology. This might seem to be too much of a knife-edge, but defence of the position is no doubt warranted by the extent to which psychology has encouraged critical, objective analysis of behaviour both at the level of general study and in attempts to solve problems of practical psychology. However, the list of threats to its position is not complete, for there is a fifth problem posed by those critics who question whether the social sciences really can be objective in any sense like the physical sciences, or even whether the physical sciences themselves have a single objective method.

Nidditch (1968) expresses neatly this possibility of scepticism:

> Science is not simple nor uniform; it is constituted by a wide range of activities, discoveries, and modes of thought which are themselves extraordinarily varied and whose tendency is progressive proliferation.

He goes on to mention Polanyi's view that scientific beliefs are *not* determined solely by observed facts. One has to take into account the whole process of enquiry and discovery that constitutes science. Science is not just the published article but all that leads up to it. Feyerabend, in his article on 'How To Be A Good Empiricist' in the Nidditch volume, argues that:

> You can be a good empiricist only if you are prepared to work with many alternative theories rather than with a single point of view and 'experience'.

Goldman (1969), discussing the social sciences, points out how they lack the degree of agreement about their nature and goals that prevails in the physical sciences. Moreover,

> When it is a question of studying human life, the process of scientific knowing, since it is itself a human, historical and social fact, implies the partial identity of the subject and the object of knowledge.

This is a truth which psychological objectivists tend to turn away from. The researcher can be God in his own laboratory, but, again in Goldman's words, 'scientific thought is only a *means* for the social group and for humanity as a whole'.

A number of philosophers have argued that some of the concepts typically used by psychologists are either lacking in explanatory force or fail to make explicit the element of value implicit in them. Louch (1966), for example, in the course of a searching philosophical polemic, concludes that:

Psychology's successes are essentially successes in the mechanics of control, and not in the explanation of normal human action.

Whatever units of behaviour the psychologist selects they do not add up to a study of human behaviour, for this is inseparable from the implication of purpose, meaning and intention—that is, standards of reference or achievement proposed by human beings for themselves. Peters (1958) pursues a similar line of argument with reference to the concept of motivation. Men 'act in accordance with ... normative laws—which they themselves create'. Motivation refers to directed action and we speak of motives when a man's conduct is being assessed against some standard. An explanation of motive is typically sought when some accepted standard of conduct appears to have been abrogated.

Ayer (1964), however, suggests that other motives may be unquestioned simply because the answers are obvious, posing no problems. Ayer also argues that being rule-governed does not prevent behaviour from being causally explained, for it is the agent's *valuation* of the rule that constitutes a factor in his motivation. Similarly, with the argument that social context must be invoked to explain certain kinds of behaviour, one can argue that social factors enter the reckoning only through their influence on the agent. The individual behaves according to the norms of his social class, not through the abstract fact of class membership but through the concrete psychological fact of subscribing at least tacitly to what he understands to be expected of him. Ayer, therefore, is inclined to assimilate motives to causes and, still more strongly, to assert that causal explanation is not ruled out even if there are other aspects of the situation that do not belong in a pattern of causal explanation.

Perspective on psychology and education

Scientists or scholars sometimes say that science or scholarship are attitudes of mind. Of course they are not *merely* attitudes of mind, but the point is that neither are they *merely* bodies of accumulated knowledge or sets of techniques. The argument of the present chapter has been planned to encourage a critical attitude of mind in the study of educational psychology. One is not dealing with simple things and there is no reason for expecting simple answers, even if it is perfectly reasonable to *strive* for as much simplicity as can be achieved without distorting or ignoring evidence. The urgency of practical problems may drive people towards oversimplified views. This does not matter too much, provided everyone recognizes that such views are governed by expediency and are not substitutes for the arduous pursuit of true and complete explanations.

Student teachers, experienced teachers, educational administrators and parents confront different practical problems in education. Psychology cannot tell any of them what they *ought* to do, for this depends on personal and social evaluations of what activities are most worth-while, not on empirical accounts of how people behave in fact. Since educational aims are never finally and indisputably agreed, but are necessarily liable to challenge and change, some disagreements about educational psychology arise from conflicting assumptions about educational aims. But psychological theories about human behaviour are also both diverse and, in the very nature of scientific enquiry, subject to modification. Here too, therefore, one should expect a considerable measure of uncertainty, variety and change. The educational psychologist is not just like the bare-back circus rider nimbly bestriding two horses, but rather like such a rider whose horses may go off in different directions or turn into several entirely different kinds of animal. The rider may finish by doing the splits between an elephant and a kangaroo.

Reverting to literal analysis, one sees that education and psychology are doing different things from one another, but also that each within itself contains a considerable variety of interests and ways of analysing situations. The educator has to think of political, economic, social, religious, historical and practical pedagogical considerations as well as of psychological theories and techniques. The psychologist has to think of statistical, physiological, servo-mechanical, psychoanalytical and other models of behavioural analysis, and only incidentally of the utility of any of his theories in education or in any other possible sphere of applied psychology. There is the further problem that, even if educational aims were agreed within some limited context and only one mode of psychological analysis selected as a guide in achieving the aims, the problem of interpreting and applying a psychological model to a specific educational situation can be a major one. Such a problem may be dignified as a problem in applied psychology, but it seems likely that the process of application will be governed by different kinds of human judgment (including principles of expediency, morality, etc.) and not just by principles of scientific psychology.

Thus far psychology has been accepted on its own terms as the scientific study of behaviour. To complete this perspective it is necessary to recall what has already been argued more fully, that there is a whole area of study, the philosophy of science, which does not accept scientific explanations at their face value, but instead attempts to analyse what exactly constitutes a scientific explanation. This is not the question of whether a particular scientific explanation is a good one or a bad one, but of what criteria must be satisfied before something can count at all as any kind of scientific explanation. It may be that even the physical sciences differ among one another in their explanatory criteria, even if one is most often reminded of common criteria such as respect for logic, mathematics, and careful experimental control of evidence. When one turns to the social or human sciences, such as psychology or sociology, the nature of the problems that arise makes it more difficult to observe strictly the common criteria of the physical sciences. Considering that the human factor is a constant threat to ideal objectivity even in studying the physical world, it is not surprising that it should be as great or greater when the observer and the observed are both human, as in the study of human psychology.

These problems about psychology as a science are quite well recognized by many professional psychologists, although some still seem to subscribe to a naïve objectivism—either unaware of, or choosing to neglect, the problems of defining 'objective' or of being objective in more than a trivially obvious way. Few psychologists choose to recognize the problem of whether human action can ever be adequately explained solely in terms of an empirical science of psychology. It seems obvious that psychology can offer explanations of a sort, namely, filling in gaps in our systematic knowledge of behaviour and mapping out the less obvious interrelationships—a functional account of behaviour. But it has been argued that, even if this is explanation at all in any rigorous sense, it is not sufficient explanation, for it leaves out the fact that, in humans, behaviour is meaningful in relation to norms or standards that persons propose for themselves. 'Needs' do not just occur but are defined by our assumptions and values. 'Growth' too is a value-laden concept; each day in a baby's life is a step nearer death as well as adulthood, although the adult-dominated world unsurprisingly takes its own flourishing as the unquestioned norm.

A deeper penetration of this problem would take one too far into the realms of philosophy, but, briefly, the problem is that a scientific account of behaviour may not be a *sufficient* account of human action, for the latter has to include some account of the individual and social norms that guide action. This at once involves one in two kinds of problem beyond psychology—the problem of how to validate such norms (a philosophical problem), and the problem of the influence of major social institutions on behaviour (a sociological problem). While it is not the purpose of this book to concentrate on such problems, they will be kept in mind as particular topics are studied from a mainly psychological viewpoint.

To recognize the problems and limitations attached to a study like psychology does not mean that the psychological game is lost before it has even started. Psychology has dispelled a great deal of misconception (even if it has, like most studies, created some), and has accustomed people to looking more critically and objectively at theories of behaviour. It has created techniques of measuring behaviour and models of understanding behaviour, some of which have been quite fruitful in clarifying both practical and theoretical questions, even if they fall short of physicists' standards (which, in any case, may be only partly relevant). It is a complex study and requires a readiness to tolerate complexity and variety. Although this first chapter strikes various sceptical warning notes, the following chapters will not sustain this tune, but rather look at specific themes within educational psychology as constructively as possible, attempting to take just account both of the problems facing educators and the possible contribution of psychologists to the partial solution of these problems.

The adult as learner and teacher 2

In the previous chapter it was argued that it would be a mistake to imagine that psychology or education or the practical relationship between them were simple. Any progress in understanding depends at least on recognizing the considerable list of diverse elements entering into educational practice and psychological explanation. This chapter turns attention to the double learning problem that faces teachers— the problem of their own effective learning of relevant knowledge, skills, and attitudes; and the problem of helping pupils or students to learn effectively. The saying. 'Don't do what I do; do as I tell you,' suggests that there may be a gap between the pedagogy that adults think suitable for children and what they consider suitable—or, perhaps more accurately, feasible—for themselves.

So many different things are expected of any one teacher and, of course, the range of expectation increases enormously as one considers the variety among teachers—variety of age, education, professional preparation, teaching service, personality, social background and, on top of such factors, all the variety of children and subjects taught. This makes it necessary to take a look at the whole question of the teacher's role before going on to consider the psychological and pedagogical factors that influence the student as learner, and then some of the problems that face the student in his role as teacher. Briefly, this will mean looking at the teaching-learning situation in terms of discipline, the structure of learning, and motivation. Finally, there will be some discussion of the problem of teaching young teachers to teach.

The meaning of role and personality

The concept of role represents a point where sociology and social psychology meet. Role refers to any category of social behaviour for which there is a fairly definite set of norms—the role of father, daughter, teacher, pupil, general, priest and so on. In more abstract terms, it is the set of public expectations attached to a socially defined position or status like those illustrated. A little thought shows that the concept is not a very precise one. It seems to accommodate a number of allied but different things. To take the example of the teacher's role, there are things that people expect teachers to be or to do as a matter of fact—let us say, to be verbally fluent, to incline towards didacticism, to drive cars rather carefully, or to turn up punctually for work and do it with considerable conscientiousness. But teachers are expected to do these, and a lot of other things beside, not just because they are customarily observed to do such things, but because they are considered to be under an obligation to do them. This is made clearer if one suggests such things as setting a good moral example, encouraging respect for religion, achieving good examination results for their pupils, or accepting broad personal as well as specific instructional responsibilities. With these more demanding criteria there begins to be more possibility of a gap between *role expectancy* and *role performance*.

This is not the end of the difficulties about the concept of role, for, of course, different people have different expectations of the same apparent role, which may have one name attached to it, such as 'teacher', but include infant mistresses, public school masters, private tutors, university lecturers, educational broadcasters and a wide miscellany of others. Even if one takes an example of a more specific single role—let us say head mathematics teacher in a large comprehensive school—the occupant of the role may be expected to be scholarship-producer, efficient departmental administrator, curriculum innovator, pupil counsellor and social organizer. The balance of expectations will vary, depending on whether the expectations are those of the head of the school, parents, sixth-form pupils, first-year entrants, subordinate colleagues, heads of neighbouring departments or visiting student teachers, and so on through all of those in what is called the *role set* of the mathematics head.

A rich phraseology seems to have grown from the word 'role'. Our mathematics teacher may experience *role conflict* because he cannot quite reconcile the expectation of chalking up academic successes with his commitments to the school's social life, or of administrative efficiency with sympathetic toleration for his subordinates; or perhaps his entire school role with some conflicting role outside of the school context. He may increase his *role distance* from the whole teaching situation and seek for comfort in some less teacherly extracurricular pursuits, let us say (frivolously) dog racing and bingo. Or he may, instead, increase his *role commitment*, become identified almost completely with school life and end up as headmaster of his own school. In any case, he is bound to have an individual, perhaps idiosyncratic, way of fulfilling his role—his *role style*—and, even if he becomes a dedicated headmaster, he will have to occupy other roles for other people. He cannot be headmaster to his wife, his son or his golf-club partners. These are different roles and the whole set of such roles has been called a person's *status set*.

Apart from the problem of pinning down the concept of role in terms of who is expecting what, of whom, in what context, and whether as a matter of obligation or customary expectation, there is the further question of the individual's own interpretation of what is expected of him. This interpretation is a subtle mixture of self-knowledge, personal idealism and views about what other people think. It is presumably via this 'mixture', this complex psychological state, that sociologically defined roles operate on the individual person. Brown (1965) formulates the link in these terms:

> Roles are units of a social system and personalities are enduring traits and motives linked to a human organism. Roles and personalities are mutually determinative. The personality one brings to a role determines the manner of its interpretation.

If the concept of role belongs slightly more to sociology than psychology, the concept of personality seems pre-eminently to be at home in the realm of psychology, although, like role, it is a complex concept. Before turning to the more specific aspects of the teacher role it may be helpful to say an introductory word about personality.

In Brown's statement above the word 'enduring' is important. People have usually used the word 'personality' to refer to the relatively permanent and characteristic patterns of a person's behaviour. Popular usage has often failed to take account of how the same person in different roles may show different apparent personality traits—perhaps hard and calculating as a business colleague and yet easygoing and generous among personal friends; stern in the classroom but friendly in the staffroom. When such disparities are popularly recognized, it is sometimes with surprise, as if there were reluctance to tolerate diverse images of one person. While roles are categories that are located in social groups, personality is normally intended to refer to what is in some sense located in the individual himself. Popularly, the term sometimes seems to refer to role style, the

idiosyncrasies of role performance, rather than anything more substantial.

Psychologists, according to their allegiances, have tried to stabilize
the concept of personality via psychometrics, physiology or psychoanalytical theories. Some of the problems attaching to these ways
were mentioned in Chapter 1 and will not be recapitulated here. The
psychometric approach consists in devising various possible tests and
measures of personality, which could include psychoanalytical or
physiological data, and analysing the results of representative samples
of people to find whether any stable personality dimensions can be
established. For example, it seems that people tend to be spread along
an introversion-extroversion dimension, from those who are rather
inward-turning and less social, through the middle ranges where most
people are a bit of both, to the other extreme where some individuals
are highly social and uninhibited. Another likely dimension ranges
people according to how psychologically stable they are. There are
other scales but these are sufficient as examples, for psychometric
testing will be considered in more detail in a later chapter.

Psychoanalytic viewpoints attach great importance to the persisting
influence of infantile experience. This will be discussed in greater
detail in the next chapter, on infancy. For the present, it must suffice
to say that personality is seen as an underlying pattern of behaviour
such that some of its features are fully accessible to the conscious
awareness of the person but others operate in a clandestine way—
perhaps recognized by observers but not by the person himself. These
subconscious factors are shaped primarily by the person's infantile
relationships with his parents. At one extreme, parents help the infant, and subsequently the adult he grows into, to express and live
with his fantasies of fear and aggression and to grow in self-reliance
and normal social affection. At the other extreme less understanding
parents, themselves acting under unconscious influences, increase the
infant's sense of insecurity in the face of both reality and fantasy, and
diminish his capacity for coping realistically and effectively with the
later challenges of childhood and adulthood.

Various psychoanalytical defence mechanisms are classified—subconscious ways of protecting one's image of oneself from the threats
of the objective world. To give some examples at a relatively superficial and trivial level, one forgets one's appointment with the dentist
(repression); boasts of putting the boss in his place when in fact the
boss himself has been doing some rather plain talking (compensation);
passes the blame down the line—'the teachers are to blame; no, the
pupils; no, the parents; no, society'—(projection, and displacement);
or conjures up a picture of oneself showing the world just how
Beethoven's Ninth Symphony should be conducted (fantasy). At a

deeper level, defences like these may strongly determine a person's life style, impelling him relentlessly along certain directions or inhibiting him from others which are, in principle, equally open and available.

Physiological analyses of personality have a long history, from typologies based on the supposed influence of earth, air, fire and water, or of sanguine, melancholic, choleric and phlegmatic humours, down to twentieth-century categorizations of body-type, in which the relative balance of muscle, fat and nerve tissue is supposed to be associated with temperamental type, ranging from the comfortable, indulgent, sleep-o'-nights *viscerotonics* to the lean and hungry, think-too-much *cerebrotonics*. The complex patterns of the body's endocrine glands secreting their fluids into the blood stream seem to provide a physiological medium for some aspects of temperamental expression, but psychologists would probably want to bring our grey matter into the personality picture, and acknowledge the dependence of our conscious functioning on the cerebral cortex as well as recognizing the autonomic nervous system that regulates our emotional reactions (increased heart beat, sweating, eye dilation, skin flushing, muscular tremor, etc.). Eysenck (1953) defined personality as

> the more or less stable and enduring organization of a person's character, temperament, intellect, and physique, which determines his unique adjustment to his environment.

This seems to bring in some of the main systematic aspects of personality while leaving it clear that an individual can have a unique position in terms of his particular admixture of any factors that can be assessed.

The teacher's role and personality

The preceding discussion of the meaning of role and personality has been brief and introductory, but it will serve in the meantime for the purpose of discussing the teacher's role or, to be quite precise, teachers' roles. Hoyle (1969) suggests that the sociologist is concerned with behaviour patterns amongst groups of people, whereas the psychologist's problem is to study what makes individual teachers perform a role in a certain way. This perhaps represents the difference of emphasis, but there is no complete distinction, for sociological patterns would just be intellectual abstractions if one did not allow for the fact that they operate psychologically through individual persons, just as psychological explanations would be incomplete if

they did not reckon with the particular effects on behaviour of awareness of social norms, embodied or expressed in roles.

Hoyle, following Parsons, lists a number of 'pattern variables' or
polarities in the teacher's role. They are (1) between emotional involvement and detachment in one's teaching; (2) between aiming at
highly specific and highly diffuse teaching aims; (3) between treating
all alike in accordance with universal criteria and breaking rules for
individual cases as tends to happen within intimate groups; (4)
between regarding pupils qualitatively in terms of age, sex or something similar, and quantitatively in relation to sheer educational
achievement, regardless of other factors, and (5) between putting
selfish interests or the interests of the community (school, college,
etc.) first in one's calculations and operations. To bring out the
potential significance of these contrasts one might imagine at one
extreme a stern headmaster who was relatively detached from the
more emotional and personal aspects of education, completely set on
maximizing the school's academic achievements at all costs, inflexible
in his demands for obedience to school rules, and dominated by his
own aspiration for scholastic reputation. An opposite caricature (one
hopes this is the right word) might reveal a master who identified
himself emotionally with the whole human life of the school, set no
special premium on any area of activity, and scarcely bothered either
about rules or reputation. Since one can imagine the disadvantages of
living with either extreme, it is fortunate that most heads fall somewhere in between.

Hoyle suggests that 'the element of control is fundamental to all
sets of expectations concerning the role of the teacher', but there is
clearly much divergence of opinion about the direction in which this
control is or should be expected to operate. Supposedly descriptive
accounts of teachers' roles are sometimes rather speculative, for it is
not easy to accumulate a wide and reliable sample of what different
categories of people do expect of different categories of teachers. One
would expect the picture to be complex and to change with time and
place. Moreover, characterizations of teacher role sometimes begin in
descriptive vein but modulate almost imperceptibly to a prescriptive
vein, in which teachers almost stand arraigned before the sociological
bar for subscribing to middle-class values; for encouraging pupils to
be active, individualistic and ambitious instead of fatalistic, com-
munity-tied and content to enjoy life as it comes; for clinging to
scholastic and intellectualist values instead of social worker values;
for being conservative instead of 'progressive'; or verbally articulate
instead of materially productive.

It seems essential to recognize these quicksands of intellectual confusion that surround the concept of the teacher's role if any value is

to be derived from the concept at all. When one turns to the personality of teachers it is a salutary beginning to recall the remark of Morrison and McIntyre (1969) that:

> In almost every investigation of the personal characteristics of those who become teachers, greater differences have been found between different groups of teachers than between teachers as a whole and the rest of the population.

Nevertheless, these authors do venture a few generalizations based on empirical studies with personality scales and the like. Three of these generalizations about teachers are that:

1 they put less than usual value on what is seen as useful, efficient and economic, and more than usual value on personal relationships.
2 teachers tend to be well adjusted, emotionally stable, objective and sociable people.
3 teachers in general may be more inclined than most to behave in conformity with the social pressures which they experience.

While such generalizations have a certain interest and even plausibility, one has to consider how extremely difficult it must be to define, measure or compare such complex things as personal value systems or conformity with social pressures. Varying specific contexts influence both the definition of scales and the range of responses to them. This is often manifest when research conducted in countries (say America and England) with radically differing social or educational contexts is compared.

There have been various enquiries into what are taken to be the fundamental social attitudes held by teachers. These enquiries are based on using a variety of attitude tests, the results of which are statistically analysed to establish what seem to be the main dimensions along which attitudes vary. For example, a radical/conservative dimension would be one revealing different attitudes towards things like personal freedom, corporal punishment, religious values or the need for security. Another suggested dimension, toughmindedness/tendermindedness, would show how far any person leaned towards hard-headed, no-nonsense, spare-the-rod-and-spoil-the-child attitudes or towards tolerant, liberal, forgive-thy-brother-unto-seventy-times-and-seven attitudes. Other scales, particularly relevant to teaching, attempt to range people between 'progressive' and 'traditional' ideologies, and between religiously altruistic and more specifically utilitarian orientations towards educational tasks. McLeish (1969) characterizes a Progressive-versus-Traditional-Ideology scale as distinguishing 'between those respondents who favour or disfavour a dynamic, activity-centred, secular based educational process which accepts change and is founded on a permissive philosophy rooted in the view that spontaneous growth is better than a forced development'.

Although there is bound to be considerable interest in the findings of enquiries based on the use of such scales, it is necessary to keep in mind that attitude-testing is a difficult and insecure territory, that the names used to designate various scales may suggest a greater measure of psychological clarity and simplicity than is warranted by the diverse tests and populations from which they derive, and, of course, that attitudes, while they may constitute some of what is meant by personality, need not have the permanence that is sometimes required as part of the concept of personality. Nevertheless, some attitudes seem to be relatively long-lasting and, with increasing years, perhaps increasingly difficult to change, and, therefore, less distinguishable from personality.

McLeish reports a comparative study of attitudes among a mixed population of 290 men and 291 women teachers, student teachers and education lecturers. He took account of religious and political allegiances as well as various attitudinal dimensions like those exemplified in the last paragraph. The sample included English, Scottish, Commonwealth and American teachers and students. In this particular sample, which, as McLeish explicitly recognizes, cannot be assumed to be representative, there were various differences. For example, the education lecturers and English teachers attending advanced courses tended towards the Progressive end of the Progressive/Traditional Ideology scale, whereas Commonwealth teachers and the English graduate student teachers tended towards the Traditional end. The English group showed a relatively high, the Scottish a relatively low, degree of Tendermindedness. The Scottish group showed relatively high, the American relatively low, scores for Anxiety.

There were also differences associated with sex, age, religion, politics, professional experience and job satisfaction. These have to be studied in the monograph itself, but it is perhaps not too misleading to mention as examples that the women were apparently more radical and power-oriented than the men; that the older teachers were more opposed to corporal punishment, and slightly more radical and satisfied in their work than the younger; and that atheists and agnostics, as well as Roman Catholics, tended to have most extreme scores. It is essential to keep in mind that, in addition to any technical imperfections in the representativeness of the samples or in the consistency of the test results, such studies must always confront the problem of devising valid psychological interpretations. The names attached to various dimensions may suggest that they are more permanently founded or more akin to commonsense psychological concepts than is the case.

Whatever role, personality or attitude a teacher may have in fact, we know the pattern that is favoured by children. Evans (1962), summing up the results of empirical enquiries, writes:

> Children like teachers who are kind, friendly, cheerful, patient, helpful, fair, have a sense of humour, show an understanding of children's problems, allow plenty of pupil activity and at the same time maintain order. They dislike teachers who use sarcasm and ridicule, are domineering and have favourites, who punish to secure discipline, fail to provide for the needs of individual pupils and have disagreeable personality peculiarities.

Perhaps not very surprising, and, as a practical guide, a counsel of perfection, but still a useful reminder or check list for a young teacher attempting to spot possible lines of self-improvement.

Student teachers obviously occupy a role which has its own peculiar problems. Although these problems are regarded sympathetically on the whole, there are exceptions. The student may have to teach in a school which is characterized by rigidity of outlook and method compared with other schools of its kind, or compared with the student's own outlook. At the other extreme, a student may be so imbued with the scholastic values of the university dons who have taught him for three years that he has difficulty in appreciating the differing needs of 70 to 90 per cent of the population. In practice, very many student teachers are *not* in particularly rigid school atmospheres and are *not* themselves so inflexible that they cannot gradually develop less academic aims and methods for appropriate situations. They face the perennial problem found by all teachers of striking the right balance between rigidity and flexibility. Equality of educational opportunity, by the very meaning of education, must mean opportunity to improve in some way. The teacher would not be doing the job he is paid to do if he stultified the possibility of improvement because of either excessive tolerance or excessive intolerance. One extreme might be summed up in the saying, 'It doesn't matter what you're doing so long as you're doing something'; the other in the saying, 'Whatever you're doing, stop it!'

These points, however, are not completely distinctive of the student teacher's role, even if they affect him in a particularly sharp way because he is a beginner. What is more distinctive is the fact that the student teacher lacks the *formal* authority that attaches only to being one of a permanent employed staff, and, therefore, has to depend on personal authority and on the general tone of the school, which may or may not be helpful. Secondly, the student teacher by the very nature of his position is both less clear about what he should be trying to do and less skilled in devising and implementing detailed practical schemes for achieving any end proposed. It is these intrinsic and unavoidable weaknesses of his role that make it necessary for him to do the three typical things that student teachers do—analyse what should and can be done (educational theory), study recognized and possible methods of doing what ought to be done, and practise the detailed skills of implementing aims and methods in the classroom. Although educational theory is the favourite whipping boy among these three, some classroom and school practice is shockingly bad because it has no clear aim or because the aim itself is indefensible, except perhaps as an expedient to fill time. Educational theory is out in the public stocks, almost inviting assault, while much educational practice escapes attention provided that its sanctum, the classroom, is reasonably quiet. Practice makes perfect, but not necessarily in an activity that deserves perfecting.

The psychology of adult learning

Before pursuing further the psychology of teaching, and particularly student teaching, it may be useful to look first at the student's other role, of learner rather than teacher, and see whether any aspects of this may illumine the teaching role or facilitate insight into the problems of those younger learners who constitute the learning population of schools. People who are teachers in one context but learners in another do not always, or even often, notice how they adopt different attitudes, depending on which side of the learning fence they happen to be on at a particular moment. As teachers they may be demanding, puzzled by poor pupil response or irritated by minor misdemeanours like lateness or interruptions. As learners they may gripe at their teachers' excessive demands, be slow to respond in discussions, or interrupt the pattern of the work by lateness or other casual behaviour.

Although student learning tends to conjure up a notion of learning that is academic and abstract, a great deal of student learning is of practical skills. This is obvious in such cases as a dental student practising tooth-filling, a medical student practising diagnostic routines, a scientist practising laboratory skills, an engineer carrying out a practical project, a linguist spending a period in the country where the relevant language is spoken, or an education student doing periods of school practice. However, the question of practicality is a relative matter. The examples given all involve activity of a fairly definite and public kind. Something can be seen happening, and in most cases, something which is publicly interesting as well as publicly manifest.

But all of those skills are intellectual functions too. They all depend on abstract analysis as well as public performance, symbolic as well as physical operations. Similarly, if one tries to think of learning that might seem more purely academic, let us say mathematics or literary appreciation or philosophical analysis, these are not just things that happen in one's head. They are public performances, except that they typically take the form of written or oral utterance. These utterances in turn produce changes in the views people form about relevant aspects of the world, and these views cause people to act on the physical world and on one another in drastically different ways.

It seems, therefore, that the apparently less 'practical' subjects are considered so only because their effects on the physical and social world are less immediate and less obvious, not because they are necessarily less influential. It will not do to compare the least influential aspects of philosophy or mathematics with the most influential aspects of science. One must compare the power of atomic theory with that of communism or Christianity. It can then be seen more clearly that abstract ideas, elusive as they may be for the scholar, let alone the man in the street, are one of the most potent means of change, regardless of the particular study in which they originate. One must conclude, therefore, that when student learning is disparaged for being academic or verbalistic, it is not because of the intrinsic irrelevance of academic study but because so many get stuck half way—able to toy with the language and concepts but not to grasp them firmly in a penetrating or balanced way, or to see how they can be given force and meaning for people at different levels of understanding. The college or university student, fresh from distilling his wisdom into examination answers, may have difficulty in redistilling it into educational change in a school classroom.

Student learning is bound to run far ahead of what the man in the street calls 'experience' (an ambiguous word, often obscuring the problem of how, if at all, a person has benefited from what he has undergone). The reasons are that so much of human thought is abstract and symbolic rather than concrete or pictorial, and that symbolic thought, acting particularly through speech and writing, enables the human mind to imagine possibilities very much faster than a person can construct or explore these possibilities in physical terms in the world. Students, therefore, have a double problem here—of disciplining their intellectual imaginings and explorations on the one hand by ordinary experience of the world (which tends to take a long time), and, on the other, by learning to appreciate the fact that most people have less capacity for abstract and theoretical thought but often considerable capacity for a balanced and realistic appraisal of the possibilities of their own social worlds.

The problem of relating student learning to the contexts of non-student life can be still more sharply appreciated when one recalls that most students have some difficulty, and some a great deal of difficulty, in mastering the context of student life itself, let alone relating it to anything else. Even the school sixth-former, with his special measure of liberty and responsibility, is relatively highly programmed or groomed by his mentors compared with most university or college students. The student finds himself free from customary restraints; responsible to a great extent for programming his own studies; excited, challenged or upset by the variety of intellectual and emotional temptations that beset him; uncertain or ignorant (if reluctant to admit it) of how to take effective lecture notes, write essays and reports, contribute to formal discussions, prepare for advanced examinations or establish a balance between work and play, social commitment and academic success. Psychologically, the student learner passes through the problems of self-definition of late adolescence into the young adult phase of polishing that definition and beginning to implement it, quite as soon as a young married worker in a particular professional and geographical context.

The detailed characteristics of this psychological transition obviously depend on a multiplicity of factors. By the time a student reaches college or university (some would say much sooner) his personality, with its intellectual and emotional structure, is already largely determined by genetic inheritance, family upbringing, social class, scholastic training and general experience. His chances of success or failure in higher education are already loaded in terms of favourable or unfavourable features of his whole past upbringing and education. But there is still room for manoeuvre. The shaping atmosphere of a particular college or university, year group or department, room mate or social clique, girl friend (or boy friend) or professor, athletic club or ideological group, current fashion or predominant social problem, professional orientation or vacation experience—or some complex combination of such factors—shapes the boy or girl into the young man or woman in a way that soon threatens to defy fundamental alteration. As time passes only radical changes in circumstances are likely to change modes of living—and even then probably not at a fundamental psychological level.

Some institutions of higher education have always concerned themselves more than others with the entire personal education of their students, but the traditional emphasis of universities has been on intellectual, and perhaps moral, discipline rather than general personal and social welfare. This is still so today, except that there has been some increase in the welfare responsibilities recognized and accepted and some diminution at least in that kind of detailed moral supervision insisted on in past times. There are, of course, considerable variations in these matters among universities within any one country, and still more if one looks across national boundaries. The development of student health and student counselling services in one form or another represents a recognition that student learning cannot be detached from the personal and social context within which the student lives. Any effort to diminish psychological impediments to learning has more than psychological importance. There are questions of moral obligation to help students make the best of themselves and of economic obligation not to waste the community's money on ineffective learning. Sometimes, of course, it will make sense on all of these counts to advise a student to enter a different course of study or a different walk of life.

The increasing recognition of the contextual factors just discussed, which can influence student learning so powerfully, may in time make student teachers more sympathetic to similar but more wide-ranging contextual considerations in schools. However, the student teacher does not typically have either the detailed local knowledge or the formal power to do very much about this aspect of school learning, other than to be sympathetically open-minded and sensitive to chance manifestations in his pupils of wider social and educational problems. What the student teacher is empowered to do is to teach children, whether in lessons of various kinds or via projects in which pupils may be active over a considerable period of time.

The project method in any of its guises is meant to forestall the possibility of a teacher following excessively academic, expository, teach-and-test models of teaching, taken over from his own college or university experience. This is not a guarantee, for the project method can be either lively and educative or wooden and ineffectual, but at least it may remind the teacher that learning is supposed to be, and be felt as being, active, self-directive, interesting and purposive. Anything resembling the traditional notion of a taught lesson offers more temptation for the teacher to do most of the talking, on the pattern of a lecture, and for the pupils, unless enthusiasts, to do as little as possible except evade individual attention from the teacher.

Talking too much and asking too few questions of too few pupils are characteristic features of beginning teachers in lessons of the talk-and-question type. It is unlikely that this is *caused* by the student's extensive exposure to lectures, but university lectures, textbooks and examinations do offer ready models of expository monologue rather than exploratory dialogue. The *cause* of excessive expository emphasis, one might speculate, is more likely to be lack of confidence, ingenuity and control in a situation of open dialogue. This, in turn, may depend on deeper personality traits rather than pedagogic experience, for some young teachers, with the same exposure to lectures, are still better communicators from the start.

Apart from the question of the human and social context of learning and the possible marginal influence of long exposure to a particular pedagogy (lectures and examinations, for example), the question of defining clearly what is expected seems to arise in relation to both student and pupil learning. A student may ask himself, exactly what books should I buy and study in detail? What kind of lecture notes should I take (some lecturers perhaps seeming to say relatively little and others ridiculously much)? How long is an essay supposed to be? What must I know for the examinations? What credit do I get for my laboratory record? And student teachers, particularly before their first school practice, want detailed answers to a great range of problems. Much anxiety and ineffective learning arises from lack of clear specifications. But giving clear specifications, like preparing the computer programme, is the hard bit of the exercise. Student teachers in their turn learn how pupils need the most specific information about what they are expected to do, and even then will produce comic caricatures of the teacher's intentions and utterances.

No mention has yet been made of the psychology of study in the sense that it is expounded in students' texts on the subject, although all that has been said can be related to a couple of major psychological principles—that, if anything is to be learned, the conditions of achieving the learning must be generally rewarding to the learner, and the conditions of learning must be such as to facilitate making whatever discriminations have to be made. Learners do not persist if the process is entirely unrewarding and they cannot learn if they do not perceive clearly what requires to be learned. These principles may seem blatantly obvious—and, in a sense, they are—but not so obvious in the educational practices of some teachers and institutions.

The psychology of study is to some extent a matter of common sense, except that the sense is not always as commonly observed as might seem desirable. Partly it is a question of knowing what one wants to learn and setting about it in a systematic fashion, but, as has already been suggested, learners do not always even know precisely what it is they do want, or are expected, to learn. The sheer volume of material confronting a university student—extensive lecture programmes, examination and course work requirements, substantial textbooks, madly long reading lists, unfathomable libraries—demands a ruthless discrimination which, when dons so often lack it, can hardly be easily attained by students. Then there is the problem of establishing regular and economic work habits in a student world which seems to offer at any time a hundred exciting invitations to do almost anything but study. A possible answer to this problem is that it is better to have a modest but really hard-working study programme which leaves sufficient time for fun and games than to have no programme at all, or one which is so unrealistically ambitious that the student snatches at any excuse for escaping from the schedule, and possibly works only at half-stretch even when he obeys it.

Another important aspect of the economy of study is the question of what one *does* in the name of private study. Some (admittedly, not all) copying out of notes and leafing through of books is just a dead routine. It may often be more profitable to revise work by thinking up, or looking up, various questions about it and then trying to outline from memory how an answer might go. Alternatively, discussion of topics with fellow students may gradually implant key ideas, lines of criticism or techniques of procedure more effectively and interestingly than solitary gloating over notes and texts. Problems and anxieties are lightened by being shared and the social stimulus of some cooperative learning acts as additional motivation for the task. This is said without disparagement of purely private study which is obviously essential as well.

Certain very specific practical problems arise in student learning which require considerable initiative to solve, despite the increasing tendency for universities and colleges to be more helpful than they once were. Essential books may disappear just when the course work absolutely requires that they be consulted. A lecturer goes from one confusion to another with no one daring to ask for recapitulation or clarification. Several tutors demand work at the same time. Individual departments act as if there were no one else in the universe, let alone university. While many dons and students are very good at ironing out such problems, there are always some who are impeded by their personalities from doing so. Solutions may be simple in principle, but the psychological problem of communication is real.

One of the most helpful contributions to the practical problem of study comes from the psychology of remembering. It was shown by earlier experimenters that things were better remembered

1 if the learning was spaced out to some extent over several separate periods of time,
2 if one tried to recall the learned material actively instead of simply reading it through repeatedly (which makes one too dependent on the presence of the book or notes),
3 if one avoided learning different but similar kinds of thing, one immediately after the other (for the degree of similarity seems to encourage confusion of the two),
4 in some cases only, if one learned a unit to be remembered (say a

poem) as a whole rather than in bits (for one tended to lose the necessary connections between the bits), and

5 If one overlearned the material in the first instance—that is, went on learning it beyond the minimum practice necessary to achieve a first correct recall.

In these traditional psychological tips for students there was already recognition of a feature of memory which has come to be stressed increasingly, namely, its intrinsically dynamic nature. The meaning of this dynamism is hinted at in the phenomena of active recall and of interference ((2) and (3) above), but the idea was more fully and fascinatingly developed in the work of Bartlett (1932), who showed how memory was not a matter of retrieving carbon copies of past learning from some imaginary mental storehouse. Instead it was a process of actively reconstructing past experience—a reconstruction in which all kinds of transformations took place. Freud, of course, had earlier described some of the psychological transformations that he saw as significant in his view of human mentality—the lapses of tongue or pen which sometimes had a deeper psychological point. Bartlett extended this notion by experimental study of what might have seemed quite neutral perceptual stimuli.

In fact, the subjects of the experiments manufactured their own significance in order to facilitate recall—simplifying and standardizing visual percepts by missing out non-standard details of the stimulus; magnifying details that struck them as significant at the expense of parts of the stimulus that struck them less significantly; or, in the cases of strange stories they were asked to recall, simplifying the outline, omitting details that did not seem to fit, and generally rationalizing the story into a form and context that made it more familiar and less puzzling. If one thinks of the difficulty of getting reliable and consistent witness to the ordinary happenings of everyday life it is easy to understand why memory should be viewed as a transforming, reconstructive operation rather than a simple retrieval operation. But educational practice has not reckoned with this phenomenon. It has recognized it (schoolboy howlers alone should have ensured that) but has regarded it like a technical defect in a machine—something which could conceivably be put right and the machine perfected—instead of as an intrinsic feature of the 'machine'. Some may reconstruct more quickly and, if they are more critical people, more accurately, but even accurate remembering has its own selective bias and personal slant, if only in the things it misses out.

It would seem then that a student teacher faced with his own and his pupils' problems of recall should formulate a remembering technique based on accurate, clear, vivid, and systematic registering of the material to be learned,

recognition of the fact that remembering is a transforming operation, not just by accident when it goes wrong but always, even when it is relatively accurate, and

active recall, public and social use of the material, and an alert attitude towards the tricks that memory plays.

While some of these points may have a marginal relevance to 'remembering' practical skills—for example, where some verbal routine is used as an adjunct to the skill, like the MSM or mirror-signal-manoeuvre mnemonic of a driving handbook—remembering how to do something is really a different sense of the word. You do not need to think at all. If you once learned to swim and can still swim, one might say, although rather oddly, you remember how to swim.

Students, like pupils, acquire knowledge, skills and attitudes. These interrelated things are widely diversified in accordance with different branches and levels of study. Examination systems play a key role in defining their detailed character. Examinations require a display of knowledge, skills and attitudes, some of which will continue to be specifically relevant to a person's professional and personal life, others of which will rapidly fade away through disuse and lack of reward after the examinations are finished. It is difficult to assess the value of what is called knowledge-for-its-own-sake (presumably meaning knowledge for which there is no *immediate* use rather than literally useless knowledge). It is presumably knowledge whose utility rests mainly in the personal satisfactions it offers—such as admiring one's own or other people's intellectual skill, or enjoying the sheer pattern of what is studied; both of which pleasures may be intensified by their capacity for contributing to agreeable social communication among interested experts. Also, such knowledge has the long-term utility of upholding the standards of honest enquiry and just appraisal on which more immediately applicable studies must depend if they are not to be governed by fashion and expediency alone.

It would seem that a sound psychology of study should take account of these points. If the student or pupil concentrates for at least part of the time on knowledge and skills which give intrinsic pleasure, and which are seen to be of fundamental and general importance, he should be better able to sustain that knowledge and these skills because of their agreeableness and their long-term usefulness. Unfortunately, some fundamental things are too difficult to give pleasure to many, and hand-to-mouth expediency is a powerfully tempting alternative to long-term solutions. Nevertheless, students undoubtedly and probably school pupils too should be guided by a psychology, and perhaps one has to say philosophy, of study that goes beyond the technical tricks of memorization or examination-passing.

The psychology of teaching

One can stand back from the actual job of teaching and talk about teachers' roles and personalities, experience and attitudes; but it is necessary also to look more closely at teaching as a practical activity and consider how psychology might contribute to the direct under-standing of that activity. It should be obvious by now that one of the main psychological contributions is to the general understanding of human behaviour, for this is often of direct practical value in under-standing oneself and one's pupils. Such understanding aids tolerance and insight and encourages a healthy scepticism towards casual opin-ions. It depends on the study of a wide range of problems like those discussed in great detail in other chapters of this book. This para-graph introduces a broad and general look at the problems of disci-pline, learning structure and motivation that confront particularly the student teacher trying to teach a class of children.

For analytic convenience discipline, learning and motivation may sometimes be discussed separately, but they are closely interrelated. The beginning teacher may want to receive an instant-mix formula that will solve his problems quickly, but this is impossible, for the problems are too varied and arise in dynamic, not static, human situa-tions. It is necessary, therefore, to try and grasp the main regulative principles and steadily correct one's performance in accordance with them. Even at a single moment a complexity of factors must be taken into consideration—the nature of the current programme a class is following, the pupils' abilities, the patterns of behaviour that are customary in that particular class, the idiosyncrasies of particular teachers, the tone and tradition of the school, the social and educa-tional characteristics of the home backgrounds, the educational materials available, and the student teacher's own knowledge, skill in human relations, personal standards and degree of specific pre-paredness. In order to succeed one has to *accept* conditions that are not alterable in the circumstances, alter conditions (normally minor ones in the first instance) that can be altered and yield advantage, work out the practical aims and methods that seem likely to match the learning stage of the pupils, and exploit one's own stronger talents in giving the whole operation life and purpose. It is a complex task that is not mastered overnight and, indeed, not finished ever. It depends on looking for what *can* be beneficially done rather than dwelling upon what apparently cannot.

A handbook for student teachers contained the advice, 'Students should seek to secure good discipline by good teaching—which interests the children—and by efficient classroom administration—which prevents opportunities for disorder'. This is formally sensible but one can sympathize with the student who felt that it was also an insubstantial truism. The probem is how to do it. There may be a tendency to look for solutions through discipline or motivation, as if these were detachable instruments of learning, when, in fact, an appropriate structuring of the learning task may achieve the learning and dispel problems of discipline or motivation. If pupils are given learning tasks which they have the means of tackling, which form part of a consistent and progressive programme and which can gain them general commendation, this alone will go far to avoid problems of discipline or motivation.

Much indiscipline and lack of interest spring directly from setting tasks beyond or beneath pupils' capacities, or not ensuring that they know the strategies for tackling the tasks successfully, or not commending success when achieved. Discipline and motivation are, in a sense, techniques of engineering success through the detailed structuring of learning situations, rather than devices for injecting a shot of order or interest into chaos and boredom. It follows that a student teacher must expect some indiscipline in some classes until he gradually masters the art of structuring learning. Where the school has already created strong structures, the student teacher will have fewer problems. Where it has not, he will have more.

Morrison and McIntyre (1969) mention three points that have detailed practical importance in relation to discipline. The first is that the teacher must communicate to the class that he knows what is going on around him. This means that the teacher must react positively to what he sees and hears. Turning a blind eye is mostly not a relevant precept, for it allows minor misbehaviour to escalate into major, and extends the area of behaviour on which the teacher apparently has no definite views. Non-reaction is sometimes a product of not knowing what view it is expedient to take, but, in this case, it is probably better to express any plausible and definite comment or instruction, and then, if events prove one mistaken, correct the situation equally definitely in a spirit that shows the teacher to be fair but still in authority. Some student teachers hesitate before this need to assume authority, in however friendly a spirit it may be exercised. They defer to the pupils as if they were equals; but pupils are equal only in a general sense as human beings, and not in the sense of being equally fit to speak on those matters on which teachers are trained and paid to be the authorities.

The second point is that there tends to be less deviant behaviour

where the teacher can effect smooth transitions from one clas
activity to the next. This too is a difficult art. Everyone likes to finish
off something he has almost finished before going on to the nex
activity. The teacher, therefore, has to anticipate all terminations o
activity and allow a kind of drinking-up time before moving on
Moreover, he has to have instructions for those who may have t
finish the job on another occasion as well as for those who are on th
point of finishing now. Similarly, in beginning new activities, th
getting ready of necessary books, instruments or materials must b
planned almost like a military exercise (unless there is lots of time)

There must be enough of everything and rapid strategies for def
ciencies ('share a book'; 'use your jotter instead'; 'get a pencil fror
the spares box'). Interruptions are characteristic of classwork. Th
teacher must minimize them by anticipating problems and by refusin
to tolerate those which do not warrant distraction from the mai
flow of class activity. He must accustom the class to self-regulatin
strategies for recurrent situations so that the right things happe
automatically without specific programming for every occasion.

The third point is that creating over-permissive situations may lea
to disorder and ineffective learning. This problem has been mentione
earlier. It sometimes springs from misconceptions about child-centre
education, which is not meant to encourage children to do as the
please, but to educate them, on the basis of their existing interests an
capacities, in relevant directions under a teacher's sensitive but pos
tive guidance. The problem may also be encouraged by a youn
teacher carrying over into his dealings with pupils a kind of non
critical universal tolerance which may (or may not) be all righ
among undergraduates but which is almost an abuse of school pupil
who are entitled to more positive help in finding their way throug
problems they certainly cannot solve for themselves. A third source
misconceived permissiveness is the vague notion that children cann
be blamed for their misdemeanours, for they are all a product of thi
that or the other. This is an intellectual confusion. The fact tha
everything has causes does not alter the other fact that we can and d
improve ourselves and others by taking appropriate action. And
fourth source is, of course, psychological uncertainty about one
own authority in respect of either the children or what they are sup
posed to learn. This is something which may deserve sympathy b
cannot justify an educational policy of *laissez-faire*.

There is an interesting contrast between Hoyle's suggestion, quote
earlier, that 'the element of control is fundamental to all sets
expectations concerning the role of the teacher' and the remark
Skinner (1968) that 'educators are seldom willing to concede that the
are engaged in the control of human behaviour'. Skinner's poin

made by philosophers as well as psychologists, is that, since the teacher is bound to control his pupils' behaviour—even if negatively by inaction and consequent strengthening of random influences—he might as well learn to control it by effective methods with a view to shaping it in worthwhile directions. Skinner's policy, illustrated in the technique of programmed learning which will be discussed later, is to analyse any learning into the appropriate series of small successive steps which build up into the final complex performance, and then get the learner to go through the resulting programme, which is devised so as to elicit easy correct responses at each step. Success at each small step rewards or reinforces the learner's activity until he finds that he has mastered the programme without any special difficulty.

This contrasts with much traditional learning which, although based on sequential study, did not always require the learner to make an active response at each step, or ensure that the steps themselves were sufficiently small and closely related to guarantee that the learner responds correctly rather than wrongly. Much poor discipline, learning and motivation spring from the fact that the teacher does not make the steps in learning sufficiently small and clear, and does not give more than a small proportion of pupils the sustaining satisfaction of success and cumulative power. This is made worse by the common reluctance to allow for slow learners who may simply not be ready to start the programme nominally suitable for their age. In such cases the teacher may struggle pointlessly to put the roof on a house whose foundations have not been laid.

Skinner is critical of teaching based on what he calls 'aversive control'—that is, on fear of unpleasant consequences, whether any of the traditional scholastic punishments or the 'punishment' of being tested or of being expected to reach ever higher standards. He attributes to such forms of control the blame for a variety of things, from verbal and physical attacks on teachers (the instruments of aversive control) to anti-intellectualism and vandalism. He thinks that, in conditions of aversive control, 'one of the easiest forms of escape is simply to forget all one has learned, and no one has discovered a form of control to prevent this ultimate break for freedom'. These speculative views are open to challenge—one could argue, for example, that the ultimate break for freedom is limited by society's own (possibly necessary) aversive controls—but they also offer a challenge to some aspects of teaching practice.

Although discipline, learning and motivation depend so much on organizing a suitable exercise at the right level of difficulty, this is a detailed and demanding task, depending on a thorough knowledge of the learning resources that might be used and of the pupils who will use them. Both require time, experience and ingenuity—again, no easy formula. The task is made more difficult by the fact that teachers are almost always confronted by a wide range of individual talent, and, therefore, have to diversify their efforts even for a teaching task which may seem on the surface a simple and unitary one. This is obviously so where a class of children has a rather wide range of general ability, but the problem does not disappear with more highly selected groups, for these confront more demanding learning tasks, which consequently once more scatter the performance of the group. If one took a group of first class honours graduates in a particular subject, their teachers would probably say that Mr A was better in this branch and Miss B in the other.

Really serious problems of discipline, learning and motivation are associated with schools in areas which are themselves socially and educationally backward or handicapped, with poor material and human facilities and traditions which may be not only educationally weak but positively anti-educational. The general psychological principles of carefully graded and well-rewarded programmes of work are equally applicable here. Difficulties arise because teachers may assume that the details of the programmes can be the same. This can result in a programme of mutual resentment rather than effective learning, with both pupils and teachers frustrated by their failure. There is no easy solution in the worst cases, but the lines of solution are clear. Teachers must find the tasks, however simple to begin with and regardless of conventional assumptions, at which socially handicapped children *will* succeed, and start building from there. Secondly, they have to make the whole school even more unremittingly rewarding than is absolutely necessary in an area where parents and community traditions themselves reward scholastic effort. And thirdly, they have to understand the detailed character of their pupils' social background, making allowance for the direct handicaps, nourishing the virtues intrinsic to the community, and yet slowly widening the horizons of its young members.

Student teachers always want to know about the place of punishment in learning. Psychological experiments on punishment have sometimes shown that punishment, possibly by emphasizing attention to a certain associated stimulus, can improve some simple learning in the laboratory. Psychoanalytical studies may associate punishing tendencies with infantile experiences or fantasies relating to punishing or being punished by parents, particularly in connection with the infant's sense of sexual matters. Adult sex too can have aggressive as well as tender aspects, from early adolescent physical teasing to the ordinary patterns of love-making. When this aggressive aspect becomes punitive in character (sadism) it may be morally judged as a perversion, or, amorally, as a statistical abnormality.

Teachers as a whole tend to reserve some rights of punishment, whether official or unofficial corporal punishment, verbal punishment (which can be gross), special reports to parents, exposure to class contumely (*school* class, one had better add in these sociological times), or other punitive devices. Some teachers and parents are very anti-punitive—one could almost say punitively anti-punitive, in the way that there are militant pacifists. Punitive attitudes in adults, whether or not in infants, are often a response to being punished. The dog bites you; you kick the cat. Fashions and traditions in scholastic punishment vary from country to country, each naïvely finding the practices of the others abhorrent. The Scots with their brutal strap; the English with their sadistic cane; the Russians with their crushing collective reproach; the Americans with their compulsive freedom to conform—it is easy to caricature.

It seems odd that anyone should think that the place of punishment in education is a simple one. It is an area in which the teacher has to search out both his own psychology and his philosophy of life, and in which it is necessary to explain fully what one is talking about rather than imagine that the concept of punishment is clear and unambiguous. Much of what teachers do and say is deliberately intended to associate unpleasant consequences with undesirable behaviour. Some of their conduct is unintentionally hurtful, either through ordinary inadvertence or through the escape of a suppressed feeling of animosity. The teacher must work out his own position. The above considerations are some of the relevant ones. People learn mainly through being rewarded, at least for some of the time, but punishment too in a general sense is part of the pattern. Punishment is hardly what one would call a good thing (although it seems to be if it is your team that dishes it out), but neither is it an entirely avoidable thing.

It has been shown that the scholastic performance of pupils is affected by whether their teachers express high or low expectations of them. It also appears that teachers' expectations and, therefore, to some extent, achievements, can be influenced by suggestions from others about a class, for example, that it is bright or dull. And certain assumptions about social class have been shown to influence teachers' expectations of pupils. Obviously these factors must operate within limits. No amount of expecting will turn a really slow learner into a really fast one. But, within the relevant broad limits for any class, one of the teacher's main instruments of discipline, learning and motivation is his reasonably high expectations—the standards that he sets.

An important detail of this as an educational policy is that pupils must always be given some room for personal manoeuvre—a way of redeeming failures or returning to grace if they have been reprimanded. Adults are so touchy about their self-esteem, and yet they may insult children openly and build up a stereotype of pupil laziness or stupidity which encourages the very things it purports to condemn. As in so many aspects of teaching, the key skill is a kind of regulative or balancing operation—in this case, sustaining reasonably high expectations and standards but also offering constant fresh opportunities for those who fall by the wayside. Skinner, who used pigeons for some of his experimental studies in the shaping of behaviour, writes, 'In deciding what behaviour to reinforce at any given time, the basic rule is "Don't lose your pigeon!" ' That applies to human learners as well.

Teaching to teach

What has been said already implies quite a lot about how to become a good teacher. If the main points were to be listed as a set of directives they might run something like this:

1   The concept of the teacher's role is highly variable and ambiguous. You must consider the many conflicting expectations and decide which limited number of non-conflicting ones you intend to try and meet.

2   The student teacher's role is in some ways particularly difficult because of the limitations of being a beginner, and because of the special conflict between personal and training ideals and the first experience of actual school circumstances. You must be patient and positive, doing what you can rather than bemoaning what you cannot.

3   Defining your aims clearly and practically, studying methods of achieving them, and practising the implementation of the chosen methods, are all necessary. If things go wrong, you must do your fault-finding at all three levels.

4   Personality in the colloquial sense of vivacity may be a positive aid to good teaching, but personality in the psychological sense is a complex concept. Good teaching is not tied to one kind of personality. Much good teaching is based on the steady build-up of relevant skills. If you really want to teach you should consider what the skills are and start taking the necessary steps to acquire them. Since they are complex this will take a long time. So-called 'born' teachers have simply, by chance or good fortune, made an earlier start on acquiring skills that happen to be relevant to teaching.

5   Some teaching skills depend on the student's own study skills, and both teaching and study skills depend on understanding the

circumstances that favour effective learning. Some of these factors are technical, but it is also important to develop general psychological understanding. You should consider how the detailed points made in the chapter apply to yourself.

6 Two important psychological principles of learning are that what has to be learned should be as clear and systematic as possible and that the process of learning should, in general if not always, be enjoyable and rewarding. Much, perhaps most, student and pupil failure derives from not establishing patterns of learning which embody these principles.

7 Discipline, learning and motivation are three vital associated factors in successful teaching. You must study the learners and the available learning resources, devise learning programmes that will facilitate successful progress and ensure general commendation, and keep the way open for slow learners. This is a complex, detailed, and never-ending task. You are right; there is no royal road.

8 There is nothing mysterious about indiscipline or poor motivation. They spring from the specific detailed factors discussed earlier. You have to diagnose the operative causes and apply the appropriate remedies. In the worst possible situations, where all of the dice seem loaded against you, you have to soldier on, setting your sights realistically, concentrating on improving human relationships and trying to keep a sense of humour. If you have no sense of humour or talent for public human relations, you had better get out of the situation and try something else.

9 In cases of scholastic desperation the question of punishment is bound to arise. This is another complex problem, but some of the relevant considerations have been mentioned. You must strike your own mean between punitive excess and a flabby policy of *laissez-faire*.

A question that has received increasing attention is how to teach student teachers to teach. Taylor (1969) makes a key point about the problem when he writes:

> The perceptual load for the beginning teacher is a heavy one, and it is to be expected that students will favour methods that 'work', and are relatively uncomplicated, over those that demand a greater range of teaching skills and sensitivity to class and individual feedback that they may not yet possess.

Morrison and McIntyre (1969) review some of the alleged shortcomings of professional courses for teachers, mentioning the well-known facts that students tend to place a high value on teaching practice, and to seek more emphasis on practical demonstrations of specific methods, on problems of 'class management, discipline and establishing satisfactory relationships with pupils', and on learning how to use 'group methods' and how to teach slow learners.

Morrison and McIntyre themselves appear to emphasize the value of psychological training in observation skills, so that teachers may become more sensitive to their pupils' actual experiences of learning. They mention the possibilities of students working in pairs so that they may learn to observe one another's teaching; of using the technique of micro-teaching, in which short lessons embodying specific aspects of teaching are taught to a handful of pupils and the lesson video-taped for subsequent analysis, discussion and revision; and of having students play assigned roles in simulated classroom situations as a means of exploring the dynamics of such situations.

Morrison and McIntyre (1969) and McLeish (1969) discuss various enquiries into the influence of college training on students' attitudes and skills. Some of the enquiries are British, some American; some refer to colleges of education, some to other colleges. A rather variegated picture emerges, with the demonstrable effects of college education appearing somewhat limited. On the other hand, some influence can be shown, and there is the perhaps more important practical consideration that, if only demonstrably effective activities were valued and encouraged, a great number of enterprises might be closed down, research establishments and schools as well as colleges. Some bread must be cast upon the waters. Research enquiries into complex educational processes can be valuable as a means of getting more accurate information about what the processes seem to be achieving, but, since new and varied goals are constantly proposed and since the question of goals is intrinsically contentious, it is quite illusory to imagine that sufficiently large programmes of empirical research could somehow penetrate to the heart of things and tell us once and for all what we ought to do. Researchers must admit this when pressed, but they sometimes write in tones which suggest the opposite.

Flanders (1964) discusses studies in which his system of *interaction analysis* was applied in certain class teaching situations. He used seven categories to describe the talk of the teacher, two to describe pupil (or, in American usage, student) response, and one to describe silence or confusion. The categories were (1) accepting student feelings, (2) giving praise, (3) accepting, clarifying or making use of a student's ideas, (4) asking a question, (5) lecturing, giving facts or opinions, (6) giving directions, (7) giving criticism, (8) student response, (9) student invitation, (10) silence or confusion.

He also used six general categories for various periods of activity other than talk alone. These were (1) routine administration, (2) evaluation or correction, (3) periods of introducing new material, (4) teacher-student planning, (5) class discussions, and (6) students working at their desks or in groups.

Then he used five scales of student attitudes—(1) liking the teacher, (2) finding school work interesting, (3) feeling that rewards and punishments were administered fairly, (4) feeling free to make some important decisions and to direct oneself at work, and (5) disabling anxiety manifest in certain paranoid reactions to the teacher's authority.

Flanders claims, on the basis of his empirical studies, that pupils achieve more and have more constructive attitudes where a larger proportion of the teacher's statements are indirect rather than direct, that is, where they encourage expanding activities rather than restricted activities among the pupils. Successful teachers, on top of their mastery of the subject matter being taught, tend to be better at

1 providing a range of roles, from the fairly active and dominant to the more reflective and supporting, achieving compliance but also encouraging student initiative;
2 assuming one role or another at will;
3 understanding the principles of teacher influence and translating these into appropriate courses of action; and
4 observing current conditions sensitively, objectively and diagnostically.

He recognizes the sensitivity of teachers about detailed studies of their teaching behaviour and advocates a policy of obtaining teacher participation in the whole planning of such enquiries. This must be genuine, not just nominal participation. His detailed advice deserves study, especially by those who seem to think that schools are just convenient laboratories for researchers.

The work of Flanders has been described in a little detail because it is suggestive for anyone who might want to analyse his own teaching more systematically, because it reminds one of some of the main factors that mediate a teacher's influence on pupils, and because his suggestions about successful teachers fit in with what has been said earlier about discipline, learning, and motivation. He is also sensible on the general question of encouraging educational innovation, stressing the need to consider the individual's emotional as well as intellectual position.

Reactions that are less than positive must be recognized, analysed, and tested in situations free of threat if a realistic approach to innovation is to be taken.

He realizes that co-operative ventures among teachers themselves may provide a useful social support for programmes of experiment or change.

Perspective on the adult as learner and teacher

This chapter has attempted to outline the psychological problems facing the young adult who is at the same time student and beginning teacher. His own personality is already shaped to a large extent by about a couple of decades of life and education, although there are useful skills and attitudes that he can still acquire before going out into the professional world. An understanding of the general psychology of learning is doubly relevant to him as student and teacher. Some of the most important general principles of learning have been stated and some of their more detailed practical implications have been spelled out, both in relation to student learning and to learning by pupils in schools.

Although some student teachers come to the task of teaching with the advantage of personal skills developed over a long period, any seriously interested person can begin to acquire or improve relevant skills. Because of the complexity and unlimitedness of the teaching task, there can be no question of quick or all-purpose solutions. It is a practical art and must be developed by practice. On the other hand, only the right kind of practice, critically regarded, will produce serious improvement. Some student teachers, carried away by teaching practice, fail to realize that they may be perfecting themselves in pointless or even undesirable activities.

Even where the general activity is valuable in principle, deficiencies in organizing it may arise from vaguely conceived aims as much as from faulty methods. Some bad teaching is associated with defective skills in personal relationships, but much arises from sheer ignorance and lack of intellectual penetration. The teacher just does not know enough about his subject, his children, his available resources or the characteristics of his own personality. If 'theory' means knowing why you ought to be doing something and why certain ways of doing it are better in principle than others, one could make the paradoxical suggestion that there is nothing so practical as theory.

Nevertheless, it is obvious that the problem of translating principles, however specific, into detailed practice must be a perennial one for the student teacher in particular, although for all teachers in some degree. There is a point at which no more general advice can be given. It is necessary to get down to fieldwork in the classroom and to detailed study of methodology. Techniques like micro-teaching or interaction analysis may help, but there will always remain the challenge for each individual of simply accepting the responsibility and authority indissociable from the teaching role. He must try what he can and correct himself as he goes—a formidable self-regulative endeavour. Psychology cannot do the detailed job for him, but a knowledge of developmental patterns, the psychology of learning, techniques of assessment, the psychology of individual differences and some other areas of study, should reduce the chances of falling into pedagogical pitfalls which have trapped many in the past.

It is not easy to run the practicalities of education in close harness with psychological analysis. The former is inescapably complex, the latter must simplify by delimiting the field and conditions of empirical enquiry. However, the attempt in this chapter to drive the two-in-hand at least illustrates the problem. It illustrates some of the points made in the first chapter and is a bridge to the next series of three chapters dealing with developmental psychology. Adult learning is built on a long earlier experience. It is now time to look at that earlier experience, both for its general illumination of psychological development and for its direct relevance to the more specific problems of the successive stages of education from infancy to adolescence.

3 The psychology of early childhood

Young children evoke a natural warm response in most adults—even if not always to the extent of the woman who said of babies, 'You can't see one without feeling you'd like to have another, can you?' Some of the things that particularly interest the lay observer are also centres of interest for the professional child psychologist—the manifest processes of rapid growth and learning, the clear response to environmental shaping, and the width of individual variation in such responding. The parent's ordinary concern with the problems of rearing his own children is matched by the psychologist's interest in whether different child-rearing practices have demonstrable long-term effects, whether the child is indeed father to the man. There is the hope too—perhaps fleeting and forlorn—that in infancy one might be able to see something of the basic patterns of human behaviour before they become obscured by the complexities of subsequent education and experience.

What makes this hope fleeting is the fact that complexities seem to crowd in from the very beginning. This is reflected in the variety of possible beginnings that can be made. The psychoanalytically inclined might plunge into the subtleties of 'the nursing couple'—the intimate and psychologically potent experience shared by the newborn infant and his mother. A biological start leads one into talk of zygotes, chromosomes and genes; foetal development and perinatal risks. The psychologist as behavioural scientist may want to emphasize experimental studies of how infant behaviour can be conditioned, or as developmentalist may want to start mapping the sensorimotor and preconceptual stages made known by Piaget and his followers. The psychometrist will be looking for the earliest opportunity of applying some standardized test, or at least some standard developmental test or schedule. The comparative psychologist will be comparing human infant development with the corresponding patterns in other species —mice, cats, birds, dogs, sheep or chimpanzees. The list of beginnings could be prolonged but, if we select a general biological starting point, other aspects will soon make themselves manifest.

Earliest growth and behaviour

Even within a biological framework one could argue for two starting points—a fertilized egg cell (zygote), or the wider socio-biological context of a man and woman who not only create this zygote but normally provide the shaping context in which the resulting new human being will grow. The wider human aspect is there from the start and continues to be the dominant one for those living through the situation rather than analysing it in physiological or behavioural terms. Although this may seem tritely obvious, it is salutary to recall how remote the scientific analyst's perspective may be from the perspective of typical parents. However, physiological and social perspectives do meet ultimately, and it is convenient to begin with the former.

All the inherited factors that will influence the new individual are already embodied in the nucleic acid chemistry of the zygote, with its twenty-six pairs of chromosomes derived from the original fifty-two of the parent cells. Each pair of chromosomes has its tens of thousands of genes—the ultimate chemical units transmitting hereditary influence. As the original zygote divides into two cells, and these into four and so on until the whole human body is created, the chromosomes are reproduced in each new cell. Male sex is determined by an X chromosome from the female parent linking with a Y chromosome from the male. Female sex is determined by an X chromosome from the female parent (who has only Xs) linking with an X from the male (who has both X and Y). This genetic chance sets the scene for all the ensuing human differences associated with sex. Social custom interacts with physiological fact, strengthening or moderating the influences of the latter. Some incidental physical phenomena are genetically sex-linked. For example, colour blindness occurs in about every twelfth male but only every hundredth female; and haemophilia (failure of blood clotting) manifests itself, as a rarity, in men but not at all in the women who nevertheless transmit its genetic basis. Other human characteristics, such as hair colour, are determined in complex ways by the patterning of other groups of genes.

The zygote takes four days to travel down the four inches of the

Fallopian tube and five or six more to become imbedded in the wall of the uterus. At two weeks the new embryo is about one-fifth of an inch in diameter. By eight weeks it is about an inch long and from this stage until birth is called a foetus. Gesell describes it almost poetically: 'Loosely moored to the placenta by the delicate umbilical strand, the fetus floats freely in the surrounding fluid.' By twelve weeks there is a three-inch body weighing about three-quarters of an ounce, the nose and eyes are developing, the external genitalia are distinctive, certain bones are well outlined, and there is a beginning of neuromuscular development. Scott (1968) reports the foetus as being active for 15 per cent of the time at four months and for 35 per cent of the time at eight months. A foetal age of twenty-eight weeks is reckoned to be typical of the point at which the foetus may live even if prematurely born. Throughout prenatal growth the foetus is nourished by the exchange of nutrient substances and waste products through the semi-permeable membrane of the maternal placenta, but the mother's blood does not flow directly into the foetal system and there are no neural (nerve tissue) connections between the mother and foetus. This is a brief and cursory outline of the physical story. Fuller accounts can be studied in many books, including Breckenridge and Murphy (1968) and Mussen, Conger and Kagan (1963).

What matters in the present context is the general character of foetal development, (1) because it reminds one of the basic character of the physiological endowment and growth on which psychological growth depends, (2) because the prenatal world provides the first environmental shaping of the new organism, and (3) because postnatal growth has such a direct line of continuity with foetal development, despite the dramatic change from floating in a sac of fluid in the maternal placenta to the postnatal form of dependence represented by a newborn baby, breathing and moving in the outside world but still needing to be fed, cleaned and cuddled by the mother. The new baby may be anatomically complete (even that only in a sense) but physiologically many functions are obviously lacking, and will appear only with further physiological growth as well as appropriate environmental stimulation.

Various prenatal and perinatal environmental influences may have important effects on the new organism. Some effects are associated with maternal age. The foetal death rate derived for mothers under twenty and over thirty-five or forty, although not very high in itself, is higher than for mothers in their twenties. The form of mental defect called mongolism too, although not common, is commoner in the babies of older mothers. Other physical factors which can harmfully affect foetal development and the birth of the new infant include maternal malnutrition, certain drugs (thalidomide being notorious), excessive exposure to X-rays, the occurrence of German measles in the mother during the first weeks of pregnancy, and maternal syphilis. Excessive emotional stress or tension in the mother may, through its chemical effects in the blood stream, influence foetal development or make the process of birth more difficult. Unfavourable attitudes towards the prospect of having a baby might, therefore, make the baby's development and birth more hazardous and distressing, a kind of circular physiological-psychological pattern.

Correspondingly favourable attitudes and favourable physical developments may be mutually confirmatory by the same means. The outcome is that a newborn child may enter a welcoming world after nine months of relatively 'sympathetic' sustenance in the womb, or an unwelcoming world after nine months of relative 'antipathy'— an antipathy which the mother may or may not recognize consciously. Of course, one must be cautious about interpretations, for it is difficult to collect valid data about maternal attitudes and emotions, and they might, in any case, be based on deeper temperamental or environmental factors rather than incidental, temporary attitudes. Moreover, where unconscious influences are attributed to a person's behaviour and physiological functioning, the onus is upon the attributor to show some objective evidence for his hypothesis.

Early infancy already illustrates some of the key themes of human development. One is *the wide range of individual variation* in any human characteristic. Even within one family, and obviously to a much greater extent when many families are considered, infants differ in weight, appearance, placidity or activity, patterns of feeding and sleeping, and, as they develop, in rates of acquiring the early motor skills, including walking and talking. In the first year or two these variations may strike parents as curious products of chance, which they are in a sense. However, as the child moves towards four, five or six years of age and becomes exposed to slowly increasing social and educational expectations, the range of individual differences becomes all the more conspicuous, with some children of four acquiring scholastic skills such as reading while, at the opposite extreme, others demonstrate their relative retardation by the persistence of levels of ordinary behaviour associated with earlier rather than later infancy. Since infancy, regarded generally, is a period of very rapid human development, it shows only too vividly this characteristic phenomenon of behavioural variation among individuals. The speed of such differentiation in infancy has caused educators to give much thought to the problem of how to help certain slow developers, handicapped in infancy by lack of education stimulation, and consequently, in the later years of childhood and schooling, by lack of the intellectual foundation which their more fortunate peers have gained from favourable home circumstances.

A second developmental theme illustrated in early infancy is *the self-activating character of human behaviour*. The foetus already generates its own movement in the womb. While some of the baby's movements, like sucking, are physiological reflexes, he soon shows a kind of 'will of his own', stimulated by the still developing mechanisms of his own neuromuscular system and not just by outside stimuli. Soon the toddler is making his own explorations of the physical world—even in defiance of possible adult attempts at constraint. These are early versions of the creative aspect of human behaviour—'creative' meaning here that the organism, via the brain particularly, can radically transform the input of sensory stimulation and not merely react to it in simple predetermined ways. One might sum it up by saying that, however we succeed in mapping out the regular patterns that can be expected in most human behaviour, one thing that must be expected is a fairly frequent occurrence of the unexpected.

A third theme is *the continuity of human development*. There is, of course, genetic continuity. The infant will differ from his parents, but within broad limits set by his physical inheritance from them. Then there is environmental continuity. The infant tends to continue under the same major environmental influences associated with his parents' background and way of life. Because of the relative consistency of the influences, their effectiveness virtually from the point of conception into adult life and the large proportion of the child's time during which they are the dominant forces, it is no facile matter to alter their effects, unless by taking the child from his parents and rearing him in a different community entirely. Within the pattern of hereditary and environmental continuity there is another continuity in the gradualism and orderliness with which any individual life evolves. Prenatal and postnatal development manifest a common order of evolution of various physiological and behavioural functions, even if the pace and details of the evolution vary widely, as already noted, from one individual to the next. Children do not talk before they walk, or read before they talk.

And, finally, there is the continuity of the child-as-father-to-the-man. The infant does not just respond in isolation to an infinite number of separate human incidents. His particular adult world consciously and unconsciously schools him in particular modes of response—modes which will differ depending on whether the infant experiences love and security or impatience and fretfulness in his earliest nursing, varied or monotonous stimulation in his earliest social and intellectual development, the social and physical concomitants of wealth or of poverty, the monopolistic family position of an only child or the possible slide from king of the castle to dirty rascal in an increasing family, and doubtless on a variety of other factors. Some of these early lessons in responding may persist into adult life, for they are sanctioned over such long periods from such potent emotional sources in the family.

These three features—individual variation, self-activation and continuity—are clearly manifest in infancy but also typical of all human behaviour. There is another feature which is more particularly characteristic of infancy rather than of other periods, although it exists in some degree in other periods of life. This is the phenomenon of wide variability from time to time within the behaviour of the same individual. Parents will comment how their child can turn suddenly quite ill and yet, within a short period, return to a contrasting state of only too abundant health and vigour. An infant will be all tears one moment and all joy and mischief the next; now an aggressive demon, now mummy's poor baby; coy on first meeting but subsequently quite forward.

Older children may vary in tests of intellectual ability or attainment from one occasion of testing to another. Infants can still less be counted on to deliver a typical performance on a particular occasion. Proud parents may sometimes express mild disappointment when little John or little Elizabeth fail to show their brilliance on appropriate public occasions. And, of course, if the occasion happens to be an interview for admission to nursery school or some other school, that is just too bad. No wonder that middle-class parents are sometimes driven to consider how they themselves can impress the infant mistress if their children cannot, like the normally hatless mother who bought a hat specially for the occasion.

Although there is such variability even within individual performance in infancy, various scales of motor, verbal, social and adaptive behaviour have been established as a rough map of normal infant development. These do not correlate highly with later measures of intellectual ability and do not give very high levels of consistency even within themselves, but it may be that one must simply be satisfied with this lesser degree of consistency. It is better than completely casual observation and estimation. However, one of the most important schools of child development study—that of Piaget and his followers—has been less concerned with establishing psychometric norms and more with unravelling, by analytic observation, the character of the processes by which cognitive development takes place, by which intelligence is created. An account of this will serve both to summarize the general pattern of development in early infancy and to introduce the mode of analysis associated with Piaget's name.

Piaget does not attach firm ages to his suggested stages of development, but, roughly speaking, the first or *sensorimotor* stages runs from birth to about eighteen months or two years, and the second or *preconceptual* (or *preoperational*) stage occupies the next years up to about six or seven. Throughout all cognitive development Piaget thinks in terms of two complementary processes of *assimilation* and *adaptation*. The organism takes in aspects of its environment and makes them part of itself. To do this the organism itself must change to some extent. The baby, armed with an innate sucking reflex, can take milk from his mother's breast (or a bottle, of course) and nourish his own body, but he must also adapt to his mother, learning by practice to suck *effectively* and to adjust to other aspects of his mother's life routine. As a toddler he becomes able to explore a wider environment and assimilate it by his own self-activated movements, but here too he must adapt, learning slowly how to adjust to slippery surfaces, hard edges, large obstacles, parental obstructions and so on. These complementary assimilations and adaptations are life-long, and Piaget emphasizes that they are based on the organism's self-activating character. He does not accept a purely stimulus-and-response account of behaviour but rather insists on the significance of central shaping, presumably in the brain, although he is not particularly concerned with the physiology of the process but with its functional character.

In earliest life this assimilative-adaptive process is more manifestly and simply physiological in character. That is why it is called the sensorimotor phase. The baby's behaviour can be summed up in a fairly short series of simple '*action-schemes*', based, like sucking, on innate physiological reflexes, but quickly and gradually extending into simple adaptive acts, such as are necessary even for breast-feeding. At a later stage of development, while the *basis* of cognitive development must obviously still be physiological, Piaget uses the term *operation* in his own technical sense to signify any cognitive function that is assumed to underlie more complex behaviour, even if this function is not as physiologically obvious as a baby sucking or a toddler taking his first exploratory steps.

The term 'operation' is unfortunate because it commonly denotes *any* deliberate action, whereas Piaget intends to refer to the logical rules which govern certain classes of action. Mussen (1965, p. 265), for example, says, 'An operation is an invariant rule about environmental events or the relations among symbols.' And Piaget and Inhelder (1969, pp. 96–7) describe operations as '*actions* characterized by their very great generality ... reversible ... always capable of being co-ordinated into overall systems ... [and] common to all individuals on the same mental level'. In other words, the operations may be actions, but only when these actions are logically patterned. This will become clearer when the psychology of later childhood is discussed. For the present chapter it may help to give some sense of the meaning of 'preoperational', applied to infant behaviour which is not typically governed by logical considerations.

The word 'scheme' or 'schema' (plural, schemata) is sometimes used to refer to sensorimotor functions like a baby's act of feeding or, at later stages of development, to wider logical functions governing human behaviour. The agent does not have to be consciously aware of the scheme; he could act logically without being able to give an account of the logic under which he acted, just as one can drive a car without being a motor mechanic. Piaget and Inhelder (1969, p. 4) define a scheme as 'the structure or organization of actions as they are transferred or generalized by repetition in similar or analogous circumstances'.

Piaget considers it an arbitrary matter when one chooses to speak of 'intelligence' in the sensorimotor period. One might say that a baby able to get sucking promptly and successfully at nipple or teat was an intelligent little chap, but one would not want to attach an IQ to the performance. A toddler showing signs of eager and effective environmental exploration in his second year might invite a more plausible, if still provisional, ascription of intelligent action.

The sensorimotor period can be divided into substages, but these should not be overstressed compared with the general pattern of development. At first the infant simply exercises the ready-made sensorimotor schemata, such as sucking, with which he is endowed. In the second substage he may begin to integrate separate simple action-schemes, for example bringing his thumb to his mouth and sucking it as readily as a food-giving nipple. In the third substage, perhaps around four and a half months there is a start to the co-ordination of seeing and grasping and the baby will show so-called 'circular reactions', such as repeatedly making a string of rattles shake. In the fourth substage he shows more ability to conceive of desired results separately from known means of obtaining them, and in the fifth, around eleven or twelve months, he searches for new variants of established action-schemes for getting what he wants. Finally, in the sixth, he finds new means not just by physical exploration but by simple insights into the structure of particular situations.

The movement of the sensorimotor period is, then, from simple innate reflexes, through increasing co-ordination of simple action-schemes, to simple purposeful exploration and control of particular situations that catch the attention of young infants. The infant's growth in intelligence or adaptability in this context must obviously depend on the amount and variety of educative stimulation he receives and on his having suitable opportunities to exercise and extend his action-schemes. At first the infant does not even distinguish himself from the world of objects. He and they are one. What Piaget calls 'a kind of general decentering process' brings the infant to an awareness of his own distinctness and of the distinctness of separate objects in the physical world. Piaget does not care to detach cognitive from affective development, as psychoanalytic theory may sometimes appear to do. Mothers are not just sources of basic affection but simultaneously sources of cognitive or intellectual stimulation for their infants. Through both channels, affective and cognitive, mothers wean their children psychologically from the individual sensorimotor universe into the universe of objects and people.

Between two and seven the range of a child's assimilation and accommodation widens greatly. This is most strikingly demonstrated in his transition from the protected world of the family to the wider, more demanding, but also potentially stimulating world of school. During this period the child still tends to be dominated by the action or image of the moment, flowing readily between the worlds of play and 'reality' without a sense of sharp difference. Although his elementary powers of reasoning may be growing, he is still readily influenced by limited perceptual aspects of a situation. If beads are poured out of one glass into a taller, thinner one he may judge that they have increased in number, for they look more. He cannot at five appreciate that what is on the left hand going in one direction must be on the right hand going in the opposite direction, or that the middle object of three in a row is simultaneously on the left of one extreme and on the right of the other. These are 'operations' belonging to a later age.

In the preoperational stage children cannot form stable categories or argue at all logically. Their confusions are a common source of harmless mirth, from early examples like the infant who lavishes 'Daddy' on any creature vaguely resembling his genuine progenitor to later ones like the beads-in-jars case quoted above. The three-and-a-half-year-old may be able by touch to distinguish an open from a closed geometrical shape, a surface with one or two holes from one with none, or a ring from a circle—but he cannot distinguish a circular from a square piece of cardboard. The former are topological features not requiring for their recognition the sense of a fixed reference system implicit in Euclidean geometry.

Analogously, in 'moral' behaviour, the young child can recognize the force of parental authority, but is incapable of genuine moral appraisal, for that too requires the intellectual capacity to grasp first of all the purport of a set of stable rules and, subsequently, the subtler problem of interpreting rules flexibly to achieve equity. Infant reasoning proceeds in what Vygotsky called 'chain reflexes'—sugar like milk is white, milk like sauce is in bottles, sauce and meat go together, meat and tarts have to be cut up, etc. There is no formulation of an overriding principle that they are all things for consuming. The child follows a principle of resemblance but changes the criteria from step to step. Hence the young child's liability to blatant 'cheating' in games.

Language in early childhood

After the sensorimotor period, from about eighteen months to two years, a most important development is that of the symbolic (or semiotic) function whereby infants come to distinguish and represent things by language, mental image and gesture. An early form of this function is the imitation of something even in its absence, or playing symbolically at some action such as sleeping or quarrelling. Later, the child evokes reality in words or drawings. Piaget thinks of deliberate imitation as an accommodation of the self to external models, whereas symbolic play allows the child to transform reality in terms of his own needs. The age range two or three to five or six is the typical period of symbolic play. It may be used to symbolize emotional conflicts—working out parental conflicts on one's dolls, for example. Language enables the post-sensorimotor but preoperational infant to represent long chains of action quite rapidly, to range beyond immediate space and time in his imagination, and to represent complex action sequences in single, relatively simple verbal structures.

Of course, the infant's earliest speech is based on vocal and cognitive development in the sensorimotor period. The baby's vocalizations (grunts, gurgles, sighs, whimpers, cries, screams, etc.) acquire some sort of meaning at least for his mother, and by one year or later he understands the reference of some of his mother's speech, whether the forbidding intonation of the utterance 'no' or the concrete significance of 'ball' or 'drink' or 'bye-bye'—for the major developmental achievement of the period is upright locomotion, not verbal fluency. A vocabulary of about five words is not untypical for eighteen months, although, characteristic of the wide range to be expected, exceptional infants can range up to as many as a hundred words (Breckenridge, 1969, p. 346). The two-word sentence appears at about eighteen months to two years ('Baby fall,' 'Mummy go,' etc.), and endless What and Where questions through the third and fourth years, with a subsequent increase in Whys, Hows and Whens.

Young children can say only short sentences, even if they may know quite large vocabularies. Brown (1965, p. 288) quotes examples of how children reduce the length of sentences uttered by their mothers as they imitate her. When mother says something brief, like 'Wait a minute', the child says, 'Wait a minute', but when she says, 'That's an old-time train' he shortens it to 'Old-time train'. Nouns, verbs and, to a lesser extent, adjectives, have a better chance of imitation. Inflections (such as *s* for a plural or *'s* for a possessive), auxiliary verbs (is, can, etc.), articles (a, the), prepositions and conjunctions are liable to be dropped, as in a telegram. Since the former class of words (so-called *contentives*) also tend to be more strongly stressed in speech, while the latter (so-called *functors*) are less stressed, sound as well as sense contribute to the pattern of differential imitation. Just as the infant imitating maternal speech follows the order of the model but drops the functors as described above, so mothers frequently recapitulate their infants' speech, keeping its order but expanding it by adding the functors. Baby says, 'Baby highchair'; mother says, 'Yes, baby is in the highchair'.

There has been considerable controversy about how precisely language is acquired. Behaviourists have represented language as a set of motor responses like any other set, developed and shaped by the reinforcing factors in the individual's environment. From this point of view, thought is simply a kind of subliminal or 'interiorized' speech. Information theorists have represented language as a self-sustaining, self-regulative machine system, with each new input changing the state of the system, which in turn alters the character of what is next admitted as input. Piaget and Inhelder (1969) see language as one aspect of human symbolizing, resting on earlier logical structures.

> Language does not constitute the source of logic but is, on the contrary, structured by it. The roots of logic are to be sought in the general co-ordination of actions (including verbal behaviour), beginning with the sensorimotor level, whose schemes are of fundamental importance.

Brown (1965) stresses the complexity of language evolution in his remark that:

> The very intricate simultaneous differentiation and integration that constitute the evolution of the noun phrase is more reminiscent of the biological development of an embryo than it is of the acquisition of a conditioned response.

And Chomsky (1959, 1967), rejecting the view that language is acquired simply by a process of 'discrimination learning', and that exposure to language is equivalent to being taught a language, says of the child:

He learns the language because he is shaped by nature to pay attention to it, to notice and remember and use significant aspects of it.

In other words, part of the language function is innate, for no purely environmentalist explanation could explain the infinite creativity of even a young child's utterances—not a random creation of novelties, but a patterned variation based on an inner sense of order or structure. These contrasting views are mentioned only to illustrate that the genesis of language is a controversial topic. It would be an inappropriate digression to pursue the technicalities of the controversy here. What can be appreciated briefly is that language, while obviously a social product and highly susceptible to development or neglect through social forces playing on the young child, is not necessarily to be represented as a *mere* product of social shaping. Its creative aspect—in ordinary expression, not just in the context of the literary arts—suggests an element of intrinsic or autonomous patterning somehow rooted in the biological nature of the human species, even if there are shadowy precursors in the more limited symbolizing activities of the higher animals.

Whatever view is taken of the fundamental problem of language, most practical attention is given understandably to those aspects of children's linguistic development which can be directly related to the family and wider social environment. The linguistic poverty of families at one extreme of society contrasts with the richness and articulateness of linguistic stimulation at the more favoured extreme. This represents not just a differentiation in terms of superficial features of language—refined or coarse, lah-di-dah or down-to-earth, a spade or a bloody shovel—but a differentiation in the cognitive structure or intellectual equipment that the child has at his disposal for analysing physical and social situations, and particularly for coping with the expectations embodied in the school system.

The growing interest in this matter has turned people's attention to the possibilities of manufacturing educational stimulation programmes that might compensate the linguistically disadvantaged child for the defects of his family background. This poses technical and social problems, for no part-time programme can achieve the consistency of influence exercised by the family itself, and, on the side of social morality, there is the problem of educating the culturally disadvantaged without alienating them from their own families. Part of the answer may be to concentrate on securing positive family, and particularly maternal, co-operation in any educational programme, for this could contribute to the solution of both the problems just mentioned.

Personality in early childhood

Recalling Eysenck's definition of personality, quoted in the preceding chapter, one may wonder whether an infant has enough 'stable and enduring organization of . . . character, temperament, intellect, and physique' to count as personality at all. And yet the child of three, four or five does increasingly seem a little person with 'his unique adjustment to his environment', even if, as a newborn babe, he looked more organism than person. The problem is how to comprehend the complex interrelations of the four aspects of personality mentioned. Character is the moral evaluation made by society of a person's behaviour; it is obviously influenced by having enough intellect to grasp principles and enough vigour of temperament to act on them. This is hardly applicable to infants, who must rely on their parents' consciences, not their own.

Although the idea of character may seem premature for the period of early childhood, psychoanalytic writers have suggested that later character is influenced by infant experiences of feeding, toilet and sex. These three areas of experience have been thought to generate three developmental phases—the oral, in which the infant's concern is with its mouth as the dominant means of influence and gratification; the anal, in which the infant experiences power, achievement and possible gratification or guilt through delivering or withholding his faeces; and the genital, in which his sexual organs become the focus of attention and concern. Adult personality problems may then be traced to a *fixation* at one of these infantile phases. Infantile experiences of gratification, frustration, aggression or guilt are supposed to generalize to adult modes of reaction. The big businessman, piling up wealth, becomes an 'anal-retentive' type or, making a display of his wealth, is compared with the infant showing off the good 'job' that he has done. Depending on early nursery habits and experience, adult character might be rigid and restrictive or flexible and tolerant, guilt-ridden or conscience-free, with consequent implications for the person's moral attitudes and behaviour.

Infantile sexuality has been particularly stressed by psychoanalysts in the Freudian tradition. Children between two and five are certainly interested in sexual anatomy and in the origin of babies, and, despite common adult disapproval and discouragement, practise self-stimulation and indulge in other forms of sex play (playing at doctors, etc.). The child may develop anxiety centred on sex if his first naïve sexual pleasure runs into severe parental disapproval or punishment. Apart from this source of potential conflict and anxiety based on direct physical aspects of sex, young children may be influenced by the psychosexual aspect of their relationships with parents. For example, the famous Oedipus situation is supposed by Freudians to recur in the young boy's jealousy of his father and rivalry for the mother's affection ('I'm going to marry *you* when I grow up, Mummy'). The corresponding Electra situation for girls is, of course, 'I'm going to marry Daddy'.

An important aspect of these psychosexual relationships is the process of *identification*, whereby the young child comes to accept particular persons as models for his own behaviour. The infant copying his mother's or father's commonplace tasks (sweeping the floor, washing the car, etc.) is an obvious example, but the process goes much further. The boy who identifies with his mother rather than his father may eventually fall short of common norms of masculinity. The girl who identifies strongly with a masculine model (perhaps an older brother) may become tomboyish. Much of this modelling of behaviour takes place without conscious awareness on the part of the participants. Parents unreflectingly as well as deliberately encourage or discourage kinds of behaviour that they feel to be appropriate or inappropriate for boys or for girls. An example of this sex-typing that has been experimentally demonstrated is the tendency of parents to tolerate, and therefore encourage, more aggressive behaviour in boys than in girls. Such a phenomenon in infancy could be considered to fit in with (not necessarily to produce) the later differences between the character of boys and girls, with the former much more prone to all kinds of delinquency and aggression.

Psychoanalysts have pictured early character formation as a process in which the child naïvely and unconsciously absorbs or introjects into his own nature what he takes to be the approbations and disapprobations of his parents. This is no intellectually objective process, but rather an emotional sense of love or hostility, coloured by the irrational feelings of fear or guilt associated with the child's own urges and desires (the *id*) as well as by the overt behaviour of the parents in relation to any of these guilt areas, such as sex. It generates a kind of precursor of conscience, the supposed *superego*, a setter of standards for the unconscious, emotional aspects of behaviour. Successful development might then be envisaged as a process whereby the conscious mind of a person, the *ego*, established a dominant role in this imaginary psychic structure—harnessing the *libido* or psychological energy of the unconscious without accepting its crude directives.

The speculative side of this psychology, based on relatively unsystematic and uncontrolled observation and on generous extrapolation by analogy, cannot be expected to commend itself to experimentalists. How does one collect precise, systematic, reliably observed and recorded data about such matters for a truly representative sample of infants? How does one follow up this sample into adult life and make an independent and reliable assessment of their adult character traits? And if there were any marked correlation between earlier and later data, how would one prove the causal character of the relationship? Infant experience and adult character might together depend on some third factor rather than on one another.

Psychoanalytical views of this kind must be regarded, therefore, as clinical rather than scientific guides. Feeding, toilet and sex are certainly areas of potent interest and potential conflict for young children. Eating and sex continue in adult life to be sensitive areas, liable to generate intense gratification, frustration or conflict. They are functions that are biologically fundamental and that, at the same time, provide a major means of individual self-expression within the framework of subtle social disciplines. The analogies between infant behaviour in matters of food and sex and the language and behaviour of adult dining and loving are interesting. But broad analogies do not constitute a theory of character formation, even if they facilitate an interpretation of certain details.

Sears and others (1957) studied the toilet training of a group of American children in relation to the affectional character of the mothers and found that severe training by mothers who showed little affection produced more emotional upset in the children, whereas severe training by mothers who were more openly affectionate had no ill effect. They also found that the setting of high standards for other aspects of the children's behaviour did not make their toilet training more upsetting. This illustrated how even the immediate emotional effect of toilet training may depend on a variety of interacting factors and should warn one against yet rasher generalizations about any longer-term effects of specific training in early infancy on later character.

Erikson (1965) recognizes more fully the biological and social contexts within which psychological processes take place—for example, the fact that 'babies control and bring up their families as much as they are controlled by them'. Although 'the first demonstration of social trust in the baby is the ease of his feeding, the depth of his sleep, the relaxation of his bowels', Erikson envisages a series of eight stages in which, expressing the positive side, man achieves

1 trust and hope, rather than basic mistrust;
2 self-control and willpower, rather than shame and doubt;
3 initiative and purposiveness, rather than guilt;
4 industry and competence, rather than inferiority;
5 a clear sense of identity, rather than confusion about one's role;

6 intimacy and love, rather than emotional isolation;
7 creation and procreation, rather than stagnation;
8 ego integrity, which is a kind of summary of the preceding achievements—the ability to accept oneself for what one is and can be, to
follow appropriate leadership in the various realms of life (political, economic, artistic, scientific, etc.), but also to act as a responsible leader where one can—or its opposite, despair.

This may seem more like a moral than a psychological formulation
and is perhaps both. The positive end of these scales or polarities
could be regarded as a recommendation for the good and happy life.
However, regarded simply as notional psychological scales, they
could be considered to assort people not into two extreme classes but
into an infinite number, with most people having both positive and
negative aspects to their identity, and only smaller numbers standing
out as being conspicuously well or badly integrated as persons. Each
stage of life would contribute to a person's eventual psychological
standing as an adult. Man brings to his social institutions 'the rem-
nants of his infantile mentality and his youthful fervour' and receives
from these institutions 'a reinforcement of his infantile gains'. This
view of infancy as the period of first social lessons in the direction of
trust, confidence, initiative, competence, sense of identity and love
has the merits of *prima facie* plausibility and of allowing the importance of later stages of development. It remains speculative and
general in character, but this has advantages. It may not be tied down
to experimental demonstrations or psychometric tests, but neither is
it tied too exclusively to any specific physical function of infancy.

Regarding character as an aspect of personality—the potentiality
for moral behaviour—one might say that preschool children have
little capacity for being moral in any strict sense. They are in a pre-
moral phase, dominated by adult authority in practice and deeply
influenced by feelings of love or hostility, confidence or guilt, which
they cannot understand and which their parents may or may not
understand. Nevertheless, infants are effectively schooled into particular sex roles, which have indirect moral implications, and into
general attitudes of competence and confidence or withdrawal and
guilt, which also influence the personality substructure of later moral
development.

Defence mechanisms found in adults can be seen as readily in the
behaviour of young children—withdrawal from the scene of action
(running to mummy), regression (sudden changes from big wild boy
to crying baby), conscious denial or subconscious repression of
threatening events (mummy and daddy *don't* quarrel), and, of course,
the universal projection (*he* did it). These defences, when used only

sporadically, are psychological safety valves, but, if a child does not have a preponderant chance of behaving constructively and realistically, then his whole psychological character may become marked by a particular brand of escapism or practical ineffectiveness.

This negative pattern of behaviour is particularly likely to occur in children deprived of normal maternal care, such as those brought up under certain kinds of institutional care. It is now well recognized that terms like 'maternal deprivation' or 'institutional care' need careful attention, for they can mean so many different things, some of which matter and some of which do not. One thing that matters is that the young child should receive a sufficient variety of sensory stimulation, as a normal child does through the surroundings and happenings of his home. (A different kind of indicator of the importance of sensory stimulation is the fact that adults, when deprived experimentally of as much sensory stimulation as possible, find the situation rapidly intolerable, and suffer from hallucinations and panic.) The other thing that matters is that the young child should have the physical, social and emotional experiences that express affection and co-operation. Physical care alone is not enough. It must be a physical care that communicates affectionate warmth. Institutional care which embodied variety of stimulation and consistency of felt and expressed affection could avoid some of the ill effects of 'maternal deprivation'.

Children who have had neither normal affectionate mothering nor an adequate substitute seem to suffer in various ways. They seem to develop more slowly, to show listless or depressed behaviour, to be more dependent on adults, and, in the worst cases, to be incapable of affectionate personal attachments. Bowlby (1965) describes the symptoms of what he calls 'separation anxiety' in hospitalized infants. Below six months infants do not fret particularly as a result of separation, but after about six months they are very likely to be fretful, distressed or psychologically 'frozen'. Bowlby suggests that the instinctual response systems of crying, smiling, sucking, clinging and following become associated with attachment to a specific mother figure. When the mother is not available there is protest behaviour and separation anxiety. The behaviour of mother-deprived babies is matched by the comparable behaviour of certain other species in similar circumstances, such as the monkeys described by Harlow (1965).

If serious maternal deprivation represents a threat to even normal preschool development, children who do receive warm affection and varied stimulation gradually become readier for and capable of wider social participation. At first infants play individually, although one can sometimes see them eyeing one another with curiosity. At about two years they may play alongside one another—digging in the sand, for example—copying one another, but not co-operating in any way. Gradually more co-operative forms of play emerge and these pass from a phase of loose organization to more highly organized joint play. Primitive sympathetic responses include crying when another child cries and comforting a playmate by putting an arm around him. These small beginnings of non-egocentric response could be considered as stages in early character development, even if naïve egocentricity tends to dominate and acts of 'unselfishness' to be adult-contrived.

The development of the young child's character has now been sufficiently outlined to show some of the interrelations of character, temperament, intellect and physique. Physique is perhaps least important at this stage, provided it is reasonably free from specific defects. However, an aspect of physique that is and continues to be important, because of the differential social response to it, is whether it is a male or a female physique. If, of course, there is any validity in the small association claimed between physique and temperamental or emotional type, presumably it exists at least potentially in early childhood, but the matter seems to be speculative at present. Since favourable upbringing tends to show advantageously in all aspects of development, the more intelligent youngster will tend to be of good physique as well.

Similarly, as has been described above, the sympathetic stimulating upbringing that facilitates socialization and the beginnings of a stable character also tends to encourage cognitive growth and great competence in dealing with physical, social or purely intellectual problems. Temperament, considered as the person's basic modes of emotional response—outward or inward turning, stable or erratic, slow or quick, subdued or forceful—is perhaps most difficult to assess in infancy. Babies differ in degree of activity or passivity, and in the readiness with which their innate responses can be conditioned to appear in the presence of novel stimuli. Older preschool children seem to show a certain consistency in the amount of aggressive behaviour they manifest. But it is not easy to detach constitutional factors in temperamental development from the environmental factors with which they interact, or an attempted factual account of infant development from the social and moral evaluation of different patterns of development which each society makes through its parents. That is why fact so readily, whether or not justifiably, tends to lead on to prescription.

The psychology of child rearing

In view of the theories about the influence of childhood experience on personality, there has been increasing interest in the investigation of whether child rearing practices can be shown to determine general personality traits. Sears and others (1957) studied child rearing practices in two Boston suburbs in the 1950s. Three hundred and seventy-nine mothers were interviewed for two hours each. The transcribed interviews were rated on 188 different scales. The evidence, therefore, is based on inference from mothers' verbal reports, with consequent possibilities of imperfection either at the reporting or the inferring stage. The child behaviour that was most often and severely punished was aggression. More permissive mothers experienced more aggression, less permissive less; but physical punishment was associated with more aggression, whereas psychological methods of control (warmth as a general rule, but withdrawal of love for wrongdoing) seemed to accompany a more effective development of conscience.

Other studies have confirmed these suggestions about aggression. Bandura and Walters (1959), for example, compared twenty-six very aggressive boys with another group of boys matched with the first for socio-economic status and intelligence. The aggressive boys experienced less guilt, more physical punishment from parents and more emotional rejection by parents. This, of course, does not tell us whether the aggressive boys' behaviour was *caused* by their parents' treatment or whether the treatment was the parents' desperate reaction to their children's inherent aggressiveness. It has been shown that children will readily imitate another person's aggressive actions, and, consequently, the punishing parent may be giving the child a lesson in aggression, not in non-aggression.

Sontag and others (1965) used detailed information about children up to ten years of age from the files of the Fels Research Institute for Study of Human Development to establish an association between emotional and intellectual traits. It seemed that preschool children who showed more aggressiveness, self-initiation and competitiveness tended to advance more rapidly in intellectual performance. Between six and ten the same pattern persisted. The scales used in this enquiry included emotional independence from parents, aggressiveness in peer relationships, self-initiated behaviour, socialization, friendliness, general competitiveness, anxiety and parental emphasis on school achievement. Many studies have shown that children whose mothers give them an orientation towards achievement, by commending their achievements in the preschool years, tend to achieve more both then and later.

Thomas, Chess and Birch (1963, 1968), in their New York longitudinal study, have studied since 1956 the development of a group of children, systematically collecting reported observations by parents, making their own direct observations in various situations and interviewing parents to ascertain their attitudes and behaviour towards their children. They took a special interest in nine aspects of behaviour:

1 *activity-passivity* the balance between these;
2 *regularity-irregularity* the balance between these in hunger, sleep, etc.;
3 *intensity-mildness* the relative vigour of behaviour;
4 *approach-withdrawal* the child's response tendency towards new situations;
5 *threshhold of responsiveness* the intensity of stimulation necessary to evoke a response to sensory stimulation;
6 *positive-negative mood* whether typically cheerful and smiling or miserable and wailing;
7 *adaptability* ease with which child's response to a new situation can be modified in a desired direction;
8 *distractability* ease with which new stimuli distract the child's attention from an ongoing activity;
9 *persistence and attention-span* the degree to which a child persists with an activity despite distraction and difficulty.

It seemed that young children's temperamental profiles remained relatively stable on these scales, the relatively adaptable continuing to be adaptable or the relatively distractable to be distractable. A small proportion of children later showed marked disturbances of behaviour; these tended to have temperamental profiles characterized by irregularity, negative mood, withdrawal, intensity of response and slowness in adapting. This suggested that some children might be inherently more difficult to manage, which, in turn, might create a more stressful situation for their parents, who might then occasion further disturbance in the children.

One child rearing practice already mentioned is that of psychological rather than physical control. One aspect of psychological control can be the use of particular contexts to make explicit the general social rules that are applicable. There is a social class difference in the extent to which this is done. Working-class parents more commonly, though not without exception, deal with each situation in itself, directing or compelling the child into the preferred course of action: ('Stop that or I'll smack you'; 'You're going to your bed'). Middle-class parents obviously use direct action too, but more often they will elucidate the reasons for their own prescriptions, gradually familiarizing the child with the principles of approved behaviour through expressing them in words ('Daddy's had a busy day, so you'd better not beat your drum any more just now. You can do it again tomorrow'; 'Run along to bed now, for you want to be up early tomorrow to go and spend your sixpence. I'll read you a story as soon as you're in bed'). This latter form of control has been called universalistic, for it uses particular occasions to communicate general ideas, while the other form is called particularistic, for it provides only a directive for the immediate situation.

Douglas and Blomfield (1958) found, with their national sample of 5,386 children born in 1946, that maternal care declined steeply with lower social group and increasing family size. These mothers made poorer use of antenatal services and their children were more often prematurely born ($5\frac{1}{2}$ lb or less at birth) and more often died in early infancy. For the total sample of children, separation from mother during the first six years appeared to have little effect, but, among children sent away from home, there were more reports of nightmares, thumb-sucking and subsequent attendance at child guidance and speech therapy clinics. Up to the age of five, no great disturbance was reported among children from homes broken by death, separation, etc. The children of working mothers seemed as emotionally stable as others, and children who were potted early achieved earlier cleanliness and less bed-wetting.

There is a great deal of fashion and not a great deal of sound theory about child rearing practices. They vary from place to place, from family to family and from decade to decade. One must be wary of generalizations. Experimental or observational enquiries are faced by many difficulties. It is difficult to show that any specific practice is the effective cause of some specific effect on personality. It is difficult to be sure that concepts like weaning, toilet training or maternal deprivation are precisely defined, for they can certainly mean different things to different people. It is difficult to ensure that any rearing practice and any personality trait are defined *independently*, for it is easy to find oneself 'proving' theses such as that 'maternal deprivation' (indicated by a child's withdrawn, unresponsive reactions) causes 'personality defect' (indicated by exactly the same criteria).

Assessment techniques are another source of error, with varied use of mothers' recollections, trained observers' records of behaviour in play groups or nursery schools, or analytic ratings of other people's records. When mothers' recollections of the same events have been recorded at two different times, many disparities have been revealed. Psychologists usually give reassurances about their own reliability, but do not always bother one with the detailed evidence which would justify the confidence. The search for uniformities may lead to an underestimation of chance differences of reaction due to unsystematic details of a particular occasion of observation or experiment. If any kind of rearing practice seems associated with some personality change, it may be difficult to establish the time-scale of the influence—whether it is fleeting, or persistent, or permanent, in the life of the individual.

The nominal concern of psychology is with fact rather than value, and with persons (or, as the Es, or experimenters, like to call them, Ss—that is, experimental subjects) rather than institutions. But practically every theory of early psychological development and every enquiry into it confronts one with the pervasive complications of value systems, implicit or explicit, and social institutions which sometimes seem to override the influence of individual psychology. Those theories of development which stress the significance of early childhood may underestimate the major changes that can occur in later childhood and adulthood, or the fact that psychological stress belongs to all stages of life and is not the infant's monopoly. Infants may belong in a common stressful environment, and yet one becomes disturbed while the other develops normally. Similarly, in intellectually unstimulating families some children still turn out bright even if more turn out dull. And the stimulating atmospheres of more fortunate families still throw up their crop of dullards. These diversities of human development are not an argument for ignoring those tendencies that have been genuinely defined and demonstrated, but they do constitute a warning about too facile conclusions.

Perspective on early childhood

Compared with other species human development is slow. This is reflected in comparative gestation periods—3 weeks for a mouse, 9 weeks for a dog, 5 months for a sheep, 9 months for a human. Compared with the general pattern of human development, growth in the preschool years is very rapid. If one looks at different aspects of growth, human growth is very variable. At five years of age the child's brain has reached 90 per cent of its eventual adult weight, his stature 40 per cent of its adult measure, and the reproductive organs only 10 per cent of their adult size. If one makes physical measurements in different historical periods or in different social classes there are systematic differences. Five-year-olds from upper-middle-class homes are on average an inch taller than those from the homes of unskilled workers. London five-year-olds in 1959 were on average three inches taller than London five-year-olds in 1910.

If one looks at the developmental pattern of any single individual, a certain consistency is manifest even in infancy. This is not surprising, since genetic and environmental factors are liable to reinforce one another. But the preschool child is still variable even in relation to his personal norms of behaviour. Different circumstances upset established rhythms, or precipitate regression to less adaptive modes, or stimulate progression to higher levels of adaptation. If one looks across the developmental patterns for a large sample of children the range is wide. At five some are already little scholars, others scarcely ready for any schooling. Children of the same family (siblings) resemble one another more than unrelated children, but still vary widely. Non-identical twins, born at the same time but derived from two separate zygotes, resemble one another rather more because of their more similar environmental situations. Identical, monozygotic twins resemble one another more closely again, for their genetic constitution is the same as well.

Common physiological and behavioural functions evolve within the individual according to a relatively fixed order—the motor areas of the brain before the sensory, the visual areas before the auditory, walking before talking, and so on. Certain kinds of physiological maturation are necessary before the child is ready to attempt any behaviour which depends on it. At the same time readiness is a relative notion, for environmental stimulation or the lack of it may advance or retard effective readiness. Readiness is not a pure physiological concept; it is inseparable from the assumptions and expectations of parents and societies. It can be wrong to force a child who is not ready (let us say, to be continent, or to begin reading), but also wrong not to encourage readiness by appropriate contrivance. Recent years have witnessed more concern about lack of educational stimulation than excess of it.

In earliest infancy children perhaps invite most comparison with animals. Born with a set of innate reflex responses they can adapt to a simple life of eating, sleeping and excreting—thanks to the free maternal welfare service which is atuomatically there for babies in all normal circumstances. Babies will smile, but, in the first six months, this is a reflex response that can be evoked by any suitably face-like stimulus, not a sign of infantile gratitude or benignity. Only after six months does the infant develop social smiling which favours his mother and not strangers. Innate reflexes, from the earliest months, can be conditioned so that a reflex response is made to some novel stimulus (turning the head, let us say, for the sound of a buzzer as well as for the touch of a nipple). One approach to the analysis of behaviour is to see it as the product of a continuing multiplicity of such conditionings, together with their generalizing to associated stimuli and responses. Thus the baby who responds with contentment to his mother's affectionate feeding might be supposed, by a process of stimulus and response generalization, to end up as the happy adult who likes people and is good at dealing with them.

Although stimulus-response mechanisms, with generalization, may account for some aspects of behaviour, many psychologists do not see them as a sufficient account, and prefer to stress the significance of central or brain processes, actively transforming behaviour, whether conceived in servo-mechanical terms or in terms of Piaget's schemata. Language behaviour in particular has evoked heated controversy and the opponents of stimulus-response psychology stress the species-specific and inherently creative character of language, rather than any view of it as *merely* a generalization of non-verbal action responses to the set of discriminating verbal responses constituting language. Whatever one's basic psycholinguistic viewpoint, it is clear that language is of tremendous importance in infancy, both in relation to the development of intellectual or cognitive efficiency and in relation to the emotional exchanges that shape the infant's socialization and early character development.

Although it seems obvious that a child's personality must be influenced by his early upbringing, it has been less easy to *prove* that any specific feature of child rearing has a specific lasting effect. Some of the difficulties of proof have been mentioned. Apart from such particular difficulties, there is a general difficulty about obtaining the resources and facilities necessary to follow a sufficiently large sample of children over a sufficiently long period of time. Even at the end of the enquiry, the results may have to be considered as relevant only to a limited geographical area or historical period. By the time they are published people may be pointing out how social conditions or parental assumptions and manners have changed since the enquiry took place.

It seems that psychological enquiry has not produced a unified theory of early childhood but has refined our conceptions about this period of growth. The significance of sex in infancy, for example, has been blatantly ignored or suppressed, subsequently overstressed in the enthusiasms of post-Freudian speculation earlier in the century, and is now viewed in a cooler, more balanced way, although, of course, there are always some parents stuck at the suppression or magnification stages. Toilet training may have no specifiable effects on personality but encouragement to cleanliness without forcing or insistence seems a convenient and harmless policy. Freud's mythical mental structures may be unnecessary but, translated into more specific socio-biological relationships, they remind us of some of the subtleties of human interaction and of the emotive base on which cognitive functioning rests. It may be difficult to manufacture emotional warmth or cognitive stimulation for those preschool children who do not receive one or the other from their families, but it seems desirable to recognize their apparent influence—as a basis for understanding and tolerance if not immediately efficacious educational reform.

The educational implications of the psychology of early childhood include the importance of helping more mothers to understand how young children are shaped by individual affection, tolerance, and variety of stimulus and experience, or by the lack of these. Although this can be stated in general terms, it cannot be done in general terms, but depends on the combined influence of all kinds of institution, from domestic science courses in schools and nursery facilities in the community to television programmes and the contents of women's magazines. It is difficult to separate the psychology of early childhood from moral assumptions (in a broad sense of 'moral') about how young children *ought* to develop. It is one responsibility of teachers to study the interrelationship of fact and obligation in this area and communicate their sense of what is feasible and desirable through their general dealings with pupils (future parents). The community has a political responsibility, which is well recognized if not always acted on, to develop the supporting institutional structures (nursery schools, play groups, advisory centres, compensatory education programmes, etc.) which also contribute to narrowing the gap between the actual and the ideal.

The psychology of middle childhood 4

Somewhere between 5 and 7 years of age, depending on their nationality, most children start going to school. The powerful influence of the family and the home neighbourhood continues but is supplemented and modified by the extra social and intellectual demands which society makes via its schools and teachers. It is convenient and not entirely arbitrary to apply the label of middle childhood to the ensuing period up to between 11 and 13 years of age, during which some form of general elementary, primary or preparatory education fills much of the child's time.

There are at least two reasons for considering this period as having some distinctive psychological character. One is that it corresponds roughly to Piaget's developmental stage of concrete operations—the stage in which children gradually increase their capacity for reasoning consistently about concrete phenomena. As children approach 7 they slowly cease to be so completely at the mercy of the temporary perceptual impressions which dominate preoperational thinking. And as they approach 11 to 13 they slowly become able to pursue logical and abstract reasoning, more independently of concrete examples. The other reason for roughly defining a period of middle childhood is that it is a period of relatively steady physical, social and intellectual development, lying between two other periods, infancy and adolescence, which are somewhat more dramatic both for speed of growth and for the implications of that growth. Freudian psychology, with its emphasis on sexual factors, thought of the period between infancy and puberty as one of *latency*, although this term can hardly be favoured by anyone who wishes to stress the considerable cognitive and social changes that take place between 5 and 12.

Even if the definition of middle childhood has some psychological warrant, there is also some arbitrariness to it. Educational legislation fixes the age at which children must go to school and sanctions particular patterns of school organization, such as a division into primary and secondary schools. It is easy to assume that divisions of convenience are also fundamental psychological divisions. But consider some of the scholastic variations. Different countries require children to attend school from different ages between 5 and 7. A varying proportion of children attend nursery schools or classes from the age of 2, 3 or 4. The next administrative division after 7 may be 9 or 10 (beginning of 'middle school'), 11 or 12 (beginning of 'secondary school'), or 13 or 14 (beginning of 'public school'). Moreover, whatever age or stage is selected, the children at it will cover a very wide psychological range, influenced by inherited characteristics and differing environmental opportunities. The more obvious cases of precocity or backwardness are a commonplace of observation at all ages. One must, therefore, allow sufficiently wide borderlands at either end of the period of middle childhood discussed in this chapter.

The period of first schooling

The focus of psychological interest is not precisely the same in different periods of childhood. There is general developmental continuity, but public schooling is such a major social institution, embodying powerful forces of tradition or reform, that child psychology must be, to a great extent, the psychology of children adapting (or not adapting) to school requirements. The psychology of early childhood has a different emphasis—child rearing practices in the family and neighbourhood and the early foundations of personality (including intellect). The psychology of adolescence has a different emphasis—the problems of transition out of childhood altogether and into adult life.

The diversity of ages at which a child may have his first experience of an organized society of children outside the family has already been mentioned. This experience may be of play group, nursery class, nursery school, kindergarten or infant class or school—and under private or public auspices. Whatever the form of organization, the experience is one centred on play and simple socialization in the first instance but moving towards somewhat more scholastic expectations as the child approaches 7. Children who go to play groups or nursery classes may do so of necessity, because their mothers are out working, or by choice, because their mothers believe that it is educationally beneficial. Although the benefits of nursery education have not been clearly proven by experimental study, they have been enthusiastically and plausibly asserted by those with relevant experience. More particularly, it has been felt that, if socially favoured children commonly have the additional social and educational advantage deriving from nursery education, socially deprived children have a still stronger claim to the same advantages. The Plowden Report (1967) says of the latter, 'They need above all the verbal stimulus, the opportunities for constructive play, a more richly differentiated environment and the access to medical care that good nursery schools can provide.'

This educational prescription is quite closely related to some of the main psychological realities. The child who receives little verbal encouragement or explanation is liable to do and experience less, and to develop limited means of coping with what he does and will experience. At the same time, the verbal stimulation must obviously be matched by diversity of actual experience if it is to mean anything to the child. In the course of educational history some teachers and theorists have put too much emphasis on words alone, just as others have overstressed non-verbal experience and underestimated the importance of verbal structuring and expression. The real question is how to work out the best use of both. One aspect of this is the clarification of the rather vague concept of readiness, which refers to the fact that children's learning cannot be precipitated or accelerated beyond certain limits, but does not mean that these limits are absolute or that performance within them cannot vary over a wide range, depending on the psychological skill exercised by parent or teacher.

Children's play is one of the most important devices for moderating social and educational pressures. It offers a respite from adult expectations but also a device whereby the child can explore aspects of the physical and social world on his own terms. Adults are better able to explore their problems in verbal terms and do indeed spend a great deal of time recounting their joys and sorrows to one another. It is a commonplace of adult conversation to see someone recount the same personal experience or problem to a great succession of friends and acquaintances. But, on top of that, adults also spend a great deal of time in playful exploration of the world, in all the many leisure activities which bring a relaxing respite from routine demands and yet develop their own sophisticated skills, whether of gardening, comparing football teams, dress-making or mountaineering. These aspects of adult life may help to suggest some of the significance of play for children, for they too explore problems and develop skills through play. The exploration or working through of problems via play is all the more important for children as they may lack either the verbal sophistication or the appropriate audience which help adults to accommodate themselves to their own experience.

Erikson (1965) refers to the 'cycle of anger and anxiety' that may be generated in a child when he feels coerced and manipulated rather than self-controlled. This can lead either to impulsive self-will or self-coercive, stereotyped, repetitive behaviour. Play is a major means of allowing a child to control himself rather than be controlled. Virginia Axline (1947) describes how play may be used with deliberate psychotherapeutic intent. The therapist must observe the following principles:

1 Quickly establish a warm, friendly relationship with the child;
2 Accept the child exactly as he is;
3 Establish a permissive atmosphere in which the child can freely express his feelings;
4 Recognize the child's *feelings* and reflect these to him in a way which helps him to gain self-insight;
5 Leave the child free to make his own choices and institute his own changes;
6 Avoid directing the child;
7 Avoid hurrying the child along;
8 Establish only such limitations as are necessary to anchor the therapy to the world of reality and to help the child accept his responsibility in the relationship.

This non-directive therapy is not outlined for detailed discussion but only to illustrate how play, as self-controlled or self-directive activity, may serve an important psychological function in developing a child's autonomy and relieving him of adult pressures which sometimes become intolerable, as indicated by outbreaks of naughtiness or by withdrawal from situations structured by parents or teachers. Piaget and Inhelder (1969) refer to the function of symbolic play in working through emotional conflicts and making the conflict more tolerable, if necessary by the child giving himself a different role, so that he is the one in authority, the one who gives the orders or administers punishment, instead of mummy, daddy, or teacher. Adults, too, refurbish their own roles as they recount their experiences.

Play, then, seems to be a function that may relieve emotional tensions, facilitate assimilation of experience at the child's own level (since there is an inevitable gap between child and adult structurings of the world), encourage the development of personal autonomy and give practice in social and physical skills. The freedom of play gives scope for the workings of preoperational cognition up to the age of 7. Even without emotional complications, the child of 5 or 6 is readily dominated by appearances rather than by what adults consider reality. If a dozen red counters are put exactly alongside a dozen blue the child will agree that they are equal. But, if one set of counters is spaced out more widely, he will decide that the two sets are numerically unequal. If the child under 7 is asked to show what an arc of wire will look like when it is straightened out, he does not appreciate the transformation. The ends of the straightened wire are conjectured to match the positions of the ends of the arc.

Although it has been suggested that play may be a socializing influence, this does not mean that young children play co-operatively in any full sense. Piaget and Inhelder (1969) put it this way, that, in games with rules, such as marbles, 'nobody loses and everybody wins at the same time, for the purpose is to have fun by playing for oneself while being stimulated by the group and participating in a collective ambiance'. Similarly, young children do not so much converse as talk to themselves without listening to others—a phenomenon, of course, which may be observed in adult 'conversation' as well. In that aspect of social behaviour which is the precursor of moral behaviour the young child, in Piaget's view, shows typical *heteronomy*, that is, a morality of obedience to the rule of another, normally the parents. A corollary of this is what Piaget calls *moral realism*. The child attaches more importance to the actual effects of action than the underlying intentions. It is worse to drop the dinner set accidentally than to smash a plate in a temper, to tell an exaggerated story than a small lie.

These various psychological factors help one to understand why play and 'reality' are less distinct in the world of childhood before about 7 years, and even later. As Flavell (1963) puts it, 'the child . . . feels neither the compunction to justify his reasonings to others nor to look for possible contradictions in his logic . . . he thinks but cannot think about his own thinking.' That is why schooling before 7 must particularly exploit the characteristics of play and develop favourable learning attitudes by slow and varied activity-steps, tempting the child along rather than forcing him. 'Tempting' does not refer to verbal wheedling, although that may sometimes be apposite, but to contriving patterns of habitual and varied activity that provide an agreeable and stimulating, even demanding, context for educational advance.

The more favourable a child's home background, obviously the more demanding his schooling can be, but those with the least favourable backgrounds, whether intellectually or emotionally, need more preparatory time to develop progressive attitudes and habits. The ideal policy for the latter appears to be a combination of greater patience and understanding with earlier and more intensive educational stimulation, but educators are still exploring in the so-called educational priority areas exactly how this policy can be made effective, sometimes in the face of major disadvantages, such as inadequate human and material resources and traditions of hostility to education.

Cognitive development after seven

Marion Blank (1968) refers to 5 to 6 years as a period of major changes in thought and behaviour. 'The child at this age is not simply characterized by a sudden growth in control of behaviour by language, but also by better attention, greater ability to delay, growth of different conceptual categories, greater frustration tolerance, etc.' Piaget sees 6 or 7 as a rough dividing line between the stage of pre-operational or preconceptual thought and the ensuing stage of concrete operational thought. A typical feature of the transition is what Piaget calls *decentering*. The child, hitherto centred on his own view of the world and dominated by the chances of his own perceptions of it at any particular time, gradually develops a greater capacity for achieving a more intellectually stable view of the physical world which is not upset by every incidental change in appearances.

The infant of one year has already achieved a measure of constancy in the perceptual realm. He treats an object as the same, even if it casts different images on the retina according to different perspectives. But it is only after about 7 that children achieve *conservation* of substance, weight (about 9 or 10), volume (about 11 or 12), and other physical characteristics. That is, children slowly come to appreciate that a given amount of substance (say clay) stays the same however you change its shape into fat balls or thin rolls, that a pound of feathers is the same weight as a pound of lead, and that a half-pint is a half-pint whether it is spread out in a shallow bowl or vertically elongated in a narrow beaker. In other words, certain physical characters remain constant even if others change. Similarly, numerical relationships, such as $1 + 7 = 4 + 4$, are recognized after 7, whereas the child between 5 and 6 may consider the left-hand term smaller if his eye catches the 1 or larger if it lights on the 7.

Lovell (1962) carried out conservation experiments with junior school children and showed how there is a gradual increase in the proportion able to conserve the ideas of quantity or weight, but also how there is a proportion at each stage who are in a transitional stage, beginning to appreciate conservation but not, as it were, fully convinced. Thus the proportion achieving conservation of quantity rose from 36 per cent at 7 to 86 per cent at 11. But, even at 11, 13 per cent were in a transitional stage and 5 per cent had not achieved conservation of substance at all. For conservation of weight, the proportion of children mastering the concept was 4 per cent at 7 and 74 per cent at 11. At the latter age 13 per cent were in a transitional stage and 13 per cent had not achieved conservation of weight at all. Lovell comments, at the end of his book, that 'the junior school child has a limited capacity for varying one factor at a time, holding others constant, and appreciating what he is doing'.

Some of the important concrete operations are (1) classification according to some consistent principle (e.g. units, tens, hundreds), (2) seriation (e.g. listing children in order of ages, heights, etc.), (3) recognizing correspondence (e.g. A-1, B-2, C-3, etc.; or three red rods correspond to one dark green rod), (4) constructing matrices or double-entry tables (e.g. a table with two columns, for boys and girls, and three rows, let us say for their average ages, heights and weights), and (5) understanding the principle of reversibility (e.g. that $4 + 3 = 7$ can be reversed by $7 - 3 = 4$; or $6 \times 3 = 18$ reversed by $18 \div 3 = 6$). Preoperational thought does not allow a child to conclude that a red box is smaller than a blue when he has seen only (1) that the red is smaller than the yellow and (2) that the yellow is smaller than the blue. He has to *see* the red and the blue together, whereas, after 7, he appreciates the *transitivity* of the relationship and can *infer* $R < B$ (red less than blue) from seeing $R < Y$ and $Y < B$.

Piaget gives, as an instance of a classification problem, the case of a child confronted by twelve flowers, of which six are primroses. He can point out the flowers and point out the primroses, but, if asked before the age of 8 whether there are more flowers or more primroses, he may be unable to grasp the relationship of the set of flowers to its subset of primroses. Other relationships that perplex children are those of time and cause. Lovell (1962) suggests that 'average children have little understanding of the time period of one year, until they are at least nine years of age', and Piaget (1969) points out how the notion of time requires the ability to order events in temporal series, to understand the idea of duration, and to handle 'temporal metrics'.

The preoperational period is a precausal period. The young child's 'causal' explanations are in terms of the purposes that things serve for him. Thus 'night' is 'so we can go to bed'. The physical and psychical are confused. The 5–6-year-old's dreams are 'little material tableaux which you contemplate in your bedroom'. For the 7–8-year-old they are in the room but originate in your head. For the 9–10-year-old they are simply in your head. Again, when Piaget investigated the explanations offered by children between 5 and 12 for the dissolving of sugar in water, the youngest thought it simply disappeared, those of 7–8 thought it was there but without weight or volume, those of 9–10 that it was there and conserved its weight, and only those of 11–12 realized that it also conserved its volume and slightly raised the level of the water.

These examples of some of Piaget's leading ideas about the 7–12 period of childhood must suffice for present purposes, except that his ideas about moral development will be mentioned in a separate section of this chapter. Those who want to appreciate the detailed character of the work done by Piaget and his followers must dip into Piaget's own voluminous writings and into one or other of the systematic critical accounts of his work, such as those by Hunt (1961) or Flavell (1963). However, it is desirable to make some evaluation of Piaget's analysis and to consider what relevance it may have for education in the primary school.

Piaget's investigations have had some of the merits and defects associated with psychoanalytical enquiry, even although the problems he has studied and the theories he has proposed have been so different. The similarity resides in his use of the detailed case study which teases out the threads of a child's thinking in the face of various problems, although Piaget's problems are contrived and more definitely cognitive whereas the psychoanalyst's just happen and are basically emotional. This kind of individual study is rich in interesting detail which would not be elucidated by simply getting a child to do a standard intelligence test. It elucidates processes rather than just indicates their summary outcome. The conspicuous shortcoming is the one that the standardized intelligence test is so carefully designed to avoid, namely that the children studied constitute no definite and representative sample. It has been left to Piaget's followers in other countries to enquire about the representativeness of his findings. Broadly speaking, they tend to confirm the order of his stages but to reveal variations and irregularities in the manner and the chronological ages of passing through the stages. Lovell (1962) points out that children may be at a preoperational level on one set of tests but at an operational level on another.

Criticisms that have been made of Piaget include his tendency (1) to elaborate considerable theoretical superstructures on small amounts of empirical evidence, (2) to disregard such problems as the function of intelligence and the influence on it of education, socio-economic factors and chronological age, (3) to count on children's verbalizations as a faithful reflection of underlying psychological structures, despite the many possibilities of misunderstanding implicit in this mode of enquiry, (4) to overemphasize the consistency of his own theory and underemphasize the range of individual differences in children, and (5) to be satisfied with qualitative rather than quantitative evaluation, despite his purport to be scientific (unlike the Freudians and Jungians whom he implicitly reproves for their 'lack of concern for verification').

The concept of a *stage* of development poses problems. If this is to mean more than an arbitrary or convenient division of the whole continuous course of development, one must establish that the divisions are based on some principle. One principle is that certain phenomena always appear in the same order, for example, that children never appreciate conservation of volume before they appreciate conservation of substance, or moral intention before conformity to parental edicts. Piaget seems to meet this requirement. A second principle is that certain phenomena should always appear at certain chronological ages, and Piaget's theories meet this requirement to some extent, although with more variations and irregularities. A third principle is that, if the stages are meant to be stages of intrinsic maturation rather than mainly products of environmental influence, the appropriate phenomena should be evident regardless of environmental variation, provided that the environment is not highly abnormal. This requirement is partly met by the fact that Piaget's findings have been broadly confirmed in different countries, but there is still a gap between Piaget's relative neglect of environmental factors and the extensive insistence on environmental shaping which pervades the work of those who have used traditional intelligence tests in their psychological enquiries. Piaget's stages are plausible but not firmly defined by unambiguous tests.

Traditional tests of intelligence were often devised for practical purposes, such as educational or vocational guidance or allocation. This meant that they recognized and embodied a functional definition of intelligence. If anyone objected to the notion of intelligence test performance, one could drop the word 'intelligence' and claim at least that the particular test score, whatever it really measured, did have a known relationship with some later performance, educational or vocational, and was marginally useful in guiding those whose test score was known. Many have recognized that the concept of intelligence is bound to embody a value judgment. One may climb a rock face intelligently without being able to tackle a mathematical problem intelligently, one may handle people intelligently without being able to solve scientific problems intelligently, and vice versa in both cases. We use the word 'intelligent' always to denote efficient ways of doing things but in contexts where very different kinds of efficiency matter. Piaget, with his predominantly theoretical rather than practical interest in the development of intelligence, and with his emphasis on central processes rather than social shaping, does not pursue these considerations.

Piaget's idea of cognitive development as a series of achievements of *equilibrium* between the organism and the environment, between assimilation of the environment and accommodation to it, is quite interesting but also rather vague. Piaget and Inhelder (1969) assert that 'intelligence constitutes an equilibration between assimilation and accommodation', but this is a very unspecific view, compared with either that implicit in the traditional intelligence test (which is operationally clear, whatever further validity it has or lacks), or the analyses of the detailed shaping of behaviour which experimental psychologists have carried out in their laboratories (which are also operationally clear, whether or not they are adequately validated or relevant outside the laboratory).

Attempts have been made to advance children's achievement of certain of Piaget's stages by giving them special training, but it seems that this is possible only within very narrow limits. This tends to confirm the general impression left by Piaget's theories that nurture must, at least to a considerable extent, wait on nature—a view that conflicts with that of the most enthusiastic environmentalists, who seem to envisage that almost anything, in principle, can be contrived by environmental manipulation. However, the conflict may not be as real as it seems at first sight. As so often in psychological study, one must consider what measuring scale is being applied to a situation. Despite the detail of his observations, Piaget is charting the broad stages of cognitive development. It is obvious that there is considerable variation within any stage. This may have major practical implications, including the possible importance of manipulating various environmental influences to achieve greater educational advantage. What is a minor feature on Piaget's large-scale picture may be a major feature when viewed through the lens of educational practice.

The main educational relevance of Piaget's theories lies in giving teachers a clearer idea of the varying character of cognitive development. Teachers must always have recognized the wide range of individual differences in children of the same age even if they ignored them in practice or dealt inappropriately with them, but none can have differentiated the qualitative differences between cognitive stages with such system and detail as Piaget has shown. Piaget has made it more difficult to think of intelligence as a single characteristic which is present in small quantities or low power at earlier ages and large quantities or high power at later ages. He has made it more difficult to think of children as little adults, or even of younger children as littler versions of older ones. Instead, one sees in greater detail how children at different ages and stages are differentiated in the detailed characteristics of their cognitive and moral outlooks.

In terms of curriculum planning and teaching method this means that schools must strike a subtle balance between stimulation and patient waiting—a policy which can be stated truistically without benefit of Piaget's support, but which should benefit in its implementation from Piaget's detailed ideas. Piaget's work confirms and underlines the lesson of ordinary teaching experience (not always learned, however) that primary school children must learn through direct perception and action. Only as they move into early adolescence do they begin to develop powers of abstract rather than concrete reasoning—and some do not develop extensive powers of abstract thought even then. Piaget's elucidation of the logic of children's reasoning about physical quantities, numbers, causation, time, space, etc. should help teachers who study the evidence to appreciate that primary schooling is not just a set of conventional programmes to be gone through somehow or other, but must, if successful, be related to the child's own nature. This has been more readily recognized in respect of the child's emotional nature, but Piaget has elucidated the cognitive nature which is no less important. Indeed, Piaget is reluctant to separate the two.

Creativity

If Piaget's theories represent one advance on traditional concepts of intelligence, the work of those who have investigated 'creativity' represents another attempt to extend the meaning of intelligence. The interest in creativity has been associated with a feeling that the traditional intelligence test posed a limited range of problems requiring single fixed answers, whereas some intellectual endeavour is characterized by more freely exploratory thinking and by the possibility of a range of different possible solutions to a single problem. Creative intelligence does not simply tick the correct answer but manufactures its own answers, which have to be evaluated in more complex terms than right or wrong. Since 'creative' has become so widely used with reference to school activities, almost to the point of meaninglessness, it is useful to consider what psychologists have meant by it.

The typical mode of enquiry has been to get children to do tests that are more open-ended than conventional intelligence tests. They may be asked (1) to give as many examples as possible of things that move on wheels, (2) to give as many uses as possible for a shoe, a brick, etc., (3) to state similarities between milk and meat, or any other pair of things allowing variety of response, (4) to find simple geometrical figures concealed in a more complex figure, like the problem pictures in children's puzzle corners, (5) to make up different endings (moralistic, humorous or sad, for example) to incomplete fables, or (6) to make up associations for various line patterns. Since there is no single correct answer, there is a problem about scoring responses, but scores that may be used include the number of different responses, or the number of unusual responses as measured against the group as a whole. Thus many children might suggest that a shoe could be used to throw at a cat, but few that it could be used to catch a mouse.

Applying such tests along with conventional intelligence tests, investigators then attempt to identify groups that are relatively better on the 'creative' or the conventional problems, and to study whether there are further differences between the groups. For example, Wallach and Kogan (1965) studied 70 boys and 81 girls aged about $10\frac{1}{2}$, and found that ten measures of creativity correlated with one another to an average extent of ·4, that the intercorrelations of ten measures of general intelligence averaged ·5, and that the correlation between measures of creativity and intelligence was ·1. This indicates that there is a moderate but not high degree of consistency among the creativity tests and among the intelligence tests, but very little consistency between the two sets. The tests within each set may be measuring *something like* the same thing, but the two sets themselves seem to be measuring something quite different. One of the special features of this enquiry was that creativity was assessed painstakingly in as natural and unforced conditions as possible, to avoid any distortion that might arise from imposing tests arbitrarily on children in conditions which might be inimical to creative expression.

Wallach and Kogan also made assessments of the children's general class behaviour, using such questions as the following:

1 To what degree does this child seek attention in unsocialized ways, as evidenced by such behaviour as speaking out of turn, continually raising his hand, or making unnecessary noises?
2 To what degree does this child hesitate to express opinions as evidenced by extreme caution, failure to contribute, or a subdued manner in a speaking situation?
3 To what degree does this child show confidence and assurance in his reactions towards his teachers and classmates, as indicated by such behaviour as not being upset by criticism, or not being disturbed by rebuffs from classmates?
4 To what degree is this child's companionship sought by his peers?
5 To what degree does this child seek the companionship of his peers?

They then compared general behavioural and educational characteristics with creativity and intelligence scores and established a matrix like that in Table 2.

These are just a few points from the extensive material collected in this enquiry. Boys in the High/Low category tended to avoid thematic conceptualizing (that is, developing trains of thought by association on a theme), although it was demonstrated that they were capable of this mental activity. More creative children were tolerant of deviant instances of any category, and, since they tended to manifest moder-

Intelligence	Creativity	Class behaviour
High	High	The girls were not only sociable, self-confident, and successful, but also disruptive and exuberantly attention-seeking. Showed moderate anxiety—like the Low/Highs.
High	Low	The children were confident and academically orientated. They were sought out socially but did not themselves seek out others. The least anxious group.
Low	High	These children were least confident and least sociable. They were disruptive and attention-seeking, but as an 'incoherent protest' rather than an expression of exuberance. Showed moderate anxiety like the High/Highs.
Low	Low	These behaved quite confidently and sociably, but were the most anxious group.

Table 2 Intelligence and creativity: findings by Wallach and Kogan (1965)

ate degrees of anxiety, Wallach and Kogan suggest that 'creativity need not be all sweetness and light'. Boys who were characterized as defensive in attitude (for example, denying that they ever lied or ever felt unhappy, despite the virtual universality of such phenomena) tended to be less creative. Wallach and Kogan doubt whether creativity can itself be created, except by creating a tolerant atmosphere for it to flourish in if it is there at all.

Butcher (1968), reviewing research into creativity, says that 'there is some agreement that the primary school years are particularly important in determining whether creative potential will come to fruition'. Some factors that have been considered detrimental to creative development are a strong orientation towards academic success, succumbing to the pressure for conformity exercised by children in a peer group, and submission to the common preference of teachers for orderliness and compliance rather than eccentricity and dissent. Guesswork has often been a teacher's term of condemnation in the context of school tasks, whereas guesswork, at least of a certain kind, has characterized some creative work even within such disciplines as science.

Despite the interest of psychological studies of creativity, the concept needs to be regarded critically. Creativity tests may measure something different from general intelligence in its traditional psychometric sense, but the difference is not very sharp. Moreover, just as the traditional tests can be criticized for not making explicit what intelligence means (as distinct from how it may be measured), so it is far from clear what creativity tests really measure. Fluency of verbal association or ingenuity in imagining original uses for bricks is not quite what one has in mind when thinking of *really* creative work.

It has already been pointed out that the concept of intelligence embodies an element of value judgment. This is certainly not less so with creativity. There is a sense in which everything that people *do* is creative. If something is simply happening to one, then by definition one is neither doing nor being creative. But to call all action creative empties the word of power. It is more useful to reserve the term for the more limited class of actions whose products are of exceptional value. This is still a relative matter, for a child's or student's work may be exceptional compared with his classmates' and yet quite commonplace if the field of comparison is widened. If 'creative' becomes simply a term of classroom encouragement for children who are doing anything more than copying the teacher or other pupils, or following some prescribed routine, its significance must be enfeebled, especially as the criterion still implies a kind of conformity to the teacher's own limits of originality. It may be sound educational policy to encourage all children to be adventurous and exploratory, but it is another matter to assess the significance of those who display outstanding and original talent, regardless of special educational policies. Creativity is a theme that pre-eminently requires philosophical as well as psychological attention for its clear understanding.

Moral development

Just as a good deal of schooling (not all) in past times has attempted to shape children cognitively without sufficient or accurate regard to their actual cognitive capacities, so has moral education been earnestly imparted on a basis of adult demands rather than child potentialities. 'Spare the rod and spoil the child' is an understandable *adult* expression of the tension between ideal and reality. Since it is frequently so agreeable to be bad, there can be no question of dispelling the tension completely and making virtue an inevitable pleasure. However, some psychologists have attempted to clarify aspects of moral development in childhood, even if the picture remains far from simple or clear.

In Piaget's sensorimotor period there is, of course, no moral possibility at all, except perhaps in the sense that emotional experience then may in some undefined way colour later modes of social response, and therefore, indirectly, of moral response. In the pre-operational period, between about 2 and 7, children become increasingly aware of themselves as separate persons and develop persisting affections or antipathies towards other people. The wilful negativism that may occur in a child of about 3 is a stage in this discovery of independence and autonomy. Socialization takes place through parental shaping and also through very gradual accommodation to children of similar age (the peer group). The child's social actions and his cognitive understanding of them advance inseparably. The preschool child cannot imagine another person's point of view and cannot act except in accordance with his own urges or sheer obedience to parental authority. As mentioned earlier, even the speech of children at play up to 6 is essentially egocentric—not, that is, necessarily selfish or self-referring, but simply tending to disregard the existence of other children. Morality, if one can use the term at all at this stage, is based on a combination of affection and fear in relation to the parent.

After the age of 7 children develop more sense of mutual respect. Again this is a product of combined social and cognitive development, and it is marked by a growing sense of justice. The preoperational child regards the rules as God-given or, virtually the same thing for him, parent-given—sacred and unalterable. After 7 there is more sense of the rules as deriving from agreement among contemporaries. The child moves from heteronomy to autonomy, from obedience to responsibility. He may still be more concerned with equality of treatment and with observance of the agreed rules rather than with any regard for equity and flexibility, which are more likely to be found in adolescence than middle childhood.

Bull (1969) suggests that heteronomy in early childhood has a more positive function than Piaget allows. He considers the parent-child relationship more complex, and the influence of socio-economic background, sex, intelligence and the 'affective content' of the child's upbringing more significant. In his own study of 360 boys and girls between the ages of 7 and 17, Bull made estimates of the development of conscience on the basis of various moral tests. For example, the children were invited to identify an ideal person (they often chose themselves!) to list virtues or vices in order of importance, to identify what was morally right or wrong in a short story, to suggest reasons for various moral actions, and so on. One of Bull's main general findings was that development of conscience was more closely associated with intelligence in the case of the girls but with socio-economic status in the case of the boys. He speculated that the girls, through greater power of sensitive verbalizing, may develop greater moral autonomy, whereas the boys, less well equipped in this respect, may be more under the heteronomy of their environment. It may be, of course, that boys and girls are differentially shaped morally by different adult expectations.

Kohlberg (1963) posed a set of relatively complex moral problems in story form to 100 boys between the ages of 7 and 17, from different social classes. He created a matrix of 180 categories derived from considering 30 different aspects of morality and 6 developmental stages. The 6 stages might be summarily characterized thus:

1 Behaviour is orientated to obedience, sanctioned by fear of punishment.
2 Behaviour is orientated to achieving the individual's own pleasure.
3 Behaviour is now orientated to a more stable concept of role, characterized by the endeavour to maintain favourable relationships with others and sustain their approval.
4 Behaviour is orientated to sustaining recognized authorities ('Teacher says', etc.).
5 Behaviour is now guided by self-accepted moral principles, in the first instance, the principle of individual rights under mutual agreements.
6 Behaviour is guided by individual principles of conscience.

If these six stages were translated in terms of one of Kohlberg's aspects of morality (for example, the question, Why be moral at all?) they might run as follows:

1 In order to obey the rules and avoid punishment.
2 To obtain rewards, and have favours reciprocated.
3 To avoid disapproval.
4 To avoid censure by authority and resulting guilt.
5 To maintain the respect of an impartial observer.
6 To avoid self-condemnation.

Kohlberg, on the basis of very detailed scoring of his interview data, concluded that there was an invariable sequence of moral development and that individuals showed a certain degree of consistency in the pattern of their evolution through these stages. He sees the pattern as something much more complex than Piaget's relatively simple story of transition from heteronomy to autonomy.

Psychoanalytic theory relates moral development to the child's earliest experiences of fear and envy in relation to parental power, and his subconscious absorption or introjection of the standards that are *felt* to prevail in the exercise of that power. This aspect of development has also been discussed in terms of identification—the process whereby a child seems unconsciously to model himself on parental behaviour, or his vision of parental behaviour. This may be rather like the case of certain primitive (and, indeed, not so primitive) people who feel that an object or pattern of behaviour taken from someone with particular power may enable one to enjoy similar power for oneself. The world of fashion is a good civilized example. In similar style the young child apes his mother or father to savour the power and pleasure of their authority. It seems that the child's conscience is likely to be strongest where parents have been both affectionate in manner and reasonably firm and consistent in their moral training, perhaps not too surprising a conclusion.

Mussen and others (1963), discussing prejudice in middle childhood, refer to evidence of lower-middle-class children between 5 and 8 in Philadelphia showing religious and racial prejudice that reflected parental attitudes. These attitudes were not deliberately instilled in the children but communicated by unconsidered assumptions and actions. In another study quoted by Mussen the attitudes of 106 white New York city boys between 8 and 14 years of age were studied before and after a four-week stay at an inter-racial camp. It seemed that those boys whose prejudice increased tended to be 'hostile, defiant youngsters who perceived the world as cruel and unpleasant and felt they were frequent victims of aggression', while those whose prejudice diminished 'manifested fewer aggressive needs, less hostility toward their parents, fewer feelings of restraint, and generally favorable attitudes toward society'. These illustrative examples remind one how parental influence and general personality factors may bear upon attitudes that have moral significance.

The problem of moral development will recur in the next chapter on adolescence, but the preceding paragraphs give some sense of how psychologists have tackled the problem, with particular reference to middle childhood. This should suffice to show the importance of certain factors and also the great number of difficulties in the way of a general theory. Moral standards vary within and between societies. Moral knowledge, moral judgment and moral action are different, even if associated, things. Any one is difficult to define and test. Factors like intelligence, sex, personality and moral training may (or may not) make big differences. To confront the genuine complexity of the problem forces one, as with Kohlberg, to limit the number of people investigated. To aim at representative samples and control of extrinsic variables like intelligence, social class, etc., forces one towards superficiality—if not impossibility. One can perhaps only admire those who have made various attempts, even if their analyses leave so many problems unsolved.

Psychology and the primary school

Much of what happens in schools must be determined by educational tradition, current social and political pressures and various consider-ations of expediency. It is naïve, therefore, to think of psychology as something that might or ought to be able to solve educational prob-lems on its own. Psychology can be only one contributor among others and, if a list of its special contributions were made, it might include these:

1 Psychologists, through all their attention to the detailed patterns of child development and to the interplay of intrinsic and environ-mental factors, have sustained that part of the whole enterprise of education which requires accurate attention to what can really be expected of children at various stages. 'At the heart of the educational process lies the child,' says the Plowden Report. The psychologist might well agree, provided that, as environmentalist, he could add, 'At the heart of the child lies the educational process.'
2 Psychologists, by devising various tests, particularly of intellectual capacity and attainment, and by establishing what is the typical achievement on such tests of different groups of children, including the *range* of typical performance, have facilitated the identification of and provision for special educational needs (slow learners, educa-tionally subnormal, highly gifted, etc.).
3 Psychologists, through their many detailed analyses of scholastic skills, such as reading, have greatly widened our understanding of such skills and the range of teaching materials available to foster them. They have not produced single best solutions but rather extended the range of possibilities and the power of looking at these possibilities in a critical but constructive way.
4 Psychologists, through their opportunities of studying individual children more extensively and intensively than a class teacher may have time to do, have helped to sustain and extend an awareness of the multiplicity of factors, and particularly home influences, which may produce scholastic or behaviour problems in school. This has its frustrating side for teacher and psychologist alike, for it is sometimes easier to diagnose the malady than to alter the situation causing it. But there has also been a certain increase of understanding and tolerance, helping teachers to live with, if not alter, a difficult situa-tion.
5 Psychologists, through their extensive studies of learning in animals and humans, have provided at least an interesting back-ground for sharper thinking about learning in the classroom. Some-

times they have advanced highly specific techniques, like programmed learning, but, more generally, they have liberalized thinking about learning rather than provided detailed techniques.

These points have already been or will be illustrated in other sections or chapters. The rest of this section will deal mainly with psychological (and partly sociological) enquiries into general problems of primary education, and particularly four researches (here marked A–D) reported in detail in the second volume of the Plowden Report. (A) Appendix 6 of the Report discusses infant starters. The sample consisted of between 227 and 255 children who had recently started school, and was drawn from a larger 1964 national sample of children of various ages. Information was collected from teachers, mothers and school doctors. The variation in sample size arose because of slightly differing numbers of completed returns from these three sources. For example, fewer children in rural areas attended the school clinics for the medical examination. Since the total sample is small, and, of course, any subsamples (for example, into boys and girls) still smaller, some of the statistical summaries of evidence do not give grounds for firm conclusions. However, some miscellaneous points are worth noting.

Sixteen per cent of mothers considered their children difficult to control, compared with 11 per cent of the wider national sample including older children. About half of the children were in a class of 31 to 40, a quarter in a class of more than 40, and a quarter in a class of 30 or fewer children. Teachers thought that about a quarter of the children showed some distress at leaving their mothers when they came to school, but half of these appear to have settled down after a week. Twenty per cent of the distressed group (that is, 5 per cent of the entire infant sample) were distressed for a month or more. There was no difference in distress between boys and girls, except that it seemed commoner in boys over 5 but in girls under 5. The teachers also assessed the children on a three-point scale for tiredness at the end of the afternoon. Only 5 per cent of boys and 2 per cent of girls seemed markedly tired. At the other extreme, 48 per cent of boys and 61 per cent of girls showed no signs of tiredness.

The teachers assessed the children's need for adult support and their powers of verbal expression. Eighteen per cent of the boys (and 26 per cent of those boys over 5 years of age) showed marked need of adult support. Ten per cent of girls showed such a marked need, with no difference between those under and over 5. In verbal expression, 30 per cent of the boys were rated Good and 20 per cent Poor. The corresponding percentages for the girls were 41 and 12. Among those over 5, 24 per cent of the boys were rated Good but 46 per cent of the

girls. The medical enquiry did not reveal many behaviour disturbances in the children. As an example of manipulative development,
three-quarters of the children could dress themselves, but 62 per cent
could not do up shoe laces and only 15 per cent could do so easily.

(B) The main enquiry into parental attitudes and circumstances in
relation to school and pupil characteristics is described in Appendix 3
of the Plowden Report. Conclusions are based on 3,092 interviews
conducted in 1964 mainly with the mothers of a representative
national sample of children in the top junior, bottom junior and top
infant classes of 173 English maintained primary schools (that is,
children aged about 10–11, 7–8, 6–7). Families were classified on the
basis of paternal occupation and the Registrar General's system of
classification, giving the pattern in Table 3.

	Category	Percentage
I	Professional	4
II	Managerial, including self-employed	14
III	Non-manual, clerical, including minor supervisory grades	11
	Skilled manual, including foremen	48
IV	Semi-skilled	16
V	Unskilled, labourers	6
	Unclassified	1

Table 3 Paternal occupation of primary school children (Plowden
Report, 1967)

Over one-third of the mothers were in paid employment, the lowest
proportion by social class being 18 per cent in class I. In at least 8 per
cent of the homes one or both natural parents were missing. Over
half of the parents had completed their full-time education by the age
of 14, and 63 per cent of the fathers and 81 per cent of the mothers
had had no further education since leaving school. The proportion of
families in which at least one member had had some experience of
selective secondary education ranged from 88 per cent in class I to
15 per cent in class V. In about a third of families neither parent had
ever belonged to a library. The proportion of children taking home
books from school or library ranged from 95 per cent of class I to
73 per cent of class V. Sixty-one per cent of children in the top juniors
were given homework, but 75 per per cent of parents wanted home-
work for their children, with little social class difference in demand.
Three-quarters of parents hoped at this stage that their children
would stay at school beyond the minimal leaving age. Seven per cent
wanted them to leave as soon as possible.

Seven per cent of families (but 17 per cent in social class V) had no running hot water in their homes. Ten per cent (but 19 per cent in class V) had no fixed bath or shower. Five per cent (but 11 per cent in class V) lacked a garden, yard or play space for either shared or exclusive use by their children. Thirteen per cent of the children played mainly in streets which were not designated 'play' streets. Sixty-two per cent of the children were at schools that their brothers or sisters attended or had attended, and 20 per cent indeed in schools that their mothers or fathers had attended. Most parents would have preferred a *slightly* earlier start at school for their children, and some (ranging from 42 per cent of class I to 15 per cent of class V) would have preferred half-day schooling to begin with. Only 6 per cent of parents in class I but 27 per cent in class V had not talked with their child's class teacher. Only 11 per cent of parents were not completely satisfied by arrangements for seeing the class or head teacher. Most parents preferred their children to be taught in separate ability groups—59 per cent of parents with children in top infants and 70 per cent of parents with children in top juniors. Parents were satisfied on the whole with school discipline—preferring, if anything, that it should be firmer.

G. F. Peaker, in Appendix 4 of Plowden, reports that, on the basis of the 1964 national survey, variation in children's school achievement is more closely associated with parental attitudes than with either home circumstances or the characteristics of the schools. Among the school variables themselves the most important seemed to be the quality of the teaching. Although parental attitudes seemed so influential and were not closely conditioned by material circumstances alone, Peaker does not claim to see clearly *how* persuasion can be exploited to encourage parents in their increasingly positive attitudes towards education.

(C) Appendix 9 of the Report deals with Wiseman's survey of 2,300 10-year-old children in 44 Manchester schools. The number of variables studied was 87, giving 3,741 intercorrelations. These correlations were furthered analysed to clarify any underlying structure of the complex situation under review. The variables included:

1 twelve tests of reasoning and attainment;
2 assessments of schools on a five-point scale (for things like first impression, quality of the building, quality of equipment, library, classroom space, recent reorganization, streaming, corporal punishment, homework, out-of-school activities, attitudes of staff to the inquiry, quality of the head and staff, examination technique and 'progressiveness'); and
3 assessment of various home and environment factors, including

material shortages, broken homes (divorce, decease, fostering, emotional tension, etc.), father's occupation and criminality.

The most significant finding was the importance of Home variables compared with those for either School or Neighbourhood in producing variation in educational achievement. Statistical factor analysis showed that 72 per cent of the test variance (or variation) could be explained in terms of a single factor. This factor is obviously partly a product of environmental shaping, and, when the environmental component was analysed, it seemed that School contributed only 18 per cent of the effect and Neighbourhood 20 per cent, whereas Home contributed 62 per cent. Wiseman suggests that adverse home effects perhaps require two measures in particular to combat them—more nursery education and more social work training for teachers.

(D) The National Child Development Study, on which Appendix 10 of Plowden is based, began with 17,000 babies born in England, Scotland and Wales between 3 and 9 March 1958. The part of the study reported in Appendix 10 refers to the English children when they were between about 6½ and 7, between October 1964 and July 1965. Most of the educational data were available for 10,963 children, and the number of completed Parental and Medical Questionnaires received by mid-August 1965 was 7,985. Six forms of assessment were used—(1) an 'Educational Assessment' booklet, (2) the Bristol Social Adjustment Guide, (3) the Southgate Reading Test (a word-recognition test), (4) a 'copying designs' test, (5) the 'draw a man' test, and (6) a problem arithmetic test.

Most of these children settled down quite well at school, but a quarter were thought to remain unsettled for up to three months or longer, and boys took longer than girls to settle. The parents of about half the sample showed an active interest in the child's schooling; a minority appeared to lack interest. The children of interested parents, and of fathers with higher occupational status, tended to be better readers. Early starting at school was associated with better reading and arithmetic, and independently of occupational class factors. Boys did better at arithmetic and girls at reading. About 3 per cent of 7-year-olds were non-readers, 24 per cent poor readers, and almost half 'had not achieved a sufficient mastery of this subject near the end of their infant schooling to use it as an effective tool for further learning'. Five per cent were receiving special help because of backwardness and teachers estimated that a further 8 per cent would benefit from such help. Many more boys than girls need such help.

About 30 per cent of both boys and girls were reported to be faddy about food, and 30 per cent to throw an occasional temper tantrum. Between 1 and 8 per cent of children were reported as showing the following behaviour frequently – 'difficulty in settling to anything for more than a few moments; destroying their belongings or those of others; frequently disobeying parents; being upset by new situations; and bodily twitches or mannerisms'.

What general conclusions are to be drawn from enquiries of the kind just described? They try to elucidate problems, not by experiment or clinical analysis, but by the statistical analysis of information derived from samples that are designed to be genuinely representative rather than arbitrary. Some of the assessments used (individual ratings of children, schools or homes, for example) are less reliable than others (carefully standardized tests, for example). The statistical analyses themselves usually provide at least some scope for dispute among experts. An attempt to abstract some of the leading indications of the research does not do justice to the wealth of information clearly (in one sense) embodied in the original reports, and yet the sheer amount of detail in the original report makes it difficult for even the intelligent layman to abstract what is most valid and important. Much of the information is sociological, even historical, in character. In other words, it conveys facts and attitudes that may be accurate in 1964 but different at a later period. These are some of the technical problems accompanying issues that are themselves intrinsically complex.

On the positive side, these enquiries are especially interesting because of their attempt to obtain definite and representative measures. The social information reminds one of factors acting on very many children which are radically different from the factors taken for granted in the teacher's middle-class world—factors which have often in the past been forgotten in practice even if acknowledged formally. Some of the findings are not what everyone would expect, and, where they do match common expectations, they delimit the validity of these expectations more than casual opinion typically does. It is interesting that parental attitude shows such *magnitude* of influence, and perhaps a cause for concern that school influence appears to have such a modest role. The teacher still can console himself with the fact that quality of teaching seems to be important within the school's total contribution.

One of the most important outcomes of enquiries like these has been the initiation of programmes of compensatory education to try and give especially the worst handicapped city centre schools extra resources to meet the social and educational deficiencies of the children attending them. Hunter (1964) listed some of the possible features of compensatory education programmes for United States slum children. His list included these:

1   Educational priority for the enterprise of getting children to read.
2   The school to be a community centre, with clubs and welfare centre, open day and night and all year round.
3   Parents to be visited in their homes, given occasional employment in schools, fetched as well as invited to PTA (parent-teacher association) meetings, and entertained in other than middle-class, coffee-evening style.
4   Pupils to receive, if necessary, individual special tuition and home-work supervision from senior pupils, college students, adults, etc.
5   Pupils to have their horizons widened, especially by school trips. 'They may know a great deal about a number of things the middle class child knows little about: sex, the police, drinks, gang fights, family brawls, and the like. But they know little about the city beyond their own neighbourhood.'
6   Team teaching in schools, with two or three teachers devising a varied programme of individual, small group, and large class work.
7   Ungraded primary schooling, in which it is 'easier for the teacher to accommodate himself to the drags and spurts of the child'.
8   Special rewards for teachers in slum schools, and 'a heavy dose of the sociology, politics, and economics of the slums in their curriculum', so that they do not overstress middle-class ways and values, which they may be especially prone to do if they themselves are of working-class origin. At the same time, Hunter attempts to be realistic in his comment:

> The goal is to make it possible for those with the inherent capacity, strength, drive, and intelligence to make it to middle class income and way of life if they so choose. This is the desirable status in America, no matter how you cut it. This does not say that all the values and attributes of middle class life in America are exemplary. They are not.

Considered in terms of psychological control, measures like the above count on changing attitudes and motivations, partly by manipulating rewards, partly by restructuring situations so that children are exposed to educative influences for longer periods and in more effective ways.

Compensatory education itself has not gone uncriticized, both as theory and practice. On the practical side, it is difficult both to ensure that recommendations like those of Hunter or of the Plowden Report are effectively implemented and to demonstrate that clear, specific educational benefit has followed from specific educational practices. On the principle of compensatory education itself, Bernstein (1970), for example, has suggested that 'it distracts attention from the deficiencies in the school itself and focuses upon deficiencies within the community, family and child'. He suggests that, if one spent as much time on working out how the schools could build on children's existing social experience as we do on contemplating Piaget's stages of development, then so-called culturally deprived children might get a more challenging education.

Bernstein himself is perhaps compensating here for some of the influence of his own papers on the place of language in socializing children. The middle-class child, exposed to a great deal of verbal explanation and exhortation, becomes quite familiar with an order of meaning that has been called *universalistic*. In other words, particular events are related consistently to general or universal principles of explanation or justification. The working-class child is more familiar with a *particularistic* order of meaning. Situations and problems are dealt with on an *ad hoc* basis, in the light of current convenience. There is less explanation of why and wherefore, and any explanation is less verbally explicit. Bernstein now seems to be suggesting that the working-class child is not 'linguistically deprived', but only that his ability to be fully explicit, to use what is called an elaborated rather than restricted language code, is limited to fewer contexts and more specific conditions than in the case of the middle-class child. Whether this refinement of analysis makes a major difference to the main situation is perhaps a matter for debate.

Perspective on middle childhood

This chapter has stressed cognitive development in middle childhood —both its intrinsic character, as suggested by detailed studies of the Piaget type, and its shaping by various environmental influences, as revealed by socio-psychological researches like those reported in the second volume of the Plowden Report. Many of the factors emphasized in the preceding chapter on early childhood continue, of course, through middle and later childhood. Although the school may offer supplementation of, even rivalry with, the home environment, the latter still with some consistency determines the emotional and intellectual climate within which a child must find his personal centre. Modes of response established in infancy are typically sustained, albeit in relation to increasingly complex challenges and capacities. The language of the home, the mother tongue, still exercises its distinctive power, limiting or expanding a child's intellectual and emotional horizons.

Nevertheless, the start of schooling marks a great expansion of a child's world, socially, intellectually and emotionally. The society of other children alone greatly increases opportunities for extending human sympathies, getting new ideas and practising new skills. On top of this, the more organized teaching of the school gradually imports skills like reading and counting which add to a child's powers of enlarging and analysing his own experience. And on top of these, the social ideologies that are implanted by tradition and political action in schools as institutions (and that find expression in buildings, curricula, patterns of organization and styles of teaching) bring the child into a realm of experience that goes far beyond that of the family.

Ideology permeates the whole of schooling. Some of this ideology is political or religious or moral. Some is a kind of independent scholastic ideology which may elevate educational achievement in a rather narrow sense from an obvious desideratum into an autonomous religion. Psychological wisdom has to be pursued in such ideological contexts. But ideology permeates educational psychology itself. There are worlds of difference between those who pursue the supposedly intrinsic pattern of human development along the lines of Piaget and his followers and those who do so along psychoanalytical lines; and between either of those and the environmentalists who endeavour to pin numbers on the educational variance due to school, neighbourhood, or home, or due to various ways of organizing schools or educational systems. There is no necessary evil in this ideological complexity. Rather it is inevitable. Sound policy lies in keeping a cool head and distinguishing between reason and faith.

The psychological ideology that has perhaps received least adequate attention in this chapter is the psychoanalytic. One psychoanalytically influenced philosophy of education can be studied in A. S. Neill's *Summerhill*, for that series of essays is a stimulating and entertaining introduction to the idea of a schooling based on frank respect for human emotion and personal autonomy, and disrespect for scholasticism with its neglect or repudiation of children's own curiosities and fears. Neill is able to write vividly from personal experience, without the constraints of attempting to establish conclusive generalizations by experiment or statistical survey. He is mentioned here, not because the details of his views cannot be disputed, but because he reminds one that the development and the education of children *as experienced by them* is not a matter of developmental stages or socio-economic categories, but of whether they are treated with appreciation and respect, and their emotional needs met as well as the intellectual.

There are good excuses for falling short on these latter criteria. Teachers often have to deal with large numbers of individuals in far from favourable circumstances. While teachers often impose part of their own scholastic burdens, illustrating a kind of scholastic masochism, it remains that there are also pressures from parents and society at large to give priority to measurable scholastic achievement, despite the evanescence of most of such achievement at every level of the educational system, and despite the demonstrable need of so many people for help in coping with their personal problems rather than with those of the English or arithmetic textbook. The teacher's problem is moral or philosophical as much as psychological. In the present context one can only hazard the opinion that teachers would sometimes do better to give more time to meeting the anxieties and curiosities of their pupils and less to the so-called demands of the school programme. But there is no universal guide, for circumstances vary so much, and scholastic skills themselves are both an essential part of education and potential contributors to emotional as well as cognitive development.

Ordinary children can be most attractive in middle childhood, because of their vitality, enthusiasm and combination of naïvety and mischief. But, of course, they can also give themselves, their teachers and their parents headaches if their energies are not channelled skilfully and firmly along educative paths, or if their problems and handicaps are not diagnosed and dealt with before the child digs himself into a rut of failure or misbehaviour. The teacher's skill is tested at two ends—providing a variety of suitably demanding outlets for brightness and exuberance, and of progressive but less demanding programmes for slow learners. This is partly an organizational problem that can be mastered only gradually by increasing familiarity with the children, their backgrounds and the educational resources available for the class programme.

To treat children as individuals in a large school class is a counsel of perfection, but a few fairly simple general psychological principles can at least take a teacher nearer the impossible ideal. One is the recognition of the extent and persistence of individual differences and the consequent need for varied treatment at all ages. A second is that serious educational failure at any stage commonly requires that the teacher go back to the stage at which the child does not fail, and build up from there. The common inconvenience of this does not alter the necessity. The only other line of attack is to modify school programmes so that slower learners are not rushed beyond their capacities; but there will always be some pupils at every stage who require in part the educational treatment of a previous stage.

A third principle is derived from the second. Cognitive achievement and emotional achievement are indissolubly linked, but emotional stability and understanding are in some ways more basic necessities. This means that finding a real base line for a child's progress in work or conduct may imply going back not just to an earlier scholastic need, but to an earlier or more overriding emotional need—perhaps to resolve some anxiety or express some feeling that has been held in. To create opportunities for expressing these emotions can be a major contribution to the child's scholastic progress, not just his personal ease of mind. This is said without any intention of denying that there is a minority of graver disturbances which need more than classroom 'psychotherapy'.

A fourth principle is that any learning programme, whether aimed at scholastic, rational or emotional improvement, is more likely to succeed if it mostly brings success and reward to the learners, and if it is structured in a consistent way. School children may be a captive audience nominally, but they are just like adults in the readiness with which they can withdraw at least mentally from what does nothing for them, or be confused by lack of consistent pattern. It is not difficult to find a reward for children, for they feel highly rewarded by acquiring new skills, but, of course, it is a detailed pedagogic problem for the teacher to ensure that the children's efforts do lead to their acquiring skills.

Between 5 and 12—perhaps a tenth of a person's whole life but more like a third of the most formative part of it—children are transformed intellectually, socially and emotionally from babies of the family to quite independent boys and girls, broadly equipped with the elementary skills that society requires of everybody. Boys and girls are made more different than human biology makes them by the differential treatment of adults ('Boys will be boys', 'Girls don't do that'). 'The world of the small boy,' says Tanner (1961), 'is a world of tooth and claw, where physical prowess brings prestige as well as success, and where the body is more an instrument of the person than in anyone except the athlete in later life.' This does not prevent boys or girls from having affectionate 'crushes' on one another, even if companionship tends towards a single sex basis.

At 12 boys and girls are on the threshhold of puberty—indeed, some of the girls particularly are across it. The ensuing period of adolescence brings a mutual interest between boys and girls that adult pressure can no longer deny. But adolescence also brings other major intellectual, social and emotional advances and problems, and these will be the subject of the next chapter.

The psychology of adolescence 5

Adolescence, like middle childhood, is a concept that is partly warrantable in psychological terms and partly arbitrary. The spurt in physical and particularly sexual growth which characterizes adolescence gives the period a certain biological definition. The completion of formal schooling and entry into wage-earning employment or specialized preparation for such employment give the period social definition in terms of a transition from the economic dependency of childhood to the relative independence of early adulthood. The completion of the *general* intellectual growth measurable by intelligence or reasoning tests, as distinct from subsequent *specialized* intellectual development based on particular lines of study or work, makes its contribution to the whole concept of adolescence. These factors constitute a kind of developmental core that one would find in some form in any society.

Arbitrariness, or at least debatability, enters the scene as one tries to achieve more detail and precision, or to define the 'real' problems of adolescence, for here the picture, as always, is made complex by the great variation in individual patterns of development, and by the varying evaluations of adolescence made by different societies and different groups within societies. Some boys and girls of 12 are cognitively ready to cope with a quite demanding programme of secondary education; others still need help with learning to read. As an example of variation in the physical realm, British girls may have their first menstrual periods anywhere within a normal range of 10 to 16 (the average age being 13·1 years); and boys' sexual development, although not so clearly typified in a single event, may start anywhere between 10 and 15 and be completed physiologically anywhere between 14 and 18. These varying patterns of development are further influenced by social response to them. To some extent the maturer child invites maturer treatment. In fact he often gets it, but, if he does not, life may be made unnecessarily difficult for him.

Psychologists have portrayed adolescence in different terms at different times. At one time it was viewed as a mainly biological or physiological phenomenon—relatively sudden in its onset and dramatic in its resulting stresses. Then, as a corrective to this, there was an emphasis on the gradualness of adolescence, on the elements of continuity rather than discontinuity with adjoining periods. Mead's studies of adolescence in communities like Samoa drew attention to the influence of cultural patterns (in the anthropological sense) on adolescence. This suggested that the problems of adolescence may be partly the problems or absence of problems that the adults in any society create for their growing children. Further general considerations include the possibility that adolescent problems are partly the problems that adults themselves feel in living with adolescents; that some at least of adolescents' own problems are not distinctive of their stage of life but could be matched by the stresses and strains of any period of adult life; and that 'adolescent' or 'juvenile' modes of response, in a derogatory sense, may be identified in some who have left their teens far behind.

These introductory remarks may help to keep adolescence in a balanced perspective. The later part of this chapter will deal with some social and emotional aspects of adolescence, but the first sections sustain the theme of continuity with middle childhood by reviewing cognitive, creative and moral development in adolescence.

Cognitive development in adolescence

From about 12 children slowly become able to solve problems by logical reasoning and not just by inspecting concrete evidence, and to take into account all of the logical possibilities of a problem rather than just a limited number. Piaget, with his associates and followers, has illustrated this development by reporting the response of children of different ages to simple scientific problems. For example, why do corks, matches and some pieces of wood float on water, whereas keys and stones sink to the bottom?

Children of 9 or 10 appreciate that, in some sense, light things float and heavy things sink, but have difficulty (1) in comparing the weights of the *same volume* of two substances (the idea of density) and (2) in comparing the weight of a given volume of a substance with the *weight of the same volume of water* (the idea of specific gravity). The prelogical child cannot operate the idea of constant or fixed volume, nor the further idea of using the weight/volume ratio of water as a standard by which to compare the weight/volume ratios of other substances. By 12 some children begin to grasp these concepts, and by 14, as reported by Inhelder and Piaget (1955), a subject being tested on density problems may say directly:

I take a wooden cube and a plastic cube which I fill with water. [The cubes are the same size.] I weigh them and the difference can be seen on the scale according to whether an object is heavier or lighter than water.

Another commonly and justifiably quoted test is the one with the colourless fluids. The child is shown four numbered flasks containing colourless, odourless fluids. The fluids are not named but are (1) diluted sulphuric acid, (2) water, (3) oxygenated water, and (4) thiosulphate. There is a fifth bottled labelled g containing potassium iodide. The experimenter produces two glasses that contain clear liquid and look exactly alike. He pours a few drops of g into each, and the watching child sees that one liquid turns yellow but the other is unchanged. The child is now given two empty glasses and the original five bottles and invited to produce yellow.

It might be necessary to add g to a mixture of all four colourless liquids, or to a mixture of three of them (123, 234, 124 or 134), or to a mixture of two of them (12, 13, 14, 23, 24 or 34), or to only one of them (1, 2, 3 or 4). In fact, the mixture that gives yellow is $g + 1 + 3$. Number 2 (water) can be added but makes no difference. If number 4 is included it will bleach the mixture. Children who are still at the stage of concrete operations may try mixing all the liquids or go through the two-at-a-time mixtures, but they tend to become less systematic at the level of three-at-a-time mixtures. They may try one or two of them arbitrarily, whereas the older child at the stage of logical or formal operations has a stronger grasp of the whole matrix of possibilities and the need to go through them systematically.

Peel (1960) illustrates the development from intuitive to concrete to logical thinking in children's answers to questions about a paragraph on Stonehenge (with accompanying picture). One question was, Do you think Stonehenge might have been a fort? Why do you think that? And four sample answers were these:

A, aged 7·7 A temple. (Why?) Because people live in it.
B, aged 9·1 I think it might have been to stop the enemy charging through. (Why do you think?) It looks like it. The bricks would stand up. The enemy could not force through quick enough and they'd be killed.

C, aged 10·5 No. There was not a war when Stonehenge was being used. (How do you know that?) There were no battles before Jesus was born. (How do you know?) No answer. (Supposing there had been how would you know?) No answer.

D, aged 14·0 I think it would be a temple because it has a round formation with an altar at the top end, and at a certain time of the year the sun shines straight up a path towards the altar, and I think that it was used for the worship of the sun god. . . .

Peel (1968) has also underlined the deficiencies in adolescent logic, particularly the failure to eliminate alternative explanations of phenomena. Only older and abler adolescents seem likely to pursue an eliminative strategy. Of course, even clever adults frequently prefer the first plausible explanation rather than pursue laborious alternatives.

The reasoning of educated adults, indeed, is something of a warning against basing too many assumptions on Piaget's stage of logical operations. One can see that logical reasoning is the appropriate conclusion to cognitive development but also that only some people exemplify its operations, and then with many imperfections. Adult reasoning may not be distorted by the perceptual irrelevancies that lead young children astray, but, as advertisers fully recognize, a pretty girl is well calculated to abate the full force of male rationality at least. To take a more academic example, graduate teachers (and others) typically find a certain difficulty in handling such concepts as a *statistically representative sample*, or a *correlation* between two variables, or *statistical significance*, despite the importance of these concepts for certain kinds of valid educational argument.

Adults generally, like adolescents, will often follow an argument in concrete terms more readily than one that is abstract—football 'perms' and betting odds before a mathematical statement of the same principles. And many conclusions are jumped at rather than reached by systematic logic. Cognitive development at any stage is a complex concept, and not least so at adolescence. Piaget's tests or traditional intelligence tests assess important aspects of cognition, but specific education makes a radical difference to cognitive equipment. People acquire the cognitive powers associated with established disciplines, whether of mathematics, engineering, literature or *haute cuisine*. And they exercise these powers under the influence of personal motivations which may modify cognition extensively. The psychology of cognitive development must include the psychology of emotion, ambition, prejudice and inertia as well as of sheer reasoning capacity.

Adolescent and adult creativity

The general character of psychological studies of creativity and some of the associated problems were discussed in the last chapter on middle childhood. The present section is concerned with enquiries into creativity in adolescents and adults. One of the enquiries that has provoked most critical discussion is that conducted by Getzels and Jackson (1962) into the performance on creativity, intelligence and scholastic achievement tests of 292 boys and 241 girls aged between 12 and 17 who were attending a Chicago high school. Two small groups of pupils were identified, one relatively high in creative test scores and one relatively high in intelligence test scores. Although the latter group had an average superiority of 23 points on intelligence test score, the high-creative group was slightly superior in scholastic achievement. Critics have pointed out that, although none of the creativity tests correlates as much as ·4 with the intelligence score, neither do the creativity tests correlate very highly with one another. Earlier psychologists have recognized the existence of *minor* factors in test performance which might be labelled 'creativity', but the *major* independent factor (conventionally labelled general intelligence) accounts for most of children's scores, whether on tests called intelligence tests or tests called creativity tests. Using special labels or even having superficial differences does not imply of necessity that different tests are measuring different things. One can use a dull wooden yardstick or a bright folding metal metre tape and be measuring length in either case.

Hasan and Butcher (1966) conducted an enquiry of the Getzels and Jackson kind into a fairly representative sample of Scottish school children. The Scottish study, unlike the American, showed quite high correlations between IQ and creativity scores. Indeed, IQ correlated more highly with total 'creativity' score than did nine of the ten separate creativity tests themselves. And, when high-creative and high-IQ groups were formed, it was the latter who scored significantly better on two tests of attainment. Butcher (1968) mentions the possibilities that creativity should be regarded as closely associated with intelligence rather than independent of it, and that it might exercise a more significant influence in people with a minimum IQ of 120 rather than throughout the whole range of intelligence.

Hudson (1966) got boys in various grammar and public schools in the south-east of England to do tests of intelligence, spatial reasoning, vocabulary and general knowledge, together with 'open-ended' tests of the kind associated with the 'creativity' label. Two examples of the open-ended tests are (1) an invitation to draw an illustration to the title 'zebra crossing' and (2) an invitation to comment on any of a couple of dozen controversial statements, such as 'Genuinely creative people don't need to wear strange clothes'. The boys were then roughly categorized into 30 per cent *convergers* (those substantially better on the intelligence tests), 30 per cent *divergers* (those substantially better on the open ended tests), and 40-per cent *all-rounders* (no marked bias either way). Hudson discusses some of the features of these groups.

The convergers tended to be physical science specialists, the divergers arts specialists, although it was the latter who were inclined to analyse objects in terms of general categories. The diverger was not lacking in concern for facts or logic but was less tied to seeing the world in preconceived patterns. Convergers were more likely to approve of being obedient, of accepting expert advice and having set opinions, and of mixing well socially and being personally neat and tidy. They tended to concentrate upon the impersonal aspects of their culture and to be cautious about expressing feelings.

On the basis of his own work and of studies of distinguished scientists by MacKinnon, Roe and McClelland, Hudson goes on to speculate about the possible genesis of creativity, and of differences between convergers and divergers. His speculation draws on psychoanalytic concepts as well as on empirical studies. Briefly, it is suggested that the converger is brought up by parents who are themselves convergers. The parents are shy of displaying affection and convey their distaste for 'gush' to the child. They are prepared to express affection indirectly by bestowing approval on the child's achievements in impersonal matters. Such achievements, therefore, become a 'haven from embarrassment, from criticism and from emotions which are disruptive and inexplicable'.

By contrast, the diverger's mother is supposed to disregard her child's practical achievements and hold out a promise of direct love, which, however, she may or may not fulfil. This experience commits the child to involvement with people rather than impersonal pursuits, but he still feels unsure that people will really deliver the security and love he needs and therefore tends, like the novelist or student of literature, to keep his involvement at one remove from first-hand relationships. Between these hypothetical extremes of convergence or divergence lies a hypothetical 'hybrid', possibly typified by the psychologist, who shares the diverger's interest in the study of personal relationships but also accepts the scientist's ideal of impersonal rationality. The hybrid has experienced close parental affection, perhaps too insistently, and 'tries, by the application of his detached rationality, to reduce the threatening emotional charge to measureable proportions'.

In some final remarks about original thought, Hudson suggests that convergent or divergent bias does not determine originality but only the field and style in which it is likely to manifest itself. Characteristics that he sees as typcial of original thinkers are single-minded persistence, self-confidence, aggressiveness and a taste for risks. This pursuit of an ideal, in whatever realm, may originate in the child's fear of independence or isolation. In a final psychoanalytical speculation, Hudson pictures the pursuit as a kind of nympholepsy (a yearning for the unobtainable nymph), with the intellectual harbouring subconsciously the fear that his yearning is an incestuous one for his own mother. Self-protectively, he comments that 'the tight-lipped will express incredulity ... yet what I have said still seems worth saying'.

Hudson himself recognizes that some of the differences he found between convergent science pupils and divergent arts pupils may be an educational by-product. 'Both arts and science teaching look like systems of cultural indoctrination and it would be odd if they had no effect.' Whether or not one goes the full way with Hudson's psychoanalytical musing, it is plausible to expect that motivations generated within the family should play some important part in the emotional characteristics that accompany different levels and kinds of intellectual striving. Schooling may provide something for the original rebel to rebel against. But, beyond that, schooling provides the necessary groundwork on which any complex intellectual achievement must be based.

There does not seem to be any proven scholastic formula for creating creativity, but teachers—at least those who themselves are not one-hundred-per-cent convergers—might sometimes ask whether they have struck the right balance between the convenience of conformity and the sometimes less convenient policy of supporting and stimulating young people in their own constructive endeavours. Systematic enquiries have shown clearly that one of the commonest complaints of the ordinary adolescent is that schools have enforced trivial conformities and curtailed the sense of personal freedom which adults demand for themselves. However, this leads one away from the psychology of adolescence to the question of the convergent and divergent functions of schools as institutions.

Moral development in adolescence

Since both 'moral' and 'development' are intrinsically complex concepts, it is not to be expected that 'moral development' can be easily defined or measured. Moral development means at least something like increasing individual capacity to recognize different interests and claims in a human situation, to weigh these up in some rational and not purely selfish manner, and to act in accordance with the decision that meets these requirements most closely. In the nature of things, moral development is not something that just takes place. All development is influenced by circumstances, and moral development particularly so, for this high human ideal obviously depends on (1) socially and culturally inherited moral principles, (2) a socially and culturally transmitted code of rationality which provides a means of sustaining and revising them, and (3) various educational measures to uphold practical allegiance to the principles, and social and legal sanctions against their infringement. In these ways all societies try to make it pay to be moral, even if the specific content of their moral codes may vary, or their success in obtaining conformity to them.

This means that many of the problems of adolescent moral development are problems about the characteristics of a society's current ideals, the merits or demerits of these ideals, and the relative effectiveness of various patterns of moral education or social and legal sanction. Delinquency—transgression against the laws of a country—sometimes appears as a most dramatic challenge to the society's general norms, but this will be discussed in a separate chapter. The present section is concerned more with studies of non-delinquent moral thinking or behaviour. Actual moral behaviour is not at all easy to study in a way that allows of valid psychological generalizations, but the classic study of Hartshorne and May (1928) attempted an experimental attack on the problem.

They tested large numbers of children aged between 11 and 16 with various paper-and-pencil tests of honesty. There were about twenty tests which gave the children opportunities of cheating without, as they were mistakenly (dishonestly?) led to believe, being found out. The correlations between the same individual's results on different tests were low, averaging 0·2, with a range from 0·12 to 0·32. It was concluded that resistance to the temptation of dishonesty was determined more by the situation than by the individual's general character. However, the small correlations were at least positive and other researchers have found a small degree of consistency in the test performances of their subjects.

The children's honesty did not appear to vary with age, but it did with intelligence. Some other enquiries have confirmed that the more intelligent do better on moral tests, but others have found differently. It has been suggested that the more intelligent may either have less need to cheat, or more shrewdly suspect the likelihood of being found out. The Hartshorne and May enquiry has been criticized for the superficiality of the tests of honesty, for the immaturity of the younger children (who might not be expected to show moral judgment in a really developed form), and for the failure to elucidate in any detail the processes of children's moral thinking.

Havighurst and Taba (1949) report on a study of the development of moral character in children born in an American town, Prairie City, in 1926 and who were in their teens at the time of the enquiry in the early 1940s. The traits they selected to represent moral character were honesty, responsibility, loyalty, moral courage and friendliness. They found more consistency in these traits than appeared among the Hartshorne and May honesty tests. Intercorrelations ranged between 0·36 and 0·77. Havighurst and Peck (1960), reporting a second character enquiry by the Chicago Committee on Human Development, discuss 34 children born in 1933 and studied over 8 years. One cannot, of course, prove much on this basis, but the authors stress the apparently close relationship between character and the way the parents had treated the children. They propose a theoretical framework of analysis with five moral stages:

1 *Amoral* like the young infant or the adult psychopath;
2 *Expedient* acting to suit one's own purpose;
3 *Conformity* wishing to do what others do, for fear of disapproval;
4 *Irrational/Conscientious* guided by inflexible, internal standards and haunted by guilt feelings;
5 *Rational/Altruistic* guided by stable principles and able to assess objectively how actions will affect oneself and others.

Kohlberg's work was described briefly in the last chapter. Graham (1968) discusses the results of using Kohlberg's analytic techniques with a sample of about 300 English children aged 12 to 15. He suggests tentatively that intelligence is important in respect of general level of moral judgment, but that social class differences are slight, once the groups are matched for intelligence and for the kind of school attended. He refers to the attempt by Bradburn (1964) to find out if moral judgment could be improved by training. She compared children of 10 whose teacher had a reputation for developing sound moral attitudes (using praise and encouragement) with children whose teacher was not highly regarded in this respect (critical, punitive and forbidding). The data for comparison derived from questionnaires, rating scales, records of co-operative and unco-operative behaviour (carefully observed in systematic time-samples) and observational records of teachers and children. The children with the 'better' teacher showed up better, but one year later, when both classes had moved to the same secondary modern school, the differences were much less. Both teacher and school 'climate', she concluded, had important effects.

The Eppels (1966) studied the moral attitudes and opinions of 250 working boys and girls, aged between 15 and 18 attending two day-release colleges in central and east London. The tests they used were:

1 Sentence Completion ('If I had my way . . .'; 'It's wrong to . . .', etc.), investigating attitudes to (a) personal relations, (b) concepts of justice, (c) responsibility, (d) goals and aspirations, and (e) authority and independence.
2 Moral Beliefs—inviting free comment on statements such as 'A person who has stolen only a few times is not really dishonest'; or 'When you accept a job you should complete it regardless of what makes it difficult to do so'.
3 The Rosenzweig Picture Frustration Test—cartoons presenting a frustrating situation, e.g. 'Pardon me, the operator gave me the wrong number,' and inviting a verbal response, e.g. 'Okay it's not your fault' or 'And you get me out of bed at 2 a.m. just to tell me that.'
4 An Essay on 'The Person I would Most Like To Be Like'.

The young people's responses were made anonymously so that they should feel free to be frank.

Much of the interest of the Eppels' study lies naturally in the detail of the response, which must be studied in the original. The young people felt that adults had a false and hostile stereotype of the young. There was need for better communication between the generations, but the prime responsibility was adults'. They viewed their own generation (the young) favourably but realized that they did not always live up to their own ideals. Friendship was highly valued and, while 'popularity, good appearance and a capacity for getting on well with other people were all dominant themes in their self-image', they were not 'besotted by the false glitter of the prizes of affluence and materialism'. Couldn't-care-less attitudes were generally repudiated but also the idea of obligation based on authority alone. The boys particularly took a flexible view of honesty—perhaps, the Eppels suggest, a realistic appraisal of their own capacity for it. Marriage and family life were esteemed highly. Forty per cent gratuitously referred to their concern about world insecurity. The Eppels conclude that, all allowances made, these young people did have a serious concern about moral problems. Adults might influence them, but by example not precept, and only if they showed 'a very high tolerance of frustration', not expecting dramatic or exclusive moral victories.

Piaget and Inhelder (1969) suggest that the achievement of formal or logical thinking in early adolescence creates 'an added dimension in the application of ideal or supra-individual values'. He admits the importance of family, school and society in the process, but perhaps not sufficiently in relation to their actual influence. The comments of Peters (1960) are relevant, that Piaget shows the distinction between a morality of custom and rational morality to have application in the thinking of children and adolescents, but does not show how the transition from one to the other morality can be fostered, or explain why rational morality commonly *fails* to operate in the adult mind.

Peters, turning to the Freudian account of moral development, suggests that it may help to explain how people fail to develop moral autonomy or, alternatively, develop exaggerated, obsessional allegiance to particular rules, through psychological *fixation* at some stage of infantile development; but that it does not explain how rational morality develops positively. It does not explore how moral rules are passed on to children, whether by conditioning, reward and punishment, verbal authority, imitation, suggestion, learning 'by experience' or rational instruction—all different modes of influence. This listing of variables reminds one once more of the formidable complexity of this area of study. It seems doubtful whether one can ever expect to achieve more than a piecemeal analysis, but it is still worth trying at least to see what factors are relevant and note the small fragments of empirical evidence that have been gleaned about some of them.

Physical and sexual development in adolescence

Before going on to discuss some aspects of social and emotional development in adolescence it is convenient, if not essential, to look briefly at the significance of physiological development. Skeletal maturity, a physiological index of the degree of development of the skeleton as shown by X-rays, is a standard reference point in this context, and the more advanced a child's skeletal age, the earlier the onset of adolescence. Tanner (1961) points out that, although the normal menarcheal age range is 10 to 16 in chronological terms, girls typically begin to menstruate within a narrower skeletal age range of 12 to 14. Moreover, girls who menstruate early tend to have had an advanced skeletal age as far back as the chronological age of 7. There seems to be a general growth factor which causes children to be advanced or retarded as a whole. Girls are ahead of boys in skeletal development from before birth. And boys or girls who mature relatively early seem to do better in tests and examinations and to be well regarded for behaviour by their teachers.

Menarcheal age, height and other physical measures are genetically determined to a considerable extent. The correlations between sisters, or between mothers and daughters, for menarcheal age and for height are about 0·4. Climate does not seem to affect rate and pattern of growth, but Tanner reports American negroes as being ahead of American whites in motor development. The daughters of upper-social-class families may reach puberty two or three months sooner than those of lower classes, and it is claimed that this may be associated with parental intelligence and attitudes, not just with economic conditions. One of the most discussed phenomena of physical growth is the so-called *secular trend*, that is, the tendency over many decades for children to mature earlier. This means that each generation has been almost an inch taller than the preceding, and that in Western Europe menarche has been reached about four months earlier for every decade that has elapsed since 1840. A girl today may expect to menstruate on average ten months sooner than her mother. And, in Tanner's words, 'the present-day 14-year-old *is*, in physique and very probably in brain maturity also, the 15-year-old of a generation ago'.

One of the obvious physical features of adolescence, as of infancy, is the relative speed of growth. Mussen indicates that boys between 13 and 15 may increase in height by an average of 8 inches (range 4 to 12 inches) and in weight by an average of 40 pounds (range 15 to 65 pounds). Twenty per cent of the gross body weight of an 8-year-old may consist of muscle. By 15 the percentage is 32, and by 16 it is 44, with boys becoming more muscular but at a later age than girls. Girls improve in motor co-ordination, strength, speed and accuracy up to about 14, and boys up to about 17. Sexual development is, of course, a prominent feature of early adolescence, extending typically to about 16 for girls and 18 for boys, with wide individual variations. Psycho-sexual development obviously continues beyond these limits.

Kinsey (1948 and 1953) discusses the nature of sexual development in preadolescence and adolescence. His data derived from interviews with between 5,000 and 6,000 white American-born males and a similar number of females. The samples covered a wide age range. Although his enquiry was severely criticized on various grounds, including the possible unreliability or unrepresentativeness of the data collected, some of his points still seem worth mentioning. Preadolescent sex play by both sexes (Mother-and-Father or Doctor games, for example) is common between 8 and 13, but, subsequently, boys have an earlier and more frequent experience of orgasm than girls. By orgasm is meant a general release of neuromuscular tension after sexual arousal. Kinsey claimed that most boys (92 per per cent) had experienced this by 15, whereas a similar proportion for his female sample was not reached until the age of 29.

He rejects the Freudian sequence from sexual narcissism (self-love), through homosexuality (love of the same sex), to heterosexuality (love between the sexes), for about half of the males and three-quarters of the females in his samples reported never having had any experience of physical response to the same sex. Partly because of sexual fears, and partly because of justifiable privacy, it is difficult to obtain reliable information about sexual behaviour. And because there is such a tendency to jump at rough and ready conclusions, whether out of brashness or prudery, it is difficult to account for the many subtle gradations of sexual behaviour. A child between 8 and 13 may consort socially with those of the same sex, possibly or possibly not indulge in homosexual play, have at least nominal opposite sex friends, and again possibly or possibly not share sexual explorations with them.

A *Sunday Times* report (1970), on the basis of an enquiry by Gorer into sex and marriage among 1,987 English men and women, aged between 16 and 45, questions Kinsey's suggestion that males are most sexually potent in their late teens. Part of this difference may arise from different definitions of potency. In Gorer's sample those who reached puberty earlier, stayed longer at school or came from fairly prosperous homes, had *some tendency* to have more frequent sexual intercourse subsequently. The medium length of betrothal for the married English was around eighteen months, with couples in the skilled working class often marrying within a few months of meeting. Forty-six per cent of the men and 88 per cent of the women claimed to have been virgins at the time of their betrothal, but Gorer reported a 50-per-cent increase, compared with twenty years ago, in the proportion of young people approving of sexual experience before marriage. The relevant data could be tabulated as in Table 4.

Sample of 1,987, English men and women, aged 16–45	Premarital sex experience	
	For men	For women
Men in favour	63 per cent	46 per cent
Men not in favour	27 per cent	43 per cent
Women in favour	39 per cent	23 per cent
Women not in favour	49 per cent	68 per cent

Table 4 Opinions about premarital sex experience
(Figures as reported in the *Sunday Times*, 29 March 1970)

Schofield (1965) conducted an enquiry by interview into the sexual experience of just under 2,000 young people between 15 and 19 living in London and certain other areas of England. It will be noted that he had about the same size of sample for a study of a four-year age range as Gorer is reported to have used for a thirty-year age range. This is very important, for, when a small sample is broken down by age, sex, social class, etc., the subsamples are very small. There were between four and five hundred in each of Schofield's four subsamples of (1) boys aged 15–17, (2) boys aged 17–19, (3) girls aged 15–17, (4) girls aged 17–19. Five stages of sexual experience were invest-igated—(1) little or none, (2) kissing, with possibly breast stimulation over clothes, (3) sexual intimacy short of intercourse, such as breast stimulation under clothes, and genital stimulation or apposition, (4) sexual intercourse with only one partner, and (5) sexual intercourse with more than one partner.

Ignoring age differences and comparing all the boys with all the girls, the percentages at each of these five stages were as in Table 5.

Stage	1	2	3	4	5
Boys, 15–19 years	16	35	29	5	15
Girls, 15–19 years	7	46	35	7	5

Table 5 Adolescent sex experience
Percentages adapted from Schofield (1965), p. 42

Taking age into account, boys of 15 were typically at stages 1 or 2, and boys between 16 and 19 at stages 2 or 3. The proportions at stage 4 were small but the proportion for stage 5 jumped to 20 per cent at 17 and 33 per cent at 19. As for the girls, the girls at stage 4 repre-sented a small proportion, although it increased to 10 per cent at age 19. Few girls at all were at stage 5, which accounted for only 13 per cent (compared with the boys' 33 per cent) even at age 19. It must be remembered that this is a *cross-sectional* study. The sample of each age group consists of different people. It is not a *longitudinal* study in which the same people are followed up throughout several ages.

Schofield's enquiry is valuable for the sense of proportion, in a statistical as well as general sense, that it gives. About a third of the 19-year-old boys and a quarter of the girls had experienced sexual intercourse, but two-thirds and three-quarters respectively had not. Even at 19 years 30 per cent of the boys and 37 per cent of the girls were at stages 1 or 2, the stage of kissing and light petting. Boys tended to seek sexual adventure, the girls romantic relationship. When first sexual intercourse took place it was often in the parental home. But, if parents provided the locale, they often failed to provide supporting advice on sex. Two-thirds of the boys and a quarter of the girls learned nothing about sex from their parents. Girls having inter-course mostly left the question of contraception to the boys, but a quarter of the boys never used contraceptives, and less than a half made a practice of always doing so. Sexually experienced boys 'were gregarious and outgoing, even hedonistic'. The girls tended to have a strong desire for freedom from family influence. Promiscuity in a strict sense was not common. It was estimated that 12 per cent of the boys and 2 per cent of the girls had had more than one sexual partner in the preceding year.

Keeping in mind studies like those just referred to, what can one say about the psychological significance of the physical and sexual developments that take place in adolescence? Although sexual development is complex, some of the major shaping factors are clearly identifiable. Whatever view is taken of them, it is perverse to ignore their existence. At the core there is some kind of universal socio-biological pattern. Males are driven physiologically to initiate sexual behaviour, females alone are physiologically able to have babies. This does not mean that sexual satisfaction in itself is not, in some sense, as important for women as for men, but it does mean that the psychological and social concomitants are different for the two sexes. If one could, *per impossibile*, imagine a race of young adults created out of the void, free from all knowledge of past custom, one would guess that they would soon start procreating and re-establish all the customs and problems that in fact confront young adults.

But there is no point in further speculation, for the actual situation is that the biological core of sexual relationship is and must be powerfully charged with social custom. Even so-called rebels must rebel in relation to the pattern that exists, and normally their rebellion itself cannot be completely original, but rather modelled on centuries of rebellious custom. Procreation itself is obviously a strong social as well as physiological urge. Contraception makes it possible to detach sexual satisfaction from procreation, but this does not eliminate the urge to procreate. Before contraception was so conveniently or efficiently practised, it may have been sensible to observe that people wanted to make love, not just make families. Now that things are different, it seems appropriate to observe that people still want to make families as well as make love.

It may seem trite to refer to this socio-biological core of sexual behaviour, but this is not strictly so, for many people speak as if the social or biological aspects were detachable, or as if the whole phenomenon varied arbitrarily with circumstances, regardless of features and problems of sexual behaviour which are universally and objectively there—for example, the sheer problem of making or sustaining such a special relationship in any stable form at any time in any society. Nevertheless, much of the interest and challenge of this problem does arise from the varying general norms of different societies. This is the second major factor shaping sexual behaviour. In past times, this intercultural variation may have been a source of casual curiosity rather than practical concern, but, with the present speed and range of international communication, there is more tendency for the norms of powerful nations to establish themselves as points of reference or conflict in countries which otherwise might have pursued their own customs unreflectingly. As sexual behaviour and attitudes have become more widely and frankly portrayed in books, films and the theatre, adolescents have experienced models of sexual behaviour which differ in some ways from those of the past.

The third factor, or group of factors, is family influence, moral and religious norms, individual intelligence and sexual opportunity and stimulus. Each of these could perhaps be viewed separately, but, for the present purpose, they are grouped together to represent the direct impact on the individual of the norms and circumstances of his own family and peer group. The broad patterns of sexual behaviour may be associated with a socio-biological urge variously conditioned from one society to another, but within any one society interest naturally centres on the finer details of the pattern. Is sexual behaviour inhibited on its physical side by narrow moralities, or on its psychological side by clinical amorality and detachment from the rest of human culture? How far is sexual opportunity available in completely human contexts, offering sexual satisfaction in relation to consideration for other people and associated values, or in incompletely human contexts (much of commercial sex, for example) where sexual satisfaction is partial on the 'consumer' side and either non-existent or irrelevant on the 'supplier' side. How far do family or school succeed (or fail) in developing positive and intelligent attitudes towards sexual behaviour, in which positive and intelligent attitudes are so rewarding and their opposites so destructive—and this in terms of general culture and morality as well as of personal happiness?

In our society, and doubtless in any society not predominantly ruled by custom, sex must be a highly charged topic, generating unstable outlooks in some people. The practical problem must, therefore, be one of moderating diverse views and encouraging attention to a broad range of facts and attitudes. Much of this moderating is already institutionalized in such institutions as marriage, the law, the churches, and so on. But it could be argued that these have not done much that is necessary for the problems of sexual behaviour as they surge up most dramatically in the growth spurt of adolescence. Many of the most unavoidable facts of sex in adolescence (masturbation, petting, etc.) have been avoided. Marriage has been glorified (appropriately!) as an institution but adolescent preparation for it neglected.

The study of the psychology of adolescence does not by itself solve the problems of adolescence, but it has tended to dispel some of the darkness from the topic of sexual development. It has developed a more complex model of the role of sex within a wider pattern. It has spread reassurance about what is relatively normal and, on the psychoanalytical side, has suggested some of the ways in which a person's conception of his sexual identity and role shape his general responses to other people and to the ordinary problems of life. But the psychological perspective, in this sense, is not enough. It has to be combined with experience of people, of literature, and of the human sexual tradition in the broad sense, whether romantic, Rabelaisian, or in any other mode. The psychological perspective itself may be profitably expanded into the broader context of the next section—on social and emotional development in adolescence.

Social and emotional development

Freud once summed up the function of man as being *lieben und arbeiten*, to love (physically) and to work. 'Make love' has been a seductive call in every age but, having given *lieben* its due in the last section, it is time to look at *arbeiten* in this. Men and women make families, but they must also make a living to feed their families, and make a regular activity both in order to fill their half-century of life between youth and age and to give themselves social identity and significance. The bonds of love give people the most *intense* feeling of significance, but the nature of man in a larger society requires as well the more *extensive* kind of significance associated with work in the community.

One of the most striking features of the adolescent's entry into employment is that it is made at such different ages by different classes of adolescent. The great proportion who leave school as soon as they can are suddenly switched at 16 from the specialized and protected world of school to the differently-demanding world of young adult employment in industry or commerce. Others take up employment at 18, while college and university students first earn a permanent living between 21 and 26. There are problems about what might be considered the protracted adolescence of students, but they have advantages of prolonged education and well-marked routes to specific and desirable careers, which are not enjoyed by those entering work at 16. The latter enter the working world before they have really completed adolescent development, further handicapped by shorter education and fewer vocational guideposts. It is not surprising that one trend of educational thinking is towards righting this uneven balance.

Carter (1962) studied a random sample of 200 Sheffield boys and girls who, at the age of 15, left five secondary modern schools for work in 1959. Each school leaver was interviewed three times—early in the last term at school, three months after leaving school, and one year after leaving school. The first interview was held at school, the second either at home or at work, and the third at home. Most of the subjects were the children of skilled, semi-skilled, or unskilled workers, and they were mostly of average intelligence. School did not mean much to most of them, but, whether it did or not, all were glad to enter the larger world of work. Even after a year's experience of the realities of employment they still valued their work for the status and income that it gave them.

Parents mostly let the school leavers make up their own minds about what they wanted to do. There was little discussion, no systematic approach to the problem, and apparently little efficacy in the activities of school careers masters or youth employment officers, even if these behaved conscientiously within the scope of their available facilities. Two-thirds of all the boys aimed at jobs in the five categories—(1) steel and engineering, (2) electrician, (3) woodwork, (4) building and painting/decorating and (5) motor mechanic. Sixty per cent of the girls wanted to be office workers or shop assistants. The pattern of jobs held after a year was similar to that on first employment, except that there were fewer boys in steel and engineering and more in various dead-end jobs (van-boys, etc.). The manner of looking for jobs was typically spasmodic and casual. Parents and relations found as many jobs as did the youth employment service. Over a third of the boys and girls changed the particular job they were in during the first year. Reasons were both diverse and complex.

Most had some apprehension about exactly what to expect on entering employment but adjusted rapidly to their new conditions, only a few remaining worried after a year. They did not see the transition to work as a really trying period. The possible child-orientation of schools was not a virtue but a defect in the eyes of those who saw themselves as youths or young adults, not kids. They were glad to escape from schoolmasterly authoritarianism, punishment or ridicule for mistakes, and exaltation of the 'beautiful and spiritual' in a world that was really ugly and materialistic. Actual work was better than vague talk about purpose in life. But it was not the work for itself that mattered but work for the status it conferred. Getting on with work mates was important, and having a supervisor who was human, fair and tolerant.

About two-fifths of the boys, and a third of the girls *at work*, went to Evening School, Day Release School or both, but Carter points out that courses and teaching were not necessarily as closely geared to the young people's needs as would be desirable, that many were receiving no further education at all, and that further education in the context of some jobs is unnecessary or unprofitable. An argument may be put forward for the benefit of general education, but, where the schools have failed to 'sell' general education, can further education colleges be expected to succeed? The amount of spending money allowed to the boys and girls varied widely, from fifteen shillings or less to more than a pound (1960), with boys tending to get more and girls less. During the first year at work attendance at youth clubs declined, cinema attendance increased slightly, and by the end of the year one-fifth of the boys and a third of the girls went dancing at least once a week. A third of the boys and nearly two-thirds of the girls went out regularly with a friend of the opposite sex. Most dropped their school interest in sports. 'Only a handful of boys and girls read books at all: there were only a few or no books in the homes of most, and reading was not a habit.' Parents varied widely in what they tolerated or did not tolerate in the realm of their children's leisure-time activities.

Wilmott (1969) studied a group of adolescent boys or young men aged between 14 and 20 living in Bethnal Green, east London. These numbered 246 and were interviewed by a team of ten young male interviewers in the summer of 1964. Forty-two were also asked to keep a diary for a selected week and twenty attended the Institute of Community Relations to record further interviews. Most of the boys spent some or a lot of their time with a group of their peers, and two-thirds had a male 'best friend'. The male peer group was 'a crucial social unit in the lives of the adolescent boys'. At about 15 or 16 mixed teenage parties became commoner and by 19 or 20 more than a quarter were engaged to be married. Those with steady girls tended to be regular visitors at the homes of relations, particularly the girls'. Membership of youth clubs and organizations rose from 32 per cent at 14 to 53 per cent at 16 to 17, then dropped to 15 per cent at 20.

Of the boys whose fathers held non-manual jobs, 25 per cent were or had been in grammar schools, compared with 14 per cent of the sons of skilled manual workers and 9 per cent of the sons of the unskilled or semi-skilled. The boys were critical of school for its remoteness from their lives, or the impracticality of its offerings, or the lack of specific vocational relevance. A fifth liked all of their teachers, two-fifths liked most, a fifth liked about half, and the remaining fifth 'a few'. Two-thirds sympathized broadly with school rules, while one-third were more critical. Schools were sometimes felt to demand too much, or to offer too little, or to be alien from the local community.

Of those boys who had jobs, 54 per cent were in skilled manual jobs, 25 per cent in non-manual jobs and 21 per cent in semi-skilled or unskilled manual jobs. Relatives and friends were as important as the youth employment service in helping them to find jobs, and more important in helping them to change jobs. About four-fifths were generally satisfied with their jobs, just over two-thirds with the pay, and almost three-quarters with the prospects. Forty-four per cent had not changed jobs at all, but a third of the semi-skilled or unskilled boys had been in five jobs or more, compared with a sixth of the skilled or non-manual. Nearly a third of the fifty-two boys who had been most critical of school rules had been through five or more jobs, compared with a tenth of those who had been generally sympathetic with school. Job satisfaction was reasonably high at 15 and 16, waned at 17 and 18, then picked up again at 19 and 20.

The Government Social Survey made a study of *Young School Leavers* (1968) for the Schools Council in 1966. A random sample of 149 maintained schools in England and Wales supplied the pupils, parents and teachers who were interviewed. Within these schools random samples of pupils and ex-pupils were drawn, and the eventual total numbers interviewed were:

Teachers (including heads)	1,489
Parents	4,546
13- to 16-year-olds	4,618
19- to 20-year-olds	3,421

A very large amount of interesting and important information was generated and it is possible here to mention only some of the more striking elements of it.

Fifteen-year-old leavers, parents and teachers had some different ideas about which school objectives were very important—leavers and parents putting much greater stress on career objectives and money management, teachers putting relatively more stress on personality and character development and on school clubs. There was wider agreement, however, about some other matters. Quite high proportions of pupils, parents and teachers thought that developing independence, learning about right and wrong, behaving confidently making the most of oneself and speaking well, were very important. Very few pupils or parents and a minority of teachers saw drama or poetry as very important. School subjects were classified as useful, useless and boring/interesting. Table 6 (p. 133) shows some of the findings, with the figures in brackets indicating the percentage who responded to various subjects in the ways indicated.

Reasons given for finding a subject boring included (1) not understanding it, (2) monotony and repetitiveness, (3) poor teaching or explanation, (4) not having anything active to do, (5) seeing no use for the subject, (6) not liking the teacher, and (7) finding the subject old-fashioned ('It's just dead', 'It's all about the past').

Over half the 15-year-old male leavers and a third of the 16-year

Boys
Useful and Interesting Metalwork (63), Woodwork (60),
English (51), Maths (48), Science (46), P.E. and Games (44),
Technical Drawing (43), Geography (40), Current Affairs (39).
Useful but Boring Mathematics (19), Foreign Languages (12),
English (11).
Useless but Interesting Art and Handicraft (11).
Useless and Boring Music (48), Religious Instruction (30),
Foreign Languages (26), History (19), Art and Handicraft (14).

Girls
Useful and Interesting Housecraft (82), English (69), Commercial
Subjects (61), Needlework (51), Maths (44), and Current Affairs (42)
Useful but Boring Maths (22), Foreign Languages (13).
Useless but Interesting Art and Handicraft (13).
Useless and Boring Music (34), History (22), Foreign Languages (20),
Religious Instruction (19), Art and Handicraft (15), Science (14),
Geography (13).

Table 6 School leavers' opinions about school subjects (Schools Council,
1968). Percentages in brackets

olds went into manufacturing and engineering jobs. About a quarter
of the 15-year-old female leavers also entered these fields, with
another 30 per cent entering service occupations involving dealing
with people, and 31 per cent entering clerical and office work. By
19 or 20 almost a quarter of the young women were looking after
homes and families, one-third were still in office work, and just under
a fifth were in service occupations. Although almost half the boys
and more than half the girls still at school felt some nervousness about
the prospect of first employment, they preferred the prospect to
school and looked forward to increased freedom and independence.
The 19–20-year-olds were generally happy in their jobs, but 19 per
cent of the young men and 15 per cent of the young women would
have preferred a different type of job. The pattern of further education
among the 15-year-old leavers is shown in Table 7.

15-year-old school leavers	Men	Women
Had studied for a qualification	44%	19%
Further education without study for a qualification	18%	24%
No further education	38%	57%

Table 7 Further education of early school leavers
(Schools Council, 1968)

The things that 15-year-old leavers valued were having a job they liked, their families, being treated as grown up, having a good time while they were young, earning money and having friends to go around with. The girls, not surprisingly, valued clothes, hairstyles and appearance. The boys' main spare-time activities were watching television or listening to radio (50 per cent), outdoor or indoor sporting activities (43 per cent), and just being with friends (19 per cent) or going to the cinema (16 per cent). The girls' were watching television or listening to radio (54 per cent), going dancing (37 per cent), going to the cinema (25 per cent), sewing/cookery/making things (24 per cent), reading (24 per cent), just being with friends (23 per cent). The survey sums up the difference between early and later school leavers thus:

> It can be seen that 15-year-old leavers differed most of all from those staying on at school in the quality of their home backgrounds which were much less favourable for leavers; in being very much less inclined to have any intellectual or academic interests; and in being much more generally of an active than a sedentary bent and more interested in practical constructional activities than were stayers.

The three studies by Carter, Wilmott and the Government Social Survey remind one—and, of course, more vividly in the originals than in a brief abstract—of important aspects of the social and emotional context of adolescence, particularly as it is experienced by the large proportion of young people whose fate is least like that of students and teachers. The significance of adult status, a reasonably satisfying job, the peer group, the family and sexual partnership stand out clearly. The family is a social and emotional anchor point. The peer group gives relief from the family's older-generation pressures and allows discussion and action on an equal footing. A job may give personal satisfactions of its own, but certainly raises one's status in the family and among peers, and gives more money for enjoyment and self-development through leisure activities. Sex may be a bit of a lark to begin with but soon changes into a more serious affectionate commitment.

Schooling could come out of it worse, but still does not emerge brilliantly. No doubt allowance must be made for young adults looking back with hindsight on a period when they were still just older children, or for older children more eager to grasp the first fruits of adult life than to think about the second crop. But, even when such allowance is made, these enquiries leave a sense that schools could do more (and probably now have done more) to meet the psychological yearnings and, indeed, the personal interests of young people who are not destined for prolonged study or academic careers on the whole. Apart from this, chance seems to play too large a role in the shaping of these young people's lives. The means of guiding them into the most suitable jobs and encouraging them to persist with appropriate forms of further education are not sufficiently developed, although, as Carter realistically points out, some of the obstacles are very real ones.

Adolescence may be the period when Piaget's stage of formal cognitive operations or of moral autonomy *can* be reached, but there is something almost too intellectualized in this compared with the social and emotional realities of the adolescent pictures just looked at. The psychology of the family, the social psychology of the peer group and psychosexual development through courtship to making one's own family seem more relevant studies. Practical activities, customary morality, and concrete or pre-logical thinking seem more characteristic of adolescence for large numbers of young people. Social learning, powerfully shaped by class and neighbourhood institutions and norms, is as important as patterns of intrinsic cognitive growth. It is a complex task to unravel how such institutions and norms are created or changed. There remains in addition the no less complex problem of finding whether or how any principles of change can be effectively controlled and manipulated, and the contentious as well as complex problem of deciding how far and in what directions they *ought* to be manipulated.

The emphasis in this section has been on the great majority of adolescents who leave school either at the earliest opportunity or quite early. Despite all the problems that they face, the limitations of their education and the chanciness of the guidance they receive, it would be wrong to over-dramatize their disadvantages. The 'school of life' also has its advantages, and it is interesting that Wall (1968) should say that 'even for highly intelligent adolescents from stable and cultivated homes, it is doubtful whether verbal-intellectual education does more than provide an incidental respite, and incidental food for thought on the problems which vex them'. Wall goes on to suggest that teachers should be as well equipped 'to discuss the human relationships that are basic to friendship and love, or how to find one's way among compelling interpretations of life, as they are to teach mathematics and geography'.

The adolescent whose education is prolonged may derive long-term advantages, but he faces some special short-term problems. He enjoys enhanced educational status but not the status that accrues with earning one's own living. The student continues to be financially dependent on his parents or some public authority. Reactions to this are varied. Some demand independence from parental finance but accept public subsidy as a kind of civic right that is deemed not to infringe one's independence. Others are still sensitive about dependence on public funds and seek to have such subsidy viewed as a kind of salary for the 'work' of being a student. Apart from this question of financial status, the fact of being in some sense *in statu pupillari* obliges students to compromise for a longer period with the adult world before fully entering it. The demand for 'participation' in the adult world and some of the positive response to it, such as the reducing of the age of majority from 21 to 18, represent attempts to modify this situation. But, just because of their wider intellectual power, students particularly have to learn to live with their awareness of the gap between actuality and the millennium, not only now but always in the nature of things.

Looking at the social and emotional aspects of adolescence as a whole, one might say that there is a common element in the problems facing all young people—the element of transition from the dependence of childhood to the independence of adulthood, from physical immaturity to maturity, from school to work, from friendship to love. But, at the same time, these common problems are infinitely diversified by the wide variety of social and educational contexts in which they are met. This tends to lead one beyond the discussion of adolescence into discussion of the nature of society itself.

Perspective on adolescence

Perhaps it could be debated whether such a thing as perspective on adolescence is possible. Equipped for better or worse by a dozen or more years' upbringing in a particular family, neighbourhood and school, each young person is thrust by physical growth and social expectation towards the challenges of adult life. Each must improvise and experiment his way towards a relatively final definition of his own identity—in social, sexual, vocational and philosophic terms, as Wall reminds us. Parents and teachers, long accustomed to the dependency role of their children, find themselves at least mildly strained and sometimes seriously upset by the gradual repudiation of this role. The children—no longer children—have had such care and affection and expense lavished on them, only to go their own sweet (or sour) ways. Mother is challenged by some little poppet that her son fancies, while father loses his daughter's affection to a hirsute or pimply youth.

Some parents, carefully avoiding authoritarianism, swing to the possibly as disastrous extreme of withdrawal from responsibility. 'They have to make up their own minds, haven't they? They'll do what they like anyway.' Many parents, for one reason or another, are not able to communicate very extensively or effectively with their adolescent children, and, in the key realm of sex, such inability seems to be the norm, although there is, no doubt, a great deal of tacit and tangential communication that may be important. The growth of their children away from the family must fill some parents' minds with a sense of threat to their own established family patterns and assumptions, a sense of their own lives moving out of the stage of child rearing responsibility, and a sense of life's dynamism passing to a younger generation.

'Criticism and fault finding without constructive suggestions for changes are,' wrote Elizabeth Hurlock (1949), 'fairly universal among all adolescents, regardless of intellectual level.' This comment would probably strike sympathy in many adult minds and be reciprocated by adolescents—with the substitution of a reference to adult fault-finding. Certainly many adults seem obsessed by the incidental froth of adolescent life, by vagaries of fashion and by delinquencies which, while serious, characterize a very tiny proportion of young people and are not necessarily more (or, of course, less) abhorrent than those of older people. Over-reaction to minority phenomena, excessive moralizing on slender evidence and with small effect, and failure to estimate highly enough the moral correctives that exist along with the moral corrosions of adolescent society—these are some other things that contribute to poor perspective on adolescence.

Another obstacle to perspective is the vast diversity of the phenomena. Adolescence is dramatic but also gradual. It is physical maturing but also the product of education and work. It is the completion of *basic* cognitive and moral development, but also the response to widely differing social circumstances, educational opportunities, intellectual capacities, political climates, personal temperaments and family loyalties. Since the circumstantial factors vary in historical time, there is no reason to assume that adolescence should amount to the same thing in different eras—even if the socio-biological core ensures that it does not amount to something *entirely* different.

There is a special plasticity to the period of adolescence. The effects of previous upbringing can hardly be sloughed off, but inevitable change in the young adult's physical and social situation at least widens the field of personal action, not just inviting but forcing individual choice. Each choice is a further step towards identifying the final adult self. There are limits to the possibility and desirability of manipulating adolescence by social control, but a policy of widening adolescents' range of opportunity and experience, within their varying capacities to cope with this, seems a defensible one educationally. It is not a facile policy, for adolescents are very widely differentiated in their capacities, and, moreover, the differentiated needs of the community necessitate differential education of those who are to meet these needs, however large a common core the educational system may have.

The educational 'implications' of adolescence are perhaps as complex as adolescence itself, but several points stand out. Young people want to be treated like adults and it is for educators to consider how far they can meet this desire. 'Treating like adults' cannot mean just token gestures, for adults expect genuine respect. It cannot mean giving the adolescent all he wants, for adults do not accede to every want that another adult expresses. It must surely mean granting satisfaction and asking satisfaction, and helping young people practically and without blame to remedy their own defects, whether in reading or social skill, knowledge or moral understanding. It must mean frankness, including frankness on topics like sex which have been swept under the mat in the past. But frankness must apply in expressing moral implications as well as in spelling out the vivid facts of life. A partial frankness is not frankness.

But education is not a set of spot remedies. The larger patterns of education that extend throughout secondary schooling as a whole provide adolescents (or fail to provide them) with the knowledge and tools of intellectual analysis that can strengthen their handling of their own problems. It is not the present intention to enter into details, but there seems to be a need for patterns that are more specifically related to adolescents' actual problems. Whatever general intellectual equipment the schools dispense, a fair proportion of it should be sufficiently specific for young people not to question its utility. The evidence of the surveys mentioned earlier does not suggest that this is an impossible ideal, for there is partial appreciation of some of what the schools already do.

Anyone hesitates if he is uncertain and adolescence is bound, though sheer inexperience, to be a period of uncertainties. Adolescents must be expected to waver backwards and forwards, now behaving childishly, now showing fully adult responsibility, now making an erratic bid to exercise some power that they have not mastered. An older person may be tempted to see the occasional childishness as typical, the display of responsibility as surprising, or the exercise of power as something better handled by a competent person (like himself, of course). Such reactions are understandable, but adult consistency would seem to demand that adults foster every striving of adolescents towards responsible adulthood and avoid focusing attention on their backslidings.

The formula just suggested is doubtless a counsel of perfection, requiring a superhuman independence on the part of adults. But how can one be independent after investing decades of affection in children who naturally come to take it for granted? Viewed in a general social perspective, adolescents are only one fragment of the population. They themselves could survive to live an adult decade for almost each adolescent year of their lives. If adolescents are to be treated like adults they must be expected to live along with adults of diverse ages and conditions. To demand *too* special a status for youth is to demand the prolongation of childhood.

6 Learning and learning theory

The preceding three chapters have outlined some of the main features of human development from birth to adolescence. The concept of development is a broad one. It may suggest some inevitable pattern of growth or unfolding, but this is an inadequate analysis. There are broad stages and patterns that seem fairly characteristic of human beings and that set limits to what a child can be expected to understand or learn or do at any particular age, but equally characteristic is the great range of individual variation at any age, a product of differing environments and endowments. The environmental variations and effects remind us that one part of development is a product of learning, not of sheer growth or maturation. Learning was discussed with deliberately pragmatic emphasis in the chapter dealing with the adult as teacher and learner. It is now time to look more closely at the whole concept of learning.

No psychological theme illustrates more effectively the difference in perspective between psychological theorist and educational practitioner. The teacher is typically interested in how to cope with the learning of particular knowledge, skills and attitudes, with slow learning and failure to learn, with practical motivation, and with behaviour problems incidental to poor learning. The psychologist has often appeared to be more concerned with animal learning, physiological mechanisms and rather abstract theories to account for laboratory findings. This had led some learning theorists, in the psychological sense, to protect themselves by avowing frankly that their work has nothing practical to do with teachers and pupils. Another reaction is illustrated in Skinner, who repudiates learning theory but expatiates at length on the relevance of his animal learning experiments to human learning. And, of course, the practical device of programmed learning is associated with Skinner's work, even if not derived directly from it. A final illustration of hostility to learning theory from within the psychologists' camp can be taken from Welford (1968) who, with reference to skill learning, damns both Gestalt psychology and learning theory:

> These broad generalizations are really a sign of immaturity: they do less than justice to the complexity of the organism and of its functioning, so that they are inevitably either incomplete or so broad as to be of trivial explanatory value.

Learning theory: reasons for its study

These views could be used to justify by-passing learning theory completely, but, for several reasons, the present chapter will pursue more of a compromise line. It will not review all of the main learning theories as Hill (1963) has so lucidly and usefully done, but rather indicate (1) how psychologists, like Gagné (1965) for example, have classified kinds of learning, (2) what kind of evidence has been presented in support of learning theories, and (3) what major kinds of learning theory have been constructed. It may be that learning theory has virtually no relevance to practical human learning, but it seems reasonable to look at some of the evidence before pronouncing judgment. Moreover, even if the relevance proves limited, learning theory, by its emphasis on experiment, may at least remind one of the contrasting casualness of some everyday speculation about human learning which is the main concern of teachers and of the present discussion.

Although psychological learning theory has been introduced with a note of caution and reserve, there are some further positive reasons for giving it attention. The first is that one typical mode of scientific analysis is to look at the particular mechanisms that help to constitute a complex phenomenon and to look at these mechanisms in simpler forms prior to unravelling their complex forms. The study of animal learning serves this mode of analysis, for the linguistic, intellectual and social complexities of human life are either non-existent or much fewer in number among animals. A second reason is that the assumption of evolutionary continuity makes it interesting to see what parallels there are between human learning and animal learning. Some of the confusions about this hardly seem necessary. One might say to those adhering to doctrines of human uniqueness, Can you see no resemblance with the higher apes? And to those who like to talk about the 'human animal', Can you see no difference? This is perhaps one of those points where intellectual detachment breaks down. Both those who do not want to recognize differences between species and those who do not want to see resemblances are unbiological and unscientific.

A third reason for looking at so-called learning theory is that theories concocted on scientific principles have effects and practical implications that go beyond science. At least some creative scientists, and many of their lesser brethren together with interested laymen, tacitly or explicitly generalize into the general field of human affairs theories that are only *scientifically* substantiated in relation to laboratory experiments. One version of this effect is the assumption that human societies can or should be managed essentially like scientific laboratories. Psychological learning theory has generated two major general views of what human beings are supposed to be. On one account (connectionist theories) human behaviour is thought to be completely explicable in terms of complex relationships between stimuli impinging on the brain from the rest of the body and outside it and muscular responses, including those of speech, to those stimuli or to other physical events in the brain. This view abhors references to mind, thought, emotion and all the other traditional 'mentalistic' language of psychology.

The contrasting view (cognitive theories), associated with earlier Gestalt (that is, 'pattern' or 'shape') psychology, tends to present both animals and human as creatures who, by their very nature, perceive the world in significant patterns and learn by 'insight' rather than mechanical stimulus-response processing. In physiological terms this view may be called 'centralist' because it would tend to stress the positive shaping influence of the brain on manifest behaviour. Connectionism, on the other hand—at least in some earlier forms—could be called a 'peripheralist' view of man, for it tended to stress stimuli received through the sensory organs and muscular responses in the peripheral limbs of the body. It seems quite important for the layman, the teacher, to know whether connectionism has proven him unjustified, or at least unscientific, when he uses the mentalistic terminology which he typically does, or whether cognitive theorists can help him salve his mentalism, possibly in a revised version. It may also be valuable for him to know precisely why, when he talks about children behaving in a certain way because they have been 'conditioned' to it, he is using 'conditioned' in a sense that has little to do with the meaning of conditioning in connectionist psychology.

There is another fairly important approach to learning that has grown in popularity and that generates its own particular model of human behaviour. That is the servo-mechanical model, already mentioned in the first chapter. The human organism is likened to the various mechanical or electrical machines which can initiate new operations in response to change in physical conditions. The cistern fills: the ballcock stops the further flow of water. The room temperature reaches the selected level: the thermostat switches the electric fire off. Lunch time approaches: the worker starts to watch the clock. The teacher expatiates abstrusely: the pupil switches on to daydreams. The servo-mechanical model invites detailed analysis of the specific processes relating to a desired result. It does not imply that humans *are* machines, but it does challenge one with the question of how far they are *like* machines.

While it is suggested that the reasons just given are sufficient to justify looking at learning theory and its associated laboratory experiments, this look will be influenced by the ulterior motive of studying human learning in its complexity, including the complexity of humans themselves, the objects of their learning, their institutions, their explicit techniques and their varying circumstances.

Simpler varieties of learning

The first four of the eight varieties of learning suggested by Gagné are (1) signal learning, (2) stimulus-response learning, (3) chaining, and (4) verbal association. (1) *Signal learning* is the same as classical or respondent conditioning as studied by the Russian physiologist Pavlov (1849–1936). Some critics would object to calling this learning at all, for it is so remote from what learning means in human contexts. The word 'conditioned' is sometimes used as if the precise psychological concept was intended when, in fact, all that is meant is 'influenced' by something or other. There may be little idea of the precise mechanisms of the influence, and it is certain that the mechanism of conditioning in the physiological sense will have little or no direct explanatory value for complex learning phenomena.

What Pavlov meant by conditioning was that certain intrinsic stimulus-response associations, such as a dog's salivating in response to the presentation of food, could be used to transfer the natural response to some quite new stimulus, such as the sound of a buzzer. The new or conditioned stimulus (CS) has to be presented about half a second before the natural or unconditioned stimulus (US) of food. After several such presentations the natural or unconditioned response (UR) of salivating can be evoked by the buzzer (CS) alone without the presentation of the food (US). The unconditioned response (UR) to food (US) has become a conditioned response (CR) to the buzzer (CS):

Food (US) → Salivation (UR)
Buzzer (CS) Food (US) → Salivation (UR)
Buzzer (CS) → Salivation (CR)

Similarly the human eye-blink in response to a puff of air in the eye can be conditioned to the sound of a bell:

Air Puff (US) → Eye blink (UR)
Bell (CS) Air puff (US) → Eye blink (UR)
Bell (CS) → Eye blink (CR)

Although this may seem a simple and plausible transfer operation, the diagrammatic simplicity is misleading. Conditions have to be carefully controlled to eliminate the influence of 'irrelevant' environmental stimuli. The response established by conditioning is by no means precisely the same as the unconditioned response. It may differ in intensity and it normally differs in the facility with which it can be *extinguished*. The dog will soon stop responding to the buzzer if there is a repeated absence of the natural stimulus of food. However if, after conditioning, a period of time elapses in which the buzzer signal is not presented at all, then the conditioned response will often be capable of being evoked despite the time lapse. Another feature of conditioning is *stimulus generalization*. If the dog responds to a signal of a certain tone, then it will also tend to respond to some extent to a signal of similar tone.

Dogs can be taught to make discriminating responses by presenting one tone in association with the natural stimulus of food and another without such support. If the two stimuli become more similar than the dog's perceptual capacity can discriminate, then the dog may develop behaviour analogous to that of a human being caught in a neurotic conflict situation where the factors requiring discrimination are beyond his psychological capacity. For example, if the dog had to respond to a circular but not to a flattish elliptical shape, there would be a point where it would be highly uncertain whether intermediate shapes were circles or ellipses. One recalls the Gilbertian nightmare with its 'elliptical billiard balls'.

Experiments on conditioning, or something near to it, have been done with small groups of babies under six months of age. The experimenter (Hanuš Papoušek) began with the fact that the babies would turn their heads left or right in response to the stimulus of milk from a bottle. By the conditioning processes described above the babies could be made (a) to turn their heads in response to a bell or buzzer, (b) to lose this conditioned response by extinction and then reacquire it, (c) to respond to the buzzer but not the bell, and (d) to reverse this pattern, responding to the bell but not the buzzer. The number of trials necessary to reach a specified criterion of head-turning was 177 for three-week-olds, 42 for three-month-olds, and 28 for five-month-olds, with wide individual variation at the lowest age and less at the highest. The average time taken to respond to the signal (response latency) dropped from 4·95 to 3·92 to 3·55 seconds, but, with this measure, variability of individual response increased rather than diminished with age. These experiments perhaps illustrate effects intermediate between conditioning and the next form of learning, for head-turning itself is presumably a partly learned response.

There are two important points about signal learning or conditioning. One is that it is a fairly abstract conception even in relation to animals, a laboratory conception that views the organism in relation to a tightly contrived situation and to limited physiological mechanisms. The animal is not studied in its natural free-ranging habitat. This does not invalidate the concept of conditioning, but it limits its scope. The other point is that there are few human situations in which one can see or operate on intrinsic stimulus-response patterns, for these are normally completely overlaid by learned behaviour. The teacher is concerned with how the patterns of learned behaviour that present themselves can be developed or changed into whatever new learned patterns he wishes to induce. Only in earliest infancy are there responses like breathing, crying, sucking or grasping which are intrinsic, and even these are rapidly shaped by environmental pressures.

Possibly the alarm responses of the autonomic nervous system might be considered a natural response system which could be controlled by conditioning techniques. These are the responses like increased heart beat, flushing or pallor, sweating, tremor, etc. that may accompany states of fear or anger. But these too work in harness with the conscious and intellectual aspects of behaviour, which, of course, are shaped by complex learning processes rather than conditioning. It seems, therefore, that signal learning or conditioning does enter genuinely—particularly in earliest infancy—into human modifiability, but does not illumine subsequent learning very much. Gagné quotes as examples of signal learning human responses to automobile horns, alarm clocks and teachers clapping their hands (to gain attention), but these seem to be signals in a much more complex sense than Pavlovian conditioning. They involve representational significance and are intellectually controlled rather than automatic responses.

(2) *Stimulus-response* learning is the name Gagné uses for what has also been called trial-and-error, operant or instrumental learning, or operant conditioning. He has some difficulty in distinguishing this from his type (3) learning, *chaining*, for the former—the single

stimulus-response connection—is more usually one element in a chain of such connections, as when a driver starts his car and drives off. He suggests as an example of simple stimulus-response learning a baby learning to discriminate the various visual and muscular cues that lead it to the capacity for holding a bottle and feeding from it, but the baby, were he unusually sophisticated psychologically, might consider this as much an example of chaining as the learner driver attempting to get his car moving.

The main condition suggested for stimulus-response learning is quick and repeated *reinforcement* or reward of the desired response to the stimulus, with non-reinforcement of unwanted responses. Whether the response generalizes to associated stimuli depends on how demanding the task and the pattern of reinforcement are. An infant might be induced to imitate an adult's 'please' by the visual promise of a biscuit. The 'please' response would be reinforced by getting the biscuit and might generalize to other food stimuli. A messily inclined schoolboy might be induced to write neatly by a teacher who sympathetically but firmly controlled the circumstances in which the boy gained her favour. The neat response might not generalize to work for another teacher unless she sustained the same tight reinforcement programme. Whether the response becomes extinguished depends on how often it is allowed to recur without being reinforced. Pavlovian conditioning refers strictly to the manipulation of intrinsic stimulus-response connections, whereas instrumental learning can make use of learned behaviour patterns ('free operants', as they have been called) to develop new patterns by differential reinforcement.

Animals may learn a particular response most quickly if they are rewarded for every correct response—typically, some food every time they press a lever. But, since such responses may disappear rather rapidly if the reinforcement stops, experimenters have studied various schedules of reinforcement that might sustain the learned response even with only occasional reward. Possible patterns include rewarding every *n*th correct response (*ratio reinforcement*), or giving reinforcement every *n*th minute regardless of the number of correct responses (*interval reinforcement*). Ratio reinforcement appears to give both a high rate of responding and high resistance to extinction of the response.

Gagné's examples of the chaining of stimulus-response connections include buttoning, fastening, using a pencil, catching balls, etc. —any simple instrumental sequence which is non-verbal, even if verbal cues may occur incidentally as part of the performance. Green (1962) describes chaining thus—'the organism is taught to produce, by means of his own action, discriminative stimuli which, in turn, evoke other behaviours on his part that eventually lead to reinforcement.' Chaining obviously requires prompting or cueing of the learner to get a series of responses correctly performed in the right order, and in sufficiently rapid sequence to make a smooth performance which is reinforced by attaining its implicit goal. The child begins by wobbling about on his new bicycle, gradually gains steadier control and eventually reaches the casual (if sometimes misplaced) arrogance of 'look at me—no hands!'.

(4) *Verbal association* learning refers to learning names of things, or verbal sequences (poetry, verbal formulae, etc.), or word correspondences between languages (*donner*, to give). The learner must be able to discriminate among the words and among things they refer to. Some simple verbal learning may be defective because children have not discriminated the word clearly, or not had distinct experience of what it refers to. Immediate memory for material that has not been previously learned is quite limited. Not more than about seven new words can be apprehended at one go. The beginnings and ends of verbal chains seem to be more memorable. In the process of recall units within the chain may interfere with one another. This effect is more marked the longer the chain. A person took one look at the nonsense syllables *muh, ick, huc, kuc, sar, gor, reg* and immediately reproduced them from memory as *muh, ick, reg, gar*. The use of mnemonics is an attempt to code words in a way that will make them and their order more memorable. (Number of flats per musical key, from one to seven: Battle Ends And Down Goes Charles's Father. And for the sharps, of course: Father Charles Goes Down And Ends Battle.)

These simpler forms of learning—signal learning (in the special sense of respondent conditioning), stimulus-response or instrumental learning, chaining and verbal association learning—have been studied extensively in psychological laboratories. They are associated with connectionist theories of learning, for they concentrate on the idea of stimulus-response connections in any organism (from earthworm to human being) and the dependence of more complex learning on the establishment and manipulative shaping of simpler elements in the stimulus-response hierarchy. Some connectionists have elaborated quite complex learning laws which are meant to accord with the evidence of laboratory experiments. Others, notably Skinner, have shunned connectionist theory but, unlike the theorists, made considerable claims for the relevance of connectionist experiments to human education. The connectionist language of 'reinforcement', 'extinction' and 'shaping' has crept into quite ordinary educational discourse. It seems important, therefore, to look carefully at this way of thinking.

Reinforcement, insight, or knowledge of results (KR)?

The central concept of reinforcement has stimulated much controversy. Although it is convenient to use it synonymously with reward, the meanings are not strictly the same. 'Reinforcement' is meant to oust mentalistic reference in favour of a purely behavioural analysis, whereas 'reward' is typically used in contexts that are mentalistic and assume conscious awareness of what a reward is. Even on a behaviouristic analysis, reinforcement theory has to accommodate the fact that there is human verbal behaviour which apparently analyses itself and theorizes about itself—a phenomenon not manifest in animals. Reinforcement, in strict behavioural terms, is simply increase in the rate or intensity of a particular response following the presentation of a certain stimulus or set of stimuli. It is a factual report of the existence of that particular kind of association, not an explanation of why it exists. It excludes reference to feelings, whereas reward typically refers to feelings and values in some sense.

The idea of reinforcement is connected historically with Thorndike's law of effect—the idea that learned behaviour is learned because it satisfies a basic need in some sense. This law is surrounded with problems. So long as one is shaping behaviour in a hungry animal by the use of food as a reinforcer, the process seems to have a biological and automatic basis, but animals to some extent, and humans to a vastly greater extent, also *acquire* various needs or drives. One dog might be accustomed to being taken for regular walks and be ready to learn various pieces of behaviour (carrying its master's stick, its mistress's basket) which it was trained to regard as conditions of continued walks. Another dog might be accustomed to sprawling most of the time on the hearth and have less basis for acquiring extra tricks.

And, if people are taken as examples, most of their learning depends on the satisfaction of acquired needs, for biological survival alone requires less effort than most people expend on miscellaneous learning. Needs and satisfactions are not basic objective biological phenomena, but highly relative to a vast range of differing circumstances and evaluations of life. Even in the most desperate circumstances imaginable (stories of prison camps, shipwrecks, etc.), where people are more dominated by primitive necessities, individuals still vary between less and more primitive responses.

These limitations to the significance of primary reinforcers, like food, sex or pain-avoidance, turned attention to the idea of secondary reinforcement. The infant who looks contented and settled when fed gradually generalizes his responses of amiability to the other stimuli in the environment—from the bottle or breast to the mother as a person, from her to the other members of the family, from them to the whole physical atmosphere of the home and to visitors and eventually people and things outside. The responses originally reinforced by a narrow range of stimuli (milk from a sucked nipple) come to be reinforced by a wider range of secondary reinforcing stimuli. And, of course, the responses too are generalized—from sucking to snuggling and smiling, from keeping with mother to exploring the environment and growing to accept other people as mother-substitutes, and so on by more subtle steps than can be outlined here.

The trouble about secondary reinforcement is that it is too wide a concept to have very specific meaning. Anything almost might acquire secondary reinforcing power. One paradoxical example was of a couple of children gleefully shouting, 'Oh, please smack me harder' because the smacking was part of a silly game that amused them very much. Similar if less amusing paradoxes are exemplified where people are reinforced by living conditions which are 'home' to them but which others might consider intolerable. It seems, therefore, that the attempt to understand reinforcement or the law of effect in a wider, apparently more meaningful, sense ends up with the notion that almost any stimuli may be found rewarding in some circumstances and may make some people respond more often or intensely.

Various experiments have been conducted to investigate the effect on learning of offering no reinforcement or reward, or of punishing performance rather than rewarding it. Rats will explore a maze, just as people sometimes nose into novel situations, even if there is no obvious reward such as food. They might be considered to be learning without specific reward. Rats that have had some exploratory sessions in a maze may solve it more quickly, when eventually a food reward is put at the end of the maze, than rats that have had no exploratory experience. And in some human learning experiments performance has been slightly improved when the 'reward' of a mild electric shock was given for success. It has proved difficult to reach definite conclusions from such experiments. Improved performance in the presence of 'punishment' appears to be a very limited effect. Improved performance following exploratory behaviour may indicate that learning to some extent takes place without reward, but that performance of the complete learning behaviour is evoked only in a rewarding situation.

Experiments on verbal conditioning have been conducted to find out whether certain classes of response can be evoked more often by subtle reinforcement. For example, a person might be asked to say as many different words as he could think of. Unknown to the subject, the experimenter would give a nod or murmur of approval for certain kinds of word (let us say plurals, or abstract nouns) but not for those that did not come into the selected category. He would follow this pattern for the first half of the experimental period, but, in the second half, stop expressing approval for anything. The question is whether the subject, although unaware of this plan, tends to increase his rate of utterance of the selected category in the first half and then diminish it when the marginal reinforcement is removed in the second half.

The answer is that such a pattern does often, but not always, emerge. Interpretation of the results is difficult, for, if the subject is not to become aware that the experimenter is trying to condition him, the reinforcement must be unobtrusive and, therefore, possibly rather weak. If the reinforcement is more definite, the subject becomes aware of it and is influenced not by conditioning but by knowledge of what is going on. In human teaching situations the practice of marginal reinforcement (encouragement) is common. It seems likely that there are all degrees of awareness or unawareness of such processes. The younger or less sophisticated learner may have little or no awareness that his learning is being shaped in such ways, whereas the older or more sophisticated learner may be influenced but also know that he is being influenced. The success or failure of marginal reinforcement is extensively illustrated in advertising. Presumably advertisers live in the hope that the high rate of responding to seductive women will generalize to the impressive range of products with which they are visually associated.

Annett (1969) stresses the importance of information, or knowledge of results (KR), rather than reinforcement, in achieving learning. He argues that stimuli that would normally be thought of as rewarding or punishing do not always have the expected effects. If the concept of reinforcement is broadened to include secondary reinforcement or what Thorndike called the 'O.K. reaction', then the basic nature of the concept is changed and comes closer to KR. If a reinforcer is defined as something that reinforces, that is, increases the rate of a response, then this is a circular definition, with no independent anchorage. If learning means *any* systematic change in behaviour, there is no clear criterion of what is to count as systematic change. If learning means, more precisely, a change towards some pattern that has been previously specified (so that one has an independent test of whether or not learning takes place), then the learner's knowledge of the criterion to be satisfied, and of the results of his own learning endeavour, can be seen in their full logical importance. The reinforcement principle, in Annett's view, is too limited a principle to account for the transformations of behaviour involved in learning. KR can embrace a wide variety of transformation rules and give a better account of learning. It allows for the differing amounts and kinds of information that determine the great variety of kinds of learning.

'Knowledge' is, of course, an example of the mentalistic language which tends to make connectionists see red. It might be thought that KR was regressive from a connectionist viewpoint. In fact, it is doubtful whether the proponents of KR are particularly worried by the use of traditional language, provided that it is more sharply defined in terms of their theories of information. These tend to be highly technical, but one of the main ones is the idea of reducing the statistical probability of an unwanted response. Suppose that one colour was to be chosen as the central theme of a pageant and the choice was among red, orange, yellow, green, blue, indigo and violet (ROYGBIV—the colours of the spectrum). You have to buy a new dress or shirt before the official decision is finally made. You have to guess which colour will be chosen, with only one chance of being right and six of being wrong. How might one piece of information almost eliminate the six chances of predicting wrongly and buying the wrong colour of dress or shirt? Perhaps the information that it was a Communist pageant? Or a Primrose League pageant? Or an orange growers' pageant?

Teachers questioning their classes often illustrate the process of reducing the statistical chances of unwanted responses—sometimes rather laboriously.

What's the population of Britain?
Please miss, about thirty million?
No, much more than that.
Please miss, a hundred million?
No, now you're going too far the other way.
Please miss, fifty-five million?
Yes, it's about fifty-five million.

Who can tell me about Shakespeare?
Sir, there's a Shakespeare Café in the High Street.
Yes, but this is not a lesson on cafés, is it?
Sir, he was the author of Romeo and Juliet.
Yes, and what is Romeo and Juliet?
Please sir, it's a film. I saw it on television.
Yes, but what was it before it was a film?

'The two women were tired.' Come and write the French on the
    board, Jennifer.
Les deux femmes était fatigué.
Not quite right. Remember, there were two women.

Les deux femmes étaient fatigués.
That's better. But what do you do to the adjective when it refers to
  something feminine?
Les deux femmes étaient fatiguées.
Good. Does everyone else agree with that?

Some aspects of KR are of wide interest and importance in various
forms of communication, including teaching. There are analogies
between some of the features of telecommunication (which has
particularly influenced the development of information theory) and
of ordinary human communication. How many pieces of information
or messages can one send in given circumstances and in a given time?
How important is it to supply more than the minimum information
that is logically necessary (what is called technically 'redundancy'),
as when one says, 'Well, I'll see you at the GPO at seven. All right?
Tonight on the stroke of seven at the post office.' How far can one
curtail a message without loss of information? 'Post office. Seven.
O.K.?' (You did mean the GPO? Seven in the evening? Today?)
  How can one orient people to the objective context, as in wrong
telephone dialling? (Mr Smith? No, this is Mr Jones, you must have
the wrong number. Is that not Smith the dog-catcher? No, you've got
the wrong number. But that was the number they gave me. . . .) What
makes a message stand out even among the so-called 'noise' of similar
surrounding stimuli? A mention of one's own name or interests
catches the attention, despite obtrusive rival stimuli. On the other
hand, there may be difficulty in picking out the particular Mr Smith
one is seeking in the telephone directory because of the visual 'noise'
of so many neighbouring Smiths. A school pupil may be so bom-
barded with information that it becomes all 'noise' and no 'message'.
Learning has to do with improving the ratio of message to noise.
  The KR viewpoint cursorily outlined above is more of a cognitive
theory of learning. If it has connectionist affinities, it is with the kind
of information-transmitting connections that interest telecommunication engineers rather than with the stimulus-response connectionism
that has interested so many experimental psychologists. However,
psychologists have not been completely swept away by connectionism. In the words of Broadbent (1961), 'The study of behaviour has
forced us to realize that even for animals a simple rule like the Law
of Effect will not wholly serve. Our thories must be more complicated.
. . .' And Talland (1968), criticizing the idea of explaining learning
purely in terms of mechanical connections, writes, 'Learning is manifested as much in the capacity to vary behaviour in accordance with
the situation as in the capacity to reproduce it.'
  The Gestalt and later cognitive theorists stressed the fact that some

learning seemed to be rapid and intuitive rather than slowly and mechanically acquired by practice and reward, and that learned performances were often modified for new circumstances rather than reeled off as an automatic product of past experience. Even Thorndike's cats, faced with the problem of learning how to unlatch a cage and get out of it, would begin with somewhat but not entirely random movements. Rats, as has been mentioned, may have no mental picture of the maze they explore, but they sometimes behave *as if* they did. Rats which have learned to run a maze may still reach the food box if the maze is flooded and they have to swim, using a different set of muscular responses from those used during initial learning. Apes may suddenly learn to fix two shorter sticks together to reach some food outside their cage beyond the reach of a single stick. Children and adults sometimes see all at once how to solve a problem —the now-I've-got-it reaction.

Because people have feelings of intuitively learning how to do things there is a strong temptation to erect these feelings into a theory of learning, but there are problems about this theory too. The connectionists would object to using any explanatory terms (intuition, cognitive map, insight, etc.) that would, in their view, reinstate speculative, unsubstantiated, mentalistic terminology. They may argue that sudden learning is not really sudden at all. The final performance may appear suddenly but often there has been a great deal of prior experience and practice, which has only to generalize to the new learning situation to give the appearance of miraculous insight. Similarly, adaptations of learned performance could be accounted for in terms of stimulus and response generalization, these convenient connectionist mechanisms.

Although connectionists are so hostile to 'internal' mentalistic concepts, they have to struggle with the fact that many behavioural connections are covert, to say the least. One may treat verbal behaviour as just one category of overt behaviour alongside the rest, but what goes on in the physiological 'black box' when the connections disappear from sight? This problem has generated a complex field of discussion about *mediation responses*, internal or fractional responses of one sort or another that are supposed to link the grosser, manifest responses. For example, the final overt response (the goal response) of a maze-running animal is to eat the food in the box at the end of the maze. This eating response will tend to spread to the whole food box situation. If there is no food the animal obviously cannot eat it, but it might, if accustomed to a food reward in the past, salivate, or poke about in the box, or lick it—in other words, emit *part* of the goal response. Similarly, if the animal were running the maze and had almost but not quite reached the food box, it might emit part of the goal response—just as a person might brighten up and lick his lips as he approached his favourite restaurant. This partial response has been called the *fractional anticipatory goal response*, or the fractional antedating goal reaction, or, for brief, r_G (little Argy!).

Such fractional responses can be thought of as reinforcing intermediate stages of a learned performance, linking a long sequence of learned behaviour, even though the major reinforcement may come at the end. A rat might explore a foodless maze, reinforced by the fractional goal responses left over from an earlier rewarded occasion. A person might drift in the direction of his favourite restaurant and drool over the menu in the window, even although the restaurant was shut or the prices had been raised beyond his purse.

Another group of mediating responses that has been suggested is that of *observing responses*—responses like staring or pricking up one's ears which alter the pattern of stimulation received. Among observing responses there is an important kind known as *learning sets*. A learning set is an acquired readiness to observe certain features of a situation which facilitate the solution of a whole class of problems. For example, the problem might be to choose one of two objects, A or B, and get a reward for the correct choice. The guesser does not know the principle on which the reward is given and the objects are switched between left and right positions from one trial to the next. The guesser may think that the reward depends on position (left always rewarded or right always rewarded). If he scores one success he may still make a different choice next time on the grounds that the reward may be switched from trial to trial. In fact, the operative principle is that exactly the same object (let us say B) is rewarded every time, regardless of position. Monkeys or people, with varying speed, may acquire the set for that class of problems and solve all similar problems speedily.

Mediation processes have received much attention in connection with all aspects of verbal learning. For example, Osgood's *semantic differential* analysis purports to place the affective or emotional meanings of words in relation to a small number of semantic dimensions—(1) an 'evaluative' dimension, including such contrasts as good-bad, beautiful-ugly, happy-sad, (2) a 'potency' dimension indicating the intensity of a meaning, as in big-little, strong-weak, or high-low, and (3) an 'activity' dimension indicating contrasts like fast-slow, young-old, alive-dead.

One might take a concept like 'mother' and ask people from different countries to say how the concept is associated in their minds with a given set of seven-point adjectival scales. Does the concept suggest Extremely Good, Quite Good, Slightly Good, Equally Good or Bad or Neither, Slightly Bad, Quite Bad or Extremely Bad? The concept is rated on other adjectival scales and a similar process followed for a series of other concepts (house, girl, picture, meat, etc.). At the end one has a large number of ratings of concepts by people from different cultures. The ratings are analysed statistically and it is claimed that they fit into a three-dimensional affective pattern of Evaluation, Potency and Activity, as exemplified in the last paragraph.

Osgood's speculative idea is that there could be a semantic space analogous to physical space. Just as objects, however diverse, can be partly defined in terms of common dimensions of length, breadth or weight, so concepts are imagined to be defined, at least in their affective or emotional side, by Osgood's semantic dimensions. One could, by a further speculative leap, imagine this semantic space as a mediation space, represented physiologically by detailed stimulus-response connections corresponding to what the layman might call simply the use and meanings of language. 'Meaning' might become 'statistical pattern of observed responses'. It is not possible here to go into the complexities of this kind of analysis, but it has an interesting if challengeable character.

Much more can be said about the allegedly basic patterns of learning and the learning theories based on them, but, before attempting to set these in a general summary perspective, it is convenient to look at Gagné's four stages of complex learning—multiple discrimination, concept learning, principle learning and problem solving.

More complex varieties of learning

The four simpler forms of learning have to do with acquiring stimulus-response connections and stringing these together in simple chains. *Multiple discrimination* refers to learning in which a series of associated but different responses are made depending on a series of associated but different stimuli. The stimuli *through, bough, trough, bought, tough* and *dough* are visually similar because of the common *-ough*, but different because of the associated letters. The English speaker has to learn to pronounce these *-ough*s in six different ways. *Concept formation* refers to learning in which the same response is attached to a series of superficially different stimuli. It is easy to conjure up the great variety of very different stimuli that may shelter under common concepts like 'home', 'mother', 'school', etc.

The main problem about discrimination learning is probably the degree of similarity among the things to be discriminated—a problem that stands out in psychological experiments as much as it does in common-sense experience. For any discrimination it is necessary to have acquired the stimulus-response chain corresponding to each element in the task—in ordinary language, to know thoroughly the things that have to be discriminated. The next requirement is to practise choosing the appropriate response in situations where the pattern of stimuli requires discrimination. Two features of the practice would be (1) noting cues that facilitate the required discrimination (traffic signs with red circles are mandatory; with red triangles, advisory) and (2) varying the order of discriminations required (three *plus* three? three *times* three? three *divided by* three? three *times* three? three *plus* three? etc.). The more similar the features to be discriminated the more practice is necessary.

Discrimination learning, like chain learning, seems to be characterized by considerable forgetting immediately after the learning, followed by a slower rate of further forgetting thereafter. This means that learning has to be reviewed at intervals if it is to be sustained. However, it seems that, once discriminations have been well learned, they are remembered equally well whether they are gross or fine in character. The non-reinforcement or non-confirmation of incorrect responses seems to be associated with extinction of the correct as well as the incorrect response, and the correct response may have to be relearned.

Is is hardly necessary to illustrate the relevance of discrimination learning to teachers, for so much of what they are trying to induce is just this—the power to discriminate. Although the principles of such learning are, after a fashion, matters of common-sense, it is a common sense that is as conspicuously neglected as observed. It is difficult to face up to the instability of learned discriminations at every level of sophistication. The graduate teacher is one with the primary school pupil in his reluctance to learn more discriminations than serve the immediate purpose and are supported by well-established prior learning. Simply to 'make the learning more interesting', while sensible enough truistic advice up to a point, does not radically alter the point being made here. Even with 'interest' it takes time to establish the prior 'chains' on which discrimination learning depends; and it takes systematic practice and review to sustain the discriminations themselves. Understandable reactions to external pressures (examinations, for example) and to the tedium of even 'interesting' practice tempt the teacher to press his pupils on to more demanding discriminations before the less demanding are really secured. There is no general answer to the problem. One can only be aware of it. Learning is hard and forgetting easy.

Given that the task is made as interesting as possible, that necessary prior learning has been secured (even if one considers it some other teacher's responsibility!), and that there is provision for regular review or practice of the new learning, the main remaining requisite is to have a systematic analysis of the steps, from grosser to finer, in the new learning and to explore the cues that may help learners to perceive and remember the differences they are supposed to see. Again there may be a temptation to regard this as insultingly obvious, but it is so difficult to do that the current emphasis is on prepared curriculum programmes and programmed learning—just as it traditionally has been on the textbook—rather than on the possibility of an individual teacher *by himself* working out the necessary steps. It remains that any textbook or programme is partly what the teacher makes of it. The individual teacher knows his own pupils and can explore and exploit the cues and sequences that seem to help them most in discrimination learning.

Concept learning is complementary to discrimination learning. It involves learning to ignore differences and see similarity. Monkeys can learn to respond to the *odd* stimulus in a series of problems and could be said to acquire the concept of *odd*, although their learning cannot benefit from the ancillary guidance of language as with human learning. With humans the word 'odd' can be used to emphasize the feature to be noticed and this is just one instance of the whole complex use of language for similar acts of guiding attention. Suppose one presented a young child with (1) two red balls and a white one, (2) two cubes and a sphere, (3) two long rods and a short one, and so on, and rewarded him for choosing the odd article each time. He might form various hypotheses about the secret of success before getting the concept *odd*, but thereafter he would always know which object to choose (provided no subtle tricks were introduced).

The Kendlers (1961) rewarded children (with marbles) for learning to choose the larger of two squares (or alternatively, for choosing a black square rather than a white). Once that learning was achieved they reversed the principle of reward, so that the smaller or the white square was correct. Seven-year-olds could achieve this reversal learning in an average of eight trials, whereas four-year-olds required twenty-three—a striking illustration of difference in conceptual development. Teachers know how children even of the same age vary in the facility with which they acquire new concepts. Conceptual learning differs from earlier forms in that continued practice seems to be less important. The learner's efforts must be rewarded, but once he has grasped the concept its relevance can be seen at once in similar problems.

Gagné says that 'the effect of concept learning is to free the individual from control by specific stimuli'. Typically a word is used to refer to selected properties of relevant stimuli, so that these properties are spotlighted and attended to rather than features of the stimuli that constitute no part of the properties. An 'edge' is a ruler edge, a mountain edge, a river edge, a handkerchief edge, the edge of one's patience, an edge of disaster, etc. Psychological accounts of concept learning have to confront the logical aspect of concepts. A concept does not just exist—it is a logical specification relative to some purpose. One would expect that concept learning has to do partly with the differing purposes that are assumed. A mathematical concept may be highly relevant to the teacher's purpose for his pupil, but it may not be grasped strongly if the pupil does not share the purpose. Concept learning might, therefore, on its practical psychological side, be a matter of persuading people to share one's purposes as much as doing a piece of knitting with learning chains. But perhaps such persuasion too is based on chaining.

Principle learning is type 7 in Gagné's hierarchy. It refers to learning relationships among concepts and is achieved by verbal guidance or direction of attention to the significance of the concepts involved together with experience in concrete terms of their interrelations. A principle is not really learned if the learner can only recite it verbally without being able to do the right things about it. The class may chant rules of grammar and write ungrammatically, copy out scientific laws and cook their experiments to match them, memorize theorems or literary appraisals and be inept at solving mathematical problems or exercising literary discrimination. Principle learning, therefore, seems to be close kin to Gagné's final type 8 learning, problem solving. At any rate, problem solving seems to be the test of principle learning.

As with discrimination learning, it may seem too easy to pillory the shortcomings of actual practices in relation to principle learning. The shortcomings may be associated with the sheer extent and power of human symbolizing capacity, relatively independently of concrete experience. If one considers the intellectual power of logical and mathematical analysis, of theoretical and imaginative thinking, it is not so surprising that principle learning should be apt to become detached from the solution of specific problems. The virtue of theory and imagination, if logically disciplined, is that they exempt one from the absolute necessity of testing out *every* phenomenon by personal experience. One need test out only a selection of the phenomena most critical for the principle under consideration. Science, like the arts, proceeds by leaps and bounds as well as by detailed analysis and empirical check.

The suggestion about a possible reason why principle learning in fact sometimes degenerates into formula learning does not, of course, justify the latter. But there is an unavoidable tension between the policy of rooting everything firmly in experience and the policy of leaping from principle to principle. The former ensures that you know where you stand, but may leave you standing. The latter invites you to try for the higher peaks, with the incidental risk of ending up lost in outer space. To express this in mundane terms, principle learning, it is suggested, requires a constant two-way didactic movement—from study of the concepts and the specific evidence that links them to the general principle that sums them up, and from the summary principle as a guiding light back to the specific problems and concepts that it illumines. One requires both—to see the light and to be able to manipulate the electric circuit. The tensions of the two processes are as clearly illustrated in people training to be teachers as anywhere.

Type 8 learning, *problem solving*, is given its own category partly because solving a problem typically involves concurrent learning of a higher order principle. It requires the use of lower order principles in relation to a new situation which cannot be handled by means of a single principle. Gagné refers to experiments by Katona (1940) in which the least effective learning method was to be shown how to do a series of problems, a much more effective method was to be instructed in a relevant verbal principle, and the most effective of all was to be shown changes that would be brought about by using a principle without having the principle explicitly stated. Even with sophisticated learners it may be necessary to recall relevant principles, or to direct attention to particular features of the problem, before the learner is able to find the solution. Discovery learning without such aids is unusual.

Although Gagné distinguishes concept learning and problem solving, experimental work by Bruner and others shows how problematical concept learning may be. They made use of cards with geometric shapes, but it may facilitate comprehension if the problem is converted into slightly more representational terms as follows.

Suppose that each of a set of cards carries a picture of either a Man or a Woman, and that the man or woman looks either Beautiful or Ugly, and either Old or Young.

| Man | Beautiful | Old |
| Woman | Ugly | Young |

One could form different sets of cards consisting of all the men, all the women, all the beautiful or all of any other *single* category. Or one could form a set based on any *pair* of categories, such as all the ugly women, all the beautiful old, or all the young men. Or one could form a set based on any *trio* of categories, such as all the beautiful young men or all the ugly old women. There are, in fact, 6 possible single category concepts, 12 double category, and 8 treble category—26 in all. The game can now begin.

The experimenter shows the subject a card with, let us say, a *Beautiful Old Woman* on it. This is an example of the concept he has in mind and he invites the subject to select another card illustrating the same concept. Now the concept might be *Beautiful Old Woman*, in which case the subject would be correct only if he picked up a *Beautiful Old Woman* card. But, since the card is only an example of the concept the experimenter has in mind, the concept might be one of six more:

1 Beautiful Women   4 Old
2 Old Women   5 Beautiful
3 Old and Beautiful   6 Women

Suppose that the subject, to cut down the range of possibilities, chooses a *Beautiful Old Man* card and is told that this too is an example of the concept. He can now eliminate concepts (1), (2) and (6). The concept must be (3) *Old and Beautiful*, or (4) *Old* or (5) *Beautiful*. If the subject now offers either a *Beautiful Young Woman* card (eliminating (3) *Old and Beautiful* and (4) *Old*), or an *Ugly Old Man* card (eliminating (3) *Old and Beautiful* and (5) *Beautiful*), then a positive response from the experimenter means that he has reached the concept. In the first case it must be *Beautiful*, in the second *Old*.

This reasoning has been called *simultaneous scanning*. It is effective but very difficult, for the reasoner has to try to keep all of the possibilities in mind. An easier strategy is that of *successive scanning*, for the reasoner tests only one hypothesis at a time. In the example above, given *Beautiful Old Woman* and *Beautiful Old Man*, the subject goes on to test whether the concept is *Old* or *Beautiful* by looking for positive instances of these concepts. The superiority in principle of the simultaneous scanner lies in the fact that he tests negative as well as positive possibilities with his choice of *Beautiful Young Woman* or *Ugly Old Man*.

A third strategy, *conservative focusing*, finds one positive instance of the concept and then changes one attribute at a time of that example until the concept is identified. Thus, if the concept was *Old*, the conservative focuser would offer *Beautiful Young Man* to test the relevance of *Beautiful* and then *Ugly Old Man* to test the relevance of *Old*. The fourth strategy, *focus gambling*, consists in focusing on a positive instance of the concept but subsequently varying more than one attribute at a time. In the example, after *Beautiful Old Man* the focus gambler might offer *Ugly Young Woman*. Focus gambling is a great temptation for most people. There is a chance, however small, of being lucky and one is saved the bother of thinking.

Anyone who finds this level of problem solving too difficult can relax with a nice traditional problem like that of the three missionaries and three cannibals who had to cross a river, using only a canoe that held two people, and ensuring that at no point in the proceedings was a missionary alone with more than one cannibal. Or they may prefer the problem with the glass of wine and the glass of water. You take a spoonful of wine and put it into the water and then a spoonful of the mixture and put it back into the wine. Is there more wine in the water, or water in the wine, or are they equal? And why?

Perspective on learning and learning theory

Three possible learning mechanisms have received particular attention in the preceding discussion—(1) the stimulus-response connection and its derivatives, (2) perceptual or cognitive insight, and (3) servo-mechanical or 'information' circuits. None of these matches all learning phenomena. The last is not a mechanism in a physiological or perhaps even biological sense. It is rather a logical analogy with machines—a machine model. It has the virtue of encouraging detailed analytic attention to the cognitive aspect of learning and to the variety of ways in which the human 'machine' can transform its 'input'. It could be that the brain is a servo-mechanism in some strict sense, but that has hardly been shown yet.

The mechanism of 'insight' learning or 'cognitive field perception' purports to be based on the intrinsic perceptual capacities of organisms—the tendencies of men and animals to perceive patterns rather than dissociated stimuli; to respond to the relative differences between stimuli (the bigger one, the smaller one, the brighter one, etc.) rather than to absolute size or intensity; to read sense and significance into stimuli that may be incomplete (.ngl.d); to build up 'maps in the head', like the rat in the foodless maze. A rat trained to respond differentially to dark horizontal and vertical rectangles will accept as substitute stimuli two dark circles set horizontally or vertically beside one another. A chimpanzee trained to respond to a white triangle on a dark square will generalize his response to a dark triangle on a white square. These exercises in perceptual organization and relativity appeal rather strongly to the (non-behaviourist) human being because they fit in with his own *feelings* about at least some learning. Although cognitive theorists are as lacking in detailed physiological evidence as anyone else, their emphasis on the organism's typical perceptual patterning has its merits. Connectionists, however, would feel that there is a failure to get down to the grass roots in the form of detailed connections and laws.

The connectionist is most concerned to repudiate any mentalistic anchorage for his theories, and substitute a physiological one. The stimulus-response connection is his basic mechanism. So long as stimulus and response are highly observable ('there's the bull; there's the hiker running hell for leather') the S-R connection is invitingly plausible. It is not too difficult either to get used to the idea that verbal behaviour is still *behaviour*, or that a person can both generate speech stimuli and respond to them ('Damme! I *will* go and have a pint!'). The problems begin at the next stage, where the S-Rs subside right inside the organism's black box. The husband at the breakfast table apparently emitting no stimuli whatsoever, or emitting only typical breakfast-table stimuli, may find a marginal internal S-R connection 'lighting up' which results in his turning up at the pub *twelve hours later*. Or, as one would say in mentalistic terms, he decides privately at breakfast time that he'll go to the pub that evening!

Although connectionist theory has been characterized in a general way in this chapter, and some of its particular problems discussed in more detail, no account has been given of the elaborate specific theories developed by people like Hull, Spence or Estes, for these are a study on their own. What can be said is that such theorists attempt to explain animal and human learning experiments in more detail than the cognitive theorists. They also tend to be concerned with— one is sometimes tempted to say obsessed by—scientific respectability, despite the restricted range of the phenomena they aim to explain, the limited practical and intellectual force of what is counted as 'explanation', and the paradoxical eschewing of mentalistic concepts combined with embracing speculative physiological or 'mediation' concepts.

The interest of connectionism, even for those who have not been converted to this particular religion, lies in its recognition that behaviour must be studied in its intricate detail if it is to be completely understood. Causes do not operate across space and time (or, worse still, out of space and time). There must be links. The concepts of S-R connection, reinforcement, generalization, discrimination and mediation represent some of the connectionist's main points of attack. The criticisms that were made earlier of some of these concepts do not demolish the entire system. There are considerable gaps between connectionist evidence and connectionist concepts, and between these and human learning problems. Nevertheless, some connectionist findings match some ordinary experience of human learning. There are at least similarities by analogy in fields like discrimination learning and concept formation.

In terms of learning mechanisms and associated learning theories it is, as was admitted at the start, tempting to fall in with the sentiment expressed by Estes (1960) in the statement 'No convergence is imminent between the educator's and the laboratory scientist's approaches to learning'. Much depends on the meaning of 'convergence'. Educators' and psychologists' purposes cannot converge; they are different by definition, not just by chance. But they share an interest in the ways behaviour is or can be shaped. It would be obscurantist for an educator to refuse even to consider the possible micro-mechanisms of learning. It would be obscurantist for the psychological 'laboratory scientist' to be satisfied with a set of speculative concepts that 'explained' some laboratory experiments but showed little promise of connecting with animals in their ethological setting, let alone humans in theirs.

On the question of evolutionary continuity it seems more important to study specific similarities and differences between men and animals rather than whether to call men animals. It is interesting that many aspects of human perception and discrimination can be matched, in simpler forms, in animal learning experiments, and that some animals have a certain capacity for problem solving and forming practical concepts (like the monkeys trained to choose the *odd* object; or the others trained to accept token rewards which could be exchanged, as with money, for consumable rewards). It remains that human intellectual powers are vastly greater and include the distinctive power of language, which constantly facilitates learning and problem solving, quite apart from any other functions. When humans behave 'like animals', their behaviour is often not really like animals' at all.

Gagné, whose eight varieties of learning have been used as part of the framework of this chapter, was more concerned to identify kinds of learning and their conditions of occurrence than to enter into disputes about learning theory. He calls learning 'a change in human disposition or capability, which can be retained, and which is not simply ascribable to the process of growth'. He recognizes the importance for humans of motivation, persuasion and the establishment of attitudes and values, as well as the acquisition of skills and knowledge. His hierarchy of learning is suggestive both of the dependence of complex learning on more elementary units, and also of the different character of complex learning, with its lesser dependence on routine practice and its relatively ready availability for further problem solving once acquired. And yet really new problems can be very difficult even for educated adults, unless they are cued in the direction of the solution. It would be a mistake to view Gagné's categories too rigidly. As was illustrated in one or two cases, there could be differences of opinion about which category certain instances of learning should be put into.

Learning must be associated with physiological mechanisms and changes in them. Although we have an imperfect knowledge of these mechanisms, such that our 'laboratory scientists' are driven into physiological speculation ('autonomous central process', 'transient, unstable reverbatory trace', etc.), it is not scientifically plausible that there should be a physiological match for so much behaviour and then a remnant that was physiologically inexplicable in principle as well as being inexplicable in fact (because of the imperfect state of our enquiries). What is sometimes wrongly suggested is that complete physiological explanation would give us the whole story of learning. But learning does not *mean* physiological change, even if it always emanates from or is somehow associated with physiological change. The meaning of human learning can be given only in terms of the learners' purposes, or prescriptions of what is required to be done.

This point is forcibly expressed by Michael Oakeshott (1967) when he says, 'By learning I mean an activity possible only to an intelligence capable of choice and self-direction in relation to his own impulses and to the world around him.' Louch (1966), in a more extended polemic against connectionist psychology, argues that psychology has been more successful in exploring the mechanics of controlling than in explaining human action. Stimulus-response units and the like do not add up to what is of real psychological interest—practices, habits and actions that are purposive, meaningful or intentional. 'Psychology as a science with its own explanatory laws, falls in a no-man's land between physiology and the *ad hoc* deliverances of every-day life.'

Perspective on psychological learning theory is a perspective on conflict and on a certain degree of confusion. Perhaps, as Louch suggests, we know all the practical laws of learning from common sense. One then has to explain some curiously persistent perversities of past and present educational systems in flouting these commonsense psychological laws. Psychological learning theory does not specify the law of corporal punishment, or the law of cramming, or the law of dictated notes or communication by lecture, all of which have survived for centuries in educational practice.

On the other hand the questions still hanging their Damoclean swords over the head of learning theory are, What does it explain? And in what sense of 'explain'? And what practical purpose do its explanations serve? It must now be left in its agony so that we can look at human learning and motivation in their own right, although it will be convenient to be able to refer to the concepts of this chapter without having to discuss them *ab initio*.

Human learning: intelligence, remembering and motivation

There is an agreeable anecdote about the hi-fi enthusiast who was completely satisfied when he could turn his equipment on and say, 'Listen! Not a single sound!' Those concerned with practical human learning may sometimes feel that the psychological learning theorist is a similar kind of enthusiast—pleased with the technical achievement of eliminating irrelevant 'noise' but uninterested in any subsequent performance. The typical teacher would probably prefer to hear the 'music' of some practical learning, regardless of technical imperfections in the psychological machinery by which he endeavours to produce it.

Fortunately, there is no need for an all-or-none choice between psychological theory and learning practice, for there are several learning problems which are important for the psychologist and the teacher alike. They include the meaning (or meanings) of learning, and the relationship of learning to intelligence, to remembering and forgetting and to motivation. It will be the aim of this chapter to explore some of these themes.

The meaning of learning

Gagné's definition of learning was 'a change in human disposition or capability, which can be retained, and which is not simply ascribable to the process of growth'. This is not untypical of psychological definitions—general in character but registering several important points which could be listed thus:

1   Learning is *change* in behaviour. Much behaviour is habitual, consisting in repeated *performances* of what was actively learned or acquired in the past. The saying 'We're always learning' is not necessarily matched by much, if any, change in behaviour. The word 'learning' has, of course, a special meaning where it refers to the sum of knowledge or skill that is *available* to be learned; but, where it refers to a human activity, it implies actual or potential change in behaviour.

2   'Change in human *disposition* or *capability*' registers two important points. The first has just been mentioned—the fact that the behavioural change may be potential rather than actual. In other words, the learner may, as a result of his learning, change his behaviour at some future date, despite the absence of dramatic change in the present. Much educational idealism has been pinned on such *potential* change. The other point made in this phrase is that the change may affect either what one is *able* to do or what one is *inclined* to do—two separate things. In scholastic contexts there has sometimes been a tendency to think of learning predominantly in terms of capability or even of sheer knowledge and less in terms of inclination. But inclinations as well as other aspects of personality are learned too. One could even suggest that it was of doubtful value to acquire capabilities (if they are for good rather than evil) without also acquiring the inclination towards their regular and proper employment—a truism which much educational practice has seemed to ignore.

3   There are many changes in behaviour, capability and inclination that do not last for any time. The candidate may put on a rather fine front for his interviewers but be unimpressive on the job. A man may be taciturn when sober but eloquent when tipsy. It is usual, therefore to specify that learning requires some duration (unspecified) in a capability or inclination that is acquired. Common knowledge recognizes that we never forget some of the things we learn but do forget others, whether sooner or later.

4   Finally, Gagné's definition recognizes that the word 'learn' is not used of changes in disposition or capability that can be attributed to growth—the small boy who grows tall enough to help himself with ease to the biscuits on the top shelf, compared with the small boy who learns to climb up on a chair or ledge to improve his biscuit-eating capability and disposition.

Any general definition, like that just discussed, is liable to be unsatisfactory in some ways from a teacher's viewpoint. It may be all right so far as it goes, but its generality removes it from the teacher's typical concern with specific kinds of learning—learning to read, to count, to speak French, to understand the physical world or human history. Also, it may stress the notion of learning as a static retention of some disposition or capacity, without giving enough weight to the fact that the performance which shows evidence of learning may have to vary considerably from one occasion to the next.

Some people would only say that one had learned to read, drive a car, speak French, etc. if one could read, drive, or speak *intelligently*, adapting the performance to the varying requirements of each new situation. In other words, learning would be considered inseparable from intelligence. But, since there can be different ideas about what constitutes intelligent performance, depending on the values of any-one expressing an opinion, the concept of learning may be inseparable from evaluation of what is learned as well as from how well any per-formance is adapted to that evaluation.

Many different criteria can be set up for what constitutes learning. The psychologist in his laboratory, the teacher in his school, the employer in his office, the man in the street, all may have different specifications and none can monopolize the argument. Four scholas-tic criteria will be discussed to illustrate certain problems that arise. Scholastic institutions have often been criticized for over-emphasizing the criterion of ability to recite memorized material, and examination systems particularly continue to have this charge directed against them. If the material is irrelevant to any possible practical purpose (including that of intellectual satisfaction) the charge may be justi-fied; but the ability to bring relevant knowledge promptly to mind is necessary in many practical situations, and merely knowing where the knowledge might be found is often a poor or impossible substitute. This suggests that recitative recall is not necessarily a bad thing, provided that the material itself has a good chance of being relevant to some practical purpose. Whether it is or not is bound to be difficult to decide in some cases, and controversial in others. A facile hostility to 'mere' memorizing will not, therefore, suffice. Discrim-ination is required.

A second standard scholastic criterion of learning is the ability to solve problems—on paper or in principle, even if not in relation to the detailed complexity of 'real' life. The specification of a problem establishes a more definite test of relevance than the recitation of material which may have only potential relevance to some unknown problem. It highlights the relationship of learning and intelligence as overlapping concepts. It cannot, of course, entirely escape those critics who suggest that the problems are artificial, or that writing about problems is not the same as solving them in practice, or that paper solutions are not necessarily practical solutions, or that the real problems are not being dealt with at all. Here again discrimina-tion is required. Some scholastic problems can be made more like practical problems. But it is naïve not to recognize the cost, the chaos and the disasters that would ensue from letting learners acquire all of their learning in real-life, on-the-job situations.

A third criterion is the acquisition of a disposition to go on learning, and particularly learning the next stages of what one has already learned. If learning 'takes', you show signs of wanting more of it. This betokens a commitment to learning ('learning for its own sake' as it is misleadingly called) which gives hope that subsequent learning will be as effectively done as past learning. It is clear that the continuance of scholastic or academic learning is not always a genuine token of such commitment. Individuals may be churned through the institutional learning machines, prevented by inertia from expressing their actual lack of commitment. They may be tokens of the chance influence of particular interests in the world of scholastic learning— the master or mistress, the lecturer or professor, for whom there is nothing like chemistry, French or history. The criterion under discussion is typically a disposition towards some particular form of learning rather than learning in the abstract.

A fourth criterion is the acquisition of a disposition to conduct oneself in accordance with whatever morals and manners scholastic institutions consider consonant with their more purely intellectual aims. There are, of course, cramming institutions which are presumably interested only in the narrower sense of scholastic results. And there has been some diminution in the extent to which colleges and universities have been allowed to demand standards of personal conduct except in the purely scholastic sphere. But there are problems about this form of segregationism. Can one be scrupulously honest in the study or laboratory but please oneself for other practical purposes; seriously confront the past or present problems of society for examination purposes but take a frivolous view of one's own social relationships; expatiate wisely on literature and the arts but believe that it is all *just* a matter of opinion? A literal answer may be that such things are possible; but with the corollary of either hypocrisy or divided personality.

It is not the present purpose to enter into the questions of value and policy that arise from these scholastic criteria of learning, or into the technical questions about measuring how far the criteria are satisfied in any given case. These are complex matters and become more complex if one tries to formulate the further criteria of learning that employers or laymen might add. What is of consequence for the present discussion is that 'learning' is typically used in a loose and variable sense that may include any of the notions just outlined, and that gives rise to complex problems of specification, evaluation and detailed assessment. As used by ordinary people, the concept is neither clear, simple nor value-free.

What people learn is knowledge, skills and attitudes. The traditional sense of learning as acquired knowledge continues to be widely used or assumed. Ignorance may be bliss and people may choose not to know what they do not want to, but most people would probably subscribe to the view that, if something is important in some sense, it is better to know the relevant considerations rather than be ignorant. Moreover, human beings tend to have an appetite for miscellaneous knowledge beyond the most urgent practical needs. Exchange of such knowledge is part of the common social fabric. Presumably it serves partly as a kind of entertainment and partly as a contribution to social skill, for part of any practical skill consists in knowing what is what in the realm of the skill. Skills become automatic in a sense, but the skilled person knows what he is doing. His actions, choices, and explanations (if these are sought) are related to relevant facts and principles, even although the effective exercise of the skill depends on appropriate experience and practice as well.

To know something is to be able to give the right answers to relevant questions, to be able to do the correct thing in situations to which the knowledge is relevant, to avoid saying or doing things which would show that one was influenced by incorrect information or understanding. 'Correct' or 'right' in this context is defined by the principles of enquiry that humans have evolved to deal with the different kinds of problem in which they take an interest. Each of the major disciplines—science, history, mathematics, etc.—has its own particular and reasonably coherent rules of enquiry and evidence which define what is 'correct' or 'right', what is knowledge, in that realm. Some rules—such as rules of logic—may be common to all disciplines. Others—such as the rules of experimentation—*can* apply only to experimental disciplines.

Both learning what is the case, and learning skills which depend partly on knowing what is the case, have to be defined partly in terms of the various disciplines, with their respective rules for finding out what is the case. A schoolboy who learned to recount accurately what happened in a certain scientific experiment might be thought to have learned his science only in the limited sense of descriptive accuracy. And since this principle is not exclusive to scientific enquiry, one might argue that he had learned nothing distinctively scientific at all —even if the lesson was labelled Science.

Similarly, a person might acquire sufficient skill to drive a car after a fashion, but show clearly that he lacked knowledge of some road signs, of certain special traffic hazards, of the importance of replacing worn tyres, and so on. Lack of knowledge of relevant principles can impair a practical as well as an intellectual skill. Of course, a person might be a knowledgeable and skilful driver but fail to apply the knowledge and skill because he was in a bad temper, distracted, less than sober or temporarily more concerned with showing off to his girl friend. Or he might drive in a knowledgeable and skilful way while hardly thinking about it, because his knowledge and skill were so strongly ingrained. Neither of these cases alters the fact that *part* of learning a skill is acquiring knowledge of relevant facts and principles. This is interwoven with the other part of skill learning, which consists in practising the skill until one can master all the practical problems to which it is relevant. But here it would still be argued that knowledge and skill are not utterly distinct, for intellectual understanding too is acquired only by extensive practice—typically in manipulating various systems of symbols (verbal, mathematical) rather than switches, gear levers and brakes.

The last few paragraphs amount to saying that, while verbal, mathematical and other intellectual skills are recognizably different from car-driving, bricklaying and other practical skills, the difference lies in the specific character of the various performances. It is not a simple matter of one set being all practice, for knowledge and practice are necessary in both sets. It remains to consider the relative place of the third suggested category of learning—attitude learning. This also is an aspect of learning that overlaps with acquiring knowledge and learning skills. Both the latter require at least an attitude of attention, and, moreover, an attitude of some minimal interest in the particular realm of knowledge or the particular skill to be mastered. If the knowledge or skill give some satisfaction they may in turn intensify the initial attitudes of attention and interest. If they do not, attitudes of inattention and lack of interest will supervene. Is it possible to go beyond these truisms?

Subject specialists certainly go further. A scientist may say that science *is* fundamentally an attitude of mind, a historian that he hopes to stimulate an attitude of interest in the diverse manifestations of the human situation, a literary scholar that he wants to develop more discriminating attitudes among his students. People speak of the attitude of mind that remains when much of one's knowledge-for-examinations has vanished. Such attitudes towards intellectual studies are obviously nourished and defined by the knowledge and skills which build them up, even if there is a loss of detail with disuse and the passage of time. Similarly, with what are commonly called practical skills, there is typically some attitude towards the skill, some belief about its significance and about how the skill should be applied.

Many attitudes, of course, differ from those just discussed. An attitude may be formed and developed in unthinking or half thinking response to chance circumstances. It may be a mainly emotional response to environmental influences, whether friendly or hostile.

Instead of being nourished by knowledge or skill, it may itself determine what knowledge or skill can be acquired without detriment to the emotional core of the attitude itself. A person who feels hard-bitten by society or circumstances may be capable of only a partial knowledge of his own world and may perfect anti-social skills rather than those that would be generally approved.

Religious or moral attitudes are examples of attitudes that do tend to be socially approved but still depend on emotional responses as well as (perhaps more than) intellectual analysis. Learning these attitudes takes place to a large extent by the influence of environmental chance; but, unlike criminal or delinquent or anti-social attitudes, moral and religious attitudes are also assiduously, if not always successfully, propagated by society's major institutions—the law, the schools, the churches, social convention, etc. Learning these attitudes poses major problems about what is to count as true knowledge or true belief, and about the possibility and propriety of combining the aim of open enquiry with the aim of securing moral or religious commitment by subtle emotional influence.

Acquiring knowledge, skills and attitudes—these interrelated capacities and dispositions—is a great deal of what is commonly meant by learning. This does not conflict with the psychological definition with which we began. But it can be seen that human learning requires some reference to human institutions and to the various intellectual disciplines if it is to be understood in any way which may make a major difference to what teachers or learners do.

Learning and intelligence

Learning and intelligence have sometimes been contrasted with one another—as if learning were something one acquired, whereas intelligence were something one simply had, in high or low degree. There is a measure of fatalism in this view of intelligence and it has sometimes led teachers to assume that learning achievement is largely determined by some intrinsic capacity that is unalterable or alterable only to a small extent. This attitude tends to be self-confirming, for people behave intelligently or unintelligently *partly* because of the way other people expect them to behave. The fatalistic view errs in one direction, but some enthusiastic educationists and environmentalists err in the other. They write glibly about *acquiring* intelligence as if it were freely available in packets on the shelves of the educational super-market. Some of them wax wrathful over the idea that a considerable part of general intellectual capacity depends on genetic inheritance rather than educational stimulation. Moreover, they may argue, it is the environmental and educational components that really matter, for something can be done about these.

These contrasting views alert one to the fact that discussions of intelligence are often loaded with evaluations that go beyond a detached appraisal of evidence. Items of factual and logical evidence that seem important include the following:

1 On any measure of intelligence individuals may vary from time to time. This is influenced by

(*a*) the length of time between occasions of assessment,

(*b*) the differences among tests used (verbal, numerical, spatial, etc.) and

(*c*) at least some kinds of educational experience—as when prolonged scholastic exposure gives people a readier orientation to problem solving.

2 The variation just mentioned is not unlimited. People sometimes quote extreme variations that have been observed as if these were typical variations. Extreme variations are important as examples of what *can* happen, not as guides to what typically happens. Variations in assessed intelligence should also be compared with variations in other human performances. This helps to remind one that there is a certain stability as well as a certain variability in the assessment of general intelligence.

3 Although some of the factors influencing variability can be identified (favourable homes, educational stimulation, motivation to succeed, special interests, etc.), it is difficult to *manipulate* these factors to increase intelligence. Social and family background are not easily discounted. Children even from the same homes show differing degrees of intelligence. Ideal educational programmes may have to wait a long time for the material and human resources necessary to implement them. Improvements that depend on constant individual attention are not possible for large numbers. These considerations justify neither fatalism nor optimism. They invite a realistic exploration of what can be done in particular situations.

4 Intelligence is not a thing. The linguistic convenience of using the noun 'intelligence' to refer to a complex set of behavioural phenomena tends to make some people think as if there were something analogous to a physical object that could be unearthed and exhaustively defined once and for all. But the concept is more accurately suggested in its adjectival or adverbial forms—'intelligent' and 'intelligently'. It refers to a *way* of doing things, namely the way that leads to success according to the diverse criteria of different activities.

To drive intelligently, climb intelligently, play chess intelligently, write or talk intelligently, all require different performances, governed by the rules for these different activities. Even within the range of intellectual activities intelligent performance varies. To do mathematics intelligently is no guarantee that one can give an intelligent account of social or political events. To write intelligently about literature is no guarantee that one can discourse intelligently even about the most commonplace aspects of science. This does not imply that there are different kinds of intelligence in any sense of distinct psychological faculties. It does mean that individual intellectual powers are necessarily sharpened along particular lines of interest and learning and thus become less easily distinguished from interest and learning.

5   It is partly a matter of evaluative choice what one calls 'intelligent' or 'intelligence'. One might consider some practical action intelligent because it solved a practical problem in a strikingly useful way (steered the car out of a skid, stretched the meal made for four into a meal for six, etc.). But the same person might on another occasion feel that such practical intelligence was not a very developed form of intelligence, and prefer to reserve the term for doing things like mathematics or philosophy. Then a scientist or historian might come along and suggest that mathematics was more of a specialized skill representing a very limited, even if useful, form of intelligence; or that philosophy was apt to be a bit arid and disconnected from the 'real' world of empirical study. They would probably all agree that their disciplines demanded or illustrated more intelligence than psychology or sociology. But, of course, they might still go around being psychologically or sociologically obtuse from the social scientist's viewpoint.

6   There is *some* common element running through most intelligent performances. The fact just emphasized, that intelligence is partly an evaluative concept, does not mean that it is entirely or even mainly so. It has been shown that there is a tendency for intellectual performances to be positively correlated. If people are assessed on various intellectual scales they tend to be rather good, rather moderate or rather poor at many things. This suggests the possibility of a general intellectual factor, a certain basic adaptive or problem-solving capacity underlying different particular performances. This fact that all intelligent behaviour has some common element, and yet that it also has distinctive elements determined by learning and interest, is quite simple and yet difficult for some people to grasp.

The points just made about intelligence may have suggested further how it overlaps or does not overlap with learning. It can vary within the individual like learning, but tends to be used to refer to the less variable aspect of human adaptive capacity. (This, it cannot be overstressed, is a relative, not an absolute, matter.) It can be increased like learning by appropriate educational stimulation, but—by the typical definition of the two concepts, as well as by the practical difficulties of controlling those factors that may influence intelligence most—not to the same extent as learning. It is, like learning, partly definable in terms of specified criteria to be satisfied, except that *any* performance, however pointless, may be specified and learned, whereas the criteria for intelligent performance require that the performance should economically match a *particular kind* of purpose. One might, if sufficiently agile, learn to somersault to work, but it would be necessary to manufacture a convincing purpose (a £1,000 bet?) to make it an intelligent mode of travel.

The evidence quoted in the last chapter about human problem solving does not suggest that problem solving is an exercise of 'pure' intelligence. With the help of already acquired learning, and of cues to special features of the new problem, the subject learns how to solve the problem. The more he gropes and fumbles, the more difficulties he seems to experience, the more he seems to be *learning* the solution by a gradual process. The quicker he leaps to a correct and elegant solution, the more he seems to be *acting intelligently*. Perhaps, too, the less able he is to give a reasoned account of his success the more he may be said just to have learned what to do. The more he can justify his actions, the more intelligent they may seem to be. The difference appears to be one of emphasis.

Skill learning may seem to have less connection with intelligence because sheer prolonged practice is often such a large part of the process, but even routine practice can be intelligently or unintelligently ordered in terms of economy of effort and achievement. Attitude learning may have more connection with emotional susceptibilities than with intelligence, but attitudes too can be intelligent or unintelligent, depending on whether or not they are well adapted to some purpose—which, of course, can be an evil as well as a good purpose.

Learning, remembering and forgetting

Learning involves so many complex and changing variables that there is a standing temptation to sweep some of them under the carpet, or at least fix them down so that they cannot move. This chapter is an essay on the impossibility of such a course of action. Learning, it has been shown, is of many kinds. It varies with different disciplines. It refers to knowledge, skills, and attitudes which themselves have somewhat complex interrelationships. It overlaps with intelligence, which turns out to be a slippery concept with various guises and various evaluations of these guises. It is connected with remembering and forgetting, which, when now examined, will also be seen to reflect human behaviour or thought as processes of constant transformation. Some of these transformations may follow the scholastic rule book, but more typically they follow their own rules—distorting, eliminating and adding to the sensory input to our brains or minds.

Teachers are as familiar as any with the waywardness of learning, remembering and forgetting. Because of the professional duties or expectations of teachers, this waywardness is apt to be considered as an unfortunate imperfection in the human machine—an imperfection that could have been avoided if only parents, or society, or the pupil's earlier teachers, had ensured that the machine, the learner, had been better made or better finished. In this happy eventuality, the teacher could now proceed to develop positive learning without having to tinker over past defects. The new learning would simply have to be clearly and rationally ordered, interestingly presented and thoroughly practised. This is not entirely a caricature, although it is easy to appreciate the circumstances that cause teachers to incline towards such a caricature. The psychological analysis of this theme would place the emphasis differently. Waywardness is not an irritating departure from the norm; it is the norm.

Waywardness, in the sense intended here, begins with perception itself. Perception means selective attention to the environment, including one's own body. The principles of selection include the pattern of biological needs operating at any time (hunger, thirst), and the patterns of individual experience, determined jointly by the individual's particular environmental exposure and the way his particular brain has processed the environmental input. There is no absolutely 'true' or 'complete' or 'correct' perception of any phenomenon. The terms in inverted commas are relative to particular purposes. Most people are not considered seriously insane and, therefore, it is useful not to define 'true' perception by reference to how the insane perceive the world. Scientific observation is more explicitly disciplined than casual observation, and, therefore, it makes sense to attribute a special degree of 'correctness' to such perceptions. But 'true' or 'correct' in all such contexts simply mean 'as perceived by sane people' or 'as perceived by scientists observing a specific code of observation', or whatever other such criterion is laid down and understood.

Countless historical and contemporary stories as well as experiments in psychological laboratories have shown how unreliable human testimony can be. Many human beings always will vouch, just as many hitherto always have vouched, for perceiving things that do not exist at all. And, where the observer perceives an actual event, he can be highly convinced of the accuracy of his own report while still being grossly inaccurate in fact. Apart from perceiving things that simply do not exist and demonstrably misperceiving things that do exist, people perceive aspects of things that fit in with their personal interests, inclinations and prejudices and may remain unaware of aspects that are equally available in physical terms but which do not meet any psychological needs.

This is illustrated among teachers and learners. Teachers are typically paid for what they do, and have, in any case, developed certain strong personal commitments to learning over many years. They can readily see the importance of their subject and perceive details relevant to it. The learners get no hard cash, may not get much alternative reward for their efforts (perhaps blame for their shortcomings instead), and, of course, have had less time to develop self-sufficient commitments to learning. These factors lead understandably to different perceptions of any material to be learned. The teacher may see a history textbook as exactly what his pupils need, but they may see it as just another volume in the load of books they have to carry.

The phenomenon just described is called *perceptual set*. It refers to the fact that a person is more inclined to perceive something (1) if it fits into a context that he recognizes and that matters to him, (2) if he has plenty of previous experience of the kind of thing perceived, or (3) if he has received instructions which effectively direct his attention, even if the context or the thing to be perceived is unfamiliar. This emphasizes the learned aspect of perception—the fact that we tend to perceive what we have learned to perceive. There has also been extensive study of aspects of perception that might be intrinsic to the organism rather than learned. Babies choose to look more at a face-like pattern than at a pattern that is comparable except for not being face-like. And in the 'visual cliff' experiment they refuse to approach their mothers across a safe glass surface when the intervening space is made to *seem* as if it were much lower than their starting point. These facts may suggest that some perceptual preferences appear before there has been much chance for them to be acquired by learning.

The Gestalt psychologists have made students familiar with other common patterns of perception which have been supposed to be intrinsic rather than acquired. People may perceive a certain pattern solely because the constituents are similar in some respect, or stand in close proximity, or form a regular straight or curved line, or a closed shape like a square or circle. People readily ignore minor imperfections in any such pattern. They see circles as complete even when they have small gaps in the circumference, and disregard other irregularities of pattern in favour of preferred ideal models. Similarly, with the various phenomena of *perceptual constancy*, people perceive what they expect to be there despite varying actual sensory inputs. The distant large ship stimulates a smaller part of the visual retina than it will when it comes near, but the observer typically allows for this. He can perceive a large ship when it is a small blob growing out of the horizon.

When perception itself is a subtle selective process, constituting an entire area of psychological research, it is not surprising that remembering, which must depend on some initial perception, is also a process of subtle transformation. A good deal of attention has been given to alleged differences or similarities between short-term memory and long-term memory, and between those and the initial learning on which they must be based. Learning and remembering, like learning and intelligence, are overlapping concepts. If I have just learned that *Liebhaber* is the German word for 'lover', one could say that I have learned the correspondence, or that I have just been told it and remember it. Suppose that a class of children learned this correspondence, but several days later only some could give the German for 'lover'. Is it that they all learned it but some remembered better than others? Or had those who forgot not 'really' learned it in the first place? Perhaps they attended sufficiently to echo the word on the first day, but did not really study it carefully, or repeat it to themselves, or allow it to displace some other train of thought that took their fancy at the time they were supposed to be learning *Liebhaber*. Perhaps those who remembered had been concentrating on their German in the interval, whereas the forgetters may have suffered interference from a rival learning activity.

Experimental studies of remembering and forgetting have run into this difficulty of distinguishing the effects of initial learning and of subsequent 'memory'. Experiments have been carried out in which (1) the length of time between learning and recall and (2) the amount of activity between the two were varied independently. These indicate that recall tends to be less efficient in proportion to the amount of intervening activity, but not to the sheer lapse of time. Intervening activity appears to interfere with short-term memory, possibly disturbing whatever physiological pattern corresponds to the initial learning, or preventing the learner from covertly rehearsing the initial learning in some way. Both short- and long-term memory, not surprisingly, benefit from repeated presentation of the relevant stimuli and rehearsal of the relevant responses.

Interference phenomena have been classed as proactive or retroactive (not 'provocative and retroactive interference', as in the delightfully Freudian misprint in Talland's *Disorders of Memory and Learning*!).

1 Suppose that class A had a French lesson, then both class A and an equivalent class Z had an Italian lesson, and finally both were tested on the Italian lesson. The French lesson might exercise *proactive interference* on class A's Italian, so that they were inferior to class Z.

2 Now suppose that classes A and Z had their Italian lesson first, then class A had a French lesson, and finally both were tested on the Italian lesson. The French lesson might exercise *retroactive interference* on class A's Italian, so that they were inferior to class Z.

The word 'retroactive' is unfortunate, suggesting some kind of backward causation. The terminology is presumably a product of experimental design, the actual interference taking place when the two tasks are registered in the learners' experience. The examples given above are manufactured for illustration only. It might be that one language task facilitated rather than impeded another, in which case there would be a situation of *transferred learning*.

3 This time one supposes (to give class A a winning chance for a change) that class A has a French lesson, then both classes A and Z have an Italian lesson of a broadly similar kind to the French lesson. This time class A learn their Italian more quickly and effectively, for some of the linguistic skill associated with the French lesson has transferred positively to their performance in Italian. Of course, there might be negative transfer (*Dove la plume della mia zia?*). Negative transfer may happen in situations which have superficial similarities but require different responses. Motorway-driving spreads to country lanes or country-lane driving lingers on the motorway. Patterns of historical interpretation that may match contemporary events are anachronistically applied to earlier periods that differ fundamentally in some ways from our own.

There still seems to be force in the view of Bartlett (1932) that remembering is a positively reconstructive activity rather than an activity of recovering items unchanged from some static store. Items are sometimes forgotten apparently because a person cannot establish the right context for recalling them. Then the context may be somehow brought to life and the items come flooding back. Current emotions and purposes may be reflected in the pattern of what is remembered or forgotten and in its many characteristic distortions. Selection, elaboration, rearrangement and alterations of emotional tone are all orders of the day. But these features occur too in initial learning. One of the constant problems of teachers and communicators generally is to try and control or limit the reconstructive idiosyncrasies of the learners or audience before the intended lesson or message is transformed beyond all recognition.

Practical skills, once acquired, seem to be particularly well retained. One does not forget how to swim or ride a bicycle, whereas much history or mathematics may slide rapidly into oblivion. The different physiological bases of such activities may partly explain the difference. Intellectual skills may have a more tenuous physiological hold in the human organism. But it may be also that practical skills are more genuinely practised in the first instance, and more rewarded by utility or pleasure in their exercise. Some of the intellectual skills may be too arduous to be mastered to the point of real use and pleasure by many people. Not properly acquired, they are not subsequently used, and consequently, quickly forgotten. A central problem of curriculum planning is to find ways of making intellectual skills practicable for ordinary people. For those who do master an intellectual skill it is in some ways as much a practical skill as any, except that it is practised in problem solving rather than in a standard physical performance.

Pupils and students obviously have great powers of not learning, and of forgetting what they have learned, despite their teachers' good intentions. However, teachers themselves are often equally resistant to practical principles of learning that have been supported by experience and experiment. Since there are so many things that can be learned it is not really surprising that individuals form serious learning intentions in relation to only a few of them. A great deal of forgetting or non-learning must happen because learners do not or cannot share all of their teachers' intentions. From a pedagogical viewpoint one of the first problems is bound to be this one of winning learners over to sharing their teachers' intentions. It is part of the problem of motivation which will be discussed in the next section. There is probably a tendency to give insufficient time and effort to the intention-sharing enterprise—partly because it is bound to fail for some people and some learning tasks, and partly because teachers are typically and understandably impatient to make progress with their own manifest performance in organizing lessons and completing courses of instruction. The lecturer who completes his course of lectures to his own satisfaction has 'covered the ground', even if his audience is far from having accompanied him on the intellectual journey.

Given that a learner does have a mind to share his teacher's intentions, some of the main practical problems are those of

1 training in the relevant principles of selective observation;

2 organizing learning material in systematic patterns to make it more intelligible and memorable;

3 practising the relevant skills, or active recall and analysis of the information to be learned, and distributing this practice over sufficient time to achieve the most economic learning.

There are obstacles to acting on these apparently simple principles.

1   Teachers and students become so obsessed with 'covering the ground' that they do not take enough time to formulate clearly what the principles of observation are. There is reluctance to sacrifice coverage in the hope of strengthening principle. And there can be failure to distinguish even which principles are relevant to a particular group of learners—as when a young scholar obsessed by his personal research fails to present the broader perspective that a junior student needs to begin with.

2   Most teachers try to organize their material intelligibly, but, just as they may be reluctant to sacrifice detail to principle in terms of the subject itself, so they may be reluctant to sacrifice any of the subject to the psychological perspective and capacity of the learners. It may seem easier to bemoan the learners' defects than to make concessions to them—for example, by going more slowly (or quickly), recapitulating if necessary, or sacrificing expository to discussion time.

3   The time-tabling of courses must often put organizational feasibility before ideal patterns of learning practice. Solving the routine problems of the time-table can be such a major achievement that no provision is made to confirm and link the larger units of learning. It is hoped that everything will fall into place in due course. But few learners establish broader perspectives so readily. They have to be helped towards them by special discussions and exercises.

Learning and motivation

Motivation, learning, intelligence and remembering are alike in at least one respect. Their proper understanding depends on careful thinking about what they mean as well as on the study of any empirical evidence about how they operate as psychological functions. This may seem obvious when stated in so many words, but it is very much less obvious when one knows how many people treat these concepts as distinct and almost physical entities. In fact, concepts overlap considerably and the evidence about the psychological functions implied requires subtle appraisal. There is no set of simple tips that, once specified, would enable one to motivate people. It is not a question of pressing a few appropriate buttons, but of understanding the circumstances in which people propose or accept various purposes for themselves.

It has already been pointed out, in the preceding chapter, that the concept of reinforcement is more a name for a certain kind of observed regularity than any kind of motivational explanation of why, in specifiable circumstances, certain stimuli evoke an increase in certain responses. It was also noted that reinforcement does not necessarily mean the same as reward. The two words can be used as synonyms, but also with differences of meaning—particularly where a person's behaviour is reinforced and he consciously appreciates both the fact of reinforcement and the intention of the person administering it. It is imporant, therefore, that people should not simply adopt the word 'reinforce' as a fashionable psychological substitute for what they might otherwise have called 'reward', nor believe that the use of 'reinforce' gives one a much deeper understanding of motivation. The interest of reinforcement as a theme lies in its charting of various patterns of behaviour with a view to their control, particularly in laboratory conditions.

The concept of 'drive' has been used with an intention of explaining motivation, and drives have been subdivided into primary drives (like hunger, thirst, or sex) and secondary or acquired drives (like anxiety). Louch (1966), however, argues that this concept is either redundant or platitudinous. It is redundant if the word 'drive' is used to refer only to the set of observations made in a motivational situation. One might say, the rats press the food-box lever an increasing number of times with each hour that lapses without any supply of food. Or alternatively, the rats' hunger drive increases with the passage of time. Some psychologists have represented drive as a *theoretical construct* or an *intervening variable* that is assumed to link food deprivation and food-seeking behaviour. This construct is supposed to have some kind of explanatory force. But does it add anything to a statement of the observations? And, as a statement of a generalization, is it not platitudinous? Surely everyone knows that food deprivation is associated with a tendency to look for food, and similarly with other appetitive tendencies?

The concept of 'need' is another that enjoys wide use as a supposed explanation of motivation. People do things because they 'need' to. Education must cater for children's 'needs'. And, like drives, needs can be divided into primary and secondary, or intrinsic and acquired. Since we all tend to assume that survival is a good thing, food and drink appear as unquestionable needs. It is then tempting to specify survival of a certain quality, which may allow one to add a need for affection or for satisfying one's curiosity. And this can lead on to the notion of relative needs, according to which a poor man might count as deprived if he lacked bread and water, but someone accustomed to luxury (perhaps through no fault of his own!) might have unsatisfied needs if the champagne and caviare ran out.

So long as people use the word 'needs' in relation to clearly understood and agreed purposes there is no problem. If we all agree to make omelettes then, of course, we need eggs. If we intend to live in a particular society we need to do at least some of the things which hold the society together, although there is wide scope for difference of opinion about what needs do or should hold it together. But there is no set of needs that uniquely constitute human nature or human psychology independently of the social and cultural norms acquired by being reared in a particular society and family. Human needs are the needs of the cultural norms which a society sustains at any point in time. It is possible, of course, to study how widespread any norms and needs are. Biological functions like physical survival and reproduction are obviously very widespread both geographically and historically. So are habits of social congregation, political organization and religious observance, all understood in a wide sense. But even in relation to these, many individuals have put other needs before survival, many more survive without the need to reproduce, and there are such things as anchorites, anarchists and atheists. Needs grow with the variety and quality of living. People whose every need is satisfied may look for new needs (a need to need?).

Peters (1958) points out the difficulty of establishing an independent test of the existence or termination of an alleged need. One might specify some state of physical tension or activity that was to count as an indicator of need. But a person might say quite normally, 'I need something to eat,' even although he showed no distinctive pattern of tension or activity. He might feel that he needed to listen to some music, or to go and have some exercise, or to vent his annoyance upon someone who had irritated him, but an observer might question any of these needs (in other words, question the justification of the actions), or be uncertain whether, after a while, the person was continuing the activity because he needed it or because of inertia. The person himself might be uncertain about whether certain of his inclinations were needs. He might also be uncertain about when a surmised need had been satisfied, for introspective tests of need are as uncertain as external tests.

This analysis of reinforcement, drive and need has practical relevance for educational discussion and action. First, reinforcements, drives and needs are things that human beings can create for themselves, although, of course, with very different degrees of difficulty in relation to different people and different purposes. Second, no need is independent of some supposition about what ought to be done. Even the nearly universal supposition that one ought to survive has been challenged by the choice of death, and other widely held suppositions, such as that one ought to love or be loved, are also challenged in practice—in the case mentioned, by the widespread choice of hatred and hostility.

Third, if it is argued (reasonably enough) that any society nevertheless tends to agree about at least some purposes and associated needs (food, drink, shelter, sex, a measure of social order, etc.), these needs are still susceptible of immense variation in their detailed specification, and in their order of importance as viewed by different persons. The practical importance of these three points can be summed up by saying that the educator in search of motivational control is not just or even mainly studying a branch of psychology but the whole subtle picture of actual and possible human purposes. The psychology of human motivation is the psychology of human purposes. Any practical motivational policy (sweets, detentions, prizes, commendations, certificates, job opportunities, etc.) is justifiable or challengeable on two counts—whether it does achieve what it aims to, and whether that way of achieving the aim is further defensible in terms of the purposes it assumes and fosters.

Of course, the word 'purpose' may be restricted to goals that a person explicitly proposes or formulates for himself, whereas people obviously act towards ends that they have not explicitly proposed or formulated. This may be partly why psychologists have so commonly rejected the concept of purpose—this together with the fact that the word 'purpose' in itself is no more (or less) explanatory than drive or need. The preceding argument rests on the significance of purposes as part of the ordinary shaping of individuals by society and not on any assumption that each and every individual must be able to express and analyse the purposes that influence him.

The practical problem of motivation is not one of mechanically activating the supposed springs of human action, but of finding how to share and reconcile different purposes. This means that a teacher has to relate his own purposes for a class of children to the purposes that they already have implicitly or explicitly. He has to find points of possible contact between what those particular children typically do and what he wants them to do, even between what each individual typically does and what he is expected to do. The relevant generalizations and limitations are those expressed in the whole complex study of child development in particular societies and educational systems.

It may be disappointing that there is no simple and easy general solution to the problem of extending and changing learners' behaviour and purposes, but the analysis of the concept of motivation confirms what is equally evident in practice. Motivational failure arises where there is an unspanned gap, virtually a failure of communication between teacher and learner. It is necessary, therefore, to study such gaps. Some of the common ones are these:

1 The teacher may take commitment to the learning task for granted without sufficient time and effort given to winning the learner's allegiance.

2 The teacher may misjudge or ignore or lack the facilities to cope with the fact that the learner does not have the basis of knowledge or skill prerequisite for the proposed task.

3 The teacher may use language that the learner does not understand. (Even university graduates can have striking gaps in their understanding of common abstract terms.)

4 The teacher's whole set of social and educational attitudes and assumptions may be different from or even inimical to those of the learners.

5 The teacher may be accustomed to a certain level of intellectual operation (for example, brighter or older pupils, or advanced and specialist students) and fail to change his assumptions and methods for a different set of learners (younger or duller pupils; beginning or general students).

6 The teacher may be temperamentally the kind of person who has difficulty in making personal and intellectual contact with any learners, or, in less severe cases, with the full range of learners that he is called upon to teach.

7 The teacher may not understand, or may be out of sympathy with, the character of the institution in which the learning is organized, and consequently fail to exploit institutional purposes to the advantage of his own particular educational purposes.

8 Alternatively to (7), the teacher may be so completely institutionalized that he fails to appreciate justifiable pressures for change in the institution, or for more subtly individualistic approaches to human problems arising within it.

All of these points could be recounted from the learner's point of view, but it is the teacher who is paid to tackle such problems and, therefore, one can perhaps justify an emphasis on his motivational responsibilities. One of the commonest dangers is of teaching too much too rapidly and with insufficient consideration of whether much valuable or permanent change in behaviour takes place. This practice diminishes the appetite for learning and results in much of what is learned being a fairly temporary acquisition. The solutions are varied and depend on analysis of the relevant communication gaps as listed above.

Some of the obvious principles that arise from these gaps can be readily listed. Spend more time and effort on winning learners over to any task they do not accept quickly. Aim at more learning rather than more teaching. If prerequisite knowledge and skills are lacking, do not push the learner on until the lack is made good. Take into account the varying linguistic, social and educational backgrounds of the learners. Consider what teaching changes are necessary when confronted with learners of a different category from the usual. Consider the bearing of institutional patterns on the teaching and learning to be done. If one has temperamental problems, choose a teaching job where their effect is least, organize the details of the teaching to avoid the worst difficulties, and, if neither of these is possible, don't teach!

If these various considerations conflict (as they are almost bound to), weigh up the relevant principles and circumstances and act in accordance with the assessment, accepting any defects as inevitable if they are so. It will not do to say that these principles of decision are too obvious. What is too obvious is disregard for them in practice. People choose not to apply these obvious motivational principles, pretending sometimes that there is some other hidden key that would unlock all the necessary doors. Such a key does not exist. Only detailed thought, experience, planning and correction of mistakes as one goes will work.

The mythical magic key is sometimes given the name of 'interest'. If one can interest the learners or (another vogue word) 'excite' them, or stimulate their curiosity (the fallacy of some dormant organ waiting to be touched into response), then learning is supposed to move effectively and joyously into top gear. But all of this encourages the false notion that there are detachable motivational functions that can be switched off or on by a sheer act of will. Interest, excitement and curiosity in fact always have attachments to particular people and activities.

Learners often remain uninterested, unexcited or incurious because some teachers are not really committed in action to the learning material or the learners. Such teachers (probably few in number) have gone through certain institutional motions and are now trying to put the next generation through the same motions. But very many more teachers are bound to have this lack of commitment in relation to *parts* of their work—to some of what they have to teach, or some of the learners they have to teach. It is not in these cases that there is a failure to light some flame of interest in the learners. The teacher virtually repudiates part of his educational functions or purposes, and in some cases possibly with justification. One cannot be equally committed to all worthwhile actions even within the sphere of one's own general commitments. Interest, excitement and curiosity are, in one sense, the emotional accompaniments of active commitment. All that was said about sharing purposes applies equally here.

Good teachers are teachers who have genuine rather than forced commitment to the learning task and the learners. They are people who tend to be good at the gap-spanning operations listed above. They can have these qualities together with a dramatic personal style (those presumably that are called 'charismatic'), or with an unspectacular personal style. By definition they have few motivational problems and may not feel there is any problem—until perhaps their careers confront them with the challenge of some new situation that does not resolve itself via old remedies. But most teachers (or their pupils) do have some problems of motivation to solve and, in accordance with the present analysis, they would often do well to consider whether the aim of a learning task should be altered, and not only whether some formula might turn up which would surprisingly achieve the aim that other formulae have failed to achieve. Motivation means the right aim and the right order of pursuing it, not just the short-term stimulation into action.

Despite the non-behaviourist emphasis of this section it may be permissible to conclude it on a behaviourist note that has human relevance. Broadbent (1961) draws analogies between rat and human learning as influenced by conflict and anxiety. If there is a conflict between two rewards both rats and humans rapidly choose one of the rewards as their goal. If the conflict is between two punishments there is marked hesitation and a desperate attempt to escape completely from the conflict situation. If the conflict is between a reward and a punishment in a single situation the animal or person tends to remain in the conflict situation, torn between appetite and fear.

Punishment for making a wrong choice has an effect that varies with the difficulty of the choice. If a rat is punished with an electric shock for entering one of two quite different doors, it learns the discrimination faster according to the strength of the shock up to a certain limit. If, however, the doors are similar and the discrimination more difficult, stronger shocks impede learning. This variation is called the Yerkes-Dodson Law. The analogy in human learning would be with a situation where quite high anxiety might be thought to facilitate an easy piece of learning but put the learner off his stride if the learning task were more difficult.

Punishment may establish sufficient anxiety to discourage a certain course of action in a particular situation even in the absence of the punisher. However, it is important that it be made very clear what the punishment is for, and in any case there is a strong possibility of the aversive effect spreading to the entire situation. The punished pupil comes to abhor teachers, school and all—not just his own misdeeds. Although punishment may discourage the misdeed so long as the associated anxiety persists, the misdeed, if it has already brought sufficient reward, will be readily reinstated where and when the punishment anxiety subsides.

Perspective on human learning

The preceding chapter examined some of the basic forms of learning as behavioural units in relative detachment from the complexities of human learning in human societies. The more advanced of these basic forms had a direct bearing on human learning while the simpler forms were suggestive more of the broad biological background from which distinctively human learning emerges. Various theories associated with these forms of learning were shown to have different strengths and weaknesses. They do not, of course, tell educators what to do, for that is not the purpose of theories, but they hold up different pictures of human behaviour, which could encourage different attitudes towards it.

The present chapter has continued to deal with general problems associated with learning, but it has switched attention more directly on to human learning in its full complexity. The main argument has been that learning, intelligence, remembering and motivation are complex, overlapping concepts. They are not simply specifiable things but complex and subtle variables that can be understood only by somewhat detailed analysis. They cannot be summed up in a few tips for teachers. Nevertheless, the other main part of the argument has been that the logical and psychological analysis of these widely used concepts is of tremendous *practical* importance for teaching and learning. An attempt was made to spot-light some of the precise practical problems and policies that are associated with the preceding analysis. The statement of these problems and policies constitutes a virtual instrument of pedagogic analysis that could be used as a guide by any teacher or learner. It cannot spell out detailed solutions, for only the responsible person on the spot can do that, but it indicates some of the main practical areas in which solutions can and should be found.

The problem of motivation has been discussed in some detail. This discussion has stressed the importance of clarifying aims, and of spanning various gulfs of understanding and commitment that are liable to separate teacher and learner, rather than the power of charismatic appeal. Concepts like drive, need and interest were criticized. This does not mean that various categorizations of need or interest are useless or invalid. H. A. Murray's list of viscerogenic (air, water, food, etc.) and psychogenic needs (self-enhancement status, affiliation, etc.); J. P. Guilford's list of social motives (dependency, affiliation, dominance, sex, aggression and self-esteem); A. H Maslow's hierarchy of needs, from the physiological to 'self-actual ization'; E. L. Thorndike's classification of interests (social inter course, ideas, practical and realistic activities, music and art, outdoor sport, amusement, self-indulgence); or E. Spranger's hypothetical value types (theoretical or scientific, aesthetic, religious, social economic, power-seeking)—all of these and other similar lists are valuable as an *aide-mémoire*, reminding one of factors which may be relevant to encouraging some piece of new learning.

M. D. Vernon (1969), while fully recognizing the environmental shaping of motives that has been stressed in this chapter, gives more weight to innate or intrinsic needs. She speaks of 'innate motivational tendencies which direct and regulate specific types of behaviour as well as energizing them' (*Human Motivation*, p. 12) and names fear (p. 58), aggression in response to assault (p. 61), and 'innate emotionality' (p. 83) as examples. She also refers to play, achievement motivation, exploratory and constructive activities, and social motivation to associate and seek approval, as patterns of behaviour that appear so early in the child's development and so universally in space and time as to seem more than the products of learning alone. She also reminds one of the instinctive patterns of behaviour in many animals, which might alert one to the possibility that human beings, while capable of much more varied adaptation, may also have some innate motivational mechanisms. Whether or not one can give meaning to the idea of innate motives in man, it remains very important that patterns of behaviour like those mentioned are so widespread as to be standard reference points for anyone trying to control or change their own or another person's behaviour.

Achievement motivation deserves its own notice, for it has been widely discussed and sounds like something educators should be interested in. Naming motives is an understandable convenience, but it intensifies the risk that people believe themselves to be referring to a highly specific thing. All it means is that children from as early as five or six years of age vary in their levels of aspiration and achievement when asked to do miscellaneous tasks. High, medium and low achievers are influenced by factors like competition, anxiety and parental attitudes and are liable to continue into later childhood and adult life in the achievement category in which they start. It is clearly important to keep this in mind, but it also matters that there are many different kinds and circumstances of achievement, and that the personality tests used in some studies of achievement motivation

are themselves only modestly reliable indicators of what they purport to measure.

A graduate wrote in an examination paper: 'Psychology may help
one to understand the reasons behind a pupil's problem but it rarely,
in practical terms, tells one how to deal with it; that is up to the
teacher alone.' There is considerable truth in this assertion. Only the
person responsible for action can determine the final details of that
action. Nevertheless, an analysis of concepts, like the analysis of
learning in this chapter, does have practical implications, for it
narrows down the kinds of action that are justifiable in specified
kinds of situation. It also establishes guiding principles which the
teacher or learner can apply for himself to determine what is actually
done.

8 Human learning: attitudes, systems and policies

The discussion of Learning and Learning Theories outlined some of the underlying mechanisms of learning and compared certain general models of learning as a whole. This approach to learning encourages one to attend to the details of the process, to experimental validation and to logical analysis of concepts. It at least tries to be more analytic than traditional common sense, even if its concepts and explanations are susceptible to criticism, conflict and weakness in human relevance.

The ensuing discussion of Human Learning: Intelligence, Remembering and Motivation referred to larger psychological functions—moreover, functions that are well known to common sense. However, it was argued, common sense does not always understand these functions accurately, either from the viewpoint of logic or of experimental evidence and scientific analysis. Learning, intelligence, remembering and motivation are all complex and subtle concepts in themselves, each one assessable by varying criteria and overlapping in important ways with the other concepts. This must be recognized if the picture of human behaviour is to be brought into sharper focus. But it is not just a question of a sharper picture for its own sake, but for the sake of various practical policies which are suggested by the new picture. Some of these practical policies were specified in fairly precise terms.

The purpose of the present chapter is to explore further some of the general psychological concepts that have particularly practical relevance to learning and teaching. Part of the purpose must be achieved simply by clarifying the relevant issues, but, as in the preceding chapter, an attempt will be made to state at least some of the specific policies suggested (one cannot necessarily say *logically* implied) by the analysis. Some of the topics to be mentioned are the psychology of attitudes and attitude change; particular learning techniques such as programmed learning, 'learning for transfer' and techniques for slow learners; and the problems of developing learning policies, whether at the individual level or the level of national curriculum development.

Attitudes and attitude change

We are all concerned with one another's attitudes, but people like teachers, politicians, publicists and salesmen have a more systematic professional involvement in attitude change. Teachers must take account of learner attitudes and, if necessary, build up new attitudes in order to facilitate the learning of skills and knowledge. They also commonly aim to develop certain attitudes in their pupils or students because these attitudes are considered intrinsically desirable—such as attitudes of reasonableness, benevolence or self-improvement. And they have to consider the significance of rival attitude-makers—the home, the peer group or the mass media. These practical concerns make it reasonable to look at what is meant by and known about attitudes.

Sometimes an attitude is taken to be the readiness to act in a certain way expressed by a person's words, gestures or facial expressions (he looks furious, amenable, scared stiff, etc.). It is what we impute to a person on the basis of our own expectations, a tentative prediction of future behaviour. In ordinary usage such an attitude can be short-lived ('his attitude has changed since yesterday'). It can also be wrongly attributed in two senses. We may be quite wrong in our interpretation of another person's likely behaviour, even when the clues seem very explicit. And, of course, we can be wrong about the sources of our own behaviour, the genuineness of our own comments on it and our predictions of its future manifestations. We may have a different attitude in other people's eyes from what we have in our own.

Asch (1952) contrasted the concept of attitude with that of set, the subconscious disposition to perform various habitual actions in the presence of the relevant perceptual cues (automatically enter our own street and house rather than someone else's; or rattle off our favourite piano piece). He considered that, compared with attitudes, sets usually had 'a poor cognitive and emotional content', were more effective the less one thought of them (thinking may upset some established physical skills), and were easily disrupted by changed conditions (a change of address, or an attempt to sight-read afresh the well memorized piano score). Attitudes, by implication, have substantial cognitive and emotional content (that is, systems of belief and knowledge, and emotional reactions to these), and are well sustained despite thinking about them or meeting new conditions. Both set and attitude are imprecise concepts, the difference of emphasis being between sheer readiness to perform some routine physical habit and readiness to sustain a wider, systematic pattern of action by what one does and says.

Attitudes can be considered as products of individual personality and the social or cultural forces operating in a particular community. Personality is simply more persistent patterns of behaviour, the product of the genetic aspect of temperament and the environmental shaping it undergoes. Attitudes, then, are aspects of personality. Long lasting and widely influential attitudes are not really distinguishable from personality, but it has seemed convenient to have a word for behaviour patterns that are of intermediate duration or influence, or, possibly, that derive more from environmental shaping than from genetic influence. The questions of theoretical and practical interest are: What behaviour patterns are resistant to change because of the genetic limits set on them? What patterns persist because they have been so deeply stamped in by powerful environmental influences, possibly in early childhood? And what patterns are shorter-lived, less deeply impressed and more susceptible to alteration? The available answers are less clear than the questions. And people's taste in answers is influenced by their own attitudes of optimism or pessimism about how changeable so-called human nature is.

J. A. C. Brown (1963) says that 'the most difficult thing in the world is to change minds in directions which conflict with the attitudes deeply embedded in the nuclear self'. By the nuclear self he means the sense of our own reality and persistence as developed by growing up in a particular society. Part of this is a conscious self-concept, the person's set of beliefs about what he is and what his possibilities are. But presumably the nuclear self would include also the tendencies that he manifests to others without being aware of them himself—the unconscious or subconscious self. Earlier chapters on developmental psychology reviewed some of the evidence relevant to the idea of a nuclear self. Some of the main factors can be recapitulated:

1   *Physical Temperament*   Individuals can show distinctive and persistent differences in style of behaviour even within one family. One cannot easily eliminate the influence on this of environmental differences within the family (birth order, changes in the family's circumstances at different periods, etc.), but both psychologists and parents

argue for temperamental differences, for example in placidity or excitability, that are thought to be partly genetic.

2 *Maternal Affection* Consistent affectionate care with *appropriate* encouragement towards independence in early childhood is associated with growth in a sense of security and practical effectiveness; defects in such care with insecurity, over-dependence, and, in extremer cases, various emotional and intellectual handicaps.

3 *Linguistic and Educational Stimulation* Young children who enjoy more varied experiences and learn from their parents to talk about such experiences gain a developmental and educational benefit that is not readily replaced at any later stage.

4 *Cultural Patterns* Apart from the previous point, children, by the sheer persistence and quantity of exposure to the social and cultural content of life in their own family and neighbourhood, are bound to be unthinkingly committed to some beliefs and practices that may serve them more effectively in their circumstances than alternatives that may be offered by schooling.

5 *Defence Mechanisms* People develop characteristic ways of defending their own self-concept against attack—the chip-on-the-shoulder, the self-protective irony, the hyperactivity that excludes time for questioning, the excessive humility or conceit, the repression out of consciousness of considerations that are too painful to recognize, and all the other defences, from those that are necessary for ordinary psychological survival to those that handicap by their extreme repudiation of objective realities.

None of these five factors should be viewed fatalistically as absolute barriers to change. Individuals who begin with the same temperamental inclination, affectional experience, linguistic or cultural exposure, or characteristic mode of defending the self-concept, develop much more diverse patterns of adult behaviour because of intervening experience and education. Nevertheless, even if the nuclear self is a relative rather than an absolute notion, Brown's assertion of its importance can hardly be denied and the specific elements that define it are something like those listed above.

If one wanted to narrow down this model of the nuclear self, the thing to do would be to trim off the more intellectual aspects and leave the more emotional, but this begins to misrepresent the really intimate relationship between intellectual and emotional development. The practical importance of the preceding analysis for teachers is that they can sometimes facilitate learning by making larger and subtler allowances (in time, attention, pace and pattern of work) for the emotional and cultural backgrounds that constitute most of the individualities of their pupils.

Along with the importance of the nuclear self, in the sense of our most persistent emotional patterns of behaviour, Brown stresses the influence of society in defining personality. Most people want to share the mental and emotional experiences of others, and not to feel completely out on a limb. When a person accepts a certain role in society (father, pupil, teacher, good fellow) he behaves in accordance with his perception of that role. While such role perception may itself be influenced by the notional nuclear self, it is also influenced by social definitions or assumptions of what is expected by the occupant of the role. The individual accommodates himself to the role expectation and, eventually, he may become the role. What begins as a role specification, that can be taken on or put off at will, ends up by being part of the individual's personality.

Although this tends to happen, it is obviously not without exception. A person may resolutely detach his business self from his leisure self, or occupy a still greater number of roles in relative detachment from one another. If social values and expectations themselves are changing rapidly, increasing the sense of the relativity of values, it becomes easier to detach changeable expectations from less changeable personality traits. This illustrates how concepts like personality themselves are susceptible to change, depending on the context in which they are discussed.

The argument so far has been about the possible sources of the most persistent attitudes in the individual's personal development in a particular society. Another approach to attitudes has been to find what attitudes a group of people have to a variety of topics and how strongly they hold these attitudes. The method of assessment is to prepare lists of statements about, for example, religion, war, penal policy, race, marriage or nationalism, and then get the group to indicate individually their degree of agreement or disagreement with the statements. The question is whether each set of attitudes is quite distinct or whether statistical analysis of the results demonstrates overlapping.

Not too surprisingly, the latter proves to be the case. People's attitudes tend to be grouped together along a limited number of underlying dimensions. As mentioned in an earlier chapter, Eysenck has proposed two major dimensions—one marking out the range between tough- and tender-minded attitudes (T scale), and the other the range between radical and conservative attitudes (R scale). Specific attitudes can be mapped out between these two dimensions, for example:

Attitude dimensions	*Particular attitudes*
Tough-minded, conservative	Favour severe penal laws

Tough-minded, radical	Favour tolerant marriage laws
Tender-minded, conservative	Favour religion and compulsory religious education
Tender-minded, radical	Favour pacifism

Eysenck's two dimensions are derived from statistical analysis of the responses of a middle-class, English sample of 750 people who completed a forty-item attitude questionnaire. It is suggested that those who incline towards the tender-minded end of the T scale may be people who are more readily conditioned, and whose upbringing has in fact established conditioned fear or anxiety responses to a larger number of things, whereas the tough-minded may tend to be less conditionable as well as less highly socialized by upbringing. These differences are also associated with differences on the Introversion-Extraversion personality dimension.

R. Brown (1965) discusses Eysenck's work in the course of a longer and excellent review of American research into the so-called authoritarian personality. This latter enquiry (Adorno, 1950) was based on four attitude tests of Anti-Semitism (the A-S scale), Ethnocentrism (E scale), Political and Economic Conservatism (PEC scale), and Implicit Antidemocratic Trends (F scale). The subjects were also interviewed and given projection tests (in which the subject makes up a story about a given picture, or responds to a speculative question). The attitude scales contained items like the following, to which the subjects had to indicate their degree of agreement or disagreement:

'I can hardly imagine myself marrying a Jew.'

'Negroes have their rights, but it is best to keep them in their own districts and schools and to prevent too much contact with whites.'

'The best way to solve social problems is to stick close to the middle of the road, to move slowly and to avoid extremes.'

'People can be divided into two classes: the weak and the strong.'

The results showed that there were varying degrees of correlation among the attitudes indicated. All were positive and they ranged in value from 0·14 to 0·86. The authoritarian personality, indicated by strong agreement with most of the attitude statements, was supposed to be one which revealed itself in (1) rigid adherence to conventional middle-class values, (2) submissive attitudes to conventional authorities, (3) aggressive attitudes to the violation of conventional values, (4) hostility to imaginative tender-minded views, (5) a tendency to superstitious and stereotyped views, (6) preoccupation with the significance of power and toughness, (7) cynical views of human nature, (8) a view of the world as wild and dangerous, and (9) exaggerated

concern with imagined sexual behaviour. The authoritarian personality was supposed to reveal itself even in childhood in a generally
aggressive orientation associated with a rigid and punitive upbringing.

The criticisms made of this enquiry provide a lesson in the pitfalls
of attitudinal investigation.

1   All of the items were stated in a positive 'authoritarian' direction.
If they were restated in the opposite direction ('I can well imagine
myself marrying a Jew', etc.), one would expect subjects to reverse
their response in each case. There should be a complete negative correlation (-1) between the two sets of responses. In fact, when the
original F scale (Implicit Antidemocratic Trends) and its 'non-
authoritarian' counterpart were given to the same subjects, their
responses had considerable inconsistency, with a correlation of only
-0.2 instead of -1.

2   When the data were more carefully analysed to discover what
factors might underlie the responses, the nine factors listed in the
preceding paragraph did not emerge from the analysis. There was a
tendency for anti-semitic, ethnocentric attitudes to be associated
with political and economic conservatism, but apparently still some
political liberals who also had ethnocentric and antidemocratic views.

3   The interviewing of the subjects was not independent of their
responses to the attitude scale. The interviewers knew how the subjects had responded on the attitude scales, and knew the kind of
hypotheses that were being studied. Consequently, they were exposed
to the real possibility of interpreting interview responses in a biased
manner. There is more significance in correlating assessments that
have been made quite independently, and without knowledge of
what someone might have in mind to prove or disprove.

4   Evidence of childhood rearing depended on recollection, and of
matters which are complex in any case. This weakens any argument
about the authoritarian personality in childhood.

5   It is possible that the result could be explained as well in terms of
the effect of intelligence, education and socio-economic status. Scores
on the F scale have negative correlations of 0.5 to 0.6 with education
and intelligence, and of 0.2 with intelligence alone. The 'authoritarian
personality' might be just an artefact of circumstances.

These and other criticisms are elaborated by Brown more fully than
is appropriate here, but what has been said should give some impression of the empirical approach to the study of attitudes. The idea
of an authoritarian personality is not really substantiated, and yet
there is obviously a partial clustering of attitudes that can understandably tantalize the researcher.

Another attempt to link diverse attitudes under a wider psychological law is represented in the theory of cognitive dissonance, associated with the name of Festinger. The theory is that it is unpleasant to entertain conflicting attitudes or knowledge and, therefore, people tend to change in the direction of reducing the amount of such psychological dissonance. In various experiments people have been rewarded for doing something they did not really like. On conventional views of reward, they ought to develop more liking for the activity the more substantially they are rewarded for pursuing it. In fact, subjects who got smaller rewards expressed more liking for the task. Festinger's interpretation is that the attitude of greater liking helped to reduce the gap between the previous dislike and the small reward for pursuing the activity.

For those who got a larger reward anyway there was less dissonance to be reduced, and so they continued to express dislike for the activity. This would fit those situations in which people seem to be more delighted with their activity the less it is rewarded in conventional terms (the wet, sweaty slog to the mist-bound mountain top— 'It was great!'). As Zajonc (1960) points out, however, there are many psychological dissonances that people seem quite ready to accept with no effort to reduce them, as in the film *The Captain's Paradise* where Alec Guinness, as the captain of a ship sailing between Gibraltar and Tangier, kept a nice little wife in the former territory while leading a wilder romantic life in the latter. Cognitive dissonance is an interesting plausible idea, but it does not explain some phenomena at all, and others only rather superficially.

Cattell (1965) postulated a number of basic 'dynamic structures' which he calls 'ergs'. They include such things as sex, fear, gregariousness, self-assertion, parental pity and protectiveness, and pugnacity. Several ergs (sex, self-assertion, protectiveness) might nourish a certain sentiment (about one's wife) which, in turn, would nourish an attitude towards aspects of one's wife (her hair-style, etc.). Similarly, other sentiments (about God, one's country, etc.) are fed by various ergs and manifested in relevant attitudes. All of these are interlinked in a 'dynamic lattice', which, however complex, is supposed to derive its motive power from the same set of basic ergs.

This has affinities with the earlier instinct psychology expounded by McDougall. Its practical importance is as a reminder of the interlocking structures of which attitudes are one feature, and of the possible dependence of all attitudes on certain basic patterns—if this is indeed a valid analysis. Cattell is sceptical about Allport's 'functional autonomy' of acquired sentiments—the idea that acquired sentiments generate their own power to an important extent. Cattell stresses the 'subtle indirect satisfactions which continue to feed the sentiment'. In other words, the highest sentiments have ergic roots. Since the very idea of an erg is something of a speculative hypothesis, there is plenty of room for argument between motivational idealists and those with *la nostalgie de la boue*.

Many laboratory experiments have been conducted to study how attitudes are influenced by such things as the group norms of the experimental subjects, the differing suggestibility of different people, the attachment of prestige or authority to a particular belief or course of action, or the presentation of conflict situations. There have also been many general studies of the techniques and effects of advertising campaigns, religious ceremonies, political indoctrination, psychological warfare and 'brainwashing'. On the whole the factors one would expect to influence attitudes do so, but not always in the simple way that might be supposed at first thought. People may be influenced at first by the fact that some statement is associated with a high- rather than a low-credibility source, but after a lapse of time this source effect may wear off. They may give clear verbal expression of definite attitudes in a psychological laboratory, but, when the experiment goes on to test their readiness to act on the apparent attitudes, some (fourteen out of forty-six subjects in one experiment) may not do so.

Among subjects who illustrate the operation of a pattern that one would expect, some nevertheless may not illustrate it. Advertising, propagandizing or indoctrinating campaigns that appear to have the usual ingredients (emotive appeal, mass suggestion, reiteration of a simple message, etc.) may still be unsuccessful. J. A. C. Brown (1963) in his discussion of propaganda, concluded that people were very resistant to messages that failed to fit their own picture of the world and their own objective circumstances, and were inclined rather to seek out views agreeing with their own. Lifton (1957), after reviewing techniques of 'thought reform' used on Chinese intellectuals (isolation in a special milieu, evocation of guilt and confession, exposure to group analysis and sanction, emotional appeals), comments that the continuance of the effects of the reform process depended on the fact that 'these responses continue to be supported and demanded by the general environment of Communist China long after the course has been completed'.

Lifton's point provides a good introduction to the consideration of how the psychology of attitudes affects teachers, for it reminds one that attitudes are sustained by the nature of continuing circumstances as well as by any originating influences. School learning and favourable attitudes towards it may depend firstly on associating it, so far as possible, with positive attitudes already sustained by the pupil's home and neighbourhood. Subsequently, the continuance of attitudes built up at school depends on their being sustained by the circumstances of adult life. The failure of these links provides a plausible interpretation of why some children do not take to school, and why almost all learners decline markedly from their peak school or college performance as soon as institutional pressures are removed.

Educational idealism sometimes expects too much commitment in the absence of any sustenance of the ideal from Cattell's ergic level. To give one example, most attitudes and interests are sustained by associated social satisfactions. It is desirable, therefore, that any attitude to be cultivated should offer some such satisfaction. In a brass-band community there is normally more future in a favourable attitude towards, and interest in, the trumpet than the bagpipes. The situation might be quite otherwise in Inverness or Oban. This argument does not imply that one can fit in only with the existing community. One never knows when there is going to be a concerto for brass band and bagpipes. It is a question of gradually and subtly attaching new attitudes and interests to existing ones rather than assuming that they will always attach themselves without special linking efforts.

Another indication for teachers is that the mass media, despite their real power, do not always have a major influence in determining people's attitudes. An unchanging diet of Conservative journalism is consistent with an unchanging habit of Labour voting. Exposure to television violence is not particularly associated with delinquency, nor apparent emphasis on sex with the actual degree of promiscuity. Where any abnormality of individual conduct (delinquency, psychological disturbance, suicide) appears to have some superficial association with a striking public phenomenon, one can be virtually certain that its roots will be in a private family situation, probably of some complexity, and that its wider social roots too will be more subtle and complex.

Young people naturally associate with others of their own age and want to differentiate themselves from the older generation, but their own families still matter very much to them, they are frequently highly appreciative of adult help if it is tactfully offered rather than brusquely insisted on, and adult attitudes and concerns often take hold of them within the relatively few years separating adolescent rebellion or merrymaking from the first responsibilities of married life. Despite the tendency towards group conformity, manifest in any case at all stages of life, young people, like their elders, are individuals actively trying to define their own individuality. They are not just standardized units in some notional youth culture, however powerfully group norms may guide them.

The influence of teachers as shapers of attitude depends on spotting what attitudes and interests it is practical to encourage in each case, and on acting constructively, consistently, sympathetically and tactfully. Where there is a background of emotional disturbance or social handicap, the teacher can count on more frequent failure to change attitudes. But it is interesting to note how many people who work with the most disturbed young people of all still follow the difficult formula just stated—constructiveness, consistency, sympathy, and tact. The first two elements affirm the teacher's or counsellor's entitlement or obligation to disseminate the values he should disseminate; the second two affirm the wisdom of doing so in a spirit of respect for the learner, who may have quite different loyalties and see no point in the alternative values offered.

Psychologists and sociologists have no *special* right to prescribe what attitudes should be cultivated in young learners, but parts of psychology and sociology are a virtual study of how people may increase contentment and creativeness or dissatisfaction and destructiveness in themselves and others. These are the parts that deal with the handicapping influence of conflict within and between individuals, and of socio-economic impediments to the wide ordinary range of individual development from childhood to adulthood. Although these parts can be mentioned separately, they do not really stand on their own. It has been argued that motivation is as much a matter of extensive detailed understanding and organization as of specific stimulation. So it is now argued that helpful general attitudes towards learning and living are as much a matter of widespread detailed understanding of individual and social psychology as of any psycho-manipulative process to give people new attitudes despite themselves.

Teachers who agree with what has been said about the power of the nuclear self, and of the roles in which people are cast (sometimes more by the chance of circumstances than any more deliberate process), may be tempted to accept a *modest* role for themselves in the matter of attitude changing. But teachers are certainly far from powerless. One noted the significance of education in the studies of the so-called authoritarian personality, and Brown's comment on the susceptibility of people to the influence of objective circumstances. Education can change objective circumstances in the shape of the new skills and ideas that it gives learners, for such skills and ideas are part of the facts of life as well as any physical or social facts. It was suggested, however, taking a leaf from Cattell's ergic notebook, that skills and ideas are all the more strongly established and sustained if they are clearly linked with humbler satisfactions, particularly social ones.

The analysis of the concept of attitude and personality should have established the practical point that the facile use of these terms is not justified. Two views are repudiated—that we know clearly what we mean, and that we have no idea what we mean by attitude or personality. There are certain conceptual distinctions that can be, and have been, clearly made. There is a great deal of evidence of different kinds which tends to substantiate certain points and not others. Both categories have been illustrated in the preceding discussion. As with most psychological analysis, much of the practical value of the analysis rests in its subtle modification of one's general picture of human behaviour. But, as with other topics, an attempt has been made to state some of the more definite policies that are at least suggested by the nature of the analysis.

Attitudes, of course, are not just things that other people have and it will not do to cast the teacher in any kind of attitude-free role. The point of typical public concern is whether attitudes are socially beneficial or detrimental, and how detrimental ones can be modified. As with other problems in educational psychology, the problem of attitudes always poses a question of social values as well as one of psychological genesis or control. Insofar as teachers may be expected to change some of their attitudes during their professional careers, it is necessary to have various institutions to facilitate the process—refresher conferences and courses, teachers' centres, proper consultation between heads of schools and their staffs and any similar mechanisms that help teachers to justify committing themselves to new educational policies.

Wall (1968) suggests that adolescent attitudes can be created or changed (1) by the teacher displaying worthwhile attitudes and behaviour with which the adolescent can identify himself, and (2) by associating satisfying experiences with any attitude to be acquired. It is not so easy to see who provides an identification model for the teacher himself, but presumably politicians and administrators can make attitude-change a more or less satisfying experience for teachers via such devices as consultation, material facilities, salary structures and in-service professional courses.

Learning systems

The definition of learning or teaching systems is an arbitrary matter to some extent, varying with the methodological fashion of time and place and with the level of generality at which one chooses to argue. To illustrate the latter point first, one could discuss in detail the respective merits of chalkboards and overhead projectors, or the best techniques of making lecture notes. Alternatively, one could go to the more abstract extreme and discuss, as has been done in earlier chapters, whether it is more effective to think of learning in terms of operant conditioning, servo-mechanisms or the social transmission of cultural norms. Between these extremes there are systems of intermediate generality like teacher education; buildings and equipment; curricula, syllabuses and examinations; and available books, particularly textbooks.

The influence of time and place is equally easily illustrated. A system of very long standing is that of setting learners to memorize material and beating them if they cannot reproduce it. It is now a discredited system; but that is less interesting than the fact that it should have persisted so vigorously for so many centuries. It represented a powerful philosophy and psychology of learning; and, of course, to say that it is discredited is not to say that it is universally abandoned in practice. There are people in some countries in our own times who have had elementary knowledge (including religious knowledge) beaten into them and survived to pursue scientific graduate studies by the most sophisticated learning methods.

Moreover, although the deterrent of corporal punishment is discredited, all learning systems have alternative deterrents in the shape of disapproval, criticism or exclusion from certain benefits, by teacher, family or community. The defensible view that reward is more important than punishment, and that satisfaction from the learning itself is more important than extrinsic rewards, seems to blind some people to the apparently inescapable role of positive punishment in society, and to the fact that even intrinsic rewards imply a kind of relative deprivation, if not punishment, for those who covet the reward but lack the means to pursue the relevant activity successfully. These considerations call for avoidance of oversimplification, but the very word 'punishment' seems to set off highly punitive responses in those most fiercely opposed to the cool analysis of the concept.

Systems less barbarous than the memorize-or-get-beaten system still share some of its formal ingredients. There must be some presentation of the material to be learned, whether via speech, writing, action or any other organized presentation or experience. There must be something done with the presentation, whether via memorizing, practice, discussion, problem-solving or any other of the usual modes of learning. And there must be some assessment of what desirable difference has been made by the learning. The popular dichotomy into formal and informal learning, with the fashionable view that the second is a good thing and the first a bad thing, perpetuates a superficial and simplistic analysis. In this context, the terms 'formal' and 'informal' are usefully employed only if it is made clear that there is a matter of degree, and if what is meant is specified precisely.

Characteristically, 'formal' signifies a relative emphasis on subject matter and on traditional specifications of aim, method and assessment. 'Informal' signifies a relative emphasis on the learner and on more varied specifications of aim, method and assessment. The words themselves justify nothing, for a sound learning policy respects both subject and the learner. Whatever the formal or informal bias, learning aims and methods have to be independently justified (Why should one learn this or that? Why should one cultivate formality or informality? What difference in learning is produced by examinations, informal projects, out-of-school visits, etc.?). Simple slogans do not answer complex questions.

The word 'system' probably has more emotive affinity with 'formality' than 'informality'. To put it paradoxically, formality is a system that believes in system whereas informality is a system that does not believe in system. Recent educational thinking provides striking examples of both modes. Informality, beginning as a reaction against existing social and educational rigidities, has led some thinkers into a naïve intellectual relativism. Since one cannot 'prove' that anything is more worthwhile than anything else, and, since people ought in some sense to matter equally, therefore each person should be allowed as far as possible to do what he wants and be equally esteemed for it.

This position is a very feeble one. People are, in some sense, difficult to define, entitled to equal respect as persons, but people and things in fact are valued differently. The practical question that arises is not to prove who is absolutely right or wrong, but to resolve differences and conflicts into defensible decisions and actions where this is necessary or beneficial. Individuals may feign opting out of this problem, but even the idea of anarchy is contingent on the idea of order, and all who would substitute a new system for an existing one still nourish their rebellion from positive sources within the existing system. In relation to learning, the point is that there is no such thing as a non-system. This may be oddly obvious, but some rebels against traditional patterns in education and society have seemed to assert the opposite. This may be because they attach the hostility caused by the content or rigidity of a particular system to the whole concept of system as such.

While one group of people are trying to get rid of system, other groups lambast the educational system for not being systematic enough. Some of these are political or economic systematizers, concerned with giving the educational system a particular direction at a particular cost, but it is the more specifically educational systematizers that will be considered here, without special emphasis on their connections with politico-economic argument. Some of this enthusiasm for systematics has clear psychological roots in behaviourism and objective testing. The argument is simple. Learning is changing specific behaviour along some desired line. What is required is (1) to specify the new behaviour in particular, not general, terms, (2) to work out the minimal programme that will produce the precise behaviour specified, and (3) to test as objectively as possible whether the new behaviours are established at the level relevant to subsequent tasks.

It is not easy to exemplify systems analysis briefly, for it tends by its very nature towards a measure of detail. However, one can cite examples that convey the essential idea. Language broadcasts for holiday-makers are presented via dramatic scenes similar to those a listener might be in during his holidays. Native speakers are employed for authenticity of speech. Vocabulary, grammar and language speed are carefully graded from start to finish. There are supplementary books and records, and sometimes other devices to reinforce the influence of the broadcasts. A parallel example is that of crash language courses for businessmen, where again the system concentrates on language that is likely to be used, but this time with a common appeal to the idea of mastering the minimum necessary skill in a short time by sheer intensity of exposure to practical language instruction. A final example might be the various attempts to analyse the acquisition of reading skill. Roberts and Lunzer (1968), for example, give a quite detailed analysis of reading as an information processing skill, and Merritt (1970) discusses some of the practical problems in a short article on primary and intermediate skills. These are, of course, just illustrative references from a literature that is vast.

It may seem that learning systems have always been with us, but the significance of systems analysis is that the job is meant to be done more ruthlessly in terms of explicit behaviour. General statements of aim must be translated into items of behaviour which can be checked as present or absent. Items which are not necessary to achieve a given general aim are eliminated as wasteful. Where one has a clear-cut utilitarian aim, systems analysis makes a good deal of sense. The problem is that some legitimate aims do not have this utilitarian precision (for example, to research into incompletely explored intellectual territory; or to understand and enjoy literature). Perhaps the systems enthusiast would argue that, however open the field of enquiry, at least some of the criteria of past enquiry are relevant to new enquiries. There should, therefore, be a system that represents the apparently most productive form of learning or enquiry at a given point in time.

Systems analysis means at least a summons to justify aims and methods in more detail than is sometimes done. So much learning and teaching effort goes into sustaining conventional pedagogic routines without any clearly identifiable behaviour change. And, even where behaviour is changed, the change may be short-lived or serve no function beyond its own acquisition—that is, provide neither pleasure, enlightenment nor other practical utility. On the other hand, enthusiasm for systematics can be misplaced if it leads to exclusive emphasis on clear immediate utility, for less clear and longer term utilities are also often important. Particularly, a background of general understanding, including knowledge and critical principles, is important in many complex operations. Sullivan (1969), discussing 'A systems approach to training in the Royal Australian Air Force', suggests the categorization of theoretical knowledge or cognitive skills in terms of whether they are essential, useful or not directly influential at all in relation to practical performance.

The two-volume *Taxonomy of Educational Objectives* by Bloom, Krathwohl and others has been, despite criticisms, a kind of bible of systems analysis. It represents the cognitive domain as divided into six broad categories—knowledge, comprehension, application, analysis, synthesis and evaluation—each of which is further subdivided. The affective domain is divided similarly into five categories —receiving or attending, responding, valuing, organizing (diverse values, etc.) and internalizing these preceding processes in the form of a general value characterization. These categories can be used as a guide to formulating and assessing diverse educational objectives.

Programmed learning

The preceding discussion has attempted to focus attention on the systematic planning of learning in a wide sense. Readers can sample what is called 'Programmed learning' by reading the following sections one at a time, keeping each ensuing section covered with a piece of board or paper until they have answered the intervening question.

1 'Programmed learning' is the term normally used to describe a particular application of the systematic planning just discussed.

  Programmed learning is a particular kind of learning that is planned . . . . . ?

2 Systematically. Programmed learning may take the form of a series

of short statements or explanations, each followed by a question to check the student's understanding, and the whole series arranged in order so as to present the material clearly and logically.

Three of the ways in which programmed learning is systematic are (a) that the length of each unit of exposition is kept . . . . . ? (b) that the presentation is . . . . . and . . . . . ? and (c) that each unit is followed by a . . . . . ?

3 Short, clear, logical, question. The idea is that with a series of short, clear and logically ordered units (or 'frames', as they are called) the learner has an excellent chance of answering the questions correctly. He is learning the correct answers and at the same time his success motivates him to go on with the programme.

A learning programme works by making it easier to get the . . . . . answers to the questions set, and so encouraging you to . . . . . learning?

4 Correct, go on. Another main feature of programmed learning is that each individual learner must make his own response at each stage of learning. A conventional textbook might share some of the systematic features of programmed learning, but it does not ensure that the learner masters each necessary unit of learning by obliging him to demonstrate his understanding of the units in order.

An important difference between a learning programme and a conventional text is that the programme obliges the learner to demonstrate that he . . . each small stage of learning?

5 Understands. The programme allows each learner to proceed at his own speed, but always with a check on whether he is really mastering the material. Regardless of individual speed of learning, each learner goes through the frames in an order that has been planned for maximum efficiency.

Programmed learning does not hold up a learner whose pace of learning is . . . . . or force the slower learner to cope all at once with . . . . . material than he can manage?

6 Fast, more. It is possible to give learners extra cues for correct responding. For example, the answer 'fast' to the last question is suggested partly by the meaning of the phrase 'pace of learning'. A cue based on meaning is called a semantic cue. But there is also a cue based on the nature of English grammar. There is a quite high probability that an adjective of some kind will end a clause beginning 'whose pace of learning is . . . . .'. A cue based on the structure of language is called a syntactic cue.

Programmed learning helps the learner sometimes with extra cues to the right response. If the cue depends on meaning it is called . . . . . ? If it depends on grammatical structure it is called . . . . . ?

7 Semantic, syntactic. A further difference between a good piece of programmed learning and most alternative forms of learning is that the learning programme is tried out with a group of the learners for whom it is intended. In the light of such a trial the programme maker can find out what defects remain, and modify the programme to match the ideal more closely.

The present illustrative section of programme has not been tried out, and, therefore, it would have to be completed and put to such a practical test in order to get rid of any . . . . . ?

Defects. And, since this kind of brief illustration is also defective in taking a lot of time and space to teach a very few points, this will be made the cue for reverting to the expository mode that is appropriate in a book not purporting to be a programmed text. It is wiser to study complete programmes. To mention four examples, Thomas and others (1963) include programmes on Elementary Electricity, and on Pythagoras' Theorem; Stones (1968) presents a programmed introduction to *Learning and Teaching*; Richmond (1965) offers a programme on the Sonnet; and Leith's *Handbook of Programmed Learning* (1966) includes sixty-six frames from a spelling programme by R. G. Middleton.

Linear programmes are those that advance in a single series of short steps and are designed to ensure a high rate of correct responding to the questions. Branching programmes are more complex, offering various routes through the programme, depending on the answer selected to key questions at each stage. The learner might have to choose one of four or five possible answers. If he chose correctly he would then be referred to the page of the programmed book on which the next section of the material was presented. If he chose wrongly he would be referred to a different page, which would help him to correct that kind of wrong answer. If he now got the original question correct, he would continue along the main-line programme—rather like an educational version of snakes-and-ladders. A branching programmed text that refers you to different pages depending on your answers is called a 'scrambled' text, for you do not read it in numerical page order like an ordinary textbook.

Whatever form a programme takes it requires a careful and detailed analysis of the structure of the learning material, so that the learning units are all there and in a logical order. It is easy to omit units on a wrong assumption that they can be taken for granted; and, with complex tasks, programmer and learner may conceive of different possible logical orders. Although machines can be used to prevent learners from going on until they have got each correct answer, it seems that programmes work as well even if the learner can 'cheat' and look ahead at the answers. Also, although the idea of making a positive response has been part of the theory of programming, it seems to make little difference whether the response is made overtly, by constructing an answer (or ticking one of several answers as correct), or covertly by just thinking of the answer one would give.

Other developments in programming include (1) the use of longer or more substantial frames as well as the short ones illustrated above, (2) the use of pictures, recordings, experiments and directed observation, as integral extensions of the verbal programme, and (3) the development of group programmes in which learners still respond individually to the presentation, but in which the presentation takes place at a fixed pace determined by the requirements of the group as a whole. The principles of carefully ordered presentation and individual response are preserved, but, paradoxically, there seems to be a move back to group work and the variety of presentation that characterizes good examples of traditional teaching. The species difference between laboratory rats and human beings reasserts itself.

Green (1962) thought that 'the basic paradigm of programmed instruction is that of the interaction of two persons', but this is true only in a limited sense. Some might say that the standard case of programmed instruction is a predetermined set of interactions between learner and programme, whereas the standard case of inter-personal reaction is a set of unpredictable interactions. Alternatively, it may be that one can more readily envisage a single paradigm for programmed instruction than for human interaction. Other interesting points made by Green include (1) the necessity of ensuring that the learner has acquired a sense of the importance of learning, (2) the difficulty of differentiating the effects of programmed learning in practice because of the interference effects from other forms of concurrent learning, (3) 'the inaccessibility of private material' as a limit on the scope of programming, (4) the widening of the gap between gifted and less gifted learners when self-pacing programmes are used, and (5) the widening of the spread of performance in proportion to increasing tolerance of wrong responses in a programme.

There is no doubt that programmed learning is an effective form of learning. The practical question is to determine where and in what forms it is most justified. (1) It can be justified as an economy in teachers' time, freeing them for tasks that are less susceptible of programming. (2) In requiring continual response from every individual it compares favourably, particularly with forms of class teaching which encourage little learner response, or which allow any one learner to respond perhaps only once or twice in a whole hour. (3) Where learners are highly motivated to master specific knowledge or skills, which will rapidly gain them (let us say) a technical certificate and an increase in salary, programmed learning can be most effective. (4) And, where a subject has not been well analysed by traditional pedagogic devices (textbooks, syllabuses, etc.), the attempt to programme it can help teachers to make a fresh and stronger analysis.

It is interesting to compare modern programming with an example of some early systematizer's efforts. For example, suppose that one opens Comenius's *Orbis Sensualium Pictus, A World of Things Obvious to the Senses Drawn in Pictures* (1672) at pages 50 and 51. Page 50 has a little rectangular picture of *Aves Aquaticae*, Water Fowl. Each bird has a number beside it. Some of the birds are clearly recognizable, others not so well drawn. On page 51, opposite the picture, there is a double column of sentences in English and Latin. They refer to the birds and the words are numbered to match the numbers in the picture. It goes like this:

The white Swan, 1.	Olor 1. candidus,
The Goose, 2.	Anser, 2.
and the Duck, 3.	& Anas, 3.
swim up and down.	natant.
The Cormorant 4.	Mergus 4.
diveth	se mergit

And so on. Not quite a learning programme in the modern sense, but nevertheless systematic, making use of a visual aid and inviting at least a set of covert identification responses between the symbols and sentence structures of two languages and between these symbols and the objects they refer to. This example can be taken as a token of the persistence of the human urge to systematize learning, whether in textbooks, encyclopaedias, scholastic curricula or learning programmes.

Learning for transfer

Transfer of learning was defined in the preceding chapter. It is the idea that the learning of a certain task may have a beneficial or detrimental effect on the learning of a later task that is partly similar but, obviously, partly dissimilar. A command of English may make one rejoice to learn that one's French travelling companion will be *fastidieux*—until this minor negative transfer is undone by learning that he will be tedious, not fastidious. But one could trust to positive transfer if offered *ein Glas Bier* in Germany and enjoy a glass of beer. These two cases differ from the third, where there is no transfer of either kind because of too great dissimilarity. Your Gaelic host invites you *Gearr sliseag de'n mhulachaig*, but you just do not know what to do.

The educational interest of transfer of learning is associated with such ideas as training the mind, mental discipline, learning to use the knowledge you have acquired in contexts different from that in which it was acquired, and the supposed superiority of certain studies or disciplines as mind-trainers (rather like the idea that nasty-tasting medicines are most effective). Transfer of learning, if it serves no other purpose, illustrates how feebly educated people may argue outside the realm of their specialism, and sometimes inside the realm of their prejudices.

1   Frequently there is no clear definition of what is supposed to have transferred. General phrases like 'well trained mind' can be interpreted to fit changing circumstances.

2   The transfer argument is often *post factum*. Mr X was a very good mathematician and became a most successful administrator; therefore mathematics trains the mind for administration. But, of course, it may be (a) that Mr X was simply a person of high general intelligence and, therefore, good at most things if motivated to tackle them at all. (b) It may be that Mr X's schoolmasters belonged in a tradition of assessing that (i) bright boys or even (ii) boys from certain kinds of home or attending certain kinds of school should study mathematics and should, if possible, be directed into senior administrative jobs. (c) It may be that senior administrators and mathematicians have a vested interest in sustaining the belief that there is nothing more high-powered than senior administration and mathematics.

3   Discounting the more sceptical suggestions of the preceding section, and allowing that a mathematical training may, in some undefined sense, make a person better at some other difficult task, one cannot avoid the fact that this transfer effect does not operate equally in all fields, for mathematicians (and all other specialists) demonstrate crass ignorance and stupidity as well as brilliant intelligence in fields outside their own (and, their specialist rivals may add, inside it as well).

4   The notion of 'difficulty' is relative when one speaks of difficult or hard subjects. What is difficult and intelligible only to specialists in one generation becomes what every schoolboy knows in the next. What is difficult when one has no mind for it becomes easy when one has. What is difficult when there is no massive effort to make it easier becomes easier when the effort is made. Problems which are complex but susceptible of definite solutions (for example, in mathematics

science, philology) have often been thought to provide real discipline, whereas problems that are complex with uncertain or variable solutions (for example in literature or social sciences) may be thought less demanding. One knows very well what is meant (the existence of clearer objective checks in the former set of subjects), but it could be argued that it is more, not less, difficult to tackle problems where there are some objective checks but also more subjective hazards.

Psychological discussions of transfer have a considerable history now. One view is that transfer takes place from one task to another only if the tasks have *common elements*, and possibly only if the nature of these common elements is made explicit for the learners. Thus you might know French and you might come across the old Scots word *chaumer*. You might or might not notice the similarity with *chambre* and realize, perhaps with a contextual cue, that it was some kind of *room*. Other psychological concepts relevant to transfer include *response generalization* and *learning sets*. The rat that has learned the response of running through the dry maze may swim through the flooded maze. The monkey that has solved a variety of problems will become more adept at such problem solving. Similarly, a human being who has acquired a so-called learning set is one who has 'got the hang of' a certain range of problems. He can solve subsequent problems more quickly. This terminology may be convenient, although all it does is to stick a label on the phenomena.

The whole concept of transfer has been trenchantly attacked by Kelly (1967). He argues that the concept is hardly necessary. Where it has a clear meaning it adds nothing to what is already implied by the concept of learning. Where it is conjectured to mean more than just learning it is not clear what transfer does mean. It is obvious that many learning tasks require, or are facilitated by, previous knowledge or skill (some algebra for later calculus; ability to drive a car for ability to enter car-racing). This does not need any concept of psychological transfer; the connection is logical.

It may be that transfer has to do with particular circumstances in which earlier learning affects later learning. Kelly lists four cases, based on whether or not the learner is acting with awareness or intention.

1 Awareness and intent. A meteorologist attempting to predict the weather is aware of previous learning and intends to use it.
2 Intent without awareness. In our ordinary use of language we intend to communicate via the learned rules of syntax, but we are not normally aware of these rules as we actually speak or write.
3 Awareness without intent. A man reared in poverty might

become wealthy but be unable to discard his earlier parsimonious habits. He may not intend to continue being parsimonious but he is aware of the habit he has learned.

4 Neither awareness nor intent. A person may have acquired a minor tic which he does not know about but which persists in adult life. He is influenced by a piece of learned behaviour without either intent or awareness.

'Transfer' might be intended to refer to any of these cases, but the differences among them are not usually recognized.

The difficulty of defining what it is that is supposed to transfer is further clarified by considering what non-transfer would mean. If a learning task shows no influence from an earlier one, it may be (1) that the supposedly transferable element was learned but subsequently forgotten; or (2) it may not have been sufficiently well learned in the first instance; or (3) it may have been learned but now be repressed because of some emotional inhibition; or (4) it may have been learned, but the learner just does not see its relevance to the new task. These are different cases and again it can be questioned whether they are illumined by the use of the terms 'transfer' or 'non-transfer'.

It seems, therefore, that transfer of learning, as a popular ingredient in the systematics of learning theory and practice, is a rather treacherous concept, whether viewed educationally or psychologically. It is difficult to pin it down to a clear and precise meaning. Some of its possible meanings seem to add nothing to more useful concepts like learning, forgetting, etc. And, if any of the possible meanings may be useful, one still has the problem that people tend not to specify what meaning they intend. There are obviously effects that can be called transfer effects and that just happen, but it would seem to be wise pedagogical policy to define what effects one wants to produce and then try to produce them, rather than trust that some mysterious underground phenomenon of transfer will work miracles.

Slow learning

Slow learning is not, of course, a system of learning (although teachers may occasionally feel that some of their pupils have perfected it as a system, if not a fine art). Slow learning is rather a problem on which to test learning systems; and the first system that is required is one which will define the scale and nature of the problem and provide means of diagnosing individual cases.

The Plowden report (1967) uses the term 'slow learners' for 'children who are genetically poorly endowed as well as those of average ability who are seriously retarded in their attainments' (p. 301) and mentions the Department of Education and Science's estimate that 'approximately one child in every ten aged over seven is sufficiently retarded to need special education, though this number is significantly greater in some areas'. Schonell (1942) found that 11·4 per cent of 317 boys and girls in a primary school were backward in both English and arithmetic and estimated that these could be divided into 7·2 per cent who were generally dull intellectually and 4·2 per cent who were of average or better intelligence. Various writers have reminded one that, at each stage of schooling, there is (and, in the nature of human variability, must be) a substantial minority of learners who still require some of the education normally associated with the preceding stage. Organizational divisions cut through the actual range of individual needs. One systematic requirement, therefore, is that stages of schooling should be regarded flexibly—particularly by teachers on the immediate 'upper' side of any division.

A second systematic requirement is to differentiate clearly between general educational rights and specific psychological diagnosis. The use of the same term 'slow learner' for a mentally defective child, a child who is generally but not gravely dull, one who is weak in a particular subject, or one who is slow only in relation to exceptionally fast competitors (in a selective school or class, for example), can cloud good judgment. Each of these is a different kind of case demanding varying educational treatment. Irrelevant differences among children should certainly not be stressed, but to obscure relevant differences hardly encourages fair treatment. The fact that categories overlap does not alter the fact that they are still roughly distinguishable.

A third requirement is for some system that can be brought into operation when slow learners get far out of their depth. The ideal plan doubtlessly is to prevent this emergency from arising, and this can be done to some extent by sufficient variety of individual and group programmes at each stage. However, it is unrealistic to overlook the very great differences among learners, and the fact that there are many systematic influences tending to sustain and increase such differences even alongside the best educational programmes. Furthermore, the rough norms against which children are assessed and scholastic planning done are themselves far from stationary. Every improvement that can be made by environmental change or educational ingenuity is a benefit to average and fast learners as well as to slow learners. This makes it all the more necessary to build alternative, remedial or recuperative systems for slow learners into the standard educational provision.

There are two different tasks. One is to establish worthwhile but

less demanding educational programmes for those who seem unlikely, even with every possible help and stimulus, to keep up with
children of average or superior general ability. One of the injustices
of past systems has been to humiliate this class of slow learner by
rubbing their noses in their own failure to reach an impossible
standard. It is not easy in practice to reconcile the urge to give a
pupil every chance and the importance of ensuring that the chance is a
real one. But it is only by working out realistic programmes and
emphasizing their own merits rather than their difference from other
programmes that slow learners can hope for both success in the task
and esteem for their achievement. This educational need is not a
temporary one to be met on an *ad hoc* basis. It is a permanent need—
part of the general need for variety of educational provision within
broad common goals.

The other task is to identify slow learning that arises from temporary disadvantages (school absence, temporary emotional upsets,
poor relationships with a particular teacher, lack of positive motivation for a particular subject, etc.). Here too it seems over-optimistic
to imagine that problems can be dispelled at the wave of a magic
wand, but alertness to the existence of handicaps and a readiness to
diagnose them and take remedial action can prevent the situation
from worsening and may set many learners back on a normal course,
despite a temporary lapse. One of the gravest dangers is that slow
learning as a product of temporary circumstances is identified as
some intrinsic feature of the learner himself. Firmly stamped as a
slow learner ('You don't seem to be catching up, Johnny!') the pupil
tends to conform to this public expectation. If one could promulgate
only one counsel of perfection to teachers of slow learners it might be,
'Never close the educational door on them!'

A system of flexible provision for learners crossing scholastic
boundaries, a system for differentiating various classes of slow
learner, and a system of differential programmes and remedial opportunities—these are three of the most important general requirements
for dealing with slow learning. Programmed learning is as relevant to
slow as to average learners. Its potentiality has been demonstrated
with children of low general intelligence and it could obviously be
used, where suitable programmes exist, for helping someone to catch
up on work he had missed through absence or similar temporary set-
back. The analytic approach required by programmed learning can
also be helpful in clarifying the nature of the slow learner's problem.
It may be that things taken for granted in relation to average learners
must be made explicit for slow learners. By this token, facile assumptions about transfer, which have been shown to be suspect for ordinary learners, are obviously no more warranted for slow learners.

It may seem that the discussion of attitudes is more relevant than that of systems to the slow learner's problem. However, it has been made clear that there is a close interconnection between motivation, attitude, and system. Certainly it is relevant to engineer satisfaction in learning for the slow as for the average learner. This is partly a matter of sympathetic encouragement from teachers, but also partly a matter of having the systematic administrative and pedagogic facilities outlined at the beginning of this section. Applying what was said earlier about the problem of teachers' own attitudes, it is necessary to provide teachers with suitable detailed training in the problems of slow learners and to make such teaching itself satisfying in terms of salary and general esteem. There are difficulties in the path of such a policy, for, just as teaching slow learners may show a small return for great expenditure of effort and patience, so the community at large may be disinclined to bestow much of its patience or reward on providing the teachers with the context they require for success.

Perspective on attitudes, systems and policies

A striking example of the interrelationship of attitudes and systems comes from the study of streaming in primary schools—that is, the practice of dividing all the children of the same age into separate classes on the basis of their supposed general ability. Lunn (1970), on the basis of an enquiry into seventy-two schools, concludes that 'a mere change in organization, such as the abandonment of streaming, unaccompanied by a serious attempt to change teachers' attitudes, beliefs and methods of teaching is unlikely to make much difference' (p. 56). The 'philosophy of education' embodied in a school's organization can genuinely influence the children's social and educational development, but only if the teachers genuinely subscribe to it. Some, perhaps many, schools still do not have the kind of institutional or interpersonal machinery that facilitates maximum commitment to some measure of agreed policy.

Curriculum and examinations reform is one of the main channels of large-scale change in educational policy. It is, ideally, a two-way channel between those trying to encourage improvements in educational programmes and others who have to put the improvements into practice (if they accept them) and who may have strong loyalties to existing curricula with which they are more familiar. The currents and eddies in this channel are complex. There must be persisting differences of opinion about at least some aspects of what ought to be done. There must be differences of emphasis with regard to central planning or co-ordination and local or individual variation. The freshness of new ideas and materials may turn as stale as what they are meant to replace unless individual teachers capture the intellectual spirit and not just the new routines. The whole topic is one where the problems of system and attitude thrive.

The conclusion to which the arguments of this chapter point is that neither attitudes nor systems by themselves can constitute any adequate educational policy. This cannot be completely obvious, for there are too many people who go around pinning their colours to one or other mast exclusively. But neither is it a matter of pinning two clear colours to the mast instead of one, but rather of weaving an intricate pattern from the two colours and pinning that pattern to the mast. Not to get side-tracked into a further extension of the metaphor, the literal need is for technical analysis of the materials and circumstances of learning, but also for the establishment of conditions which will make learning satisfying and rewarding to both learners and teachers by ordinary social criteria. Unrewarded dedication is an ideal, not a means of achieving it.

Concepts like attitude, systems analysis, learning transfer and slow learning are complex and sometimes surrounded by confusion. It is difficult to believe that some of the prevalent misunderstanding of such commonly used terms can be other than detrimental to educational practice and policy. Some of the ideas behind the general concepts are valid and practically relevant, others are not. One chapter cannot make all of the important discriminations, but some of the important ones have been made.

Policy is usually the name given to large-scale planning; it is typically, in the case of education, politically rather than psychologically determined. But politicians are prepared to use psychological arguments and, consequently, expose themselves to psychological appraisal. But policy is something that can be envisaged at different levels—political, central administrative, local administrative, individual school, individual teacher or even individual teacher confronted by one individual pupil. Whatever the actual influence of psychological understanding and insight at these various levels, it seems legitimate to suggest that some of the principles suggested in this and other chapters ought to count with educators.

The problem of slow or backward learners is often a difficult one for teachers. Its solution depends on more detailed study of teaching aids and systems than is possible in this book. It is a specialized area of study. Nevertheless, it has been taken here as an example of how systems analysis and attitudinal considerations might be related to a particular educational problem. One of the most difficult systematic problems here is that average and abler children automatically generate more reward for themselves and their teachers by making successful progress, whereas regular slow learners generate less reward for more effort. The community at large is apt to contribute exhortation rather than substantial support to the slow learner problem.

Faster learners are normally expected to set their sights higher, but so are some slower children from ambitious families. This gives rise to the problem of slow learning relative to insistence on advanced achievement. It may be general, as when a pupil is held to an academically demanding programme despite his average ability; or specific, as when a pupil is expected to aim at a particular career despite his disinclination for it. The treatment of such cases must vary with the details, and the most persistent difficulty may be to do anything about parental or headmasterly pressures. Apart from that, teachers can provide some kind of safety-valve, if only by offering a sympathetic ear to the victim. Many slow learners in this category will persist and succeed; some revolt against the entire imposition.

The preceding three chapters have concentrated on learning from various points of view, but trying to keep a balance among empirical evidence, general theory, specific conceptual analysis and specific practical suggestions. Although it is justifiable to look at learning itself as a central topic of educational psychology, it must still be related to the wider perspective of child development discussed earlier and to problems of assessment and guidance which will be discussed in the remaining part of the book.

9 Educational and psychological assessment

Some understanding of human assessment is indispensable for people, like teachers and psychologists, who exercise great influence through the assessments they make and the decisions that are taken in consequence. But educational and psychological assessment is not only a technical problem, for patterns of assessment and assumptions about them depend on wider assumptions about human behaviour and purpose—each influencing the other. With so many variables it is more difficult to sustain a clear, complete and balanced picture, but the main intention of this chapter is to attempt at least a first sketch for such a picture.

One of the most widely relevant background factors is the association between (1) length of education, (2) parents' occupational class, (3) level of intelligence, and (4) the pattern of a person's adult life and career. A typically clear and carefully argued example of this association is given by Maxwell (1969). He discusses the careers of a representative sample of 1,208 Scottish boys and girls, born in 1936, assessed educationally and psychologically in 1947 when they were eleven years old, and further studied down to 1964 when they were twenty-eight. Of the original 1,208 the number still contacted in 1964 was 1,104. Maxwell stresses the fact that, if any group is selected in terms of one of the first three factors listed, it will be selected also in terms of the other two, for all three are intercorrelated. The present purpose is not to discuss these complex phenomena, but only to state the general relationship as an important aspect of the context in which assessments and associated educational assumptions are made. Length of education, parental occupational class and level of intelligence constantly impinge upon other assessments.

Examples of cultural diversity in educational assessment are easily found. The United States has made the most extensive use of 'objective testing', whereas traditional examinations have predominated in Europe. But these traditional examinations themselves vary between stressing frequent or infrequent examination, written or oral examination, marking on a percentage or on a five- or ten-point scale, asking for a few substantial answers or a greater number of shorter answers, centralization or devolution of the examination function, etc. And the content of what is assessed varies according to national or local culture. Similarly, in the realm of general psychological assessment, the United States makes use of a very wide range of psychological tests of aptitude, ability and personality, both for research and practical purposes, whereas European countries use such tests much less or not at all.

This chapter is concerned mainly with looking inside the problem of human assessment, but the points just made may help to establish that organized assessment is very much a social function, a means of processing the members of a society according to current norms, and incidentally sustaining these norms as it does so. Challenges to assessment practices may be challenges to remedy technical defects or to substitute different norms. It may be necessary to look outside the assessment problem in its narrower technical sense. However, there is no perspective, wide or narrow, that will abolish the problem itself. One of the most tedious kinds of argument is that which harps on the gap between actual assessment and some notion of perfect assessment (or even more mythical non-assessment). The practical problem is one of improvement not of perfection or abolition.

Purposes of assessment

The fundamental questions are (1) why does one want to make an assessment? (2) what exactly is it one wants to assess? and (3) how can one make the assessment most efficiently with as few undesirable side-effects as possible? Sometimes it is easier to answer the question of why in terms of what causes one to make an assessment than to do so in terms of what justifies it. The cause may be the fact of being paid to make the assessment, or being expected to, or not having thought of questioning established custom, or believing that the custom is a harmless or even beneficial one. The more interesting question is the one of justification, and there are several interrelated categories.

(1) *Guidance and selection* constitute one justification. If individuals are to acquire the education and pursue the careers they ought or want to, then some assessment must be made of (a) individual

abilities, aptitudes and personality; and (b) individual achievement at various stages relevant to an eventual goal. The units or occasions of assessment for this purpose can vary from the class test in a particular school subject (to guide pupil and teacher about what work should be undertaken next) to the major examination, or major discussion of a school-leaver's career, which may determine very large areas of the individual's future. The word 'guidance' may be appropriate where a variety of open paths confronts the person assessed, the word 'selection' where particular opportunities can be given only to a limited number, for whatever reason. Some might consider the *diagnostic* purpose of assessment as a separate category (especially where one has in mind assessment for some special or remedial treatment, on an educational analogy with medical diagnosis), but this would seem to be a sub-category of guidance or selection.

(2) *Motivation* may be the second justification for assessment that occurs to teachers. Presumably this is a form of social motivation, or motivation based on regard for one's private or public image (the self-concept). A good or bad assessment makes one feel good or bad —at any rate, if one counts on esteem from that particular assessor or in the particular area of achievement assessed. If little Johnny gets most of his esteem from back-street exploits he may not bother about his poor arithmetic, and may be prepared to ride out the storm of the teacher's displeasure. Those children who acquire high 'achievement motivation' from an early age are likely to go on doing more work for the satisfaction it gives them, but, as suggested earlier, this is not a mysterious causal agent but the result of parental expectation and associated influences which one would expect to persist if they were strongly present in early childhood.

Since motivational factors like the desire for esteem or for social conformity operate through organized habitual channels, institutionalized assessment (examinations, etc.) provides motivation by providing such a channel. There is a premium of parental pride, teacher approval and career success on scholastic achievement, all sustaining the motivational channel of standard scholastic and vocational assessments. But the sustaining factors may be absent. Some parents do not care about schooling. Some teachers or schools do not engineer success and approval for children who cannot achieve them easily. Some careers, and their associated scholastic preparations, are irrelevant for some children. Wankowski (1969), discussing successful and unsuccessful students at an English university, suggests that the latter are students who (a) are uncertain about their short- and long-term goals, (b) have been persuaded to go to the university rather than gone by their own wish, (c) are uninterested in their studies, and (d) have relative difficulty with them.

All of this suggests that assessment can be an occasion or channel for motivation, but that other factors are more fundamental in determining whether or not the channel operates. A feature of many scholastic assessments is that the guidance (or selection) and motivational functions are confused. The assessor wants both to form an accurate and objective opinion about what has been achieved and to influence learners' subsequent behaviour by encouragements and discouragements. The slow learner may get a bonus for trying, the fast learner a penalty so that he does not develop too good a conceit of himself. Hence the tendency often observed to avoid the lower and upper extremes of a mark scale. The absolutely worthless answer gets 10 per cent because there are marks on the paper; the answer that could hardly be bettered in examination conditions gets 80 per cent because some mythical super-examinee could presumably make 100.

(3) *Maintaining publicly recognized standards* is the third justification for some assessments. This is one of several points at which assessment interlocks with wider educational and social purposes. One of the virtues of well recognized public standards of achievement is that they help people to know what is being assessed and what it signifies in a broad sense. This does not mean that such criteria are free from defect or the need for periodical review and change. But a free-for-all policy of assessing anything you like in any way you like can undermine the value of the assessment currency. In the Gilbertian aphorism, where everyone is somebody, no one is anybody. Another relevant adage is, Better the evil one knows . . . Not as an automatic argument against change, but as a reminder that one can allow more readily for the defects of a known system. One has to balance the virtues and defects of a system known intimately from experience against new systems whose qualities have to be surmised by reflection on general principles. However, even with radical change of standards, the general purpose remains. The new standards too are meant to offer some kind of public assurance. Even those most urgent to avoid the prescription of particular standards seek public recognition for their prescription of non-prescription.

(4) *Research* is a justification for assessment that concerns fewer assessors directly but may influence very many more people ultimately through its findings. Psychological assessment, or psychometrics, has made major general and practical contributions to educational assessment. The fact that there are psychologists with psychometric manias and phobias should not prevent one from recognizing the clarification of what is involved in human assessment that has emerged from decades of research and controversy. People have been forced to see what some of the main problems are, even where differences of interpretation and emphasis persist.

The interlocking of these four purposes can be illustrated explicitly. Guidance must be in relation to public standards and individual motivation. Motivation is influenced by public standards and by individual guidance. Research interests are influenced by the nature of public standards and policies, and influence these in return. Research also influences understanding and practice in guidance and motivation. Despite these interrelations, the four purposes suggested seem to be the main ones that can be substantially differentiated. There are other ways of looking at assessment that may seem broader or narrower according to one's viewpoint. For example, an administrator might think of assessment as an administrative device for allocating people to various institutions and educational or vocational treatments. An economist might think of it similarly as a tool for deriving the maximum benefit from the minimum input—a kind of quantity and quality control. Or a psychometrist might think of it as the sum of techniques available for measuring human performance on all dimensions of behaviour that could be measured reliably.

These possibilities deserve passing mention, even if they are less specific than the four-purpose analysis proposed here. Even with four purposes, it may seem that assessors have only too many lines of justification for almost any assessment practice. If one line weakens (let us say that motivation is poor despite every pedagogic effort) there is another (perhaps the defence of public standards) to fall back on. This suggests that it is not enough to recognize or state the purposes of an assessment programme in all-embracing terms. Ideally, there should be a specification that differentiates the achievement or non-achievement of the goal by clear and demonstrable criteria.

Some fundamentals of assessment

It seemed right to start with the justifications for assessment, but discussion of the What and How of assessment will be easier if some fundamentals of a different kind are interposed—the elementary ways of describing and comparing the results that emerge from assessing groups of people by any means at all. Certain common problems arise whether one is assessing intelligence, specific learning, aptitude, character or personality; and whether one uses examinations, tests, interviews, ratings, 'continuous assessment' or any other technique whatsoever.

Briefly the problems are these:

1 Against what scale is the assessment made?
2 How representative is the sample (of people or of performances) on which the scale is based?

3 What pattern or distribution of assessments does the scale produce?

4 How valid is the scale? That is, why should one believe that it really measures what it purports to?

5 How reliable is the scale? That is, why should one trust that it will give consistent results from one occasion to another?

6 How can the results from different assessments be combined or compared?

Defining the standard of comparison is the first problem. It is a question of making clear what one means by any assessment. Much of ordinary conversation has meaning only because the context is known. Suppose that someone said, 'She's a really bright girl.' That is plain enough English on the face of it. But was it said of a go-go girl in a discothèque, or the best Honours Classics graduate the professor had seen in a decade, or a con man's lady associate, or your girl-friend or wife the night she made that very special casserole, or ironically of the damsel who has just well-meaningly ruined your shirt in the laundry?

The problem with considered assessment is that people may think they know what the context is and how it compares with associated contexts, but in fact they cannot know with certainty unless controlled comparisons are made and the evidence made available. The teacher of slow learners forgets how fast *average* children are; the teacher of academically directed pupils how bright his dullest pupil is in relation to the whole population. Entire classes, schools or even regions may differ systematically from other classes, schools or regions, despite superficial similarities. Only systematic comparisons with standard instruments of assessment can provide a measurement that has more than local relevance. Many measurements do not have to have more than local relevance, but this limitation of function may involve a limitation of general esteem and value. The general reputation of a school or area provides a rough standard of comparison, but usually too rough to guarantee accurate assessment of individuals or distinguish genuine from imagined achievement.

Samples and distributions

To define the standard of comparison represented by any test requires knowledge of how the assessments are distributed and how the sample of people assessed is constituted. (The word 'test' is used for convenience, but it could be any form of assessment, from an examination to an interview). If any individual assessment is to be as meaningful as possible, it must be made with reference to a known distribution of assessments derived from a representative sample of the population concerned.

For limited purposes a person with extensive experience of a particular form of assessment might constitute in his mind a notional sample distribution from that experience. Anyone dealing regularly in a particular commodity, from selling potatoes to teaching reading in a wide-ability-range school, has some kind of reference scale validated by experience. However, there have been copious demonstrations of the variability and instability of such notional scales. Interview assessments, for example, which are bound to make use of notional scales, have sometimes been shown to correlate very little with subsequent success in the course for which the interview is supposed to select.

The problem of how to get a representative sample will not be discussed here, for it is well discussed at suitable length in many introductory and advanced statistics texts. All that must be noted is the many ways in which the representativeness of a sample may be impaired. There may be absentees when the test is given, and these may differ in some systematic way from those who are present, so that the obtained distribution is biased as well as incomplete. Even if a sample is large and representative of a particular school or area, that school or area may differ systematically from other schools and areas. An analysis of questionnaire responses cannot include those who did not bother to respond. A sample of on-the-street or round-the-door interviews may be biased by the interviewer's lack of diligence in observing strictly the instructions that would give a representative sample. A head teacher may exclude some children from a survey for a reason related to educational purposes if not the purposes of representative sampling. A soft-hearted teacher may give marginal help, or at least encouragement, to those tested, while a hard-headed objectivist sticks carefully (as all should) to the letter of the instructions. In this last case, the two samples may be equally complete but their respective performances not equally representative of their usual work.

Given that the worst of these pitfalls have been avoided, what kind of distribution of assessments is typical or desirable? School examination marks tend to be distributed in a way that reflects (1) reluctance to award very high or very low marks, and (2) reluctance to place many below whatever mark is conventionally counted as a borderline pass (perhaps 50 per cent). Interview assessments may allocate candidates into three rough categories of Accept, Reject or Provisional, with the proportions in each category obviously depending on the ratio of applicants to places. Honours examinations allocate candidates to three or four categories. Perkin (1969) reports that, of the 1967 graduates from five of the new English universities, the percentage getting first-class honours varied from 1 to 6, of upper second class from 18 to 39, of lower second from 39 to 53, and of third class from 8 to 26.

These examples give some idea of how different circumstances, conventions and purposes influence the distributions. If markers or institutions are compared they may differ in two respects particularly. They may assess apparently severely, with a low average assessment, or apparently leniently, with a high average. It may be that those who earn a low average really are not so good as the high average group, but marking scales are partly arbitrary. The performance on which one man stamps 60 per cent is stamped 50 per cent by another. The fallacy that numbers must be precise indicators comes into play and the unthinking believe there is a genuine percentage difference.

In addition to differences in apparent severity, reflected in high or low averages, markers differ in the way they distribute their marks. Table 8 shows the marks awarded to six candidates by three assessors. In this example all the markers have the same average of 60 but the scores are very differently distributed, ranging from 45 to 77, 55 to 65, and 45 to 80 respectively. The degree of variation is normally expressed by a statistic called the *variance* (σ^2, sigma squared) or by the *standard deviation* (σ, the Greek letter sigma), which is simply the square root of the variance. The calculation of the variance and standard deviation of marker Z's assessments is shown in Table 9. Taken to the nearest whole number, the standard deviations of the three markers are 10, 3 and 15. One standard deviation above the average or mean gives 70 (60 + 10) on marker X's scale, 63 (60 + 3) on marker Y's, and 75 (60 + 15) on marker Z's. These three different numbers signify the same thing, the same relative position on the marking scales as actually used. There are various techniques for expressing assessments on a common scale, even if they derive from different kinds of distribution.

Some of the ways in which assessors can partly predetermine test distributions have been mentioned. A test can be made so easy that everyone scores high marks, or so difficult that the marks are all low. It could include items intended to make finer distinctions among the ablest candidates or among the less able. This is all a matter of selecting test items for the purpose in mind. In practice it is more difficult to draw fine distinctions in respect of a given criterion among the great majority who tend to do middling well. Partly because of this, partly because of statistical convenience or expediency, the form of distribution known as a *normal* distribution has been

Candidate	A	B	C	D	E	F
Marker X	45	53	56	62	67	77
Marker Y	55	57	59	61	63	65
Marker Z	45	45	45	70	75	80

Table 8 Variation in marking. Three markers have the same average (60) but different distributions of individual marks

Scores	Difference from group average (60)	Difference squared
80	20	400
75	15	225
70	10	100
45	−15	225
45	−15	225
45	−15	225
360 (total)	(total)	1400

$$\text{Average} = 360 \div 6 = 60$$
$$\text{Variance} = 1400 \div 6 = 233 \cdot 3$$
$$\text{Standard deviation} = \sqrt{233} = 15 \cdot 27$$

Table 9 Calculating the variance and standard deviation of scores, a simplified example

extensively used in attempts to make more precise psychometric assessments. The general pattern of this distribution is shown in Figure 10.

A normal distribution has a precise mathematical formula. If a characteristic is distributed in this way it is possible to make various convenient statistical operations on the data. The average score may be called 0 and the scores of the population tested are spread out symmetrically in standard deviations on either side of this central point. Just over two-thirds of them fall closely into the centre, between one standard deviation above and below the mean. Calling the mean 0 involves the use of negative as well as positive scores, but it is possible to convert the scale into entirely positive scores. For example, the mean might be 60 with a standard deviation of 10. In that case, 68·26 per cent of the scores would fall in the range 60 ± 10, that is, between 50 and 70. Or, if the mean were 100 and the standard deviation 15, 68·26 per cent of the scores would fall between 85 and 115. Similarly, if one looks at the range between one and two standard deviations above or below the mean, 13·59 per cent of

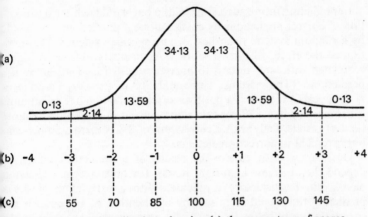

Figure 10 Normal distribution, showing (a) the percentage of scores in each section, (b) the standard deviations above and below the mean, and (c) the distribution expressed as a standardized scale with a chosen mean of 100 and standard deviation of 15

scores would fall in each of these sectors, whatever the actual value of the mean and standard deviation.

Apart from the statistical conveniences mentioned, another advantage of normally distributed scores is that users become rapidly familiar with a single intelligible pattern, instead of having to discriminate among a great variety of less stable distributions which are less well understood. At the same time, a caveat must be entered that assessments do not have to be normally distributed. Moreover, normal distribution is something that makes more sense when one is studying the whole range of any measured characteristic. Sometimes one is concerned only with a very restricted section of the whole range, in which case any normal distribution that is manufactured must be different from that illustrated by the entire range.

Validity and reliability

Knowing the distribution of a relevant representative sample on a scale, whatever it is, one can go on to assess the validity of the assessments that are made, to find evidence that the test really does measure what it claims to. The usual evidence sought is that the test correlates well with other purported measures of the same thing. Test A in commercial subjects should correlate with Test B, and both should correlate with success in commercial employment. There is no fixed standard of what such a correlation should be.

In predicting future success or failure one would achieve a proportion of correct predictions by chance alone if predictions were made by a random system, regardless of any specific evidence. The question is, therefore, whether a set of assessments is sufficiently highly correlated with later success to provide a basis for *improving* future predictions. (This assumes some stability in the correlation over several years.) If there is a positive correlation of 0·6 one might hope for something like a 20-per-cent improvement in prediction by using the test results. Only with a correlation of 0·8 is there a 50-per-cent improvement in correct predictions.

Deciding whether to use the results of a predictive test might depend then on how important it was, for other reasons, to avoid having an unsatisfactory candidate. With a correlation of 0·8 a predicting test would seem worthy of attention in any case. If the correlation were below 0·6 or 0·5 the employer might resort to the traditional test of choosing the one with the pretty face, or, more seriously, whose personal circumstances made her more likely to meet the requirements of the post. But predictive tests are often more relevant to assessing the likely success of whole groups rather than single individuals. If an employer of large numbers obtained even a 10-per-cent improvement in his selection, this might represent a large economy just because of the numbers.

The case just given is over-simplified in order to illustrate a single point. In practice there tend to be many different criteria of current performance and of subsequent success. 'Satisfactory' to one employer may mean 'fitting in completely with routines I don't want disturbed'; to another, 'showing real initiative and ability to cut out pointless routines'. What predicts one characteristic cannot be expected to predict the other. But, even where the criterion is apparently agreed (initiative, let us say), different employers may have different ideas of what constitutes initiative, and the same employer may change his conception of initiative from time to time. This kind of variability, typical of all human assessment, constitutes a warning not to regard any single validity correlation (or coefficient) with too much veneration; nor 'common sense' comments on validity, unless they specify what stable and clearly identifiable criteria are intended.

Where validity means correlation with some future criterion it is called *predictive* validity. Correlation with another test at the same time is called *concurrent* validity. The term *content* validity is used to refer to adequate and properly balanced coverage of the contents of any subject tested, and *construct* validity to indicate that a test genuinely measures some general psychological quality. A test of engineering aptitude would have poor construct validity if all the most successful practising engineers did badly on it, for the very idea or construct of engineering means the skill that actual successful engineers exercise, however it may be analysed in detail. If there were a test for newspaper delivery one would hardly talk about construct validity, for the function specified has little generality or complexity.

The reliability as well as the validity of a test must be estimated. How sure can one be that the test would give the same results if it were repeated on a slightly different occasion, or if it were marked by the same person on separate occasions, or by different markers on the same occasion? One of the well proven facts of assessment is that performers and assessors vary from one occasion to the next. Some of this variation is due to identifiable change between occasions. The performers may improve with practice or degenerate with loss of interest. The assessors may change their minds about what deserves most credit, or happen to be in a more (or less) cheerful mood. But some of the variation is a product of more elusive chances, so that there are inconsistencies with no identified cause or justification.

Reliability, like validity, can be expressed by a correlation coefficient—this time between the results from the same test on two different occasions of testing or of marking. Where a test has a large number of items, it is possible to avoid the problem that those tested may improve or degenerate on a second occasion because of their experience on the first occasion. If the test has a hundred items one treats the one occasion of testing as if it were two—one defined by doing the even items of the test, the other defined by doing the odd items. If the results for odd and even items are highly correlated, the test is considered reliable. The resulting coefficient is called the split-half coefficient. As with validity coefficients, there is no fixed standard of what is satisfactory. Similar considerations apply in interpreting correlations. A carefully constructed objective cognitive test might be expected to have a reliability of about 0·9, but tests are used with much lower reliabilities and one simply has to note that results of such tests contain more unidentified chance variation than more reliable tests.

The potential unreliability of assessors has been extensively demonstrated in school and university and in different kinds of subject, from English to mathematics. While objective tests tend to have reliabilities of the order of 0·9, assessments of examination answers or essays typically achieve reliabilities of the order of 0·5. Individual assessors may be more consistent or less consistent than this. Multiple marking of essays by four assessors can sometimes generate average marks with a reliability nearer 0·9. The use of identical sets of instructions to markers does not necessarily increase the statistical reliability of the assessment, perhaps because markers do not necessarily follow the instructions. The practical implication of this is that there is considerable scope for the influence of pure chance on assessments, and consequently on the awards and decisions associated with them. The use of larger numbers of questions or the use of objective tests can increase reliability coefficients, but at the expense of lowering the premium on more substantial units of work and on the exposition of ideas in essays. The use of a sufficient variety of assessors, modes of assessment and occasions of assessment may be a practical way of ensuring that a person's general assessment is not dominated by any single bias arising from one or more of these sources. There is certainly no point in sitting down to lament the fact of unreliability, for it will persist in any conceivable human society. The practical task, as already suggested, is to moderate the worst excesses and study improvements.

Comparing and combining assessments

Means, standard deviation. Table 11 and Figure 12 show the kind of distribution one might get from administering an objective test to a large group of people. This particular group consisted of first-year undergraduates. Just displaying the distribution is one way of presenting the facts, although there is already a minor degree of simplification and clarification in dividing the scale into a series of five-point sections. But even this amount of detail may be confusing for some purposes—for example, if one has to compare a considerable number of distributions. A common way of describing such a distribution summarily is to state the average or mean score and the standard deviation. If one calls the scores x then the mean is sometimes written as M_x or $\bar{x}$. Its calculation is expressed as $\Sigma x/N$ (Σ or Greek capital sigma meaning 'the sum or total of')—the total of the scores divided by their number. The standard deviation is written as σ_x.

The mean of the distribution in Table 11 and Figure 12 is 68 and the standard deviation 13. One can see that the distribution is not quite so symmetrical as the ideal normal curve in Table 10, but it is near enough to ignore the difference for illustrative purposes. Knowing only the mean and standard deviation (and assuming roughly normal distribution), one knows without any further detail that about two-thirds of the scores will be in the range 68 ± 13 (55 to 81), with another sixth at either end of the range. One knows how far the test spreads out those who do it, and one can give some meaning to an individual score.

Median, percentile, quartile range. Table 11 also illustrates another way of describing a distribution—one that might be more valid if the

Intelligence score	Frequency (f)	Cumulative frequency (cf)	(cf) as percentage of 152
90–94	3	152	100
85–89	12	149	98
80–84	18	137	90
75–79	17	119	78
70–74	23	102	68
65–69	25	79	52
60–64	13	54	36
55–59	17	41	28
50–54	7	24	16
45–49	10	17	11
40–44	4	7	5
35–39	3	3	2
Total	152		

Table 11 Grouped frequency distribution of intelligence scores of 152 students, with cumulative frequencies (counting from the foot), and cumulative frequencies as percentages of 152. Mean score 68 with $\sigma = 13$. Median score (middle score or 50th percentile) 69 with interquartile range (the range of the middle 50 per cent of scores) of 19. The 75th percentile is 78, the 25th percentile 59 (78 – 59 = 19).

scores were heavily skewed towards the top or bottom end of the scale. One finds out the score of the middle person when all are arranged in order from top to bottom. This score is called the median. With a short series of scores it is easy to spot the median (6, 7, 8, 9, 10—median 8). If the number of scores is even one takes the median to be halfway between the middle two (1, 6, 8, 9—median 7). In the first instance both mean and median are 8, but in the second the mean is 6 while the median is 7.

With grouped scores, as in Table 11, it is necessary to convert the individual frequencies into cumulative frequencies (3, 3 + 4 = 7, 3 + 4 + 10 = 17, etc.) and then convert these into percentages of the total (at the top of the percentage column, 152 out of 152 is obviously 100 per cent of the students). If one looks at the cf percentage column, 52 per cent of the students are accounted for up to and including the intelligence interval 65–69, but only 36 per cent up to the interval beneath it, 60–64. The middle student, the one at the 50 per cent mark, must come somewhere in the 65–69 interval. And, since 52 per cent takes you to the top point of that interval (69·5),

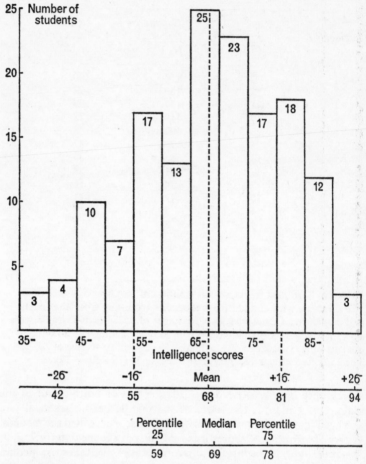

Figure 12 Histogram of intelligence scores of 152 students, with standard deviation scale and percentile scale

he must be fairly near the top. By a simple calculation one can establish that the median is 68·9 (69).

The median or 50th percentile indicates the scores of the person who is better than one-half of the group and poorer than the other. The 25th percentile similarly indicates the score of the person who is better than 25 per cent, or the 75th the person better than 75 per cent of the group. In Table 11, the 25th percentile is 59 and the 75th is 78. The range between these (78 − 59 = 19) may be given to indicate the spread of scores on either side of a median. Because these particular percentiles cut off the top and bottom quarters of the distribution they are also called the first and third quartiles, and the intervening range the interquartile range. Sometimes, presumably to make it look slightly more like a standard deviation, the interquartile range is halved and converted into a semi-interquartile range (in the case of Table 11, 19/2 = 9·5).

Any percentile can be calculated. The final column of Table 11 illustrates that the 2nd percentile comes at the top of interval 35–39 (39·5). The 28th is 59·5, the 90th is 84·5. The value of a percentile is that it tells one exactly what percentage of the group is above or below a particular score, and enables a meaningful comparison to be made between scales of assessment that may be otherwise different in character. If the students of Table 11 had been carefully assessed for good looks (a less objective matter, of course) and their scores converted into percentiles, the person at the 90th (or any other) percentile would have the same relative standing for looks as the student at the 90th percentile on the intelligence scale for intelligence. In both cases he (or she) would be judged better than 90 per cent of the group, but not so good as the top 10 per cent.

Standard error. The statistics just described can be helpful as summary descriptions ·or for comparing different sets of assessments with one another. However, the problem persists about whether the statistics themselves are derived from reliable samples. Suppose that one took a second sample of 152 first-year science students, and that there was no identified reason for expecting their intelligence scores to vary from those of the first sample. Can one estimate the likelihood of variation due to unidentified chance on the basis of the first sample's results alone? The statistic known as the standard error is used for this purpose. It is an estimate of how far an actually observed statistic might vary if one repeated the test or experiment a large number of times.

We have seen that the mean score for the 152 students in Table 11 is 68 and the standard deviation 13. The standard error for the mean (symbolized as σ_m) is the standard deviation of the distribution divided by the square root of the number of cases ($\sigma/\sqrt{N}$, or $13/\sqrt{152}$ = 1, approximately). Knowing this one can consult tables which indicate the chances of any parallel sample deviating by a given amount from the existing sample. Roughly speaking, there is a 95 per cent chance ($P < ·05$) that the mean of any other sample of the same population on the same test would be within two standard errors of the value already obtained—that is, $68 \pm (2 \times 1)$, 68 ± 2, or 66–70. Our observed distribution is a big and representative enough sample of its particular population to virtually guarantee that the mean would not vary beyond these narrow limits.

A small sample would have a mean with a larger standard error.

To take a rather extreme case, the six scores given by marker X in Table 8 have a mean of 60 and a standard deviation of 10. For this sample σ_m would be $10/\sqrt{6}$, $10/2\cdot449$, or $4\cdot25$. In other words, a variation of $\pm$ two standard errors from the mean ($60 \pm (2 \times 4\cdot25)$, $60 \pm 9\cdot5$, or $51\cdot5$ to $69\cdot5$—18 points of score) indicates a much bigger variation where the sampling distribution is so tiny. This illustrates the principle, but, of course, one would not base any generalization on such a tiny sample. The question remains, at what point then would one trust a sample? And the answer is a matter of degree, partly assessable by means of the standard error. The more one has to be sure of an estimate, the lower must the statistical variability be, or, alternatively, the wider the allowances one must make in using the evidence. It is convenient to illustrate the idea of standard error with reference to the mean, but one can calculate the standard error of some other statistics. This is discussed in relevant textbooks.

Non-parametric statistics. Statistics based on the properties of the curve of normal distribution should be used only when dealing with a distribution that is normally distributed. There are statistical tests for establishing whether a distribution is normal in the technical sense. For less precise purposes it may be sufficient to inspect the distribution and decide whether it looks near enough to normality. Or, in some cases, assessors can be instructed to distribute their assessments in a way that will ensure near-normality. Thus, if assessing any characteristic on a five-point scale, assessors might be instructed to ensure that their percentage distribution was roughly as follows:

A	B	C	D	E
10	20	40	20	10

or, if there were (let us say) eleven categories, something like this:

A	B	C	D	E	F	G	H	I	J	K
1	3	7	12	17	20	17	12	7	3	1

and to avoid the tendency to bunch their assessments, as in:

A	B	C	D	E
3	60	30	7	0

This assumes that there is either a sufficiently wide sample, or alternatively, a sufficiently finely discriminating test to spread the scores out fully.

Statistics based on a known distribution like the normal curve are called parametric. Their defining limits or parameters are known.

But distributions may not conform to a known pattern, in which case non-parametric statistics should be calculated. These are mentioned in statistics texts and discussed fully in Siegel (1956), who classifies the statistics according to whether they apply to nominal, ordinal or interval scales of assessment. A *nominal* scale is one that classifies characteristics by simple names or numbers (employed/unemployed, medical fitness A1/C3, etc.).

An *ordinal* or *ranking* scale is one that puts people in order according to some varying characteristic, but without having a fixed unit of measurement. Thus one can rank people for socio-economic status, but there is no unit that would let one say a particular step at one part of the scale was precisely equivalent to a particular step at another. There is a ladder but no standard size of rungs. Similarly, a set of examination marks expresses the candidates' order of merit. And, for convenience, we pretend that we are entitled to add and subtract marks as if any marking unit was the numerical equivalent of another. But some marks are actually harder or easier for anybody to earn—for example, those respectively at the top and bottom of the scale. In addition, the pattern of marks varies partly arbitrarily from one assessment or assessor to the next.

An *interval* scale, finally, is one where the assessments are not just an order of merit but a scale with fixed and known units, like a thermometer or a metre stick. Normally-distributed test scores are sometimes regarded as equal interval scales, but, as Siegel says, this is partly assumption, partly artefact. That is why earlier references to normal distribution in this chapter stressed its convenience and plausibility rather than any supposed absolute validity.

Correlation. The comparison of assessments depends on using the most justifiable statistics and on estimating the sampling error to which the statistics themselves are subject as well as any other errors which may more obviously invalidate conclusions. These are points that have been stressed in the immediately preceding sections. One of the direct comparisons most frequently made is that represented by the correlation coefficient (r). A correlation can be calculated either on a parametric or non-parametric basis. Table 13 illustrates the appearance of a correlation chart. The distribution of intelligence scores is the same one that appears in Table 11 and Figure 12, but it is set alongside the performance of the same students in their first-year university science examinations.

The intelligence scores have a mean of 68 with $\sigma = 13$. The examination marks have a lower mean (just over 62) and a narrower range (σ just over 8). The positive correlation of 0·6 indicates that the two kinds of test are partly measuring the same thing. The correlation coefficient, when squared and expressed as a percentage,

Intelligence scores	First-year university science marks								Total no. of students
	40 44	45 49	50 54	55 59	60 64	65 69	70 74	75 79	
90–94			2		1				3
85–89			3	4	2	3			12
80–84		1	5	6	4		1	1	18
75–79	3		3	3	4	3	1		17
70–74	1	2	3	3	7	4	3		23
65–69	2	2	6	6	3	4	2		25
60–64	1	1	1	3	3	3	1		13
55–59	2	1	4	3	5	2			17
50–54	2	1	3	1					7
45–49	2	3	3	2					10
40–44	3	1							4
35–39	1			2					3
Total no. of students	17	12	33	33	29	19	8	1	152

Table 13 Correlation of intelligence test scores and university marks (r = +0·6)

indicates the proportion of variation in each test that overlaps with variation in the other. In this case the proportion is $(0·6)^2$ per cent, or 36 per cent.

The existence of this kind of correlation or overlap points out a fact and puts a number on it only as an indication of scale. It does not explain it. Does being intelligent make one better at science, or being good at science make one better at intelligence tests? Or does the opportunity of a certain kind of education or background make one good (or poor) at both? There are more sophisticated techniques of statistical analysis (factorial analysis, analysis of variance, etc.) which can clarify some points further. But statistical analysis always requires to be supplemented by hard thought about the problems it does not solve. In some ways it is a device for avoiding certain unnecessary imprecisions and fallacies rather than for answering substantial problems by itself.

Combining assessments. Reverting to the admittedly odd marker Z (in Table 8) who awarded marks of 45, 45, 45, 70, 75 and 80, one might question whether the average of 60 represents this distribution very well. It is like an odd cook who produced *cordon bleu* meals half the time and inedible ones the other half. One would not split the difference and call her an average cook. And yet we are constantly averaging out very diverse evidence when people are assessed. Sometimes, as in many interviews, the items of evidence themselves as well as the weights attached to them are vague and variable. But even when the items and weights seem controlled, as in examinations or tests, only statistical analysis shows whether purely chance differences in the various lists of marks tilt the final results arbitrarily—increasing the number of undeserved certificates, promotions and commendations, and of undeserved failures, non-promotions and discouragements.

Those who produced standardized objective tests have to pay attention to points discussed in this chapter. Particularly they have to make clear how their tests typically distribute those for whom they are designed, on what populations (age, socio-economic grouping, etc.) they were standardized, and what evidence there is of their validity and reliability in the statistical sense of these terms. Knowledge of such factors facilitates understanding of whether it may be legitimate to combine assessments, or of how best to combine assessments, in particular cases. Test-makers are not equally conscientious in satisfying the ideal standard, nor equally successful when they are conscientious, but their criteria are explicit and they can be judged by them.

Ordinary examiners, interviewers and writers of reports have special problems and special purposes. The principles of objective testing are not enough. But that does not mean that the principles are irrelevant. It is no virtue that criteria should often be elusive and changeable, that pure statistical chances should affect practical decisions about people's careers more than necessary, or that the admittedly complex technicalities of assessment should prevent a person from trying to understand as much as he can. The tendency to look more to the value of the teacher's experience in making assessments must be supported by greater competence in the technical aspects of assessment, if those assessed are not to be at the mercy of the casual factors discussed earlier.

Some principles that seem as relevant to general assessment as to objective testing are:

1 explicit and detailed specification of what is being assessed and the weight given to each part of the assessment;
2 sampling performances sufficiently widely by means of different kinds of assessment, different assessors and different occasions of assessment (as practical substitutes for the often impracticable standardization techniques of objective testers);
3 at least comparing the appearance of the various distributions of marks, etc., to see whether there are signs of:
   (a) accidental uneven weighting,

(b) non-use of a considerable part of the purported range of the mark scale (for example, no marks below 40 or above 80 reducing a percentage scale to a 40-point scale),

(c) treating small intervals on a percentage scale (or a 40-point scale) as if they were highly reliable and significant (for example, treating 53 per cent as if it were clearly different from 50 or 56 per cent when, in fact, the chance of having a different marker might easily topple 53 to 50 or boost it to 56);

4 taking into account the relation of the sample one works with to its wider population (for example, the school in a socially handicapped or socially advantageous area, the class of slow or fast learners, etc.);

5 at least considering the possibility of using one of the arithmetical or graphic scaling techniques, fully and clearly described in McIntosh (1962), to express assessments on some kind of common scale, if circumstances seem to justify it;

6 consulting any relevant literature, such as the Secondary School Examinations Council's third examinations bulletin, *The Certificate of Secondary Education: An introduction to some techniques of examining* (1964) or Pidgeon and Yates' *An Introduction to Educational Measurement* (1968).

Perspective on assessment

Four main purposes of assessment have been suggested—(1) guidance or selection, (2) motivation, (3) maintaining standards, and (4) research. Justifying any particular assessment depends on being clear about what purposes are intended and about the detailed sense in which they are intended. It is wise also to remember that any detailed justification of this kind is necessarily related to assumptions about values in particular societies. Such assumptions are mostly taken for granted. This must be so if anything practical is to get done. But there are times for questioning basic assumptions themselves and assessment practices must be influenced periodically by such questioning. However radical the questioning, assessment in some form is inevitable and the issues raised in the first section of the chapter are permanently relevant.

Alongside the fundamental question about purposes there are other questions that are more technical, but still fundamental in their own way. Six such questions have been discussed—referring to (1) assessment scales, (2) representative samples, (3) distributions of assessments made, (4) validity, (5) reliability, and (6) the combining or comparing of assessments. Anyone pursuing these topics would have to go on to textbooks of statistics. The present intention has been to indicate the importance of certain ways of analysing assessments, with only a limited amount of specific statistical illustration to give some concreteness to the general argument.

Apart from the convenience of these elementary statistics for purposes of summary description and comparison, they should give a first sense of the meaning of statistical significance. There can be confusion between this technical meaning and the wider meaning of significance (= importance). An average difference of (let us say) 3 per cent between boys and girls on a certain test is statistically significant if we are highly likely to find a closely similar difference on repeated occasions of testing. It means that the difference is really there. But one still has to decide on other grounds whether the difference is important in relation to some specified aim—or whether it is a difference that makes little or no difference! An appreciation of statistical significance is relevant also to the understanding of research reports. The relevant parts of this chapter should enable a person to read a typical table like Table 14, even without the explanatory notes.

Test	N	Boys' mean	σ	N	Girls' mean	σ	P
1	47	12·36	6·34	46	14·09	4·84	> ·05
2	50	7·58	2·85	50	6·68	2·10	NS
3	49	8·69	2·36	49	10·29	2·68	< ·01

(a) Girls are 1·73 points better than boys on test 1. P > ·05 indicates that there is slightly more than a 5 per cent chance that this result could vary beyond acceptable limits on other occasions.

(b) Boys are 0·90 points better on test 2. NS indicates statistical non-significance. The result could definitely vary beyond acceptable limits.

(c) Girls are 1·60 points better on test 3. P < ·01 indicates that there is less than a 1 per cent chance of not getting a comparable difference on another occasion. One can have 99 per cent confidence that the observed difference is genuine.

Table 14 Significant and non-significant differences between means

Statistical analysis cannot supplant but may supplement general appraisal of the evidence on any assessment problem. If assessments are feebly based or inaccurately made in the first instance no statistical manipulation will undo the defects. But some of the points made earlier are relevant to avoiding a feeble basis. Assessment cannot be simplified beyond a certain point. Features that make the process intrinsically difficult include these:

1 one is typically dealing with a characteristic that varies subtly over a wide range, not with a few clearly defined categories;
2 one is typically dealing with several such characteristics at a time, not just one;
3 one is typically dealing with *tendencies* of varying degrees towards interrelationship of certain characteristics, not with complete correspondence or lack of correspondence;
4 one is typically dealing with characteristics
   (a) that are defined differently to some extent by different people or different measuring instruments,
   (b) whose constituent elements are differently weighted by different people, even when they agree on a common conceptual framework; and
   (c) that may overlap with one another in varying degrees, despite superficial differentiation.

These problems of range, multiplicity, tendency and definition perhaps help to explain why it is tempting to fall back on whatever shibboleths appeal to one rather than face the hard job of sorting out so many interlinked variables.

Assessment then is like juggling—it needs system and a lot of practice. Unfortunately, the professional assessor cannot hope to be as completely successful as the professional juggler. One thing or another escapes his grasp, tarnishing the act. Despite this imperfection, two objects left lying at the beginning of this act must now be picked up—the What and How of assessment, in the sense of what people are mainly concerned to assess and what ordinary methods are available to them. These themes will be developed in the next chapter and related to the idea of guidance or counselling.

Assessment and guidance

Things that teachers and psychologists assess formally or informally include educational attainments, intelligence, aptitudes, personality and character. The methods they use include examinations, tests, interviews, observations, ratings and the collection of relevant information. Assessment can be done with varying degrees of objectivity. It may be useful to clarify the idea of objectivity beyond what has already been done in the preceding chapter and to consider what kind of objectivity attaches to those tests that are called objective.

Broadly speaking, objectivity consists in giving all the relevant evidence its due weight and, particularly, not being conspicuously influenced by selfishness or purely personal bias. The words 'objective' and 'subjective' are loosely and misleadingly used for much of the time—mainly for the emotional effect of stressing what is considered to be acceptable or not. But nothing is absolutely objective or subjective. The person who is obviously distorting the evidence under emotional stress still refers to things that could be part of an objective picture. The person who gives what some like to call a 'purely subjective' opinion can usually offer evidence of some kind. And, on the other hand, the most refined, let us say computer-controlled, experiment in the physical sciences represents some personal appraisal of how research money and effort should be directed and some personal hope of acceptance, respect and even fame among colleagues.

Allowing the relativity of the concept, one can still say that objectivity is an ideal that has been well studied and many of its leading principles clearly stated—to define terms clearly in a way that helps anyone to agree whether or not they are applicable to a given set of phenomena; to attend to all the possibly relevant evidence and particularly any evidence that does not seem to confirm a proposed hypothesis; to expose any theory with its evidence to expert scrutiny and to the test of independent experiment where experiment is an appropriate means of testing (a kind of diamond-cut-diamond test); and to measure objectivity by the criteria relevant to the field of enquiry—not demanding experimental evidence for historical objectivity, aesthetic evidence for scientific objectivity or psychological evidence for logical objectivity.

Stating these principles clearly has its dangers. They may rebound on the subsequent analysis, for assessment is not a theme on which it is easy to be objective. Moreover, any achievement of objectivity is apt to be painful for those who have cause to fear objectivity in a particular area. But these risks must be taken and it will be convenient to begin with the consideration of objective tests, a form of assessment that has the temerity to label itself 'objective'.

Objective tests

Objective tests of educational attainments and of general intelligence are those that have been most widely and successfully used by teachers and educational psychologists. Their claims to objectivity are various and can be listed something like this:

1 The choice of items, their number, their formulation, their placing in the test and their degree of difficulty—these are determined by trying the test out systematically on a sample of the kind of population it is intended for, analysing the results and modifying the draft test.

2 So far as possible, the knowledge or skill to be tested is broken down into sufficiently small and clear units, so that questions with only one correct answer can be set. For example, these items might go into a statistical attainments test based on the last chapter:

(a) Multiple-choice item:
A sample of normally distributed intelligence scores had a mean of 68 with a standard error of 1. If the test were given to a comparable sample of the same population one could be almost completely confident that the mean would not vary outside the limits—

(a) 68–69?	(b) 67–69?	(c) 66–70?	(d) 67–68?	(e) 67·5–68·5?

(Tick the correct answer)

or (b) 'Constructed answer' item:

Five pupils did test A and got scores of 6, 7, 8, 9 and 10.

Four of them did test B and got scores of 1, 6, 8 and 9.

What was the median score for test A?

And for test B?

What was the mean score for test A?

And for test B?

3 The test is standardized by being given to a representative sample of the population for which it is intended and establishing the distribution of scores for that population. For example, if a test was to be used for several years and had to be relevant to all of the pupils in a city or county, one could standardize it on the basis of the scores of all of the children of a certain age in a particular year.

It is obviously particularly important that the group used to define the standardization should be either a genuinely complete group or population, or a genuinely representative sample of that population. It should also be obvious that the standardization itself can only be relatively appropriate. It is better than standards based on haphazard opinion, but, of course, there may be a radical change in the whole relevant population over a period of time. Immigration into and emigration out of the local area may change the population characteristics. New circumstances, or new educational methods and programmes, may raise or lower standards generally, or alter the character of what is learned so that old test items are no longer relevant. These are factors that need watching, but they do not invalidate standardization as a convenient procedure for giving assessments more objective meaning.

Many technical problems arise in the course of constructing a test on the principles just outlined. These can be studied in greater detail in appropriate textbooks, such as Macintosh and Morrison's *Objective Testing* (1969). Some of the problems, like those of sampling, reliability and validity, have been touched on in the preceding chapter, but something should be added here about item analysis. The first thing is to collect more items than will be needed so that those which prove ambiguous or non-discriminating in use can be discarded. Only the subject expert can decide the substance of what is to be tested. Bloom's *Taxonomy* may help some to think more precisely about whether their intention is to assess one of the many kinds of knowledge (of terminology, specific facts, trends, categories, methodology, etc.), or one of the various intellectual skills (interpreting, analysis of relationships, evaluation, etc.).

Once the draft test has been given to the first sample to be tested each item is analysed in the following way. First the distribution of results for the test as a whole must be compiled. Then the top 27 per cent (a percentage found to be convenient in practice) of those tested are compared with the bottom 27 per cent in respect of success in each item. The *discrimination index* (D) gives a measure of how well an item discriminates between those who do well or poorly on the test as a whole. If 200 were tested there would be 54 cases in the top and 54 in the bottom section. Suppose that 40 got the item correct in the top 54 and 19 in the bottom 54, D would be $(40-19) \div 54 = 0.4$. This or a higher D would be satisfactory. Were 40 top scorers to answer the item correctly and 30 low scorers, the discrimination would be unsatisfactory $(D = (40-30) \div 54 = 0.2)$.

Another index used is the *facility index* (F). It can be taken as the percentage of all candidates who get an item correct, or the percentage of the top and bottom 27 per cent together who get it correct. An F of 40 to 60 per cent would indicate a suitable item for the middle part of a test. An F well above 60 per cent might indicate a suitably encouraging item with which to begin the test, while an F below 40 per cent would indicate a more difficult item. With a knowledge of D and F one can do more precisely what assessors would presumably try to do in any case—eliminate items that make no difference, and place items partly according to their degree of facility or difficulty.

Objective tests of attainment vary almost as much as the main kinds and levels of attainment possible. They are particularly useful for clarifying the typical range of performance of particular groups of people, facilitating practical guidance and selection, whether educational or vocational. Even where other forms of assessment are of prime importance (teachers' assessments, for example), objective attainment tests can be used to adjust different teachers' or institutions' assessments on to some kind of common scale. They have also been useful in correcting casual misjudgments of educational trends by documenting the genuine changes from time to time in samples of the same population (say 7- or 11-year-old national reading standards over a period of years).

Although it is easier to see the viability of objective tests of elementary attainments, some university work too can be tested in this way—and is, particularly in the United States. One of the main obstacles to the extension of objective testing at advanced levels is the heavy demand it makes on the analytic power and the ingenuity of the tester. Where advanced problems have widely recognized importance and widely accepted solutions the effort of constructing objective tests can be justified economically. Where people are less agreed on what matters most, or on even a limited range of solutions to whatever problems are formulated, objective testing becomes less likely to be used. Assessments are then made by an elusive mixture of elusive criteria—partly explicit and objective, partly implicit and variably assessed, partly arbitrary and resistant to justification, partly sheer chance. The assessor does not know very precisely what he is effectively doing, and the person assessed is uncertain about what *he* is expected to do.

Objective attainment tests are not restricted to assessing what is called 'mere' factual knowledge, although more conventional examinations tend to put a considerable premium on just such knowledge. It is probably easier to compile tests of such knowledge whatever their form, and more difficult to test various problem-solving skills, whether analytic or synthetic, and whether demanding routine techniques or ingenious or divergent thinking. But divergency or ingenuity too benefit from some form of objective definition and test, and become vague clichés if this is not possible.

The most serious objection to objective testing may be not its inapplicability to complex skills, but the danger of encouraging an emphasis on the acquisition of approved formulae, however subtle, rather than on intellectual exploration, however elusive the signs of success in such exploration. If one were to try and make an objective test of intellectual exploration in defiance of this danger, it might have to be a test of the ability to ask the right questions rather than give the right answers. This does imply that there are answers to the question: What makes a question a right question? But scholars would presumably choose to keep the list of answers permanently open.

Objective tests of intelligence

Specific attainment and general ability are closely related, but the makers of objective tests of general intelligence have believed that there is some intellectual or adaptation factor in behaviour that differs significantly from attainments, even if the two do overlap in part, and that can be assessed by a different kind of test. Intelligence test results are certainly variable, and therefore one should not over-stress one intelligence quotient (IQ) independently of other test results or relevant evidence of other kinds (for example, social competence in an otherwise intellectually feeble person). However, while large variations can occur (particularly over longer periods of time), smaller variations are more usual.

This means that little importance attaches to (let us say) 5-point changes in IQ on a scale where 95 per cent of the population stand somewhere between 70 and 130 and 68 per cent between 85 and 115. But while a person with an obtained IQ of 110 might vary between 105 and 115, or much less often between about 100 and 120, it is not likely at all that he will drop below 100 or rise above 120. Exceptions to this general indication would be most likely where some powerful specific handicap (serious physical illness, grave emotional upset, etc.) had clearly affected one of the intelligence assessments, or where the test had been badly standardized or administered. If the occasions of assessment were within months or only a year or two of one another, the amount of variation would be less.

As with attainments tests, one of the great virtues of intelligence tests is to provide a rapid and well-controlled assessment of intellectual functioning. Teachers who know pupils well over a long time can make their own assessments, but this takes longer, is limited by local frames of reference and is more inclined to mix general personality assessments in with purported intellectual assessments. The saying that intelligence is what intelligence tests measure is facile and misleading, although not meaningless. It may sound better if one calls it an *operational* definition—one used for the purposes of observation and experiment alone—but it seems wiser to avoid the suggestion that any single measure is what we mean by the thing that is measured. We certainly mean more by 'intelligence' than the contents or results of any one test.

In ordinary usage the word 'intelligence' is so heavily charged with the intellectual interests or preferences of the person using it that there is lots of scope for misunderstanding. Intelligence must be intelligence in a particular context, and some of the critics of intelligence tests have been people who have failed to recognize the context of such tests, namely, the general personal and educational guidance of people spanning the whole intellectual range. Teachers of abler learners particularly are apt to see everything in terms of a context that is highly selective and often highly specialized. They are concerned with finer discriminations and with intelligence specifically expressed in attainments, whereas intelligence tests have been designed mostly to make broader discriminations and to do so in relative (not, of course, absolute) independence from specific attainments.

It is difficult to avoid words in an intelligence test, although verbal facility is particularly susceptible to educational influence and liable to make the test into one of attainments. One can limit the use of words, as when a tester makes a patterned chain of beads while a young child watches, and then says, 'Now you make one'. The child shows his intelligence by recognizing the pattern and copying it. Or one can easily get a child to imitate a very simple pattern of coloured blocks by showing him how to do it. Having got the idea of the game, he shows his degree of intelligence by copying a series of patterns for himself until he reaches the point where the relationships in the pattern are too difficult.

Another relatively non-verbal test is one based on items like that illustrated in Figure 15. One has to communicate the idea of completing each series by using one of the blocks provided, but then it is a matter of seeing what the relationships are. A person could still use words to aid his private thinking, but the solution of the problem does not depend on explicit verbal understandings. Raven's matrices, consisting of such test items, have been extensively used, and can obviously express simple or complex relationships in spatial form.

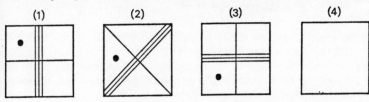

Which one of the following patterns should go in the blank square above?

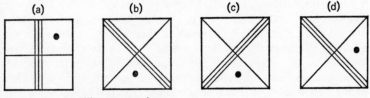

Figure 15   Intelligence test item

Other non-verbal tests are designed to assess still more complex spatial intelligence by requiring one to identify the effect of transforming or superimposing shapes in various ways.

Most intelligence tests accept the advantages and disadvantages of assuming certain educational levels, so that most people now have come across verbal and numerical items like the following:

1 If Nfssz Disjtunbt is code for Merry Christmas, write Happy New Year in the same code
2 Write the next item in each series:
   (a)   1   2   4   7   11   ..... ?
   (b)   az   by   cx   dw   ..... ?
   (c)   1   2   6   24   120   ..... ?
3 Underline the odd item in each series:
   (a) minute   second   day   mile   hour   year

(b) house cottage mansion castle horse
(c) crab lobster trout prawn shrimp
4 Duck is to duckling as hen is to   ..... ?
  Room is to house as cabin is to   ..... ?
  Decimal is to ten as binary is to   ..... ?
5 (a) Janet is twice as old as Peter, who is 5 years younger than
      Mary. Mary is 13. How old is Janet?
  (b) There was a strange people who could count only from 1 to 9
      and who meant 9 when they said 1 and 1 when they said 9,
      8 when they said 2 and 2 when they said 8, and so on. Since 5
      came in the middle they meant 5 when they said 5. If they
      offered you 7 apples, 4 oranges and 1 banana, how many items
      of fruit would you really have all together?

Items in an actual test would be more carefully planned and selected
than these illustrations, but the point is that one tries to test reasoning power—the ability to recognize relationships and make use of
them—rather than mastery of a particular syllabus. It is a question
of emphasis, not of absolute dichotomy.

If one gets a large representative sample of people to do a sample
of intellectual tests (a 'battery' of tests as it is aggressively called!)
it is possible to compare and analyse the pattern of results to see
whether each test is measuring something different, or how much
overlap there is in what they are measuring. There are various ways
of doing this analysis and these are affected by psychological preferences. Some stress the single large common element running
through such tests, others identify a larger number of factors. One
of the best known analyses of the latter type is Thurstone's seven
'primary mental abilities'—spatial ability (S), perceptual speed (P),
numerical ability (N), verbal meaning (V), memory (M), verbal
fluency (W) and inductive reasoning (IorR).

It is important to remember that factors like these are not mutually
independent. They overlap, or are correlated, with one another.
People tend to do poorly, average or well on most aspects. J. P.
Guilford and his associates have been prominent in sustaining the
American preference for multi-factor analysis. British educational
psychologists tend to follow Vernon's analysis of intelligence in
terms of a large general factor, with two major components, one
verbal and educational, the other spatial and mechanical. Butcher
(1968) reviews these and other aspects of intelligence with lucidity
and balance.

Some intelligence tests are designed to be done by whole groups at
a time. These are typically paper and pencil tests with items like those
illustrated. They are standardized on a sample of whatever popula-

tion they are designed for. The fact that they are made for large groups facilitates their standardization on large groups. Tests designed as individual tests are more difficult to standardize, partly because of the time it takes to test any considerable number of people, and partly because there is often more scope for variation in administration and scoring among individual administrators. It is significant that many individual tests get converted into abbreviated forms by some of their users—just to save time. This may be justified but represents a further attenuation of the standards of reliability and validity expected of a good objective test.

The fact of individual administration does not, then, guarantee that the test or its results will be better quality articles. It may allow an admixture of practical as well as verbal and numerical items. It may be usable over a wide age range. It may give an estimate of mental age (MA) that can be compared with chronological age (CA) and expressed in *one* form of the IQ.

$$IQ = \frac{MA}{CA} \times 100;$$

for example, $\frac{12}{10} \times 100 = 120$ for a brighter child,

or $\frac{8}{10} \times 100 = 80$ for a duller child.

But there are statistical and general psychological objections to the admixture of diverse items that may occur in an individual test.

This does not mean that such tests are useless. The original Binet test from the beginning of the century with its various revisions (Stanford-Binet, Terman-Merrill) and the Wechsler Intelligence Scale for Children (WISC) and Wechsler Adult Intelligence Scale (WAIS) have been so extensively used that there is a vast amount of evidence about them. This does not abolish all of the problems mentioned earlier, but it helps one to make allowances and better appraisals. Moreover, these individual tests are often used as part of a wider individual psychological appraisal. They provide the clinical or child psychologist with a structured situation which may give important incidental insights into the individual's problems or needs as well as a useful estimate of general intellectual functioning in relation to less verbal as well as more verbal modes.

Intelligence or verbal reasoning tests—one sometimes sees VRQ for verbal reasoning quotient instead of the old IQ—have drawn strong fire from their enemies. They are said to measure educational advantage rather than intellectual power, to encourage a fatalistic sense of limitations instead of an educative sense of potentialities, to generate quotients which sound more precise and permanent than they have any right to, and to embody a narrow or even trivial conception of what intelligence is. It would be more accurate to assert that these are some of the main ways in which intelligence tests can be misunderstood or abused rather than that any of these are intrinsic to the tests themselves. Intelligence quotients have been a vehicle for oversimplifying educational problems just as the increasing recognition of variability due to environmental factors has led to its own analogous oversimplification in the opposite direction—'L'éducation peut tout'.

It is interesting to know whether a person has an IQ of about 75 or 105 or 125, but then the interesting question is how he can squeeze the utmost advantage out of the intellectual equipment he has at that point in time. Although there is a systematic relationship between IQ and educational or occupational level, it is a very broad relationship. Within any educational or occupational category the range of IQs is wide. Within any limited range of IQs the range of effective achievement is wide. Any policy that ignores either the broad trends or the wide variation within trends is defective.

Assessing personality

Discussions of personality in earlier chapters have given forewarning of the difficulties of knowing what is meant by personality, let alone measuring it. The concept is associated with those of role (as discussed in Chapter 2) and attitude (as discussed in Chapter 8). Its popular use to signify the quality of a person who makes any strong social impact, and the tendency to contrast personality with intellect, despite their integral relationship—these together distract attention from psychological attempts to establish a more cogent analysis. But these latter attempts themselves leave a rather confused picture— now based on psychoanalytical speculation, now on statistical analysis; now on physiological typologies, now on the shaping effect of particular roles or circumstantial pressures.

The problem could be summed up by saying that personality has many different meanings, has generated many different theories about its main phenomena, and has been assessed by many diverse techniques, having in common only their relatively low statistical reliability and validity. When it is remembered how readily even objective tests of attainment or general ability fall short of their theoretical ideal, one prepares to tread warily among the greater pitfalls of personality testing. However, this does not alter that most cogent consideration—that people do assess personality and cannot avoid doing so, and, therefore, must study improvement rather than lament the meagreness of what has been achieved.

Individual tests of intelligence give scope for less objective factors to influence the assessment, but an intelligence test can be done with a greater degree of personal detachment than a personality test. The more one seeks to identify major aspects of individual personality the more the personality is liable to be activated and defended, and equally personal reactions activated in the tester or assessor. There are two exceptions. The naïve person may be unbothered by his own self-revelations, and the mature assessor may be less emotionally drawn into the emotional vortex of the person he is assessing. A third exception might be urged by some—the use of standardized paper and pencil personality tests, which may be thought to have a degree of paradoxical impersonality. These still give scope for deliberate or unwitting self-misrepresentation, although some tests include items which are intended to show up the person who lies.

One of the most commonly used assessments is simply to describe a person in terms of the traits he most obviously manifests—cheerful and resilient, cautious but reliable, etc. For many purposes no more is needed—particularly where one knows the assessor personally and also the circumstances in which he has made his assessment. This might be so in appointing a person to a certain job. Provided the necessary traits were likely to show, and undesirable ones to be suppressed if not absent, it may not matter, within this narrower context, that the person has other unspecified traits—even potentially undesirable ones.

There are, of course, limitations to this approach. There is a huge vocabulary of words referring to personality traits, and there must be extensive overlapping of meanings. People mean different things by the same word. When they agree on the general meaning, they may differ about what detailed evidence is relevant to establishing the presence of the trait. And when they agree about what evidence is relevant, they may give different weight to different parts of it and to different circumstances in which it appears. They may confuse an apparent personality trait with a temporary reaction to circumstances. It is not surprising that even common sense tries to get beyond surface traits to some deeper sense of personality structure—often in the shape of a typology.

The typological approach was mentioned in Chapter 2. Physiological typologies may have a limited validity, but the association between body type and personality is not sufficiently close or precise to be of much practical use. Typologies based on factorial analysis are more significant. Indeed, they would probably dissociate themselves from the word 'typology' because of its history of speculative categorization. Personality factors established by the statistical analysis of test results are no more valid than the evidence from which they are derived, but they do usefully narrow one's field of attention by suggesting frameworks that are consistent with some systematic empirical evidence. The two general factors of introversion/extroversion and neuroticism or instability/stability seem well established.

Just as American psychology seems to favour the analysis of intellectual ability into a larger number of overlapping factors, rather than one or two independent factors, so it has produced factorial analysis of personality on the same lines. Cattell (1965) argues for a series of sixteen factors, including dimensions like shy/venturesome or practical/imaginative, as well as wider factors like intelligence and emotionality. Cattell is particularly insistent on the need to use only dimensions that have been at least factorially validated, and critical of personality tests based on clinical intuition or general psychological speculation.

One of the attractions of using factorial dimensions is that they provide a defensible simplification of complex phenomena, but still allow for the infinite diversity of individual people. They do not divide people into too few or too separate categories, but rather indicate the relative degree to which a person shows any basic factorial trait. Even three factors, such as intelligence, stability and introversion/extroversion, make a large number of different categories possible, depending on the combination of varying degrees of the three qualities in any one person. And the layman, who does not use formal personality tests, can benefit by noting which aspects of personality seem to be best validated by empirical study and statistical analysis.

The many personality tests that have been devised cannot be discussed adequately in the present context, but brief mention of a few will indicate some of the main lines of attack:

1 Paper and pencil tests. Cattell's Sixteen Personality Factor Questionnaire (16P.F.) takes about 50 minutes to do and gives scores for each of the sixteen factors. Eysenck's Personality Inventory takes 5 to 10 minutes to do and gives scores for neuroticism (N) and extroversion (E). The Minnesota Multiphasic Personality Inventory (M.M.P.I.) requires 'true', 'false', or 'cannot say' responses to 550 items and can provide scores on a variety of scales. Cattell's Objective-Analytic Personality Test Battery has practical tests, like reaction times, as well as paper and pencil items. It is time-consuming but is intended to get beyond subjective paper and pencil responses. These are some better known examples of one large category of personality tests.

2 Projective tests. These are tests which provide some visual stimulus intended to help the person tested to express his personal concerns, worries, etc. The Rorschach test is a series of ten symmetrical ink blots. It has been claimed that three years is necessary to be properly trained in their interpretation! The test is scored for intellectual and other personality characteristics by reference to whether the responses are based on the whole blot or on details, on colour or chiaroscuro, on space or movement, and so on. The Thematic Apperception Test is based on inviting people to construct stories about rather vaguely drawn pictures, intended to encourage personal interpretations of what the pictures are about. Such tests have attracted passionate devotees and contemptuous critics, and it would seem that they are more likely to be justified (if at all) as clinical aids rather than as personality measures with any real statistical reliability or validity.

3 Concept tests. These are tests designed to make more explicit the concept a person has of himself or of some problem facing him. Osgood's semantic differential was mentioned in Chapter 6. It is based on getting a person to classify the associations suggested by a particular concept. For example, one might have to rate one's associations with the concept 'love' on seven-point scales for the dimensions valuable/worthless, fast/slow or deep/shallow. The ratings on these and other dimensions for 'love' and any other selected concepts are inter-correlated to indicate the emotional significance of the concepts for the person concerned. The name repertory grid technique is used of a similar system of analysing a person's conceptual or attitudinal repertory. (There are examples of repertory grids in Ryle, pp. 85–98.) The main relevance of such detailed analysis would be in clinical situations where, conceivably, ordinary enquiries might not have pinpointed the exact nature of a patient's psychological problem.

Personality test items vary widely in content, but, in one form or another, they typically invite explicit or implicit self-rating in relation to such statements as:

People seem to treat me badly without cause.
I would find it difficult to get up and address a large group.
I prefer a man who is sexually attractive.
I want to be first-rate in my work.
I am always punctual for appointments.
I like an activity with a bit of risk to it.
There's not much fun in doing something by yourself.
Reading is one of my favourite activities.
It mostly pays to be cautious.

In laboratory conditions such tests can be extended to include the assessment of reaction times or galvanic skin responses (G.S.R.) in various conditions; the capacity for motor adaptation; and various other variables that require special circumstances for their assessment.

Sociometry is a form of assessment akin to personality testing, although it concentrates more on the social psychology of a small group of people. The technique, expounded in detail by Moreno (1953), is based on finding out the social preferences of a group of people by reference to a specified criterion. For example, if a teacher had to arrange a class into three or four groups to go on a certain visit, the sociometric solution would consist in asking each child to write down the companions he would prefer to go with (or possibly not go with) and making up the groups accordingly. The method requires that there should be a strong, enduring and definite criterion that will evoke sincere and spontaneous choices and rejections by the members of the group. If criteria are vague or if no action will be based on actual choices, then the method is much less valid.

The pattern of choices resulting from a sociometric enquiry may reveal individuals who are centres of attraction or, at the other extreme, isolates chosen by nobody, as well as the detailed preference groupings within the class. The pattern can be expressed graphically, with arrows indicating who chooses whom, or the choices can be charted numerically. Moreno also suggested that adequacy or originality of emotional response could be assessed by a psychodramatic method. The person is urged to throw himself into a state of anger, fear, sympathy or domination towards another member of the group and his response is rated, presumably impressionistically.

Two problems about sociometry are that it is not always possible to satisfy the assumptions about a genuine choice leading to action, and that it may not reveal anything of permanent importance that is not already fairly obvious by informal knowledge or enquiry. Sociometry may be a corrective to facile assumptions about the social patterns within a group, be useful where one has to identify quickly the patterns within a new and unknown group, and may help to reveal some anomaly related to the personality of a particular individual.

A journey through these various personality tests may seem more like a visit to the fairground's hall of distorting mirrors, but without a standard mirror to validate one's genuine self. In practical situations people are able to tolerate a remarkable range of diverse personalities, provided that the owners of these personalities are able to do what is expected of them as workers, students, representatives, etc. This means that much personality assessment is done for specific purposes in specific situations. Then, since it is preferable to live and work with agreeable rather than disagreeable people, those with power to select try to satisfy themselves (and incidentally as many others as possible) on this score. And since another important set of criteria is constituted by general morality (reliability, honesty, etc.), these criteria also play a major role in validating practical decisions based on personality assessment.

Finally, in many practical situations people, even if they make assessments that subsequently seem wrong, are readier to correct the situation as they go rather than strive to make the original assessments more meticulous. None of these points is an argument against attempts to assess personality more scientifically, but they remind one of considerations which are bound to influence general attitudes towards any full-blown scientific ideal. The layman may 'peer into a factorial hyperspace' with Cattell but be less keen to make the hyperspace trip. The tester's hidden lie scales to detect our acts of distortion or sabotage may have to compete with Whyte's pleasantly mischievous appendix to *The Organization Man* (1960) on how to cheat on personality tests.

Interviews, reports and ratings

Interviews, reports and ratings are some of the principal means of personality assessment extensively used for practical purposes. It would be comforting if these took one on to more reliable ground than personality tests, but this by no means necessarily happens. Teachers have written entertaining satires on the incompetent interviewing techniques of some appointment committees. Researchers have shown how poorly interview judgments may correlate with students' later academic success. To give one example, Abercrombie (1969) studied the selection and academic performance of students at the Bartlett School of Architecture in London and found 'little relationship between the statements made at a board interview about specific characteristics of candidates, and the opinion of teachers who become familiar with their work as students over three or four years'. And the fact of considerable inconsistency among individual interviewers has been frequently demonstrated, for example, in selecting students or personnel, and in making psychiatric diagnoses.

Reports and ratings tend to suffer from several failings—(1) vagueness and generality instead of specific meaning and reference, (2) poor indication of what standards of comparison are being used, and (3) poor indication of the range of evidence on which generalizations are based, and, consequently, of their limitations. Reports may be misleading even where they seem precise. Percentage marks for subject examinations may conceal the fact that 90 per cent in, let us say, mathematics may not be better than 75 per cent in English. The character of the two mark distributions as a whole might show that the two different percentages referred to the same relative standing, the nominal difference being purely a matter of marking conventions. Reports and ratings often have a persuasive purpose—to get Elizabeth the job she has applied for, or warn Fred that he had better pull up his scholastic socks. Their defects as assessment devices may not matter so much if these latter criteria are the important ones. But they still matter to some extent, for Elizabeth may get the job but be unable to do it, or Fred be panicked into aspirations beyond his reasonable capacity.

Some poor rating results from requiring people to assess what they are not well able to. The teacher may have to report on 'conduct' when all he can do is mention whether a pupil has been troublesome in his particular class. He may be understandably tempted to attribute to the pupil characteristics (troublesome, well behaved, etc.) which really appertain to a particular pupil-teacher relationship. He may have to spread pupils on some scale when the truth is that there is no great individual difference—all members of the class having their ups and downs but performing generally on the same level. He may have to make a report or practical recommendation, despite knowing that his evidence is scanty. These practical exigencies must be set against the weaknesses of rating and reporting as such.

The advice given by psychologists is (1) to define any personality trait as far as possible in terms of actual behaviour, (2) to sample such behaviour in as wide a variety of circumstances as possible (different classes and teachers, inside and outside school, etc.), (3) to get several people to make independent ratings (a very difficult thing in practice, for what are called independent ratings are often strongly influenced by the general attitudes of other assessors, and particularly of assessors with a high ranking in the relevant social or professional hierarchy), (4) to rate traits separately one at a time, so that the halo effect (or presumably its opposite, the cloven hoof effect) does not cause one to see nothing but good (or evil) in the same person (another counsel of perfection, although workable in some circumstances), and (5) if those rated cover a wide range on a particular trait, to decide on a rough notional distribution pattern and allot people to categories accordingly (for example, the 10/20/40/20/10 percentage distribution for a wide sample on a trait that is believed to be normally distributed). Although these points are worth keeping in mind, it is obvious that many actual circumstances prevent one from making the assumptions on which the advice is based.

Interviewing, despite the shortcomings already mentioned, is likely to continue as one of the main practical means of personality assessment. To clarify this function of the interview it is necessary to identify various other functions that are liable to be served at the same time. People often fail to distinguish these diverse, legitimate functions:

1 An interview may not aim at fundamental assessment at all. It may be intended to provide only a confirmatory assessment in relation to a provisional decision made on more extensive hard evidence.

2 An interview may aim at making candidates and interviewers feel that the whole business is not entirely impersonal; or, alternatively, that every human step has been taken to make justice be seen to be done. This may apply particularly where all candidates could readily justify their acceptance but where vacancies are limited and a choice has to be made somehow. The candidate feels he has a chance to make a personal appeal, the interviewer that he has a chance to notice elusive personal merits or demerits. The justification is on humane grounds rather than superior predictive efficiency, for those chosen may do badly and those rejected be successful in comparable situations elsewhere.

In the Abercrombie study, already mentioned, 12 out of 60 students admitted in two years proved unsuccessful, while 13 who were refused admission succeeded elsewhere in similar courses. If any group is already highly selected in terms of qualifications it is not surprising that any further selection should be influenced by lesser or chance factors. People may make a fuss about the small difference between candidates accepted and rejected at critical borderlines, but this must be so where places are limited. One can try to improve the predictive power of selection techniques by statistical studies, and one can mitigate the problem by increasing the supply of desired places or opportunities. But these processes too have their limits. Some desirable things will always be in short supply, and predictive techniques, however improved, are bound to remain imperfect.

3 An interview may have a mainly persuasive function. This can range from the kind of persuasion that is near to being a directive, even if some fresh assessment enters into the situation marginally, to the kind that is more influenced by reappraisal of the interviewee's personality, although still mainly concerned with persuasive guidance. A post-misdemeanour interview with the headmaster might illustrate the first, a vocational interview where there was little choice of jobs the second.

4 An interview may have a large expressive function. Interviewers often use the occasion to air their own concerns and reflections, to

register their own significance with fellow interviewers, sometimes almost to prove not that a particular candidate should be chosen but that they are fit to be on the interviewing panel. This expressive function can interfere with assessment (for example, by cutting down the proportion of time spent in attending to the candidate). On the other hand, it may be a kind of miniature sample of the social network the applicant wants to enter. While the surface exchanges may be erratic and even trivial, both assessors and assessed have a useful chance of sizing one another up by subtle signs and symptoms.

These four possible functions of the interview may leave little space for an assessment function, except that human beings are always assessing one another in some sense of the term. What are some of the points to be remembered if the interview is a selection interview and intended mainly to achieve an assessment of personality? The self-justificatory, persuasive and expressive functions of the interview should be recognized. As has been argued, they may be useful functions; but they should not be confused with assessment. The various points made earlier about the meanings of personality, and the difficulties of any kind of reliable and valid assessment, should be recognized if any assessment is to be made in a sophisticated way, that is, with adequate specification of criteria, evidence and judgment. There should be a clear definition of what the interview is supposed to establish as distinct from other evidence already available, and enquiries should be directed sympathetically but persistently to eliciting the relevant evidence. All that was said about ratings is relevant to interviewing, for the interview assessment is liable to be a series of ratings made haphazardly and without systematic evidence.

There is a difference of emphasis between assessment in a selection interview and in a guidance interview. In a selection interview there may be a decision, positive or negative, that is in the interest of both parties; but the person assessed is typically trying to show his virtues and conceal any shortcomings while the assessors are trying to penetrate any false front and see the candidate in a true and complete perspective. This parallels the 'motivational distortion' or lie scale built into some personality tests. With the guidance interview it should be the case that assessor and assessed are working for a common goal—the best guidance of the person assessed. The person assessed typically *does* some of the assessing—a process of self-assessment, aided by the counsellor's sympathetic ear. The counsellor may *undergo* assessment in terms of whether he is really sympathetic and really knowledgeable enough to supply practical suggestions if they are relevant.

The guidance interview does not abolish motivational distortion automatically, for people can cheat themselves as well as others when it comes to personality assessment. Talking to a counsellor may help a person to discharge some pent-up emotions, explore notional and practical possibilities, and reach a more realistic appraisal of his own personality and the genuine possibilities for him in whatever situation is under discussion. Non-directive counselling, associated with the name of the American psychiatrist Carl Rogers, stresses what its name suggests—the avoidance of direct advice and the encouragement of self-analysis and self-counselling by virtue of sympathetic listening.

This is certainly the kind of counselling that the man in the street constantly seeks from his friends and neighbours—just a friendly ear on which to discharge tensions and help him work round to a cooler frame of mind. Such ears are not always too easily come by, which explains those odd 'conversations' in which both parties gabble on about their woes, each giving minimum attention to the other. Listening is hard work. Although any listener may serve the purpose (consider how some people launch forth on accounts of their private problems to complete strangers), the sympathetic uncritical listener is preferred. The professional counsellor, whatever his private views, must offer this uncritical acceptance if he is to find acceptance as a guide. This does not mean he cannot have his own standards. These standards may supply the later stages of guidance, but they cannot be thrust at people in an interview.

Part of the effectiveness of the guidance or counselling interview depends on the counsellor's insight into his own personality. It is easy to assimilate other problems to one's own, although they may really be different, and to propose solutions which might be one's own, although they are inappropriate for another person. The very choice or acceptance of the role of counsellor may be charged with some unrecognized urge to influence other people in particular ways, however subtly. The counsellor must be unusual if he does not have problems of his own from time to time, and, problems or none, he must have some personal dispositions and defences, which can be kept in their place by frank recognition but not prevented entirely from operating. Personality assessment, therefore, in the counselling interview is still subtly coloured by the inevitable personal evaluation of the interviewer, even if the evaluation lacks the explicitness that is more justifiable in a selection interview. In personality assessment no one can stand outside the circle completely, even if one acquires a measure of relative detachment.

Non-directiveness is obviously a relative matter. It is a question of style, for the ultimate aim must be to find even if not give direction.

Otherwise the counsellor would just be drifting with the person counselled. It may be valuable to be patiently non-directive where a person needs more time in any case to see his way through problems where there are considerable emotional tensions under a superficially technical problem, or where the person has already suffered so much from a sense of being bossed around (or equally destructively smothered with excessive surface affection) that respite from this state of usurped freedom and individuality is of first importance. It may be possible to be more openly directive, without harm or offence, where one is dealing with a relatively mature person ('mature' having various meanings), or where there is a clear desire for technical guidance, that is, for independent appraisal of personality, circumstances and opportunities.

The vocational guidance interview may often fit into this latter category, and *The Seven-Point Plan* published by the National Institute of Industrial Psychology gives excellent advice on the topic. The seven points of assessment are (1) physical make-up, (2) attainments, (3) general intelligence, (4) special aptitudes, (5) interests, (6) disposition, and (7) circumstances. This N.I.I.P. pamphlet must be studied in its entirety, for it is a concise and practical document that can hardly be condensed further. It reminds one of the importance of assessing effectively applied intelligence and not just theoretical potential, of probing into 'interests' to find out what exactly they amount to and whether they are accompanied by competence or not, and various other points of this kind. The plan as a whole reminds one that an interview may elicit new information, probe information already available and begin to establish a perspective on the whole situation which may facilitate ultimate decision.

One of the most important general points made is that any such plan is a plan of what the interviewer or assessor ought to find out; it is not a specification of the precise order or manner in which the finding out should be done; nor is it a means of turning bad judges of people into good judges. Study of seven-point plans or the arguments of this section is a means of improving, not of supplying, the experience and wisdom necessary to make a good judge of people.

Some may choose to classify the clinical or diagnostic interview separately from the selection or guidance interviews in their broader sense. The clinical interview is concerned with both selection and guidance—selection for an appropriate treatment and guidance towards benefiting from the treatment—but there is an implication that one starts with something wrong requiring to be corrected. The child is backward and a remedial or special educational programme has to be selected and implemented. Or he is emotionally disturbed, perhaps presenting some special behaviour problem, and the roots of the disturbances must be explored in the individual, his family and his place of work or study. While it is still necessary to follow the general rules of good assessment—comparing the individual carefully against relevant norms, etc.—it is also necessary to establish the detailed form that general factors take in the particular individual's life. What specific kinds of difficulty impede his ability to read? Or what specific family problem has upset him? And what specific remedies are practically available? Such specific problems have their own extensive literatures.

Examinations

Most of the psychological or psychometric points that should be made about examinations are made in other parts of this chapter or in the preceding chapter, although illustrated mainly with reference to objective testing. However, examinations are one of the most powerfully institutionalized forms of assessment and play a large part in the practical lives of most teachers and learners. It may be important, therefore, to underline at least some of the major points in terms of their bearing on examinations.

The discussion of the purposes of assessment is perhaps most important, for it is not always clear (1) exactly (as distinct from vaguely and generally) what the purpose of a given examination is, (2) what evidence there is of the extent to which it achieves a specified purpose, and (3) whether or not some other method would achieve the purpose better. Examinees may grasp these queries eagerly, ready to face evils they do not know rather than the evil they know, but this may be a mistaken reaction. A central problem of assessment is to know the value of the assessor's coinage, and this criterion is *roughly* met by established examinations, despite all their shortcomings. The practical need is for periodical critical review of the form, content and extent of examinations.

All that has been said about objectivity must be related to examinations, which are often criticized for relative subjectivity. Some examinations could be replaced by objective tests, but such tests cannot do all that examinations do and, like examinations, they have their own unwanted side effects. Within the examination form of assessment, it is possible to improve the consistency of the examinees' marks if they answer a larger number of short questions, but, of course, this removes the premium from longer answers. Perhaps the ability to do longer pieces of work could be tested by class or course exercises. It is also possible to get more consistent estimates if several markers assess the same work and average their marks. If this is too laborious, there is the practical alternative of having different markers assess different work from the same person, which at least increases the chance that a candidate is not elevated or shot down because of one assessor's bias.

Close attention should be given to defining (and making known to all the markers) the scale of marking and how it is to be used. Scales do not just exist in a state of nature, waiting for us to measure one another against them. It is we who make the scales to serve our own purposes. Fifty per cent is the pass mark if we make it so, but what comes first is the judgment that certain work is satisfactory. Percentage scales are purely conventional. There is nothing to prevent one from using a seven-point (or any other number of points) scale and calling inadequacy 1, bare adequacy 2 and varying degrees of adequate achievement 3, 4, 5, 6 or 7. Some of the deceptions of percentage scales were pointed out earlier.

It is particularly important to realize that discriminations cannot be reliably made to an accuracy of one or even five or more points on a percentage scale. For many purposes it does not matter that Janet's 60 per cent could turn into 55 to 65 per cent on a comparable examination, overlapping with John's 65 per cent, which might mean 60 to 70 per cent on other occasions. All assessments have a margin of variability. And, where convention decrees that a pass is, let us say, 50 per cent, candidates who just miss the mark have to be reconsidered, if this is allowed, from the point of view of general justice rather than of marking still finer discriminations. The person with 48 might have made 52 or 53 on a slightly different occasion of examining. Examiners do not usually look into the fact that anyone between 50 and 55 might have failed on a slightly different occasion. That is the way the game is played.

Although some examinations are intended only for class or school purposes, even these are more useful if the results can be compared for other classes and years in the same school. The wider the range of comparisons required (school, local area, national) the more useful it is to have some scaling test—an objective test in the same area as the examination but used only to give a rough indication of broad levels of performance, so that assessors are not unduly influenced by a limited sample on a non-objective test. Another device is to agree on the approximate pattern of distribution of marks and allot individual marks so that they do not diverge too much from the agreed pattern, unless some reason for divergence can be pinpointed. This does not always deal with individual feelings about a certain class being exceptionally good or a certain year group very disappointing. Then one has to resort to an objective test which will document changes more reliably, even if it leaves some less reliably assessable factors out of account.

The laudable attempt to mitigate the constricting aspects of public examinations (one rarely hears about their enlarging and elevating effects) has caused more emphasis to be put on the assessment of pupils' work by their own teachers. This makes it even more important for teachers to think about the matters discussed in this chapter. Apart from what has already been said, it is possible to create at least a slightly better chance of balanced and comparable assessments if teachers make and take opportunities of studying the work of other schools and other areas. The problem of moderating between the assessments of different schools has received increasing attention with the increasing attempt to avoid the imposition of external standards and assumptions on school curricula. This policy has more than technical difficulties to face, for it is external social standards of one sort or another that ultimately sanction educational policies and awards.

In addition to possibly deleterious effects on school curricula and methods alleged against examinations, the psychological stress caused by examinations has been another cause of criticism, particularly where the examination determines a person's career or public esteem in a major way. It seems likely that some of such stress might manifest itself in some other testing life situation even if there were no such things as scholastic examinations, but much of it too must be precipitated by features of the examination process that could be modified. Examples include the massiveness of some examinations, the dependence of major decisions and awards on single occasions of examining, the awesome formalities that may be attached to the administration of the examination, and the contribution of teachers themselves (no doubt with the best intentions of spurring on the candidates) and the general public (through its expectations of schools and colleges) to building up a sense of excitement or panic.

Examining must be seen in a broad, cool perspective. All societies require assessments of achievement, whether it is the ability to hunt your dinner in the forest or to profess mathematics in a university. These assessments are bound to be erratic and the only practical aim is to make them a little less so. They are bound to be painful for some and the only solution here is to mitigate the pain as far as possible. Examinations have been meant to assess people by their achievements rather than their ancestry or connections. It seems better to improve them than to lapse into an earlier world where patronage and influence held more exclusive sway than they do today.

The heads of educational institutions have a special role to play in this as in other matters. It may not be an enviable role, but it is one which allows the possibility of magnifying or moderating the influence of examinations and of discussing or prescribing policies and techniques. The choice in each case is widely influential.

Guidance or counselling

Discussing problems of assessment leads naturally into discussing problems of guidance or counselling. The guidance and counselling function as a distinct psychological and educational entity has received more attention in the United States than the United Kingdom, but there are signs of increasing attention to it in the British educational world. Child guidance has been associated here with special provision for a limited proportion of children with exceptional problems rather than with a continuous universal service to all young people.

This does not mean that guidance in the United States is an undisputed concept. Since teachers are always bound to be guides and counsellors in some sense, there are possibilities of tension and problems of status definition when a class of professionally trained counsellors hives off from the traditional teaching staff of schools. Then there are radical differences of psychological emphasis among counsellors themselves. This was illustrated in the Harvard Educational Review's issue on *Guidance—An Examination* (1962) where the following three statements are made in different articles:

1 The heart of the behavioural approach in counselling is that the environment must be manipulated so as to allow strong reinforcing consequences to become attached to the behaviour that is desired. (J. Michael and L. Meyerson.)
2 Constructive personal growth is associated with the counsellor's realness, with his genuine and unconditional liking for his client, with his sensitive understanding of his client's private world, and with his ability to communicate these qualities in himself to his client. (C. R. Rogers.)
3 The psychiatrist is the bootlegger of certain moral values (mercy and self-determination) under the guise of a medical diagnosis. (E. J. Shoben.)

The first two of these views may be exposed to the criticisms that Lady Wootton (1959) directed (rather harshly) against certain aspects of social case-work—of encouraging the condescension of 'superior psychological insight' or the mystique of 'relationship'.

Reasons for an increasing interest in guidance are not hard to find—(1) the wider diversity of young people receiving a prolonged education and requiring a wider diversity of educational opportunities, (2) the wider range of career possibilities in a complex and rapidly changing society, (3) the greater concern to involve young people in the shaping of their own destinies as one part of a democratic ideal, (4) the greater recognition of the social and emotional factors that may be more influential in a young person's education than any mainly scholastic learning, and (5) the feeling that it may make more sense to prevent problems arising by a continuous guidance programme rather than attempt to solve them when their symptoms erupt in severe and destructive forms. There is also (6), a concern with economy in the broad sense—partly a matter of getting a good public return for educational expenditure, but also partly one of getting a good return for the individual, for so much educational effort is difficult to justify on either count. The more one puts into an enterprise the less can one allow chance to play a *large* part in determining its degree of success or failure.

As things are, and even limiting oneself to vocational guidance, there is a huge disparity between the extensive systematic discussion of theories and evidence illustrated by Crites' seven-hundred-page *Vocational Psychology* (1969), or even the practical survey of the British scene in Vaughan's *Education and Vocational Guidance Today* (1970), and the casual manner in which perhaps most young people drift through the educational system and into some job or other, with little or fragmentary guidance, and little guidance oriented towards them as persons rather than as cases for disposal. Conventional assumptions linger when circumstances have changed. The problem is too big to be solved casually and requires systematic provision of one kind or another, perhaps by ensuring that all teachers receive a general introduction to guidance work while some specialize in it. It seems unlikely that there can be a complete resolution of the tension between the functions of teaching those who know in the main where they want or are expected to go and helping others to find out where they can and ought to go.

One of the earliest ideas about vocational guidance was that it was a business of matching ability and personality specifications to job specifications. The National Institute of Industrial Psychology's pamphlet *Studying Work* is a guide to job specification, matching the seven-point plan for establishing the job-seeker's profile. Crites illustrates American devices having the same purpose (see Crites, 1969, pp. 42–3). While the matching principle must be relevant in some general sense by definition, it is not so easy to turn it into precise specifications. The same people may tolerate diverse jobs, and the same job diverse people. Aptitudes, interests and personality traits, which one might hope would intercorrelate highly and help to predict job success, seem in fact to have very small degrees of overlap. Criteria of success or satisfaction in work are diverse and difficult to assess for adequate samples, although it seems that a steady 13 per cent of American samples express dissatisfaction with their work.

There has been emphasis on the idea that vocational choice is a developmental process over several years rather than a point-in-time decision (as treated in some traditional vocational guidance practice), and that it is a development from fantasy to reality thinking in terms of field and level of aspiration. Different theories have proposed explanations of vocational choice by reference to social or economic pressures, the evolution of the individual's self-concept, the exercise of existing abilities and aptitudes, the need to compromise between aspirations and potentialities, and the influence of subconscious drives or needs (driving the timorous, let us say, into librarianship or the aggressive into power tool operation).

Systems of diagnosing vocational problems have been suggested, including an interesting pattern devised by Berezin and quoted by Crites (pp. 287–8). This proposes eight areas of investigation—(1) intrapersonal conflict (between self-motives), (2) interpersonal conflict (between the person and others who matter to him), (3) environmental conflict (between the self and the situation it is in), (4) lack of experience, (5) lack of skill, (6) lack of self-understanding, (7) lack of information, and (8) the area of self-actualization, that is, of defining and achieving what one wants to become. Each of these categories can be considered in relation to three areas of the person's life—the emotional, the educational and the vocational.

There seems to be a moderate but not high correlation (about 0·4) between good or bad adjustment to work and to life in general. Personality problems are the most common cause of discharge from employment (according to studies of American employment records), but it is obviously possible to do a satisfactory job despite being personally maladjusted in some sense. Danskin (1955) instances the professional dance musician as a case where professional success may require a style of life which precipitates personal problems and upsets.

Much of the guidance a teacher may be called on to give will be educational and personal. Even that guidance which depends on information can involve difficulty in obtaining the facts and complexity in unravelling and applying them. This aspect needs central or specialized organization in a secondary school of any size. The scope and efficacy of more personal guidance depends on how accessible the teacher makes himself—temporally and psychologically. Some people are able to combine teaching quite readily with a kind of permanent openness to the personal problems of the learners. Others may have to separate these functions more definitely. Provided they are accessible sometimes, they can provide this service and probably gain more allegiance for their teaching purposes as well. In a profession so diverse as teaching there are bound to be some who are intrinsically less accessible and who may not have seen a way through their own problems, let alone anybody else's.

Apart from this last consideration, teachers' attitudes may vary systematically with the sex and social class of the pupils, and with the age and experience of the teachers, as illustrated by McIntyre, Morrison and Sutherland (1966). They found that teachers of 11–12-year-olds in a Scottish city valued pleasant and trustworthy pupils in middle-class and mixed-social-class schools, but hardworking or clever pupils in working-class schools. Older and more experienced teachers valued persistence, enthusiasm and attainment more, while younger teachers valued particularly children who behaved themselves in class, Expectations of girls were more stereotyped than of boys. It is easy and doubtless proper to draw attention to such phenomena, but it is in the nature of opinions to simplify and systematize themselves. A study of researchers' attitudes would perhaps reveal how they too were influenced by current fashions and prejudices within each field of research.

Teachers' attitudes are still very important. Pidgeon (1970) and others have shown how teachers' expectations influence pupils' aspirations and achievements. This guidance of mutual expectations is a kind that continues all the time among human beings, and it may be that skill in establishing the right expectations for individual learners is one of the most important kinds of guidance a teacher can give, apart from the guidance of behavioural example (one avoids saying 'exemplary behaviour', for that smacks of smug perfectionism). This does not solve the problem of who is entitled to suggest what the teacher should expect of himself. The teacher must feel sometimes that there are a great number of people prepared to counsel him, and that they have a tendency toward directive rather than non-directive guidance. He may wonder too whether teachers, by whatever counselling techniques, can dispel or even mitigate very much those ills which are rooted in social institutions more potent than the school.

Perspective on assessment and guidance

People have to assess intellectual attainments, intellectual potential and miscellaneous temperamental aspects of personality which vary

in importance with the character of the situation under consideration. Standardized objective tests of attainments and intelligence
have succeeded more than 'personality' tests in meeting the general
criteria which objective testers have set for themselves. It is necessary
to understand the nature of these criteria if one is to appreciate what
objective tests can or cannot do. It is necessary to understand these
criteria in order to judge whether or not any particular test satisfies
them. And it is necessary to understand them in order to refine the
operation of more traditional modes of assessment, like examinations, reports and interviews.

The number of variables, and techniques and scales of assessing
them, is so great that it is easy to play off one bit of an assessment
argument against another by disregarding inconvenient evidence
and not bothering about whether or not one is comparing like with
like. For example, it would be possible to argue from this chapter
that examinations were good things or that they were bad things—
and similarly with other kinds of assessment. The intention has been
to map out the strengths and weaknesses of various forms and areas
of assessment, and to suggest practical applications where this is a
positive possibility. Some points are points to be acted on, others to
be warned about, others to be noted for further reference.

Looking back on this and the preceding chapter, one might realize
that assessment poses a series of problems of different kinds—of
knowing (1) precisely what one means by the terms used, (2) what
the purposes of any assessment are, (3) what functions the assessment fulfils, whether purposed or not, (4) what technical problems
have to be solved if the assessment is not to be excessively influenced
by chance variations, and (5) what side effects the assessment has
that may have to be guarded against or mitigated. Since any one of
these is a theme on its own, it is less surprising that many may drift
along with oversimplified solutions rather than face the complexity
of all five themes together.

The use of assessments for specific problems of selection is readily
appreciated. The guidance or counselling movement is spreading the
idea of assessment and guidance as an on-going combined operation
rather than two widely separate functions exercised at a few critical
points in a person's childhood or adult career. This is associated with
recognition of the range of human talents and the entitlement of all
to fair and personal consideration.

As an ideal this seems commendable and it underlies much, but
not all, of what has been said earlier. Assessment and guidance must
be combined, but they are still two highly distinguishable activities.
Good intentions as a counsellor can easily distort good judgment as
an assessor. Expectation may affect performance, and giving the

benefit of the doubt is often good policy, but good intentions, high expectations and benefits of doubts are consistent with objective assessment. One can overrate as well as underrate a capacity—as illustrated in the so-called decompression phenomenon, whereby school leavers, carefully nurtured or pressurized into university entrance, flop when they have to proceed at the university under their own intellectual and temperamental impetus.

Teaching is a kind of guidance, but it is not just guidance. It has to do with initiating people into forms of understanding that society deems good for them. Society puts both a general premium on all such forms, under the general idea of education, and differential extra premiums on some forms—typically the most intellectually and personally demanding. Any philosophy of guidance in education would be something of a sham if it turned a blind eye (as can happen) to these facts. One can, of course, set about changing society's ideas about premium rates, but this is a slow process—even in revolutionary societies.

The present discussion of assessment and guidance has been in the general context of young people's educational and vocational careers. It is not possible in a book like this to go deeply into all the difficult special problems of assessment and guidance that arise, but the next chapter will offer at least a first look at some of them.

11 | Handicap and behaviour problems

The particular problems discussed in the two preceding chapters could be placed under the general heading of justice and helpfulness for the wide range of ordinary learners. It is easy to grow quickly satisfied with the rough justice of conventional practice, for conventional practice has much to commend it, despite any shortcomings. It is a matter of professional conscience for those who have extensive powers over the careers of young people to seek out every way of improving assessment and guidance, even where existing defects are minor and do not give rise to really gross anomalies. Where anomalies are gross, the case is naturally all the stronger.

While all learners should be viewed against the general background just indicated, there are some special problems that are bound to command the attention of all at some time or other, and the attention of some for most of their professional careers. The problems that will be discussed in the present chapter are those of handicap, maladjustment and delinquency. The discussion must obviously be a general one, for so much detailed work has been done on these topics, but not, it is hoped, so general as to avoid making some of the most substantial points that need to be made. Although the emphasis will be on substantive problems, these topics provide a continuing lesson on the problem of human assessment as well, illustrating the need for subtlety and refinement as one moves from the useful but rough norms of psychometrics to the challenges of special groups of people and of individuals within these groups.

Handicap: categories, incidence and attitudes

Anything is a handicap if it prevents someone from doing what he wants or ought to do. Handicap as a technical term should presumably refer to conditions such as blindness, deafness or very low intelligence, which most people would agree were disadvantageous. But there are bound to be disagreements about where the line is drawn between minor and 'real' handicap, and, of course, there can be paradoxical cases where real handicap is turned to advantage—a beggar's livelihood from defect or deformity, a serious wound that takes the soldier away from the danger of the fighting, a child's ailment that gains him special sympathy.

There are ten officially recognized categories of handicapped children requiring special educational facilities—children who are (1) blind, (2) partially sighted, (3) deaf, (4) partially hearing, (5) educationally subnormal, (6) epileptic, (7) maladjusted, (8) physically handicapped, (9) affected by speech defect, and (10) delicate. Jackson (1969), using mainly 1966 statistics for England and Wales, indicates an incidence of about one deaf school pupil in 2,300 (1 : 2,300), giving a total at that time of just over 3,000 cases. Almost as many again were partially hearing. The incidence of blind pupils was about 1 : 5,300 (giving 1,400 individuals at that time) and of partially sighted about 1 : 3,400 (giving 2,200 individuals). These handicaps are serious, although they affect fewer people than some others. They have been thoroughly studied and varied technical and educational provisions made for them. The figures quoted indicate twice as many deaf as blind pupils, and 50 per cent more partially hearing than partially sighted. With these as with other handicaps, the ordinary teacher in the primary school has to make sure that a mild degree of handicap (slight deafness, for example) is not mistaken for intellectual dullness.

Jackson's figures for physically handicapped and delicate children show an incidence of approximately 1 : 700 for each of these two categories (actual numbers in 1966 of over 11,000 and over 10,000 respectively). These categories are susceptible to more variety of interpretation. 'Delicate' is an elastic term and educational decisions about physically handicapped children are influenced by factors of general intelligence and home background, not just by a physical diagnosis. Epilepsy may affect 4 : 1,000 children between the ages of five and fourteen, but, since much of this takes mild forms (with symptoms like dizziness, confusion, falling or, in *petit mal*, scarcely noticeable wanderings of attention), only limited scholastic provision is necessary for this category. (In major epileptic attacks a child may slump down, lose consciousness, jerk spasmodically and froth at the mouth. The attacks often last only two or three minutes and what is immediately necessary is to prevent the person from hurting himself against surrounding objects and let him sleep afterwards.)

Maladjustment and speech handicap are another couple of elastic categories. Over 8,000 pupils were at special schools for maladjusted children in 1966—an incidence of less than 1 : 1,000—but six or seven times as many children were treated at child guidance clinics, and a proportion of these must have been emotionally disturbed children. The 1 : 700 children born with cleft palates will have been treated before going to school at all, but may still need some special speech help. The 1 : 100 children (4 : 100 before the age of seven), mainly boys, who stammer will need help, particularly by calmness on the part of the teacher. And Jackson estimates that 5 : 100 may need special help at one time or another with some aspect of speech, although the incidence falls with age. Speech serves such vital purposes of communication and self-expression for everyone that it deserves more educational attention generally than it actually gets.

The remaining category is that of educationally subnormal children (E.S.N.). They constitute by far the largest group for whom provision is made in special schools. There were 55,000 in 1966 and Jackson estimated the average need for E.S.N. provision to be 8 : 1,000—that is, almost twice the combined proportion for all auditory and visual defects together with physically handicapped and delicate pupils. Educationally subnormal children are those who are not suited by the standard and pace of work in an ordinary school but can make some progress, given their own programme of work, (1) moving by small slow steps, with (2) a less predominantly verbal emphasis than ordinary school programmes, and with (3) more variety to stimulate interest in tasks which may bring only a modest return for the effort expended on them.

Although IQ is no strict guide to E.S.N. classification, E.S.N. children tend to have IQs between about 50 and 70. Only 2·3 per cent of children have IQs of 70 or less; only 1 : 2,000 has an IQ of 50 or less—that is, where the IQ scale has a mean of 100 and standard deviation of 15. (Tests can have other standard deviations. Two standard deviations of 15 down from a mean of 100 gives 70, but, of course, two standard deviations of, let us say, 20 would give a score of 60—meaning the same thing as the more usual 70. Similarly, at the other end of the scale, an IQ of 130 is high if the standard deviation is 15, but, if it were 20, the corresponding score on the scale would be 140.)

Apart from all of these educational categories, there is another category which is (at the time of writing) about to be transferred from the responsibility of the health authorities to that of the local education authorities. That is children (21,000 of them in 1970) who are not able to benefit from the kind of schooling offered in a special school for the educationally subnormal but who can attend junior training centres, where they learn some simple language and social skills and receive some sensory training, for example through music and movement. Children attending a training centre from five to sixteen might begin with a mental age of about two and end with one about six or seven. Children attending a special school for the educationally subnormal might go to the school about the chronological age of eight or nine and make one or two years' normal educational progress by the age of sixteen. In terms of mental age (not to be interpreted too strictly), a child at an E.S.N. school might begin with a mental age of five or six and leave school at sixteen with a mental age of ten to twelve.

Mental age means mental age as measured by some test, exactly the same as IQ indicates intelligence as measured by some test. These are indicators of general adaptability and educability, but a sixteen-year-old is, in a wider sense, bound to have *something* of the mentality of a sixteen-year-old, even if he is intellectually very slow. Mentality can be interpreted as a quality of social adaptation to simple given circumstances as well as a capacity for varied intellectual adaptation to varying or complex circumstances. It can include useful abilities, however laboriously acquired or however specialized, and not only the all-round intelligence that comes as a gift of God, genetics or family fortune. That is why decisions about educational treatment or allocation have to take account of a person's whole social and educational adaptability—not just his abstract intellectual power.

The Scottish Education Department's pamphlet on *Degrees of Mental Handicap* (1961), although published some time ago, makes some sensitive and sensible points about categorization—the importance of complete and varied assessment, of flexibility in interpreting categories, of reviewing decisions and allocations in the light of a child's actual progress, and of erring on the side of giving children a chance at the higher of two levels if there is any doubt. The last point must not be urged just as a matter of facile optimism. Jackson has a useful statement of the arguments for and against special schools as compared with special classes in ordinary schools for the educationally subnormal (Jackson, 1969, pp. 95–7).

Small proportions of children come into further sub-categories deriving from the main categories mentioned. For example, in 1970 the number of mentally handicapped cared for in hospitals was 6,000 (*Times Educational Supplement*, 17 July 1970, p. 12). Some children suffer from multiple handicaps and have to be treated according to individual needs. The physically handicapped include those suffering from one or other of the forms of cerebral palsy which have been extensively studied both medically, psychologically and educationally. The estimated incidence is about one or two per thousand births. Cockburn (1961) makes the point that the cerebral palsied, while constituting a group (or cluster of sub-groups—spastic athetoid, etc.) from a medical point of view, do not constitute a single group from the point of view of psychological characteristics or desirable educational policies. Half of her sample of 223 children and adolescents had IQs below 70, and half of those IQs below 50. Such children, whatever else they needed, needed the educational treatment appropriate for the intellectually retarded. Another quarter had IQs between 90 and 130 and were, therefore, in the middle of the normal intellectual range or above it. Some needed special help related to sensory handicap or epileptic handicap rather than to cerebral palsy as such.

Clegg and Megson (1968) present and extend the problem of handicap in the following way. They note that about twenty out of every thousand children born will present society with a clearly defined educational problem. Two or three of the twenty are likely to spend their lives bedfast and virtually ineducable, another two or three to be capable only of simple training (see Chapters III and IV pp. 14–20 of Degrees of Mental Handicap on the 'trainable' and 'untrainable' child). The remainder of the twenty will receive education in special schools. Clegg and Megson are disposed to view this as the tip of the iceberg. They argue that there is a further considerable proportion of children handicapped by living in distress. The 'mute misery . . . rampages . . . clamant demands for affection' that may strike the teacher in school may be the symptoms of family quarrelling, cruelty or immorality, of mentally ill mothers or work-shy fathers, and of mental retardation in children frustrated by a society that has no time for those of modest ability or, as the authors more tendentiously put it, that puts the shadow of measurable book learning before the substance of total personality development.

About 14 per cent of the population have IQs between 70 and 85, between the level at which there is a possibility of needing special education and the lower limit of the middle two-thirds of the whole population. Fourteen per cent means about eight million people in the United Kingdom, or one million out of a school population of eight million. Children in this group do not need special education in the administrative sense previously discussed but they certainly need particular consideration in the ordinary schools. The demands made on teachers of these children are ambivalent. They must expect as much as possible of the children and try to compensate for the social handicaps which often compound intellectual handicap, and yet at the same time make allowances, not expect too much, and expend great patience on achieving small measures of progress. As a counsel of perfection this is admirable, but it is sometimes expounded with a facility only possible for those not doing the job themselves. As argued in Chapter 8, the teachers of slow learners need as much material support in their teaching endeavours as the slow learners do in their learning.

Social and educational handicaps can accompany one another at other points in the intellectual scale. Only one-quarter of children (1970) stay at school beyond the age of sixteen, although many more could stay on with advantage. Less than one-fifth of eighteen-year-olds go on to full-time higher education, although the corresponding proportion for many other countries is higher (45 per cent in the United States). MacArthur (1970) argues in a polemical article that 'thirty thousand children of university ability leave school every year at 15 and the problem of schools in slum areas remains largely untouched', and that 'a society which disinherits so many of its young is storing up explosive social problems for the future.'

Handicap in the narrower sense may affect only 2 or 3 per cent of the population, but the size of the percentage does not express the fact that one is referring to tens of thousands of people. One always has to note what a percentage is a percentage of. Moreover, handicap is not equally spread throughout the population but concentrated in various ways, with some people suffering from multiple handicap. An awareness of handicap and its approximate incidence must be part of a complete picture of child development, although the detailed diagnosis and treatment of some handicaps must be a specialized matter that cannot be summed up briefly.

The ordinary teacher can contribute even to the cause of the specially handicapped by encouraging an informed and sympathetic attitude to them, but intellectual and social handicap are the two forms that any teacher may have to deal with directly. The main methods available are personal tolerance and encouragement, the full exploitation of every positive lead that suggests itself, the abatement of conventional expectations if their ineffectiveness is manifest, and the abatement of institutional emphasis on scholastic achievement if more learners would benefit from some other emphasis (social, practical, etc.). The main problems that these methods confront are inadequate resources and the fact that society (that is, most people) is consistently motivated by conventional success goals but only fitfully motivated by compassion for those less capable of achieving them.

Some handicaps are identifiable by clear criteria (blindness, deafness), others by more variable criteria (partial sight or hearing), and others by highly variable and even disputable criteria ('delicate', 'socially handicapped'). A less conspicuous handicap may have more psychological and educational significance than a more conspicuous handicap in the same person. The spastic child may be conspicuous because of inability to relax the muscles and consequent rigidity of movement in the affected limbs, or the athetoid because of the uncontrollable movements of face, head and limbs to which he is subject; but, where they exist, low intelligence, social handicap or defective family care may be the more serious underlying handicaps from a practical point of view. Similarly, intellectual capacity may intensify or moderate social handicap, and social advantage or disadvantage influence the practical outcome of intellectual capacity.

These points should be sufficient warning against forming stereotyped conceptions of handicap. Thomas, Chess and Birch (1968, pp. 124–35) give the examples of three brain-damaged children with different patterns of emotional and social adjustment. Bert was intelligent and temperamentally quite adaptable; the experience of family stress produced a behaviour problem, but only a mild one. Kevin was of below average intelligence but positive in mood and mild in his reactions; he progressed slowly but successfully within his capacity and had no real behavioural disturbance. Barbara was of average intelligence but highly active, persistently irregular in response, slow to adapt, inclined to withdraw and negative in mood; she developed seriously ritualistic and disruptive behaviour patterns and was placed at seven years of age in a residential institution for training and care. The social background of the three children was similar and prosperous. Temperamental factors seemed to contribute to their different patterns of development.

Behaviour disorders—Thomas, Chess and Birch

The text for this theme should doubtless be, 'All t'world's queer 'cept thee and me—and even thee's a bit queer sometimes.' Maladjustment or behaviour disorder seems fully qualified to enter the class of elastic concepts already mentioned. It poses the question of whether a person does 'fit in' to, or behave correctly in, a given society and sometimes begs the question of whether it is a good thing to adjust to the society in any case. Despite the question of value judgments lurking behind the idea of maladjustment, it is possible to argue that there are ways of behaving that are (1) inconsistent with the widely held purposes within a particular society, or (2) inconsistent with the avowed or implicit purposes even of those so behaving, or (3) consistent with such purposes, but either (a) manifestly uneconomic in terms of psychological effort and gain, or (b) manifestly harmful in their side effects on the person himself or on those who have to live with him. These are practical questions that can be put, and sometimes if not always answered.

Thomas, Chess and Birch (1968), whose work has been mentioned in this chapter and in Chapter 3, stress the importance of considering the interactions among factors of individual temperament, factors of individual ability and general social circumstance, and factors of child rearing and specific tensions characteristic of an individual family. They have studied from 1956 and throughout childhood a group of 136 New York children from middle or upper class, mainly Jewish, families. The group is relatively homogeneous in terms of social class, child rearing attitudes (practices may vary from expressed attitudes) and intelligence. The mean IQ at the ages of three and six was 127, with a standard deviation of 12.

Forty-two of the children developed significant behaviour problems and these will be discussed shortly. All of the children have been carefully and independently rated at various times on the nine temperamental dimensions listed in Chapter 3—(1) amount of activity, (2) regularity or rhythmicity of activities, (3) intensity or mildness of response, (4) tendency to approach or withdraw from new situations, (5) responsiveness to stimuli of high or low intensity, (6) cheerfulness (positiveness) or miserableness (negativeness) of mood, (7) adaptability, in the sense of readiness to change with new situations, (8) distractability from an ongoing activity, and (9) persistence with activities, whether or not temporarily distracted.

Some methodological points about the enquiry are worth noting. Later assessments are compared not with recollections of how the children behaved earlier but with records made at the time of how they did actually behave. Different assessors were employed for different aspects of the child studies and for different periods at which the children were studied. One assessor did not know the evidence collected by others and had to make an independent judgment. 'All notations of behaviour were made in concrete, descriptive terms' to avoid excessively general categories. Subcategories were specified to further discourage too-general allocation, and global psychological labels like 'anxious' or 'hostile' were avoided.

Parents were asked to specify exactly what they meant when they gave too general accounts of their children's behaviour (see Thomas, pp. 192–5, for a practical guide to systematic enquiry about the nine temperamental traits). Ratings were made with reference to the responses of the particular child under study, not to responses or imagined responses of children in general. And, in the study of the 26 boys and 16 girls who showed significant behavioural disturbance, the symptoms of disturbance were assessed in relation to (1) whether or not they were typical in any case of that particular age, (2) whether or not they were typical of that particular child, or only isolated phenomena, and (3) whether or not they were related to any known psychopathological phenomenon. These criteria alone do not validate an enquiry, but disregarding them invalidates some enquiries.

Symptoms that were taken to be possible danger signals for behavioural disturbance were (1) the child's being seriously behind ordinary developmental norms, (2) repeated self-endangering or self-destructive behaviour, despite comprehending the existence of danger, (3) inadequate responsiveness to people or contact with the environment, (4) flagrant flouting of social conventions, (5) significant and continued disturbance in language and speech, (6) perceptual or perceptual-motor inadequacies, (7) isolation from children of the same age, or annoying or aggressive behaviour towards them, creating its own isolation, and (8) school failure despite intellectual adequacy.

The temperament ratings for the disturbed children were all compared with one another (360 intercorrelations). The intercorrelations ranged between $+0.5$ and -0.5. In other words, they were modest in size, indicating shared or overlapping variances of 25 per cent or less. The temperament traits that seemed most prominent in the statistical analysis were (4) intensity, (7) adaptability, and (6) mood, in that order. The clinical sample differed from the non-clinical in the ratings made both before, and at the time of, the disturbed behaviour, in 'excessive frequency of both high and low activity, irregularity, nonadaptability, intensity, persistence and distractability' (Thomas, p. 69).

Children who had been temperamentally more difficult to rear provided more behavioural problems, but 'easy' children could also present problems. One of these adapted readily to very demanding parental standards of outward politeness but could not subsequently sustain both this adaptation and an adaptation to his fellow pupils' expectations of less starchy behaviour; another gained kudos at home for his 'cute' outspokenness but ran foul of teachers and fellow pupils when they were at the receiving end of his cheek. The parents of 'difficult' children could react in complex ways, showing 'calm strictness, permissiveness, punitiveness, peremptoriness, dislike of some of the child's behaviour and admiration of others (i.e. other behaviours), in addition to admixtures of guilt and resentment' (Thomas, p. 81). Intensely reactive, high active, persistent children tended to react to frustration with temper tantrums; mildly active, persistent children with whining and fuss; mildly reactive, low activity children with withdrawal.

Thomas and his colleagues see six particular sources of stress and dissonance, between

1 parental practices or demands and the child's temperament or capacities;
2 home values and school or peer values;
3 different parental practices on different occasions (inconsistency);
4 one parent and another on the same occasion (interparental dissonance);
5 the child's expectations of affection and acceptance and the parents' actual feelings and behaviour;
6 the mode of functioning of a teacher or other adult and the child's own characteristics.

Of the 42 children clinically examined and treated, 32 improved and 10 continued to get worse. The numbers involved are small, but it seemed that there was no difference in the improvement rate for children who had earlier been rated 'difficult' or 'easy'. Those who were temperamentally persistent seem to improve less than others (improvement rate of 1 : 3 compared with 2 : 3).

Thomas, Chess and Birch deserve study for the general interest of their findings, the practical suggestiveness of their categorizations and for their emphasis on the complexity of interaction that goes to produce a particular behavioural pattern. They question the need for traditional psychoanalytical concepts in relation to young children, although the psychological symptoms of older children may be influenced by 'ideation, abstraction and symbolic representation, conceptualized motives and aims'. They mention the view of Eysenck (1963) that 'neurotic behaviour consists of maladaptive conditioned responses of the autonomic system and of skeletal responses made to reduce the conditioned sympathetic reactions', but do not see this as a complete explanation. (As mentioned in Chapter 6 the autonomic or sympathetic nervous system is the physiological system that governs involuntary emotional responses.)

They recognize anxiety—'presumed states of intrapsychic conflict' —as a possible product of interactional stress, but not in childhood as a cause. They would not attribute disturbed reactions automatically to maternal deprivation, to 'spoiling', or to punishing. What they consider essential for preventing or correcting maladjustment, in the sense of behaviour disturbance, is a process of prolonged and regular accustoming of the child to whatever pattern of behaviour is beneficial rather than maladaptive. This is not as obvious or easy as it may seem, for adults do a lot to encourage maladjustment by encouraging disadvantageous behaviour or by acting inconsistently. The motivation for this seemingly mad practice may be thoughtlessness, the hope of temporary peace, excessive or inadequate expectations of a child, or any of the various expressions of personal dissatisfaction within the family.

Symptoms of maladjustment

To keep behaviour disorder or maladjustment in perspective it is worthwhile recalling the many symptoms that any of us may spot in acquaintances or manifest in our own behaviour—eccentricity, frayed nerves, indigestion, anxiety, crankiness, temper, fears, hypochondria, obsessional tidiness or cleanliness, ready fatigue, suspiciousness, defensiveness, cravings for security or praise or regressions to adolescent or even infantile response. All of these are symptoms which can fall within the wide range of what must be called normal adjustment but which can, in more extreme forms, become the signs of maladjustment. Cameron (1947) distinguishes behaviour disorder by the existence of 'relatively fixed, crystallized patterns of maladaptive attitudes and responses'.

He shares a view stated earlier in this chapter, expressing it in the claim that 'behaviour pathology is to a considerable degree based upon serious defects in the techniques of sharing the perspectives common to one's own society'. He sees behaviour as a biosocial phenomenon, requiring biological and social reference for its explanation. Like Eysenck, he sees the autonomic nervous system as part of the physical mechanism for sustaining and generalizing emotional reactions. The smooth muscles controlled by the autonomic nervous system can sustain a state of tension with little fatigue. The glandular secretions of the system circulate for some time before they are broken down. Consequently an emotional reaction set off by one state of affairs, by one set of stimuli, may be displaced on to adjacent stimuli, and the emotional spiral further prolonged by reflection upon what happens. (The pupil frustrated by one teacher vents his feeling on the school as an institution, whipping it on by further reflection on the injustice he feels he has suffered.)

Like Thomas, Chess and Birch, Cameron is sceptical about some Freudian interpretations and about attributing substantive causal efficacy to motives. 'Infantile sexuality is related to adult sexuality in about the same sense that nursing at the breast is related to an adult dinner date. . . . Motive and motivation are simply verbal designations that result from our own operations in analyzing behaviour.'

The psychoanalytical mechanisms, like repression and projection, are discussed in biosocial terms, excluding or minimizing reference to figments like the unconscious.

The Underwood Report (1955) on maladjusted children expresses a view that recurs in many educational writings—'some children are not obtaining at home the love and care, the discipline or the stimulus which they need, and the school inevitably has to try to make good some of the home's deficiencies'. Its detailed practical recommendations refer to desirable scales of provision for specialist services (psychiatrists, psychologists, etc.) and to the value of discussion groups or training courses in mental health for health visitors, teachers and parents. In boarding schools for maladjusted pupils they thought anti-social behaviour had to be tolerated, but that pupils could be helped to differentiate right and wrong, partly by being given a larger share in the running of the school. They characterize a desirable school as one 'run as a benevolent dictatorship'.

---

1 *Nervous disorders:*
   Fears—anxiety, phobias, timidity, over-sensitivity.
   Withdrawal—unsociability, solitariness.
   Depression—brooding, melancholy periods.
   Excitability—over-activity.
   Apathy—lethargy, unresponsiveness, no interests.
   Obsessions—rituals and compulsions.
   Hysterical fits, loss of memory.

2 *Habit disorders:*
   Speech—stammering, speech defects.
   Sleep—night terrors, sleep-walking or talking.
   Movement—twitching, rocking, head-banging, nail-biting.
   Feeding—food fads, nervous vomiting, indiscriminate eating.
   Excretion—incontinence of urine and faeces.
   Nervous pains and paralysis—headaches, deafness, etc.
   Physical symptoms—asthma and other allergic conditions.

3 *Behaviour disorders:*
   Unmanageableness—defiance, disobedience, refusal to go to school or work.
   Temper.
   Aggressiveness—bullying, destructiveness, cruelty.
   Jealous behaviour.
   Demands for attention.
   Stealing and begging.
   Lying and romancing.
   Truancy—wandering, staying out late.
   Sex difficulties—masturbation, sex play, homosexuality.

4 *Organic disorders:*
Conditions following head injuries, encephalitis or cerebral tumours; epilepsy, chorea.

5 *Psychotic behaviour:*
Hallucinations, delusions, extreme withdrawal, bizarre symptoms, violence.

6 *Educational and Vocational Difficulties:*
Backwardness not accounted for by dullness.
Dislikes connected with subjects or people.
Unusual response to school discipline.
Inability to concentrate.
Inability to keep jobs.

7 *Unclassified.*

Table 16 A grouping of symptoms which may be indicative of maladjustment. (a) This follows, except at a few points, the lines of a classification in use in child guidance clinics in this country.
(b) For many of the symptoms listed, any and every manifestation does not indicate maladjustment, but only manifestations that are excessive or abnormal. (Appendix B of the Underwood Report on Maladjusted Children, H.M.S.O., 1955.)

Appendix B of the Underwood Report consists of a classification of possible symptoms of maladjustment as set out in Table 16 of the present work. The classification is self-explanatory to some extent. Organic and psychotic disorders particularly require medical appraisal. The terms neurotic and psychotic can be used variously by different people. For example, Cameron distinguishes psychoses as disorders which require institutional treatment, whereas Eysenck claims that psychosis is a different dimension from neurotic instability. The classification into nervous/habit/behaviour disorders is obviously fairly broad. They are all behaviour disorders, although the label may be stuck particularly on behaviour that tends towards explicit aggressiveness with disruption of other people. Nervous disorders seem to fit broadly the reaction of flight rather than fight. They are disorders in which the person himself suffers rather than others (at any rate directly), and in which the psychological mechanism seems to be inward rather than outward turning. Habit disorders include marked departures from whatever is considered within the wide normal range for such basic habits as speech, sleep, feeding, excretion, etc., and the development of habits as strong as the basic habits except that they are less useful, or positively harmful.

With so many symptoms going a-begging and so many possible interpretations it is not surprising that people may note those that suit or inconvenience them, and not necessarily others that are equally or more important. The Thomas, Chess and Birch parents were more concerned with 'mood disturbances, difficulties in peer relationships, speech problems and learning deficiencies' in their young children. Clegg and Megson (1968), reporting on 2,800 school children in an industrial population of 18,000, claim that 'there were twice as many withdrawn, timid, lethargic and depressed children as there were those described as aggressive, defiant or undisciplined', although public comment sometimes gives the impression that aggressiveness is the big behaviour problem. Aggression may be serious in terms of immediate irritation, but not necessarily more serious in terms of cumulative psychological damage than prolonged individual depression and withdrawal.

A form of maladjustment that has received considerable attention recently is that called childhood *autism*. A current estimate is of 4,000 English cases. Autistic children have been alleged to be most difficult between the ages of two and five. They may not speak and do not relate with people or situations in any ordinary way, although they may, unlike mental defectives, show cognitive potentialities at least in some areas. One mother described how her autistic child would 'rush about in a mercurial frenzy, climbing over everything, pulling out drawers and opening cupboard doors' (*The Times*, 25 February 1970) and in other ways disrupt the life of the family. As with other relatively uncommon syndromes it is difficult to get enough hard evidence to define or explain autism clearly.

Some psychiatrists have compiled typologies of abnormality, such as Leonhard's classification quoted by Fish (1968). Like lists of symptoms, these typologies may constitute a clinical check list, even if they need more refined interpretation. Leonhard's list includes the following: (1) The *epileptoid* personality (not connected with epilepsy) would reveal itself within normal limits by impulsive behaviour. (2) The *anankastic, obsessional*, or *compulsive* personality may show inflexibility, a tendency towards routine for its own sake and anxiety when routine is disturbed, persistence combined with indecisiveness, and conscientiousness combined with overprecision. (3) The *hysterical* personality may be considered demonstrative within ordinary limits, a gift for expression combining however with an excessive need for appreciation and a tendency to repress unpleasant facts, which may nevertheless express their emotional significance in the shape of physical symptoms.

(4) The *paranoid* personality may reveal excessive persistence and touchiness within normal limits, tending towards overvaluation of the self and delusions about hostility at the extreme. (5) The *reactive-labile* or emotive personality is particularly readily moved to joy or

sorrow. (6) The *cyclothymic* personality is also liable to alternate between joy and sorrow, but with longer phases of each and not necessarily in reaction to specific events. (7) The *subdepressive* personality is characterized by over-seriousness, with slowness in thought and activity. (8) The *hypomanic* personality is marked by cheerfulness, overactivity and prolixity. (9) the *anxious* personality is marked by excessive fears. These categories are mentioned mainly because they may be used by some people, but, as impressionistic typologies, they would be abhorrent to factor analysts like Eysenck or Cattell. Apart from that, they lack distinct definition even at an impressionistic or clinical level while perpetuating, by their terminology, the idea that personality is some clear thing. In fact, as has been shown earlier, it is a complex and debatable concept and all of its dimensions are surrounded with problems of valid definition and assessment.

The incidence of maladjustment in terms of special school provision has already been given (about 1 : 900), but there is an indefinite penumbra of children and young people who are psychologically and educationally handicapped to a greater or lesser degree by tensions or conflicts they cannot resolve unaided. Ryle (1969), discussing *Student Casualties*, estimates that between 1 and 2 per cent of students during a three- or four-year course may require hospital admission because of psychiatric illness. Three to 6 per cent may suffer from serious neurotic illness or personality disorder requiring prolonged psychotherapy. Six to 12 per cent may require brief psychotherapy or counselling. In addition to these severe or moderate cases, 20 per cent of students may report normal stress reactions, requiring reassurance or brief medication.

Less is known about the incidence for adolescents or young adults other than students, but Miller (1969) notes that 'adolescents will often act out at school the tensions resulting from family conflicts', and Wolff (1969), more specifically, that (1) children rejected psychologically by their parents may react with unsocialized aggression; (2) those neglected by delinquent parents with 'well adjusted' aggression; and (3) those (a) exposed to family repression ('a hypercritical, inconsistent father, a dominating mother and lack of sociability in either parent'), or (b) suffering from chronic physical defect or ailment, with over-inhibited behaviour.

The treatment of maladjustment

The treatment of a great deal of what might be called mild maladjustment or problem behaviour must depend on the homely psychotherapy that people can give one another through the ordinary channels of human sympathy and understanding—sharing sorrows, lending a helping hand or a sympathetic ear, giving a word of praise or encouragement, taking the pressure off a person when he is down, being ready to note mitigating circumstances and slow to exacerbate conflict. Sheer patience may sometimes help, for things do often change and what was a problem becomes less of a problem. A proportion even of quite serious psychological illness abates with the passage of time for reasons not fully understood. Behaviour which is regarded as seriously maladaptive at one point in time or by one set of people may come to be considered as less significant at another time or by other people. This does not imply that any forms of adaptation are as good as any others. Reasons for rejecting this view were stated earlier in the chapter.

At the other end of the scale there is the unfortunate proportion of people who require systematic and sometimes prolonged medical treatment because of serious mental imbalance (not intellectual defect in the sense of low intelligence). These do not pose primarily educational problems and, therefore, need not concern teachers, except as part of a general perspective on human behaviour. Between the extremes of medical, possibly institutional, treatment and ordinary sympathetic exchanges there is a range which includes residential schools for maladjusted children, child guidance clinics to advise on the handling of individual cases of maladjustment, social workers to look into the possibility of ameliorating general home circumstances, school counsellors to give specialized support to the informal counselling work of teachers, headmasters to develop school policies that build up the morale of various kinds of pupil, and teachers themselves to note the special problems of the children in their classes and give special attention where it seems called for. This entire network is required for various purposes and might be expected to be most efficient the more its members understood the range of problems involved and recognized the value of one another's contributions. It is this network of services that is discussed in detail in the Underwood Report.

Some maladjustment is associated with educational backwardness or failure. It may or may not be fundamentally caused by these, but, in either case, it is good therapy to try and correct whatever is educationally wrong. A child may need a second chance to learn to read, going back to an educational stage some distance below his chronological age. To acquire such a basic skill may be an important step towards establishing a point of confidence for that learner—even if he continues to be affected by other disadvantageous influences. This exercise of going back a stage or two is by no means easy, but neither is life with a youngster whose nose is rubbed deeper and deeper into the mire of scholastic failure.

Another characteristic case is the child whose whole educational orientation needs altering on to a more realistic level, for example, the child whose parents have ambitions for him beyond or below his real capacities or interests. This takes one into the realm of parent guidance but also illustrates the importance of doing what is educationally justified, for one may be able to make an educational contribution to psychological improvement where one cannot cut through the Gordian knot of a person's family history or situation. Clegg and Megson argue strongly for action on behalf of the individual child, whether or not one can redeem the family as a whole.

The guidance or counselling of parents is another way in which schools can moderate the effects of maladjustment. With serious cases this is a subtle professional job for psychologist or psychiatrist, but headmasters and teachers, through their general contacts with parents, can act as sources of enlightenment, spreading an understanding of educational and psychological processes and helping to win the sympathy at least of the more accessible parents (many, of course, are not very accessible—particularly fathers) for what the schools are trying to do.

The tendency of some teachers to overlook children whose emotional disturbance occasions no outward disruption has been noted. Here is a recognized tendency which could be corrected by systematic attention to subterranean disturbance, and tactful encouragement directed to helping such children to express themselves in one form or another, or at least to gain a sense that they were not regarded as nonentities, however much they seem to invite such a role. Another widely recognized line of treatment is that of giving more time and effort to accepting learners as people, and letting them come through as such. This means sacrificing time and effort that might otherwise be spent on getting through larger chunks of syllabus, but again one has to ask whether such time lost is really lost or gained. Each person has to strike a balance in the light both of objective circumstances and his own capacity to be a person as well as an instructor, but the sustaining of *some* maladjustments or maladaptation is partly the choice of adult society. They decide that the syllabus and certificate are more important.

All that has been said so far about the treatment of maladjustment is so eminently practical and sensible that one may ask why there are any behaviour problems left. The answer is that the suggested treatments meet the needs of very many, but are not always applied. The position is more difficult still. It seems essential to accept the fact— even if it cannot be fully understood—that some maladjustment is so deeply and widely rooted that it does not evaporate even with a lavish application of psychological or educational enlightenment. Some of the causes can be conjectured—multiplicity of social and psychological handicaps, gross abuses or impossible tensions sustained by persisting features of a particular family, the interaction of unfavourable inheritance with unfavourable environment—but, whatever the causes, the phenomenon is there.

Many books have been written by teachers who have persisted with specially difficult children either in day schools or residential schools. Their wisdom is often individual, even idiosyncratic, and not well represented by any bald summary. However, there are certain things that recur in a great number of these stories. They are (1) acceptance of the children as the persons they are, by radical abandonment of conventional educational patterns and demands, (2) persistence of sometimes monstrous and commonly highly irritating behaviour by the children, despite the new tolerance or humanity into which they are implicitly invited, and (3) the establishment of a not-too-stable *modus vivendi*, in which the disturbed children, while still quite disturbing, slowly settle to a slightly lower level of disturbance and higher level of human sympathy than originally prevailed. This is, of course, an oversimplification, but it seems worth noting that the experience of so many teachers in these circumstances is characterized by the method of radical acceptance and the reward of slightly greater humanity in some individuals.

Delinquency

Moral and legal as well as psychological problems cluster around the word 'delinquency'. For some it is just those cases of maladjustment that happen to run foul of the law; for some, those cases of moral deficiency that also incur legal penalties; and for some, any behaviour grossly offensive to their own standards. Being classified as a juvenile delinquent depends on many things other than actual conduct. If several individuals steal things of similar value from shops of a certain kind, one may go undiscovered, one be discovered but be dealt with by his parents, one be suspected but with insufficient evidence to prove his guilt, one receive police attention but a lenient disposal, one be dealt with more gravely (for example, by being sent to a residential institution).

Apart from these variations, which must arise where chance and discretion play a role, police authorities may vary their categorization of offences or their practical policy towards a given offence (greater strictness or tolerance, for example), so that statistics of delinquency reflect factors extrinsic to the behaviour of the actual or potential delinquents. On top of this, public opinion varies towards different classes of delinquency—possibly reacting more vigorously to teenage vandalism and rampaging than to the 'vandalism' and carnage wrought by car drivers. Convicted adult criminals themselves take a harsher view of some crimes than others, illustrated by hostile reactions to serious sexual crimes against children. Periodical reforms of particular legislation reflect changing ideas about criminality or delinquency, although it is easier to note the barbarity of remoter legal practices (child imprisonment, etc.) than the barbarity that future generations may see in our practices.

The general public enjoys learning about delinquency in both factual and fictional form. Even psychological or sociological discussions of delinquency would probably receive a quite high rating for general academic interest. One would not have to stretch the point too far to suggest that the general public enjoys its own minor delinquencies—the 'fiddle' on the side, the unofficial 'perk' as conceived by its beneficiary, the 'borrowings' that turn permanent, the plants or materials that do not *seem* to belong to any one and are *deemed* available to be taken, the income or import undeclared for tax or duty, the casual shoplifting, the older child who is small enough to look half-fare. There ought to be widespread sympathy with juvenile delinquents, for stealing is their predominant delinquency too.

Burt's *The Young Delinquent* (1925) is an early classic in this field of study. He compared 200 London juvenile delinquents with a matching control group of non-delinquent children of the same age and social class, and from the same school as the delinquents. He compared congenital and non-congenital influences on the two groups of children. *On the average*, the non-delinquents were exposed to one adverse congenital factor, but the delinquents to between two and three. The non-delinquents were exposed to between two and three adverse factors that were not congenital, but the delinquents to seven. Environmental influences on delinquency were most significant. Multiple causation was characteristic and 50 per cent of delinquencies and crimes in Burt's sample were attributed to a group of causes, among which the following were paramount:

1 intellectual dullness, but short of mental deficiency,
2 temperamental instability, but short of psychopathology,
3 defective family life and discipline, and
4 harmful friendships formed outside the home.

One hundred and thirty-seven of Burt's delinquents were followed up for a year or more, but only about half received psychological treatment judged appropriate. Burt claims that 62 per cent of those treated seemed cured, compared with 12 per cent of the others; 36 per cent made satisfactory but incomplete progress, compared with 23 per cent of the untreated; and only 2 per cent had wholly unsatisfactory reports, compared with 65 per cent of the untreated. Burt's general guidance for the treatment of delinquency was (1) early ascertainment, (2) treatment as part of general child welfare, (3) treatment, not punishment, (4) remedies for causes not symptoms, (5) continued research, and (6) programmes of general social amelioration.

The Gluecks (1950) compared 500 persistent male delinquents with a control group of the same size and concluded that the delinquents tended to be (1) physically more muscular in body type, (2) temperamentally more impulsive, extroverted, aggressive and destructive, (3) attitudinally more 'hostile, defiant, resentful, suspicious, stubborn, socially assertive, adventurous, unconventional, non-submissive to authority', (4) intellectually more concrete and less systematic in their thinking, and (5) socioculturally reared in unstable, affectionless and ill-disciplined homes.

Not many delinquents are markedly subnormal in intelligence (an average inferiority of only eight IQ points has been suggested) but many more are educationally backward. Homes broken by divorce or separation are commoner (perhaps twice as common) among delinquents than among 'controls'. Bad example alone does not explain delinquency, for many people exposed to bad examples do not follow them. The important point must be the significance for the delinquent of the person who gives the example. This is a corollary of the saying that ethical examples which have no personification have little force in the lives of young people. One of the most striking characteristics of delinquency is that it affects predominantly adolescent males, with a peak incidence at the age of fourteen, gradually tapering off towards the twenties. A third of first offenders are reconvicted within five years, but one-half if the first conviction was before fourteen years of age.

Hewitt and Jenkins (1946) characterized three sub-groups of delinquents. Unsocialized aggressives, or psychopaths as they might now be labelled, are malicious, violent, defiant and lacking in remorse. Over-inhibited neurotics are sensitive, seclusive, worrying types, lacking interest and energy. Socialized delinquents, who may be rather commoner than the other two types, keep bad company but are less overt in their misdemeanours and less unco-operative with adult helpers. The three types were associated with three different emphases in family rearing—active rejection, repression, and negligence and laxity respectively.

West (1967) comments on the generally disappointing outcome of attempts to improve delinquents by social or psychological therapy (West, pp. 254–7), but adds that such therapy may not yet have been properly tested by intensive application to properly selected cases. West (1969) describes the first stage of a long-term study started with 411 boys aged eight to nine, living in a densely populated, working-class, urban district. This entire group was socially handicapped (three times as many fathers in the lowest socio-economic category compared with the national average, twice as many families with seven or more children, two-fifths of the children with reading attainments comparable with the bottom 10 per cent of the general child population, half the homes without baths); those characterized as severely handicapped (1 : 8) suffered in addition from 'lax parental rules, unstable maternal personality and disharmonious and inconsistent parents'. West suggests that these features match the three factors the Gluecks found most predictive of future delinquency—'incohesive families, lax discipline and unsuitable style of maternal supervision'.

Only half of the boys who were actual or potential social problems were in touch with relevant social agencies. Boys who were rated unfavourably for conduct both by teachers and by psychiatric social workers (based on evidence from parents) showed a greatly increased liability to juvenile court appearances even before the age of fourteen. Also, the different set of teachers who rated the boys at age eleven still identified the same group of troublesome ones. Troublesomeness was correlated with all the indications of adversity, but particularly with family income. Correlation, of course, does not mean cause and effect. While a whole complex of factors, perhaps summarily indicated by family income, enters into the causation, the question of their relative influence is not answered. One indicator that seemed to be relevant at every social level of the group was popularity with peers. Whatever the social level, unpopularity with peers was associated with generally poor conduct. Poor performance on psychomotor tests was another factor that was an indicator not limited by social level.

Poor performance on a matrices test of intelligence at eight, nine or eleven was associated with subsequent early juvenile court appearances. Paradoxically, at the lowest social levels marital disharmony and maternal affection were *not* significantly correlated with children's misconduct, but above-average parental vigilance or interest in education *were* associated with children's better reading performances, and above-average child intelligence *was* associated with better behaviour. Sadly, 'an attempt to isolate and investigate a group of well-behaved boys from bad backgrounds was largely frustrated by the fact that there were so few of them'. These provisional findings of West, with their careful exposition of the procedural and logical problems that affect any possible conclusions, make an interesting study.

Mannheim and Wilkins (1955) studied a sample of 700 admitted to twelve borstals during 1946–7, taking, as a criterion of success, absence of further conviction up to 31 August 1951. Success rates varied among borstals between 30 and 64 per cent and they found that 'the earlier the career of crime was commenced the less likely were the lads to reform after Borstal training'. A record of absconding or excessive drinking was associated with failure. There were rather more lads from homes lacking a parent than among the general population but this was not associated with any higher failure rate. Neither were intelligence test score or personality ratings associated with the success/failure rate. General estimates of likely success correlated positively with actual success to the extent of 0·36, that is, a 13 per cent overlap in the variance of predictive categories and actual success/failure categories as defined in the first sentence of this paragraph. Those given a good prognosis had a 67–68 per cent success rate, those with an average prognosis a 57–61 per cent success rate, and those with a poor prognosis a 28–38 per cent success rate. In each case the first percentage refers to those in 'closed' borstals and the second to those in 'open' borstals.

The dilemma of treating delinquency is well brought out by West (1967). The work of psychiatrically directed residential rehabilitation projects 'depends upon great perseverance in establishing and maintaining close relationships with difficult characters', while 'society as a whole has little faith in the reformative effect of penal treatment, and little sense of obligation to try to make a place for anyone marked out as an official delinquent'. Trying to get in touch at all with some young people who feel most strongly alienated from ordinary social institutions has difficulties illustrated in the work of Morse (1965) with *The Unattached*. Some of her recommendations are for adolescent and parental counselling services, for more respect for people as persons in school and society, and for more informal places of social resort for adolescents.

Although there seems little doubt that individual deficiencies may contribute significantly to delinquency, some writers stress the general social character of delinquency. It is an alternative subculture in which those who cannot achieve success by ordinary ways set up their own society, governed by different norms and giving some measure of gratification in relation to these norms. Or it is an expression of unrest in a society where traditional norms may have lost their force and people do not have the capacity to substitute other norms which will give them comparable personal stability and security.

Yablonsky (1962) argues that, in disorganized American slums, there are sociopathic youths who are incompetent in relation to more demanding deviant or social groups, and who snatch desperately at a kind of substitute significance in the loosely organized life of a violent gang. The sociopath has no feeling for the victims of the gang's violence, his attitudes to sexual relationships are crudely exploitative, and his morale hangs on sustaining gang exploits, without which his violent fantasy existence collapses, revealing basic human incapacity. Yablonsky attributes part of the responsibility to the pattern of a society in which 'all youths are provoked by the mass media to desire a great variety of cultural goals they can seldom obtain through legitimate means'. The gang is a 'social narcotic' creating an acted out fantasy for its members. It creates a special form of delinquency requiring distinctive treatment, which Yablonsky discusses at the end of his book. One of his main points is that the detached gang worker must not, by a sympathetically acquiescent approach, sanction the delinquency that he is supposed to try and eliminate or diminish.

An aspect of delinquency that has received considerable attention recently is illegal drug taking. There are various books on the subject but the short discussion of student drug taking in Ryle (1969) gives a quick and balanced insight into the various problems, making clear the retreat into fantasy which drug taking signifies but distinguishing lesser and more serious concomitants of such retreats. Apart from the maladaptive aspect of drug-taking it is obvious that the 'pushing' of addictive drugs is a lucrative criminal business. The drug 'idyll' cannot free itself from the world of commerce which it sometimes nominally repudiates.

Table 17 illustrates an example of general delinquent sentencing policy in a particular year. Fining and probation are the principal means of dealing with delinquents from a legal point of view, although detention is obviously liable to be the fate of more persistent or serious offenders. There is not much evidence about the efficiency of different penal treatments, but it may be that recidivism is associated with factors other than the kind of penal treatment received. Those responsible for the residential supervision, education, and training of delinquents committed to their charge must work out their own practical philosophy, despite the absence of hard evidence and sometimes of much support from society at large.

Vocational, practical and physical training have often played, and still do play, a large part in residential treatment. It is sometimes argued that general education more analogous to that in an ordinary

Legal treatment	Under 14 Percentage of 24,439	14 under 17 Percentage of 36,544	17 under 21 Percentage of 45,193
Absolute discharge	2·6	1·9	1·0
Conditional discharge	28·5	19·3	9·8
Probation	30·6	27·6	16·1
Fine	19·3	33·1	54·7
Approved school	5·4	6·8	
Detention centre		2·1	6·1
Attendance centre	9·5	6·0	0·1
Imprisonment			2·0
Dealt with under Magistrates' Court Act, 1952			3·5
Committed to Quarter Sessions			4·9
Otherwise dealt with	4·1	3·2	1·8

Table 17 Legal treatment of indictable offences according to age group in magistrates' courts in England and Wales in 1967 (*Criminal Statistics, England and Wales, 1967*)

school should play a larger role, but the last word, here particularly, must rest with those doing the job. The careful classifying and allocation of delinquents committed to residential institutions are important considerations, but there may be considerable fluctuations in supply and demand, both with the incidence of delinquency and variations in policy.

Perspective on handicap and behaviour problems

Everyone has handicaps and behaviour problems. The top-class sportsman in his physical prime may be worried by fear of being only runner-up. The eminent research scientist may be piqued by his rival's prior publication of a new finding. The sensible married woman may have guilt fantasies about the rearing of her children. The competent classroom teacher or school head may slip into defensive rigidity or compensatory laxity in some aspects of his work. The other side of the coin is that all or most people publicly recognized as handicapped, maladjusted or delinquent, in any of the senses discussed in this chapter, are normal in many important ways. Sticking on labels encourages some quite false stereotypes. Miller (1969) makes this point in relation to adolescents—'any labelling of adolescents is liable to create difficulties'.

Two instances of physically handicapped children may serve to underline the point of the previous paragraph. Mary was severely spastic and just would not speak when she was taken at five years of age to meet the head of the infant department at the local school. Arrangements were made for her to be taught at home, but she would not speak to the teacher. She was taken to meet the head-mistress of a school for physically handicapped children, but she would not speak to her either. The headmistress reluctantly agreed to admit Mary, although she suspected that she might be mentally and not just physically handicapped. Mary settled down quite readily in the infant class, playing with the toys that were available and doing what she was asked to do, even if she had nothing to say at first. She was soon talking quite normally with other pupils, with the class teacher and with the visiting doctor, although she continued to be reluctant to speak to the headmistress or other teachers. She was not intellectually bright but extremely sensible, practical and hard-working. She loved school.

Billy came to a school for physically handicapped children at the age of eight. He had club feet and had undergone a whole series of operations. He was very backward educationally, hardly able to read or count at all. The report from his first school indicated that he was a very difficult child, given to lying and fits of temper. With a fresh start at the five-to-seven educational level, he settled down and made very good progress. His teacher found him cheerful, truthful, hard-working and very good with the smaller children.

The more conspicuous or widespread a handicap is, in some ways the easier it is to deal with it. It is at least more difficult to overlook its presence and its nature. Teachers may meet occasional cases of miscellaneous handicap which are more readily neglected because the main organization of work is geared to the unhandicapped. This can be be variously exemplified, but the case of reading difficulties is a good intermediate illustration. Clark (1970), for example, found that 15 per cent of seven-year-old pupils in the Scottish county of Dunbarton in 1966 had no independent reading skill after two years at school. This included, of course, those who could be expected to be backward because of below-average general intelligence, however assessed. The children had been absent a good deal and as many as a quarter of them had been in at least two schools in their first two years at school.

Two hundred and thirty of the 1,544 children were severely backward and these were studied more intensively. Half of the 230 still needed help in basic reading skills after three years at school. These children were nearer average on 'performance' tests than 'verbal' tests of intelligence. At the age of nine only 19 children (15 boys and

4 girls) who were of average intelligence were two or more years backward in reading. Many of these 19 had speech defects, poor auditory discrimination or poor visuo-motor co-ordination, and most came from large families. But an analysis of the specific nature of their reading disabilities showed wide diversity and no common pattern—another lesson in the importance of non-stereotyping.

Inability to read is an important educational handicap and, in ordinary schools, its elimination depends on (1) the continued opportunity to acquire basic skills after as well as before seven, (2) special consideration throughout for slow learners who take longer to reach the eventual goal, and (3) special help for a very small number of children of average intelligence, typically boys, who may need different kinds of reading treatment as late as nine years of age. These provisions depend jointly on appropriate attitudes and teaching skills in teachers and wider organizational arrangements by heads of schools and local education authorities.

A constructive approach to handicap requires realistic appraisal of the particular facts of each case together with an emphasis on what can be done rather than what cannot. These two requirements are more difficult to meet in the case of categories of handicap, like maladjustment or social handicap, which are intrinsically elastic in conception. Various ways of looking at maladjustment have been outlined. They are all at least suggestive for practical thinking. If any one point were selected for emphasis it might be the desirability of emulating the standards of Thomas, Chess and Birch for specifying problems in concrete and particular terms, and avoiding wide generalizations and concepts. But this prescription too has its problems, for few people can resist, or even be expected to resist, the convenience of conceptual simplification. Simplification is part of the purpose of conceptual thinking and different people simplify at different levels of conceptual complexity.

Social handicap in one form or another is a frequent, although certainly not invariable, concomitant of many of the other handicaps that have been mentioned. It is not a single or clear phenomenon, but a varying selection of associated factors which are relatively prominent where there is educational subnormality, serious maladjustment or juvenile delinquency. These factors are modified one way or another by specific individual or family factors which do not arise from the environment alone, but rather, in part, from genetic aspects of temperament or ability which may not be precisely specifiable, despite their undoubted existence.

There is no doubt that certain attitudes in teachers can intensify the influence of social handicap and other attitudes moderate such influence. Correct information about psychological and social facts is important, for some attitudes are demonstrably based on false information or understanding. Careful assessment by the teacher of his own educational purposes or commitments is important, for so many diverse writers, including experienced and practising teachers, refer to the importance of personal and not only scholastic education. Scholastic education is part of personal education but sometimes ousts other aspects, despite the fact that very few indeed have a limitless taste for academic knowledge (certainly not all of those who go on to an academic higher education). Recognizing the responsibility for personal education, compensating for social or other handicap, that teachers are called upon to accept, one must add that schools and teachers can only too readily be made the scapegoats for ills that are neither of their making nor within their powers of cure.

Lowe (1969), in his valuable discussion of personal relationships in psychological disorders, makes some good points about regressive behaviour. When adults regress to an earlier stage of behaviour (the temper tantrum, the appeal to be babied) the regression is never complete, but presents varying symptoms of both adult and childish behaviour. Moreover, such regression is not invariably a pathological phenomenon; it may be psychologically helpful as a temporary adaptation. This could be considered relevant to some of the behaviour of children or young people. Children are sometimes reproved (and, admittedly, sometimes appropriately) for being childish. If it is sometimes permissible for adults to be 'big babies' it is sometimes permissible for children to be childish. The childishness may indicate some area where extra help is needed towards an eventually more mature pattern of conduct.

Lowe refers to another phenomenon which is relevant to teaching, although he is writing about psychotherapy. Psychotherapists who were 'individualistic, spontaneous, open and warm with patients' were more effective than those concerned with 'correcting' symptoms, maintaining social distance from their patients and receiving deference from them. It is difficult to assess success precisely either in psychotherapy or teaching, but many would agree that warmth and spontaneity are as necessary as any kind of technical assessment of an educational situation. Both things are desirable. In educational contexts, the effect of teacher spontaneity has frequently been shown in connection with studies of new methods. Up to a point, lively teachers *make* methods work.

One can do something about minor behaviour disorders or delinquency by accurate appraisal of the circumstances and firm and sympathetic guidance or rehabilitation. A problem about more serious cases is that they are more difficult to manage by definition and less rewarding because of the lower chances of success. It is fortunate that there are some people who are prepared to seek the elusive satisfaction of tackling such difficult problems. The discussion of delinquency in this chapter is a sketch map of the problem area rather than an exhaustive account of what has been attempted, let alone what might be done. It may be that methods of advanced delinquent spotting will be improved, and that the most susceptible young boys will receive special attention before they act out their adverse 'fate', but this possibility has yet to be worked out in practical terms. It would be optimistic to imagine that any human contrivance could control completely the hot blood of youth and the inevitable margin of pure genetic and environmental chance.

Handicap and behaviour problems test one's command of the principles of assessment and guidance discussed in the previous two chapters, but they also test the human and moral response of those individuals called on to deal with them, and the political and social wisdom and effectiveness of the community as a whole. Some controversy and some failure are inevitable, but there are, within the complexity of the issues discussed in this chapter, at least some points where psychological analysis and educational experience come quite close together.

12 Psychological theory and educational practice

Educators, whether teachers, parents or administrators, are bound to hold at least some implicit or covert psychological theories about how young people develop and learn, and about how such development and learning can be assessed. In fact, because they are more articulate than average, they tend to express their psychological theories quite freely and eloquently. They may disclaim any theoretical pretentions, but this must be viewed as something of a Socratic irony. Otherwise, it would be plain naïvety.

Psychologists may seem more able to pursue psychological theories regardless of immediate practical demands, but there are two limitations on this academic ideal. One is that the community obviously expects some practical good to emerge ultimately from the theoretical endeavours that it supports, and, indeed, makes some of its support directly dependent on immediate utility, through the financing of 'applied' research. The other is that psychologists too are fortunately human. As the teacher cannot refrain from theorizing, so the psychologist is bound to emit some opinions on general practical matters, however cautiously he hedges himself with fictions about not speaking as a psychologist. In this he shares the position of all scientists.

The most useful standpoint seems to be to recognize a double need, for both detachment and co-operation. A teacher would hardly get on with his job if he was always stopping to reflect on the justifiability of the psychological concepts and theories that his practice takes for granted. An academic psychologist would hardly get on with his if he had to turn out a practical recommendation every other week. The former needs some detachment from the demands of rigorous intellectual analysis, the latter from the demands of short-term practical purposes. But there should be occasional exchanges of role in this respect. The teacher who never re-examines his own psychological assumptions and the psychologist who completely avoids questions of practical relevance alike limit their own intellectual horizons.

The relationship of psychology to teaching or education is subtle, not simple. Psychology does not generate directives for teaching. The actions of politicians and administrators in relation to education have more directive character, although these actions too are modified by the circumstances of public opinion and material facilities. Psychology, itself influenced by broad ideological assumptions (such as the pre-eminence of scientific ideals, or, within particular countries, by the political assumptions of the country), gradually modifies our picture of human behaviour by fresh conceptual analysis and empirical evidence. It may provide an occasional practical tool—programmed learning, objective tests, improved means of analysing traditional assessments, better validated tests of temperament or emotional stability—but the gradual refinement of our notions of the range of human behaviour in various circumstances, and of the causal patterns that characterize it, are as important and probably more so.

Although systematic psychology can and does have this refining influence on ordinary psychological and educational thinking, it would be self-deception to ignore the extent to which people can elude its benign operation. There are various reasons for this—lack of a sufficiently substantial and well-planned introduction to systematic psychology in the first instance, lack of opportunity or inclination to revise psychological studies that may have grown rusty with the passage of decades, readiness to tolerate second-rate psychological ideas so long as nobody threatens them with a critical approach, and the tendency to rationalize the neglect of what is sound in systematic psychology either by facile reference to its failures and shortcomings, or by claiming (but not previously demonstrating) that one knew it all already.

Teachers certainly do make free assumptions about motivation, personality, intelligence, attitudes, transfer of learning, behaviour problems, moral development, remembering and comparable concepts that have been analysed in the earlier chapters of this book. But some of these assumptions are just not good enough. They do not correspond to a sophisticated professional ideal which would expect the individual teacher to get to the bottom of relevant psychological problems and not be satisfied with whatever formula either scrapes a pass mark in a professional examination or wins an approving smile in a school staff room. The concepts mentioned are themselves sophisticated and complex. There is no reason why wisdom about them should boil down to a few trite aphorisms. And it is not just a question of theoretical purism. People do mistaken things because of their mistaken analysis of the people and situations for which they are professionally responsible.

Knowing how readily any short and simple formula is accepted instead of a more complex but more accurate statement of the truth, one might hesitate to state the 'practical implications' of psychological analysis. On the other hand, to suggest no possible practical consequence may foster the belief that there is none. An attempt has been made throughout this book to suggest fairly definite policies that might be considered consistent with the accompanying psychological analysis. Such statements of practical policy do not 'just follow' from the psychological analysis. One can claim only that they seem to correspond more closely to what is psychologically the case.

Sometimes it can be argued that the policy is common sense any way, but frequently this is not so. In many of the examples throughout the book, 'common sense' is either mistaken or grossly oversimplified. In many cases, 'common sense' is not so common as to be widely manifest in common practice. Systematic psychological study corrects common sense, and, where common sense is in some way already correct, highlights the importance of appropriate action. This does not, of course, free psychology from the need for self-correction. But the imperfections of psychology do not justify the imperfections of educational practice. Mutual sympathy rather than mutual detraction seems relevant.

It is hardly possible to give more emphasis than has already been given in Chapter 2 to the fact that psychological considerations are one set among many that the practical educator must take into account. There has been increasing interest in the second half of the twentieth century in the relationship between sociology and education. As many students say, they are not quite sure what sociology is but they would be very interested to study it. Sociology is a useful complement to the psychology of education in so far as it focuses attention on the ways in which institutions as such provide reference points that influence human behaviour.

Psychology has sometimes been harnessed to an educational cult of individualism, which could obscure the fact that an *ideal* of individualism is compatible with an *actuality* of powerful shaping of individuals by institutional norms (expressed in the family, school, social class, etc.). Sociology has commonly harnessed itself to a social cult of compensatory educational policies—first, in the sense of extending to the many what previously was the privilege of the few, then, more radically, in the sense of changing the nature of education (more 'practical', 'relevant', etc.) to make its aims fit the many. This is not the place to embark on a discussion of the complex issues that arise. What can be noted is that both of these social sciences are highly susceptible to ideological influence. This does not necessarily detract from their utility, but it does require discrimination between scientific and ideological criteria of successful theorizing.

Both psychology and sociology are educationally useful in suggesting some of the limits of modifiable behaviour. There are many circumstances where successful teaching requires an appreciation of what the teacher or school are unlikely to change, as well as of what they may change and ought to try to change. Both psychology and sociology can be educationally irritating in the occasional smugness with which their practitioners propound what ought to be done by schools or teachers, sometimes with little or no experience of what it is like to teach in the wide range of ordinary schools. The social scientist paints in the broad and easy brush strokes and expects the 'operatives' to do the detailed drudgery.

Teachers may invite this drudging role if they do not bother to grasp at least some of the main features of analytic enquiry in the social sciences. There will always be people at the extremes of any human continuum—the theorist who cannot act, the successful practitioner with no analytic understanding of his own success—but these are not the typical cases. Most people come somewhere in the middle and what matters most is to maintain open discourse among them. It is easier for those who are paid to study general problems to sustain a lively interest in them, but it would be a kind of dehumanization of teaching if its practitioners were content to act out the specific roles prescribed for them, whether by politicians, psychologists or sociologists, without taking part themselves in the role specification. The study of the social sciences by teachers is not a substitute for the practical work of education, but an ancillary discipline to help keep practical thinking from sinking into a self-deepening rut.

Psychology, in many of its branches, does illumine individual behaviour in practical ways. The individual teacher can develop and change specific practical policies within his classroom by reflection about certain psychological factors, whereas sociological understanding may be more of an aid to tolerance than to any other form of practical action in the classroom context. At the same time, the study of educational psychology, as intrepreted in this book, does not assume the walls of the classroom as the teacher's ultimate perimeter. Teachers never have been mere class instructors. Even those who have come nearest to being so have had further influences—sometimes more potent—as good or bad models of human conduct, of what being human can mean. Today, when a wider variety of education is given to a wider variety of people, there is almost universal recognition of the need for teachers to be more than instructors, even if one does not go the whole way with those who seem to conceive of them as the reformers of the whole of society.

Whatever educational aims a teacher acts on, his own character as a person is one of the main influences exerted on his pupils or students. Imitation is a powerful educative influence. Deeds talk louder than words. No quick or superficial study of psychology, sociology or anything else will contribute substantially to educational practice. It is only ideas, evidence and modes of analysis that have been mulled over for some time as part of a wider education that have a chance of refining a person's working conceptions of human behaviour and entering into his practical dealings with people. The discussions of human development, learning and assessment in this book may offer a substantial start for reflection upon human behaviour within an educational context.

Bibliography

ABERCROMBIE, M. L. J., et al., (1969), *Selection and Academic Performance of Students in a University School of Architecture*, Society for Research into Higher Education.

ALLPORT, G. W., (1966), 'Attitudes in the history of social psychology', in Jahoda, *Attitudes, Selected Readings*, Penguin.

ANNETT, J., (1969), *Feedback and Human Behaviour*, Penguin.

ARGYLE, M., (1961), 'A new approach to the classification of delinquents with implications for treatment', *California Board of Corrections*, Monograph 2, 15–26.

ASCH, S. E., (1966), 'Attitudes as cognitive structures', in Jahoda, *Attitudes, Selected Readings*, Penguin.

AXLINE, VIRGINIA, (1947), *Play Therapy*, Chicago: Houghton Mifflin Co.

AYER, A. J., (1964), *Man as a Subject for Science*, University of London, The Athlone Press.

BANDURA, A., and WALTERS, R. H., (1959), *Adolescent Aggression*, New York: Ronald.

BARON, G., and TAYLOR, W., (1969), *Educational Administration and the Social Sciences*, University of London, The Athlone Press.

BARTLETT, F. C., (1932), *Remembering*, Cambridge University Press.

BEECH, H. R., (1969), *Changing Man's Behaviour*, Penguin.

BERGER, P. L., (1966), *Invitation to Sociology*, Penguin.

BERNSTEIN, B., (1970), 'A critique of the concept of "Compensatory Education" ', in Rubinstein and Stoneman, *Education for Democracy*, Penguin.

BIDDLE, B. J., and ELLENA, W. J., (1964), *Contemporary Research on Teacher Effectiveness*, New York: Holt, Rinehart & Winston.

BLANK, MARION, (1968), 'Experimental approaches to concept development in young children', in Lunzer and Morris, *Development in Learning*, Vol. 2, Staples Press.

BLOOM, B. S., KRATHWOHL, D. R., et al., (1956, 1964), *Taxonomy of Educational Objectives, Handbook 1, Cognitive Domain; Handbook 2, Affective Domain*, Longmans.

BOWLBY, J., (1965), 'Separation anxiety', in Mussen, *Readings in Child Development and Personality*, New York: Harper & Row.

BRADBURN, E., (1964), 'The teacher's role in the moral development of children in primary schools', University of Liverpool, Ph.D. thesis.

BRECKENRIDGE, MARIAN E., and MURPHY, MARGARET M., (1969), *Growth and Development of the Young Child*, 8th edition, W. B. Saunders Co.

BROADBENT, D. E., (1964), *Behaviour*, Methuen.

BROWN, J. A. C., (1963), *Techniques of Persuasion, From Propaganda to Brainwashing*, Penguin.

BROWN, R., (1965), *Social Psychology*, New York: The Free Press.

BROWN, R. I., (1967), *The Assessment and Education of Slow-learning Children*, University of Bristol Institute of Education.

BRUNER, J. S., et al., (1966), *Studies in Cognitive Thought*, New York: Wiley.

(1962), *A Study of Thinking*, New York: Science Editions.

BULL, N. J., (1969), *Moral Judgement from Childhood to Adolescence*, Routledge & Kegan Paul.

BURT, SIR CYRIL, (1925), *The Young Delinquent*, University of London Press.

BUTCHER, H. J., (1968), *Educational Research in Britain*, University of London Press.

(1968), *Human Intelligence, Its Nature and Assessment*, Methuen.

CAMERON, N., (1947), *The Psychology of Behavior Disorders, A Biosocial Interpretation*, Chicago: Houghton Mifflin Co.

CARROLL, J. B., (1964), *Language and Thought*, Englewood Cliffs, New Jersey: Prentice-Hall.

CARTER, M. P., (1962), *Home, School and Work. A Study of the Education and Employment of Young People in Britain*, Pergamon.

CATTELL, R. B., (1965), *The Scientific Analysis of Personality*, Penguin.

CHOMSKY, N., (1967), 'Review of Skinner's verbal behaviour' in Jakobovits and Miron, *Readings in the Psychology of Language*, Englewood Cliffs, New Jersey: Prentice-Hall.

CLARK, MARGARET M., (1970), *Reading Difficulties in Schools*, Penguin.

CLEGG, SIR A., and MEGSON, BARBARA, (1968), *Children in Distress*, Penguin.

COCKBURN, JUNE M., (1961), 'Psychological and Social Aspects', in Henderson, *Cerebral Palsy in Childhood and Adolescence*, E. & S. Livingstone.

COMENIUS, J. A., (1967), *Orbis Sensualium Pictus, Facsimile of the third London edition of 1672*, introduced by J. Bowen, Sydney University Press.

CRITES, J. O., (1969), *Vocational Psychology, The Study of Vocational Behaviour and Development*, McGraw-Hill.

DANSKIN, D. G., (1955), 'Occupational sociology in occupational exploration', *Personnel and Guidance Journal*, 34, 134–6.

DOUGLAS, J. W. B., and BLOMFELD, J. M., (1958), *Children Under Five*, Allen & Unwin.

EPPEL, E. M., and M., (1966), *Adolescents and Morality*, Routledge & Kegan Paul.

ERIKSON, E. H., (1965), *Childhood and Society*, revised edition, Penguin.

ESTES, W. K., (1960), 'Learning', *Encyclopaedia of Educational Research*, 3rd edition, New York: Macmillan.

EVANS, K. M., (1968), *Planning Small-scale Research*, National Foundations for Educational Research.

(1962), *Sociometry and Education*, Routledge & Kegan Paul.

EYKEN W. VAN DER, (1967), *The Pre-School Child*, Penguin.

EYSENCK, H. J., (1963), 'Behavior therapy, spontaneous remission and transfer in neurotics', *American Journal of Psychiatry*, 119, 868.

(1953), *The Structure of Human Personality*, Methuen.

FESTINGER, L. A., (1957), *A Theory of Cognitive Dissonance*, New York: Row, Peterson.

FEYERABEND, P. K., (1968), 'How to be a good empiricist—a plea for tolerance in epistemological matters', in Nidditch, *The Philosophy of Science*, Oxford University Press.

FISH, F., (1968), *An Outline of Psychiatry for Students and Practitioners*, 2nd edition, John Wright.

FLANDERS, N., (1964), 'Some relationships among teacher influence, pupil attitudes, and achievement', in Biddle and Ellena, *Contemporary Research on Teacher Effectiveness*, New York: Holt, Rinehart & Winston.

FLAVELL, J. H., (1963), *The Developmental Psychology of Jean Piaget*, Van Nostrand.

FURNEAUX, BARBARA, (1969), *The Special Child, The Education of Mentally Handicapped Children*, Penguin.

GAGNÉ, R. M., (1965), *The Conditions of Learning*, New York: Holt, Rinehart & Winston.

GATHERCOLE, C. E., (1968), *Assessment in Clinical Psychology*, Penguin.

GETZELS, J. W. and JACKSON, P. W., (1962), *Creativity and Intelligence*, New York: Wiley.

GLUECK, S., and E., (1950), *Unraveling Juvenile Delinquency*, New York: The Commonwealth Fund.

GOLDMAN, L., (1969), *The Human Sciences and Philosophy*, Cape.

GRAHAM, D., (1968), 'Children's moral development', in Butcher, *Educational Research in Britain*, University of London Press.

GREEN, E. J., (1962), *The Learning Process and Programmed Instruction*, New York: Holt, Rinehart & Winston.

HARLOW, H. F., and ZIMMERMANN, R. R., (1965), 'Affectional responses in the infant monkey', in Mussen, *Readings in Child Development and Personality*, New York: Harper & Row.

HARTSHORNE, H., and MAY, M. A., (1928–30), *Studies in the Nature of Character: Studies in Deceit (Vol. 1); Studies in Service and Self-control (Vol. 2); Studies in the Organization of Character (Vol. 3)*, New York: Macmillan.

HARVARD EDUCATION REVIEW, (June, 1962), *Guidance—An Examination*, Harvard University Press.

HASAN, PARWEEN, and BUTCHER, H. J., (1966) 'Creativity and intelligence: a partial replication with Scottish children of Getzels and Jackson's study', *British Journal of Psychology*, 57, 129–35.

HAVIGHURST, R. J., and TABA, H., (1949), *Adolescent Character and Personality*, New York: Wiley.

HEBB, D. O., (1949), *The Organization of Behaviour, A Neurophysiological Theory*, Chapman & Hall.

HENDERSON, J. L., (1961), *Cerebral Palsy in Childhood and Adolescence, A Medical, Psychological and Social Study*, E. & S. Livingstone.

HEWITT, L. E., and JENKINS, R. L., (1946), *Fundamental Patterns of Maladjustment*, Michigan: D. H. Green.

HILL, WINFRED F., (1964), *Learning, A Survey of Psychological Interpretations*, Methuen.

HOME OFFICE, (1968), *Criminal Statistics, England and Wales, 1967*, H.M.S.O.

HOYLE, E., (1969), *The Role of the Teacher*, Routledge & Kegan Paul.

HUDSON, L., (1967), *Contrary Imaginations, A Psychological Study of the English Schoolboy*, Penguin.

HUNT, J. M., (1961), *Intelligence and Experience*, New York: Ronald Press.

HUNTER, D. R., (1964), *The Slums, Challenge and Response*, Collier & Macmillan.

HURLOCK, ELIZABETH B., (1967). *Adolescent Development* 3rd edition, McGraw-Hill.

JACKSON, S., (1969), *Special Education in England and Wales*, 2nd edition, Oxford University Press.

JAHODA, M., and WARREN, N., (1966), *Attitudes, Selected Readings*, Penguin.

JAKOBOVITS, L. A., and MIRON, M. S., (1967), *Readings in the Psychology of Language*, Englewood Cliffs, New Jersey: Prentice-Hall.

KELLY, E. L., (1967), 'Transfer of training, an analytic study', in Komisar and Macmillan, *Psychological Concepts in Education*, Chicago: Rand McNally.

KENDLER, H. H., and T. S., (1961), 'Effect of verbalization on reversal shifts in children', *Science*, 141, 1619–20.

KINSEY, A. C., (1953), *Sexual Behaviour in the Human Female*, Saunders. (1948), *Sexual Behaviour in the Human Male*, Saunders.

KOHLBERG, L., (1963), 'The Development of Children's Orientations Towards a Moral Order 1. Sequency in the Development of Moral Thought', *Vita Humana*, 6, 11–33.

KOMISAR, B. P. and MACMILLAN, C. J. B., (1967), *Psychological Concepts in Education*, Chicago: Rand McNally.

LAWTON, D., (1968), *Social Class, Language and Education*, Routledge & Kegan Paul.

LAZARUS, R. S., and OPTON, E. M., (1967), *Personality, Selected Readings*, Penguin.

LIFTON, R. J. (1966), 'Thought reform of Chinese intellectuals', in Jahoda and Warren, *Attitudes, Selected Readings*, Penguin.

LOUCH, A. R., (1966), *Explanation and Human Action*, Blackwell.

LOVELL, K., (1967), *Team Teaching*, University of Leeds Institute of Education
(1962), *The Growth of Basic Mathematical and Scientific Concepts in Children*, University of London Press.

LOWE, G. R., (1969), *Personal Relationships in Psychological Disorders*, Penguin.

LUNN, JOAN C. B., (1970), *Streaming in the Primary School*, National Foundation for Educational Research.

LUNZER, E. A., and MORRIS, J. F., (1968-9), *Development in Learning* (3 volumes), Staples Press.

MACARTHUR, B., (9 March 1970), 'Equal education still a mockery for too many', *The Times*, 9.

MACINTOSH, H. G., and MORRISON, R. B., (1969), *Objective Testing*, University of London Press.

MCFARLAND, H. S. N., (1969), *Human Learning, A Developmental Analysis*, Routledge & Kegan Paul.
(1965), *Psychology and Teaching*, 2nd edition, Harrap.
(February, 1962), 'Education by tutorial', *Universities Review*, Association of University Teachers.
(October, 1961), 'University lectures', *Universities Review*, Association of University Teachers.

MCINTOSH, D., et al., (1962), *The Scaling of Teachers' Marks and Estimates*, Oliver & Boyd.

MCINTYRE, D., MORRISON, A., and SUTHERLAND, J., (1966), 'Social and educational variables relating to teachers' assessments of primary school pupils', *British Journal of Educational Psychology*, 36, 272-9.

MCLEISH, J., (1969), *Teachers' Attitudes, A Study of National and Other Differences*, Cambridge Institute of Education.

MANNHEIM, H., and WILKINS, L. T., (1955), *Prediction Methods in Relation to Borstal Training*, H.M.S.O.

MAXWELL, J., (1969), *Sixteen Years On, A Follow-up of the 1947 Scottish Survey*, University of London Press, for the Scottish Council for Research in Education.

MAYS, J. B., (1962), *Education and the Urban Child*, Liverpool University Press.

MERRITT, J. E., (1970), 'Reading skills, re-examined' in Stones, *Readings in Educational Psychology*, Methuen.

MILLER, D., (1969), *The Age Between, Adolescents in a Disturbed Society*, Cornmarket/Hutchinson.

MORENO, J. L., (1953), *Who Shall Survive?* 2nd edition, New York: Beacon House.

MORRISON, A., and MCINTYRE, D., (1969), *Teachers and Teaching*, Penguin.

MORSE, MARY, (1965), *The Unattached*, Penguin.

MUSSEN, P. H., CONGER, J. J., and KAGAN, J., (1965), *Readings in Child Development and Personality*, New York: Harper & Row.

(1963), *Child Development and Personality*, Harper International Student Reprint.

NATIONAL INSTITUTE OF INDUSTRIAL PSYCHOLOGY (undated), *The Seven-Point Plan*, N.I.I.P.

(undated), *Studying Work*, N.I.I.P.

NEILL, A. S., (1962), *Summerhill, A Radical Approach to Education*, Gollancz.

NIDDITCH, P. H., (1968), *The Philosophy of Science*, Oxford University Press.

OAKESHOTT, M., (1967), 'Learning and teaching', in Peters, *The Concept of Education*, Routledge & Kegan Paul.

OLDFIELD, R. C., (1968), *Language, Selected Readings*, Penguin.

OSGOOD, C. E., (1967), 'Semantic differential technique in the comparative study of cultures', in Jakobovits and Miron, *Readings in the Psychology of Language*, Englewood Cliffs, New Jersey: Prentice-Hall.

PAPOUŠEK, HANUŠ, (1967), 'Experimental studies of appetitional behaviour in human newborns and infants', in Stevenson, *Early Behaviour*, John Wiley.

PEARCE, J. D. W., (1952), *Juvenile Delinquency*, Cassell.

PECK, R. F., and HAVIGHURST, R. J., (1964), *The Psychology of Character Development*, New York: Wiley.

PEEL, E. A., (1968), 'Learning and explainer thinking', in Lunzer and Morris, *Development in Learning*, Vol. 2, Staples Press.

(1960), *The Pupil's Thinking*, Oldbourne.

PERKIN, H. J., (1969), *Innovation in Higher Education: New Universities in the United Kingdom*, Organization for Economic Co-operation and Development.

PESTON, M., (1969), 'Economics and Administration of Education', in Baron and Taylor, *Educational Administration and the Social Sciences*, University of London, The Athlone Press.

PETERS, R. S. (1967), *The Concept of Education*, Routledge & Kegan Paul.

(1960), 'Freud's theory of moral development in relation to that of Piaget', *British Journal of Educational Psychology*, 30, 250–8.

(1958), *The Concept of Motivation*, Routledge & Kegan Paul.

PIAGET, J., and INHELDER, B., (1969), *The Psychology of the Child*, Routledge & Kegan Paul.

PIDGEON, D. A., (1970), *Expectation and Pupil Performance*, National Foundation for Educational Research.

and YATES, A., (1968), *An Introduction to Educational Measurement*, Routledge & Kegan Paul.

PLOWDEN, LADY, (1967), *Children and Their Primary Schools*, H.M.S.O.

POWELL, J. P., (1966), *Universities and University Education: A Select Bibliography*, National Foundation for Educational Research.

RICHMOND, W. K., (1965), *Teachers and Machines, An Introduction to the Theory and Practice of Programmed Learning*, Collins.

ROBERTS, G. R., and LUNZER, E. A., (1968), 'Reading and learning to read', in Lunzer and Morris, *Development in Learning*, Staples Press.

ROGERS, JENNIFER, (1969), *Teaching on Equal Terms*, BBC.

RUBINSTEIN, D., and STONEMAN, C., (1970), *Education for Democracy*, Penguin.

RYLE, A., (1969), *Student Casualties*, Allen Lane, The Penguin Press.

SAVAGE, R. D., (1968), *Psychometric Assessment of the Individual Child*, Penguin.

SCHOFIELD, M., (1965), *The Sexual Behaviour of Young People*, Longmans.

SCHONELL, F. J., (1942), *Backwardness in the Basic Subjects*, Oliver & Boyd.

SCHOOLS COUNCIL, (1968), *Young School Leavers*, H.M.S.O.

SCOTT, J. P., (1968), *Early Experience and the Organization of Behavior*, California: Brooks/Cole Publishing Co.

SCOTTISH EDUCATION DEPARTMENT, (1961), *Degrees of Mental Handicap*, H.M.S.O.

SEARS, R. R., MACCOBY, E. E., and LEVIN, H., (1957), *Patterns of Child Rearing*, Evanston, Illinois: Row, Peterson.

SECONDARY SCHOOL EXAMINATIONS COUNCIL, (1964), *The Certificate of Secondary Education: An Introduction to Some Techniques of Examining*, H.M.S.O.

SEMEONOFF, B., (1966), *Personality Assessment, Selected Readings*, Penguin.

SHIELDS, J. B., (1968), *The Gifted Child*, National Foundation for Educational Research.

SIEGEL, S., (1956), *Nonparametric Statistics for the Behavioural Sciences*, McGraw-Hill.

SIMON, H., (1964), 'On the Concept of Organizational Goal', *Administrative Science Quarterly*, 9, 1.

SKINNER, B. F., (1968), *The Technology of Teaching*, New York: Appleton. (1959), *Cumulative Record*, New York: Appleton-Century-Crofts.

SONTAG, L. W., et al., (1965), 'Mental growth and personality development: a longitudinal study', in Mussen, *Readings in Child Development and Personality*, Harper International Student Reprint.

STENHOUSE, L., (1967), *Discipline in Schools*, Pergamon.

STEVENSON, H. W., (1967), *Early Behaviour, Comparative and Developmental Approaches*, John Wiley.

STONES, E., (1970), *Readings in Educational Psychology: Learning and Teaching*, Methuen.

(1968), *Learning and Teaching, A Programmed Introduction*, John Wiley.

SULLIVAN, L. H., (Autumn 1969), 'A systems approach to training in the RAAF', *Royal Air Force Education Bulletin*, 6, 33–41.

SUNDAY TIMES, (1970), 'Sex and marriage', three articles published on 15, 22 and 29 March.

TALLAND, G. A., (1968), *Disorders of Memory and Learning*, Penguin.

TANNER, J. M., (1961), *Education and Physical Growth*, University of London Press.

TAYLOR, W., (1969), *Society and the Education of Teachers*, Faber.

THOMAS, A., CHESS, STELLA, and BIRCH, H. G., (1968), *Temperament and Behaviour Disorders in Children*, University of London Press.

(1963), *Behavioral Individuality in Early Childhood*, New York University Press.

THOMAS, C. A., et al., (1963), *Programmed Learning in Perspective, A Guide to Programme Writing*, City Publicity Services, for Lamson Technical Products, Ltd.

UNDERWOOD, J. E. A., (1955), *Report of the Committee on Maladjusted Children*, H.M.S.O.

VAUGHAN, T. D., (1970), *Education and Vocational Guidance Today*, Routledge & Kegan Paul.

VERNON, M. D., (1969), *Human Motivation*, Cambridge University Press.

WALL, W. D., (1968), *Adolescents in School and Society*, National Foundation for Educational Research.

WALLACH, M. A., and KOGAN, N., (1965), *Modes of Thinking in Young Children*, New York: Holt, Rinehart & Winston.

WALTER, W. G., (1953), *The Living Brain*, Duckworth.

WANKOWSKI, J., (July 1969), 'Some aspects of motivation in success and failure at university', Society for Research in Higher Education.

WELFORD, A. T., (1968), *Fundamentals of Skill*, Methuen.

WEST, D. J., (1969), *Present Conduct and Future Delinquency*, Heinemann.

(1967), *The Young Offender*, Penguin.

WHYTE, W. H., (1960), *The Organization Man*, Penguin.

WILMOTT, P., (1966), *Adolescent Boys of East London*, Penguin.

WOLFF, SULA, (1969), *Children Under Stress*, Allen Lane, The Penguin Press.

WOOTTON, LADY BARBARA, (1959), *Social Science and Social Pathology*, Allen & Unwin.

YABLONSKY, L., (1967), *The Violent Gang*, Penguin.

YUDKIN, S., (1968), *0–5, A Report on the Care of Pre-School Children*, 2nd edition, Allen & Unwin, for National Society of Children's Nurseries.

ZAJONC, R. B., (1966), 'Balance, congruity and disonance', 1960, in Jahoda and Warren, *Attitudes, Selected Readings*, Penguin.

ZANGWILL, O. L., (1950), *An Introduction to Modern Psychology*, Methuen.

Index

Topics